THE
ATLAS OF
ENDANGERED
SPECIES

THE
=== ATLAS OF ===
ENDANGERED
SPECIES

Editor: John A. Burton

Pictures supplied by Bruce Coleman Ltd

MACMILLAN PUBLISHING COMPANY
NEW YORK

MAXWELL MACMILLAN CANADA
TORONTO

CONTENTS

A QUARTO BOOK

Macmillan Publishing Company
866 Third Avenue, New York, NY 10022

Maxwell Macmillan Canada, Inc.
1200 Eglinton Avenue East, Suite 200
Don Mills, Ontario M3C 3N1

Library of Congress Cataloging-in-Publication Data

The atlas of endangered species/edited by John Burton.
    p.   cm.
  Includes bibliographical references and index.
  Summary: Describes the various animals and plants throughout the world whose survival is being threatened and the steps being taken to save them from extinction.
  ISBN 0–02–897081–0
  1. Endangered species – Juvenile literature.
2. Endangered plants – Juvenile literature.
3. Nature conservation – Juvenile literature.
(1. Rare animals. 2. Rare plants. 3. Wildlife conservation. 4. Environmental protection.)
I. Burton, John A.
QH75.A85 1991
333.95'16 – dc20   91–12611
                      CIP
                      AC

Preface *John Burton* **6**
Introduction *John Burton* **8**

Biogeographic regions map **12**
Climatic regions map **14**
Natural disasters map **16**
Pollution map **18**
Population map **20**

THE SPECIES AT RISK
22

THE PALEARCTIC REGION **24**
(Europe, temperate Asia, North Africa)

Habitat and plants *John Akeroyd* **26**
Wildlife *Tony Hutson* **32**

Species in focus **Butterflies** *R.I. Vane-Wright* **48**

THE NEARCTIC REGION **52**
(Canada, USA, parts of Mexico)

Habitat and plants *Peter Alden* **54**
Wildlife *Peter Alden* **60**

Species in focus **Migrating birds** *Tobias Salathé* **82**

THE NEOTROPIC REGION **86**
(South and Central America)

Habitat and plants *Sabina Knees* **88**
Wildlife *Chris Madsen* **94**

Species in focus **Mangroves** *Sue Wells* **114**

THE ETHIOPIAN REGION **118**
(Africa south of the Sahara)

Habitat and plants *Stephen Droop* **120**
Wildlife *Martin Jenkins* **128**

Species in focus **Tropical timbers** *Sara Oldfield* **144**

THE INDIAN AND ORIENTAL REGION **148**
(South of the Himalayas to Sulawesi)

Habitat and plants *Ruth Taylor* **150**
Wildlife *Tim and Carol Inskipp* **156**

Species in focus **Coral reefs** *Sue Wells* **170**

THE AUSTRALASIAN REGION **174**
(New Guinea, Australia, New Zealand)

Habitat and plants *Stephen Davis* **176**
Wildlife *Michael Kennedy* **184**

Species in focus **Antarctica** *Mark Carwardine* **200**

OCEANIA AND MARINE *Teresa Farino* **204**
(Islands and seas)

CONSERVATION IN ACTION
222

National Parks *John Burton with Peter Earland-Bennett* **224**
Protected regions map **240**
International Conventions map **242**
Conclusion *John Burton* **244**

Endangered Wildlife 246
Conservation Organisations 250
Bibliography 250
Index 251
Acknowledgments 256

This book was designed and produced by
Quarto Inc.
The Old Brewery, 6 Blundell Street
London N7 9BH

Senior Editor Sally MacEachern
Editor Judy Maxwell
Index Connie Tyler
Designer Hazel Edington
Maps Janos Marffy, David Kemp
Illustrations Ann Savage, Wayne Ford,
Paul Richardson, Rob Shone
Picture Research Co-ordination
Jane Lambert
Picture Manager Joanna Wiese
Assistant Art Director Chloë Alexander
Publishing Director Janet Slingsby
Art Director Moira Clinch

Typeset by ABC Limited, Bournemouth
Manufactured in Singapore by
Chroma Graphics (overseas Pte Ltd).
Printed by Leefung Asco Printers Limited,
China

10 9 8 7 6 5 4 3

Printed in China

PREFACE

An increasing number of plants and animals are becoming endangered or even being rendered extinct, and it is obvious that this is due mainly to loss of their natural environments or habitats. More difficult to identify are the reasons, and hence the possible solutions, for the habitat destruction.

One factor in the destruction is the disparity in wealth between countries of the world. This has contributed to, for example, the tragic loss of tropical rainforests. Many conservation groups in wealthy nations, such as in Europe and North America, have urged a ban on the import of tropical timbers such as mahogany. Yet for many poor countries, rainforests are among the few resources that can generate the foreign currency needed to pay for essential imports. If developing countries are to preserve their rainforests, then these forests must be able to earn as much standing as cut down. Part of the value of intact tropical forests is that they are a source of medicines, such as the leukemia cure discovered from the Madagascan Rosy Periwinkle. Unfortunately the profits from this discovery went mainly to the drug companies, instead of benefitting the forest inhabitants or Madagascar as a country, and so the decimation of Madagascar's forests continued.

A closely related issue is the link between human population growth and the destruction of wildlife. The human population is currently increasing at a rate of over 200 000 people a day. Along with increased populations come development schemes, such as drainage, irrigation and hydroelectric dams. These may be environmentally damaging in themselves and, as HRH the Duke of Edinburgh pointed out, "if such projects only result in further growth in the human population the problems are compounded. Developers may not like the idea, but as population numbers increase, the proportion of poor in the population is not likely to decrease, so that the total number of poor is actually increased."

A third factor is the ease with which we as individuals can lay the blame for environmental problems on large corporations and governments. Much of the destruction is indeed carried out by large corporations and sanctioned by governments, but individuals also play a part. In many cases the governments at fault were elected to power by the people, and corporations need the public's complicity to sell their products. Similarly, every time you vote for a politician you could be said to be condoning the policies that he or she supports. It is a sad fact that the vast majority of politicians and industrialists focus their attention on short-term measures and give long-term conservation needs a very low priority and a miniscule proportion of their budget.

However, there are glimmers of hope. For example, in the developed world, people at all levels of government and industry started taking notice of conservation issues in the 1980s. This may have been a result of nearly half a century of conservation education, through television, books and magazines. Perhaps the 1990s will see a radical change, since more and more of the leaders, both in politics and industry, will have grown up in a period when conservation was seen as a necessity and not a luxury.

INTRODUCTION

This book gives an overview of some of the problems facing wildlife as we approach the twenty-first century. The plants and animals within a region of the world share certain characteristics and these have led biologists to divide the world into biogeographical regions. While the fate of life in all regions is interlinked, this book focuses on each region in turn so that its wildlife can be examined in greater detail.

Among the species of most concern throughout the world are those confined or endemic to single islands or groups of islands. Because of their isolation and often small numbers they are particularly vulnerable to any environmental changes. In addition to the oceanic islands there are habitat "islands" on the continents, such as small mountain ranges surrounded by plains, isolated lakes, and cave systems. Also, people are increasingly creating "islands" for many parks and reserves are totally

Above *Fiddler Crab* (Uca).

Above right *Ice shelf, Admiral Byrd Bay, Antarctica.*

isolated and surrounded by agricultural lands. Research has demonstrated that there are critical sizes for islands, including reserves, below which the numbers of species that can be supported drop dramatically.

The threats currently facing the wildlife of islands and other areas include natural catastrophes, and even gradual change. The natural catastrophes that produce the most dramatic effects are those most similar to large-scale industrial pollution: volcanic eruptions. That of Mount St. Helens, USA, in May 1980 produced a plume of airborne ash and pumice that stretched almost a mile into the sky and affected the global climate for over a year. The only species likely to be made extinct by volcanic eruptions, or other natural disasters including hurricanes, tsunami (tidal waves), and floods, are those confined to islands.

Such natural catastrophes can now be manipulated by people. At a conference held in Stockholm in 1984, papers were given which showed how much environmental damage could be done by using small-scale nuclear explosions to trigger volcanic eruptions. As long ago as 1978 a Convention on Environmental Modification (Enmod 1977) came into force, and applies to the UK, USA, USSR, and over 40 other countries. This seeks to protect the world from environmental warfare and other

Left Cattleya skinneri, *the national flower of Costa Rica.*

disruptive activities. Unfortunately it is difficult to enforce, and so may be as ineffective as the various other conventions seeking to prevent the use of chemical and bacteriological weapons in war. Thousands of acres of Vietnam are still affected by the defoliants sprayed by US forces, and it may be decades, or even centuries, before they recover. Through these and countless other activities, people have become the most significant threat to the majority of species facing extinction.

The causes of extinction

Extinction is a natural process, and the majority of animals and plants that have evolved over the many millions of years since life first began are now extinct. However, over the past 400 years the rate of extinctions has accelerated. As Europeans burst from their continent and spread across the rest of the globe, they left behind them a trail of death and destruction, particularly on small oceanic islands. The Industrial Revolution enabled Europeans to spread even further afield, and destroy more and more natural habitat in their quest for resources. Having drained almost all the swamps of Europe, and cut down the primeval oak forests, the tropics were plundered. Modern medicine is allowing the last refuges of wildlife to be exploited in relative safety.

The human activities causing extinctions fall into three main groups: hunting, pollution, and habitat destruction, with overlap between them.

Hunting

From earliest times, human hunters have caused the extinction of many species. For instance, before humans colonized the Americas they contained a much greater diversity of large mammals, including mammoths and camels. With the spread of Stone Age hunters, over 100 species of mammals became extinct. Lions were wiped out in Greece in the Bronze Age, bears and beavers in Britain around the twelfth century, and the last aurochs (a wild ox) in eastern Europe in the early seventeenth century. Until the eighteenth century it was mainly large species that were hunted to extinction, and most animals managed to survive in remote areas. Then Europeans began traveling regularly all over the globe, and guns became more accurate and easy to handle. By the end of the nineteenth century, the gun had brought one of the most numerous birds in the world, the passenger pigeon, to the brink of extinction, reduced the Californian Condor to a level where its future was probably doomed, and aided the extermination of many species in the Pacific.

Today, hunting is, in theory, regulated in most parts of the world but it remains a major threat to the survival of birds and mammals in particular. Sport hunting, though the most questionable perhaps on moral grounds, generally has the least impact. Commercial hunting for ivory, skins, hides, and other products has rarely been effectively controlled and continues to lead to the extinction of species.

As the twentieth century draws to a close, though, it is probably plant species that are under the greater threat from direct exploitation. The plant equivalent of hunting, collecting, is endangering many species including rare orchids and cacti, and even rare species of timber trees.

Above *Ruffed Lemur* (Varecia variegata).

———— Pollution ————

Our food is contaminated with hundreds of pesticides and other chemicals. While we may only consume small amounts, large quantities run off into the rivers and accumulate in the soil. In addition huge amounts of pollutants, many of which will persist in the environment for decades, are being pumped directly into rivers, seas and the atmosphere. Oil slicks are the most visible marine pollutants and cause serious mortalities among sea mammals and birds. Even more dangerous, perhaps, are the hundreds of miles of "ghost" nets — fishing nets that drift in the oceans, ensnaring and drowning fish, seabirds, seals, dolphins, and turtles.

The effects of atmospheric pollution may be far more grave. In particular, some of the gases produced by industry rise up in the atmosphere and trap the sun's heat through the so-called greenhouse effect. Between them, the European Community, USA, Brazil, and USSR produce more of these gases than all other countries together. Concern that these gases will result in global warming is now widespread.

———— Habitat destruction ————

This is undoubtedly the most significant threat to the greatest number of species and is also the most difficult to prevent.

During the period 1975–1985 the world's consumption of wood increased by 22 per cent and paper production increased by over 41 per cent. Some 3 million hectares (7.4 million acres) of tropical forest were being cleared annually in the early 1980s, and by the end of the decade it was estimated that over 12 million hectares (30 million acres) were being cleared each year. In many parts of the world, burgeoning human populations are displacing wildlife in an effort to turn seemingly unproductive forests into farmland. For instance in the mid 1980s it was estimated that of over 4.6 million square kilometers (1.8 million square miles) of moist forests in Africa only 1.8 million (0.7 million) remained, and of these only 7 per cent were protected. Similar, equally depressing, statistics can be given for almost all parts of the world.

Responsibility for these problems does not rest solely on the poorer countries with their rapidly increasing populations. Fundamental inequalities lie at the root of much of this destruction Much of Europe and North America, for example, is wealthy and can (at least in theory) afford the luxury of conserving the remnants of their wildlife. Unfortunately, all too often, having depleted their own natural resources they have gone on to exploit the resources of the tropical countries. In order to repay crippling international debts, many developing countries are forced to allow wholesale exploitation by foreign companies. Japanese lumber companies, for example, are plundering the forests of southeast Asia, while conservationists may argue that with proper management such resources could be exploited in a sustainable way, few businesses and even fewer governments will consider investment over the timescales relevant to tropical forests.

In addition, it is the industrialized countries that are using the bulk of the world's natural resources. The average inhabitant of Canada, for example, uses 148 times more energy than a person in Zaire. Also, the importing countries insist on paying as little as possible for those raw materials.

The case for conservation

There are a number of arguments used to promote conservation. One contends that plants and animals should be conserved simply because they enhance the world and make it a more interesting place, and because they have a *right* to exist. Another is the materialistic one that plants and animals are useful to people. Although superficially attractive, this view is double-edged. It encourages decisions based on economic principles, which may not always be of benefit to the global ecosystem.

A third argument is that our survival depends on a healthy global ecosystem. The consequences of the spiraling human population and resource consumption will be

Above *Scarlet Tanager.*

Left *"Gerais" grasslands, central Brazil.*

as grave for us as for the natural world. When populations of any species increase, the resources upon which they depend become depleted, starvation becomes widespread, and pandemics of disease wipe out weakened populations.

As human populations have increased, people have gathered in urban areas and the potential for catastrophes has escalated. In 1986 over 40,000 people died of cholera in Africa, while since 1982 cases of AIDS have soared in many parts of the world. The toll taken by natural disasters is also great. An earthquake in China in 1976 killed over 240,000 people, while 184 million people were affected by floods from 1980-85. A volcanic explosion the size of Krakatoa or Tambora (many times greater than Mt St Helens) – and there is a reasonable certainty that one will occur within the next century or so – will kill millions of humans. A disaster is often followed by migrations of refugee populations and increased pressure on other areas and their wildlife.

Whichever justification one uses for conserving wildlife and the environment, one thing is clear: the destruction cannot continue, even in the short-term of the next few decades, without the collapse of entire ecosystems and human populations.

BIOGEOGRAPHIC REGIONS

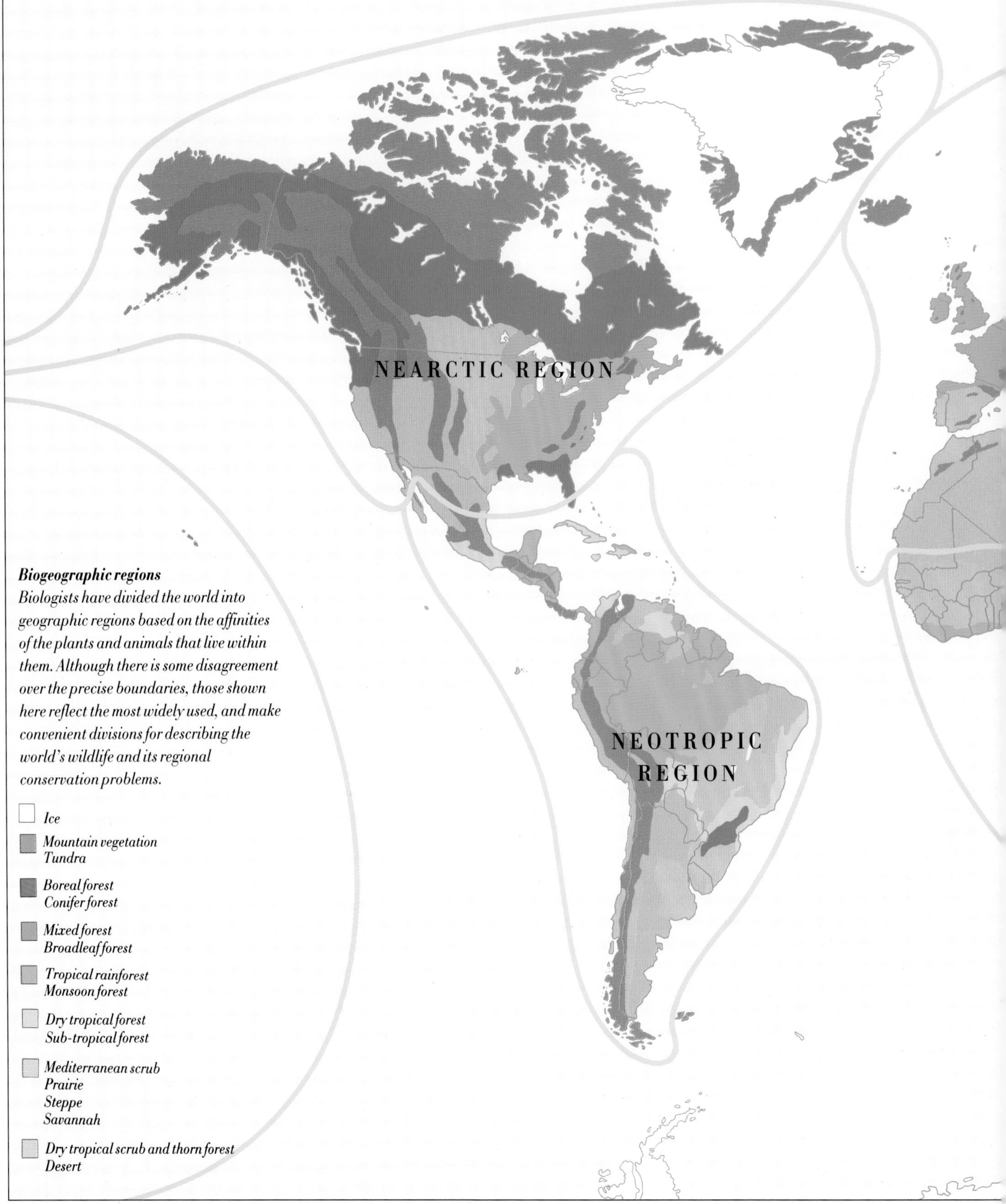

NEARCTIC REGION

NEOTROPIC REGION

Biogeographic regions
Biologists have divided the world into geographic regions based on the affinities of the plants and animals that live within them. Although there is some disagreement over the precise boundaries, those shown here reflect the most widely used, and make convenient divisions for describing the world's wildlife and its regional conservation problems.

- *Ice*
- *Mountain vegetation*
  Tundra
- *Boreal forest*
  Conifer forest
- *Mixed forest*
  Broadleaf forest
- *Tropical rainforest*
  Monsoon forest
- *Dry tropical forest*
  Sub-tropical forest
- *Mediterranean scrub*
  Prairie
  Steppe
  Savannah
- *Dry tropical scrub and thorn forest*
  Desert

PALEARCTIC REGION

OCEANIC REGION

INDIAN & ORIENTAL
REGION

ETHIOPIAN
REGION

AUSTRALASIAN
REGION

CLIMATIC REGIONS

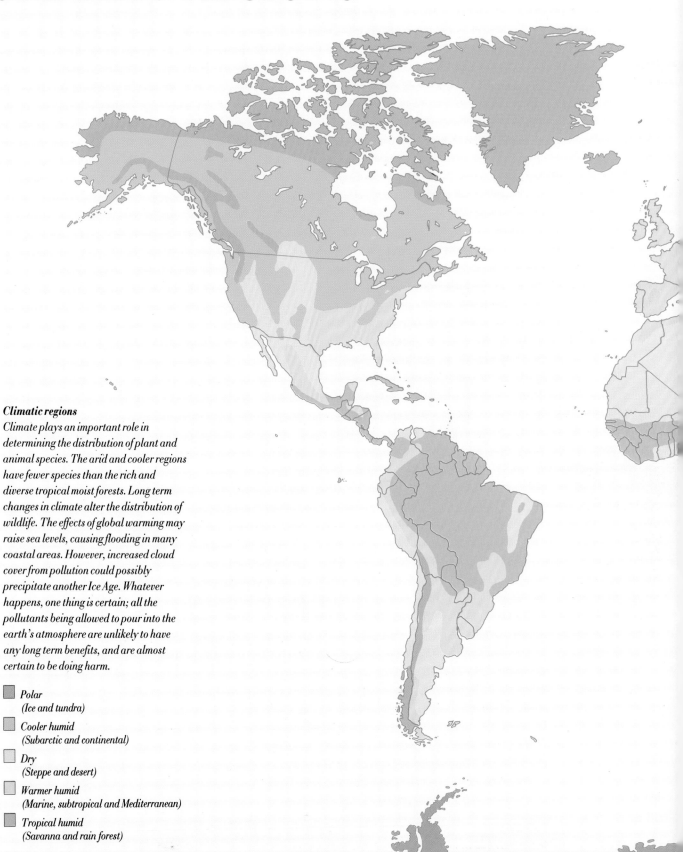

Climatic regions
Climate plays an important role in
determining the distribution of plant and
animal species. The arid and cooler regions
have fewer species than the rich and
diverse tropical moist forests. Long term
changes in climate alter the distribution of
wildlife. The effects of global warming may
raise sea levels, causing flooding in many
coastal areas. However, increased cloud
cover from pollution could possibly
precipitate another Ice Age. Whatever
happens, one thing is certain; all the
pollutants being allowed to pour into the
earth's atmosphere are unlikely to have
any long term benefits, and are almost
certain to be doing harm.

- Polar
  (Ice and tundra)
- Cooler humid
  (Subarctic and continental)
- Dry
  (Steppe and desert)
- Warmer humid
  (Marine, subtropical and Mediterranean)
- Tropical humid
  (Savanna and rain forest)

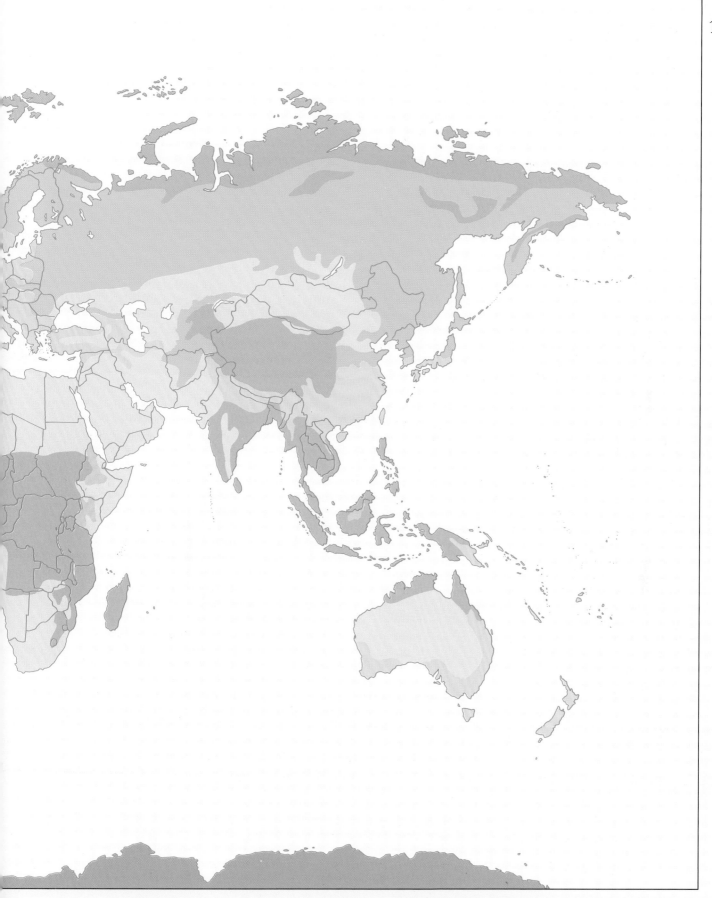

NATURAL DISASTERS

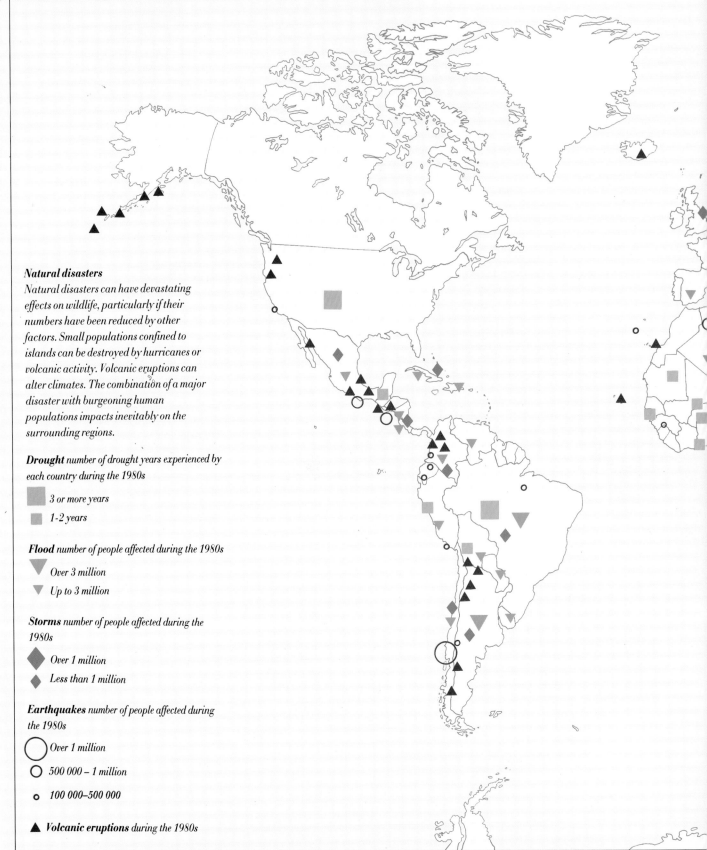

Natural disasters

Natural disasters can have devastating effects on wildlife, particularly if their numbers have been reduced by other factors. Small populations confined to islands can be destroyed by hurricanes or volcanic activity. Volcanic eruptions can alter climates. The combination of a major disaster with burgeoning human populations impacts inevitably on the surrounding regions.

Drought number of drought years experienced by each country during the 1980s

   3 or more years

   1-2 years

Flood number of people affected during the 1980s

   Over 3 million

   Up to 3 million

Storms number of people affected during the 1980s

   Over 1 million

   Less than 1 million

Earthquakes number of people affected during the 1980s

   Over 1 million

   500 000 – 1 million

   100 000–500 000

▲ **Volcanic eruptions** during the 1980s

POLLUTION

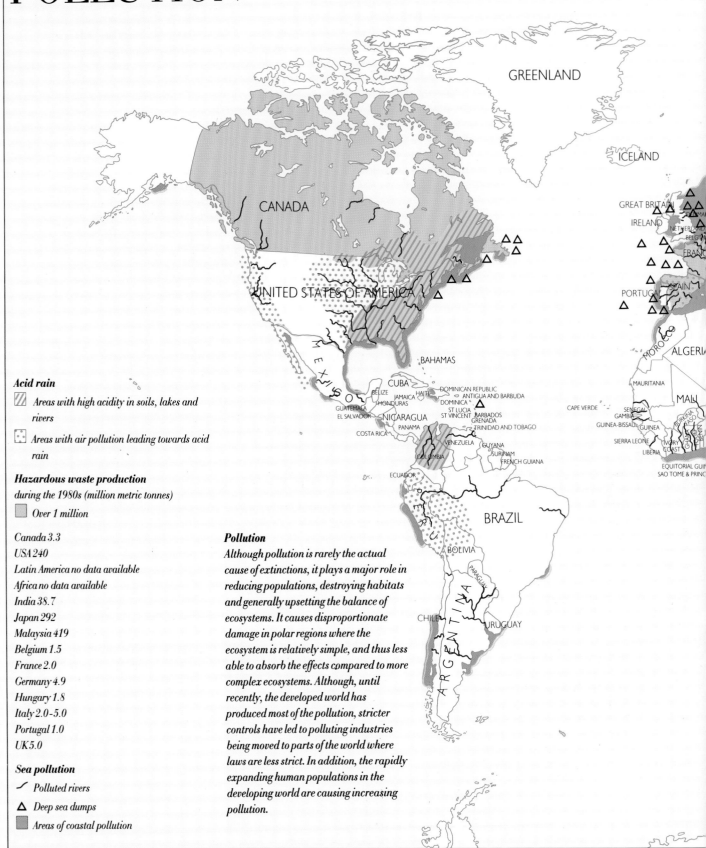

Acid rain

▨ Areas with high acidity in soils, lakes and rivers

⠇ Areas with air pollution leading towards acid rain

Hazardous waste production

during the 1980s (million metric tonnes)

▨ Over 1 million

Canada 3.3
USA 240
Latin America no data available
Africa no data available
India 38.7
Japan 292
Malaysia 419
Belgium 1.5
France 2.0
Germany 4.9
Hungary 1.8
Italy 2.0-5.0
Portugal 1.0
UK 5.0

Sea pollution

⁄ Polluted rivers

△ Deep sea dumps

▨ Areas of coastal pollution

Pollution

Although pollution is rarely the actual cause of extinctions, it plays a major role in reducing populations, destroying habitats and generally upsetting the balance of ecosystems. It causes disproportionate damage in polar regions where the ecosystem is relatively simple, and thus less able to absorb the effects compared to more complex ecosystems. Although, until recently, the developed world has produced most of the pollution, stricter controls have led to polluting industries being moved to parts of the world where laws are less strict. In addition, the rapidly expanding human populations in the developing world are causing increasing pollution.

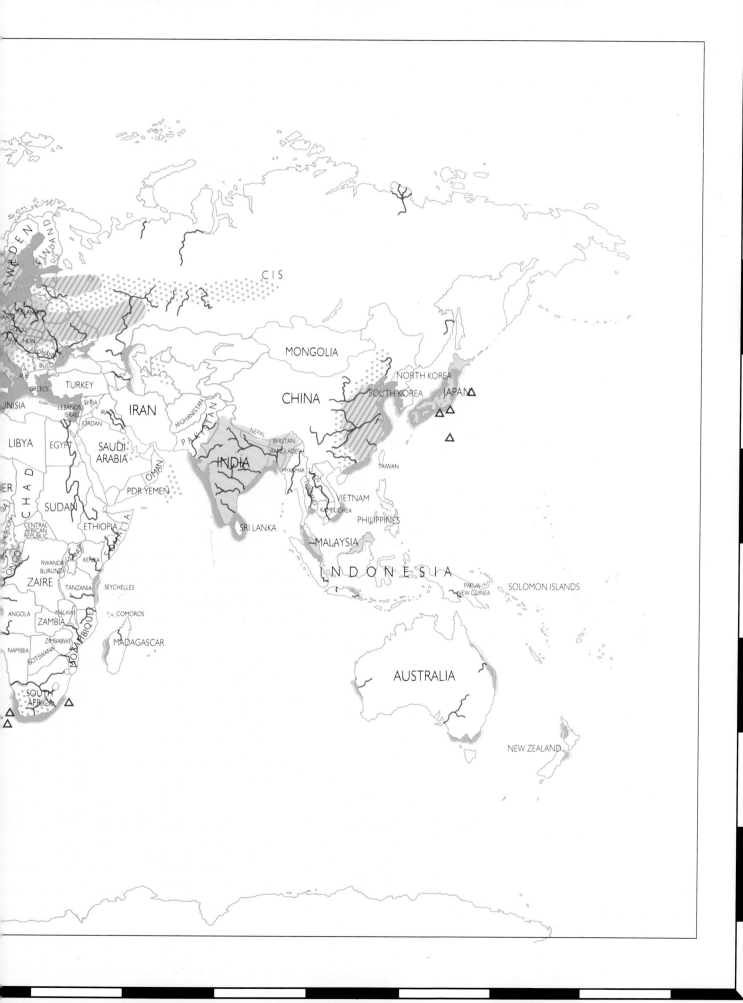

SWEDEN
FINLAND
POLAND
CZECH
AUR HUN
ROMANIA
BULG
ALB
GREECE
TURKEY
TUNISIA
LEBANON SYRIA
ISRAEL
JORDAN
IRAQ
IRAN
LIBYA
EGYPT
SAUDI
ARABIA
OMAN
PDR YEMEN
CHAD
SUDAN
ETHIOPIA
CENTRAL
AFRICAN
REPUBLIC
CONGO
ZAIRE
RWANDA
BURUNDI
KENYA
TANZANIA
SEYCHELLES
ANGOLA
ZAMBIA
MALAWI
COMOROS
NAMIBIA
ZIMBABWE
BOTSWANA
MOZAMBIQUE
MADAGASCAR
SOUTH
AFRICA

CIS

MONGOLIA

CHINA

NORTH KOREA
SOUTH KOREA
JAPAN

AFGHANISTAN
PAKISTAN
NEPAL
BHUTAN
BANGLADESH
INDIA
MYANMAR
LAOS
THAILAND
VIETNAM
KAMPUCHEA
TAIWAN
PHILIPPINES
SRI LANKA
MALAYSIA

INDONESIA

PAPUA
NEW GUINEA
SOLOMON ISLANDS

AUSTRALIA

NEW ZEALAND

POPULATION

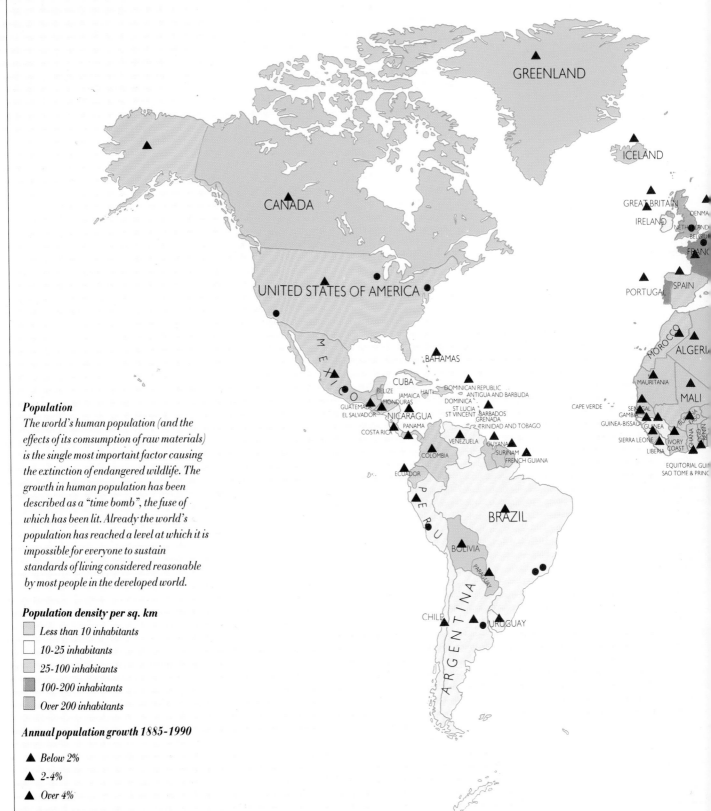

Population

The world's human population (and the effects of its comsumption of raw materials) is the single most important factor causing the extinction of endangered wildlife. The growth in human population has been described as a "time bomb", the fuse of which has been lit. Already the world's population has reached a level at which it is impossible for everyone to sustain standards of living considered reasonable by most people in the developed world.

Population density per sq. km

- Less than 10 inhabitants
- 10-25 inhabitants
- 25-100 inhabitants
- 100-200 inhabitants
- Over 200 inhabitants

Annual population growth 1885-1990

- ▲ Below 2%
- ▲ 2-4%
- ▲ Over 4%

- ● cities with over 5 million inhabitants

GREENLAND

ICELAND

CANADA

GREAT BRITAIN
IRELAND
DENMA
NETHERLAND
BELGIUM
FRANC

UNITED STATES OF AMERICA

PORTUGAL
SPAIN

MEXICO

MOROCCO
ALGERIA

BAHAMAS

MAURITANIA
MALI

CUBA
BELIZE
JAMAICA
HAITI
DOMINICAN REPUBLIC
ANTIGUA AND BARBUDA
DOMINICA
ST LUCIA
ST VINCENT
BARBADOS
GRENADA
TRINIDAD AND TOBAGO

CAPE VERDE

SENEGAL
GAMBIA
GUINEA-BISSAU
GUINEA
SIERRA LEONE
IVORY
LIBERIA
COAST

EQUITORIAL GUIN
SAO TOME & PRINC

GUATEMALA
HONDURAS
EL SALVADOR
NICARAGUA
PANAMA
COSTA RICA

VENEZUELA
GUYANA
SURINAM
FRENCH GUIANA

COLOMBIA

ECUADOR

PERU

BRAZIL

BOLIVIA

PARAGUAY

CHILE

ARGENTINA

URUGUAY

SWEDEN
FINLAND
POLAND
CZECH
AUS.
HUNG.
ROMANIA
BULG.
GREECE
TUNISIA
TURKEY
LEBANON
SYRIA
ISRAEL
IRAQ
JORDAN
IRAN
LIBYA
EGYPT
SAUDI
ARABIA
OMAN
PDR YEMEN
NIGER
CHAD
SUDAN
CAMEROON
CENTRAL
AFRICAN
REPUBLIC
ETHIOPIA
SOMALIA
CONGO
RWANDA
BURUNDI
UGANDA
KENYA
ZAIRE
TANZANIA
SEYCHELLES
ANGOLA
MALAWI
ZAMBIA
ZIMBABWE
MOZAMBIQUE
COMOROS
NAMIBIA
BOTSWANA
MADAGASCAR
SOUTH
AFRICA

CIS
MONGOLIA
CHINA
NORTH KOREA
SOUTH KOREA
JAPAN
AFGHANISTAN
PAKISTAN
NEPAL
BHUTAN
BANGLADESH
INDIA
MYANMAR
LAOS
TAIWAN
SRI LANKA
THAILAND
VIETNAM
KAMPUCHEA
PHILIPPINES
MALAYSIA
INDONESIA
PAPUA
NEW GUINEA
SOLOMON ISLANDS

AUSTRALIA

NEW ZEALAND

SPECIES

AT

RISK

THE PALEARCTIC REGION

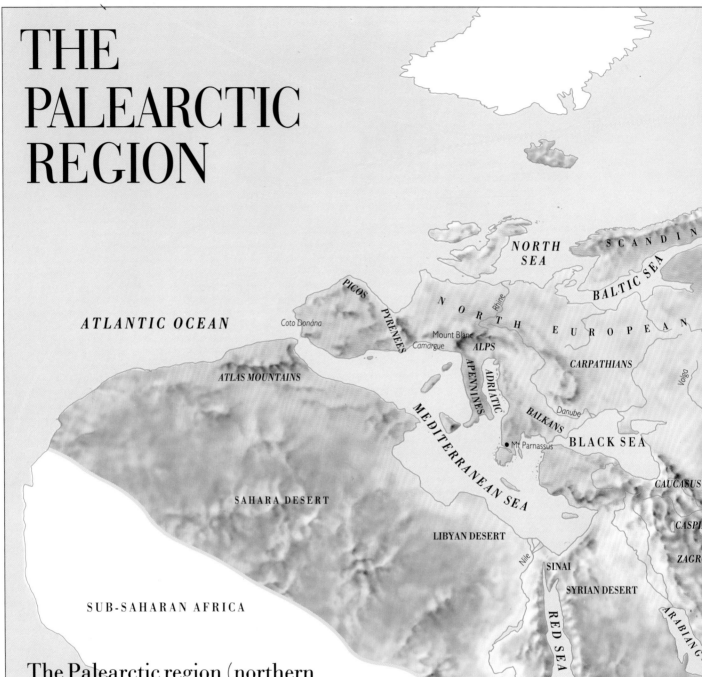

ATLANTIC OCEAN

PICOS

PYRENEES

Coto Donána

ATLAS MOUNTAINS

Camargue

Mount Blanc

ALPS

APENNINES

ADRIATIC

NORTH SEA

SCANDIN...

BALTIC SEA

Rhine

N O R T H   E U R O P E A N

CARPATHIANS

Volga

Danube

BALKANS

MEDITERRANEAN SEA

● Mt Parnassus

BLACK SEA

CAUCASUS

CASPIA...

SAHARA DESERT

ZAGRO...

LIBYAN DESERT

Nile

SINAI

SYRIAN DESERT

ARABIAN GU...

SUB-SAHARAN AFRICA

RED SEA

The Palearctic region (northern
Old World) extends from Iceland in
the west across Europe and Asia to Kamchatka
and the Bering Sea in the east and south to the Himalayas.
Many of the Palearctic habitats that exist today are fragments
of the original vegetation, particularly of the vast forests which
dominated the northern hemisphere.

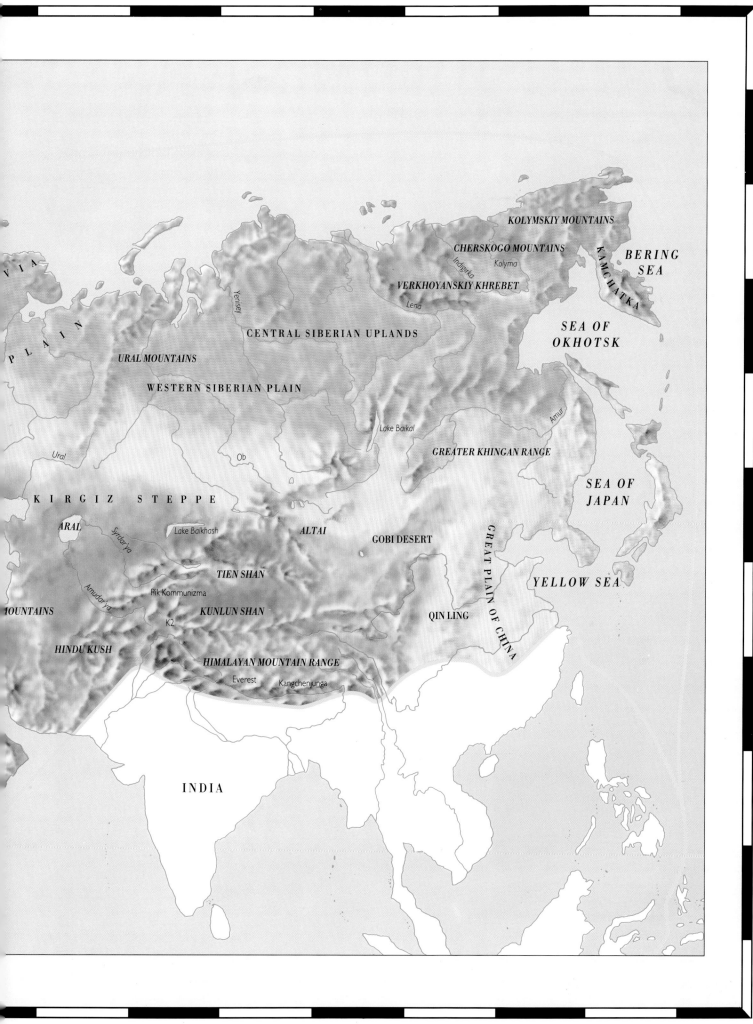

HABITAT & PLANTS

John Akeroyd graduated in botany from the University of St. Andrews, followed by a Ph.D. from Cambridge University and research fellowships at Trinity College, Dublin, and the University of Reading, including revision of Vol. 1 of *Flora Europaea*. Currently, he is a freelance botanist researching the taxonomy and conservation of European and Mediterranean plants, including identification, assessment of data for official and non-governmental bodies, writing and editing, and leading tour groups. He has written numerous scientific papers and contributed to many books.

The Palearctic region covers a wide range of climates and habitats in Europe, temperate Asia, and North Africa. These range from the cold deserts of the tundra of northern Europe and Siberia, through zones of coniferous and deciduous forests, and dry grasslands or steppes, to the hot deserts of central and southwestern Asia and north Africa. Within these zones are coastlands, wetlands and mountains, each with a further zonation that creates a graded and variable mosaic of vegetation and habitat. Comparatively recently many of these habitats have been eroded or have disappeared through human activity. Their loss threatens the region's rich resources of plants and animals.

Many of the Palearctic habitats that exist today are fragments of the once extensive tracts of natural vegetation, much of them dominated by forest, that formerly girded the northern hemisphere. The basic pattern of vegetation zonation was established some 100 million years ago, when the continental masses were assuming their present configurations. Since that time there have been countless episodes of migration, adaptation, and extinction of plants in response to climatic and other changes. These have given rise to today's complex patterns of distribution, often with isolated populations of individuals spread over a large area. One of the main factors influencing distribution has been successive cold periods, known as Ice Ages, during which glaciers spread out from arctic and mountainous regions. The other main factor has been the evolution and advancement of humans, notably the most recent species, *Homo sapiens.*

There are few records to show what plant species may have become extinct during historical times. Large mammals or birds such as the Lion or the Ostrich were recorded by writers in classical times, whereas the rarer plants were not. In more recent times, however, botanists have become increasingly concerned about the loss of valuable plant species, especially from the more populous areas of Europe and the

Right *A managed woodland in the Cotswolds, England. Humans have been managing European woodlands for centuries, the tended wood or coppices being used to produce wood for charcoal, as well as poles and laths. In Britain coppicing is a common practice, and the open woodland created is an important habitat for many flowering plants.*

Mediterranean. Many have disappeared through urbanization and road construction, intensive grazing and arable cultivation, forest plantation, drainage, fire, and pollution. Others are endangered by over-exploitation, either for particular products that they yield or for their use in an expanding horticultural industry. Above all, however, it is habitat destruction and disturbance that threatens the flora.

——— Forests: a surviving native vegetation ———

Provided there is enough water and a reasonably fertile soil, vegetation will in time come to be dominated by trees. Native forests or wildwood once covered much of the Palearctic between the tundra and deserts that delimit the region. Forests do still cover extensive areas of Eurasia and the higher mountains of parts of north Africa, but they have been severely reduced in extent and fragmented over the last 10,000 years through human management. Fortunately, the mixed landscape of woodland and agriculture that covers much of the populated Palearctic often provides as valuable a habitat for plants and animals as the wildwood that preceded it.

Temperate deciduous forest is characteristic of and largely confined to the Palearctic, from western and central Europe through to Russia, and over much of China and Japan. This type of vegetation has been especially reduced in area by human clearance for agriculture, as it tends to grow on better soils in areas of adequate rainfall. Some areas were set aside for forestry, but much forestry practice has been and continues to be destructive. Over much of the region, huge tracts of woodland have been cleared for lumber, charcoal-burning, and bark for tanning as well as to make way for grazing animals or farmland. Forests of conifers, often growing on poorer soils or in rugged or mountainous terrain, survived longer. However the resinous trees are susceptible to fire, and the safety match has represented their greatest threat, as it has to the evergreen Mediterranean oak forests.

Above *Coppicing is one of the traditional methods of managing a deciduous woodland. Each year the trees in a different section of the wood are cut down and trimmed to ground level. The stumps are cut at an angle to prevent water from settling on them and to allow the trees to regenerate. Over a period of years, the wood will contain areas of trees at various stages of regrowth, each of which will be a home for a particular group of plants and animals. The overall result is a dramatic increase in the variety of species present in a wood. The cut wood is used for a variety of purposes such as firewood, wattle fencing, stools, broomsticks, and other wood products.*

Left *Much of the Mediterranean has been replaced with second-growth forest, either as plantations or after fire-damage. The trees in this view of the Bucaco Forest, Portugal are all the same size; an indication that they are probably second growth.*

The habitats that the native deciduous wildwood supported have now mostly disappeared, with just a few areas of lowland primeval forest surviving, notably in parts of Poland and Lithuania. Happily, the trees themselves will regenerate locally and many of them occur widely in leisure areas and forestry plantations.

Plants have a remarkable ability to survive in small remnants of their native environment, far more so than the mammals and birds that need to forage for food. Patches of Wood Anemone, a widespread plant but one characteristic of ancient woodland, can often be found in hedge-banks, fields, or mountain-ledges. Their presence in an area suggests that it used to be covered by native deciduous forest. The Wild Service Tree, another indicator of ancient woodlands, survives in copses in some parts of London. A forest species that used to occur over the whole of Europe is the large, handsome Ladies-slipper Orchid. It is still present in reasonable numbers in a few parts of the Alps, but elsewhere is extinct or decimated. Forest clearance started its decline, which has been hastened by over-collection.

Evergreen forests of coniferous trees occupy vast areas of the Palearctic. The taiga of Siberia is a forest mostly of pines, firs, spruces, and larches, mixed locally with birch and aspen, and interspersed with areas of raised bog. It still forms a belt across the Soviet Union, although it is serously degraded in Scandinavia and the Baltic region. In the mountains of Europe, Asia, and North Africa, there are some fine forests of pines, spruces, firs, and cedars. A few coniferous trees have restricted distributions, such as the Serbian Spruce, which occurs only in a small part of central Yugoslavia. Fortunately, this elegant, spire-like tree is increasingly popular as an ornamental elsewhere in Europe and will certainly survive in cultivation. An even rarer conifer, the Sicilian Fir, once formed stands in the mountains of Sicily and now survives in just one remote grove. However, it is now being actively protected and propagated.

Grasslands and heathlands: a human landscape

Many grasses are drought-resistant, and large areas of eastern Europe and central Asia that are too dry for the growth of trees, together with drier parts of the Mediterranean area, are dominated by the grasslands known as steppes. These are mainly natural, although some have been created through the loss of tree and shrub cover by human activity. All are composed of drought-tolerant grasses, notably species of feather-grass *(Stipa)*. Much of the huge steppe region that extends from eastern Europe across the Soviet Union is now under cultivation, which has put a great deal of pressure on the limited areas of surviving steppe, and the many species of plants and animals adapted to live in it are under increasing threat.

When wildwood and, in wetter northern and western parts, peat covered huge areas of the Palearctic, insufficient light penetrated for the grasses and other light-demanding plants including those now known as "weeds" of cultivated land. Such plants were restricted to broken or rocky ground, or unstable or poor soil that did not allow the growth of trees. Some of these refuges still survive today, for example the astonishing plant-rich gorges of the island of Crete, and the strange mixture of Mediterranean and alpine plants in the rocky limestone pavements of the Burren region of County Clare in western Ireland.

The clearance of forests to provide pasture for grazing or meadows for hay opened up large areas of grassland. Although these are not natural environments, grassland that has been managed over successive human generations can still be very rich in species. Sadly, economic pressure has led to the abandonment of older management techniques, and modern meadows and pastures tend to be "improved"

Below *Ladies-slipper Orchid* (Cypripedium calceolus) *is now extinct or rare over most of its European range. Collecting by gardeners and for the horticultural trade is largely responsible for its disappearance.*

by artificial fertilizers. Britain has lost 95 per cent of its traditional colorful meadows, a terrible destruction of its heritage. The resulting bright green sward containing just a few species is a poor habitat for both plants and animals. Elsewhere the situation is not quite so bad, but many attractive species have been lost, such as in the traditional hay meadows of the Picos de Europa mountains of northern Spain. Bory's Gentian, a rare member of an attractive genus of mountain grassland flowers, is threatened by changes in traditional grassland management both in the Picos and in the Sierra Nevada of southern Spain.

Heathlands are another "unnatural" or managed type of vegetation with a rich flora. As their name suggests, they are often dominated by members of the heath or heather family, small or dwarf shrubs with reduced leaves and usually tiny massed flowers. Other shrubs include peaflowers such as the gorses and brooms, and grasses too may be present. Native heathlands are largely restricted to naturally broken

ground or to coastal areas. Burning and grazing, together with thin or poor soils, prevent trees from growing. However, in recent times, much heathland has been lost through encroachment of trees either naturally or by planting.

Moorland has a more peaty soil than heathland and occurs in more northern and mountainous climates. It has some affinities with the tundra of the far north, a treeless, mossy landscape with permanently frozen soil. Despite their remoteness, moorland and tundra have not escaped human disturbance. Forestry plantations have encroached on moorland and, in some parts of the Soviet Union, tundra has been disturbed by oil extraction.

Above left Drystone walls, grazed meadows, and isolated groups of trees are all typical of the intensively managed landscapes of most of Britain and Europe. However these are often old-established landscapes with a rich fauna and flora, such as this one near Chelmorton, Derbyshire, England.

Above Alpine meadows, many of which have never been sprayed with pesticides or herbicides, are often remarkably rich in flowering plants. In recent years there has been a rapid destruction of this once widespread habitat.

———— Mountains: a rich flora under threat ————

Mountains provide a wide range of habitats, from cliffs, rocks and screes, to grassland and, on the lower slopes, forest or scrub. They are fairly undisturbed compared with the lowlands, but are increasingly threatened by development for industry and tourism. Mountainous areas are often rich in minerals and the extraction of these can wreak havoc. In recent years the mountains of central Greece have been strip-mined to obtain bauxite, the major ore of aluminum. These mountains, which include the

Threats to the mountains

- Skiing damages habitats both through the construction and use of facilities and by opening up remote areas to large numbers of visitors.
- Mountain walking damages the habitats of many plants and makes them more vulnerable to picking and collecting. In some areas, such as the Alps, the flora is protected by law. In other areas, such as the Balkans and Spain, there is little protection.
- Tourist development related to walkers is damaging formerly undeveloped areas such as the Atlas mountains, the Caucasus, the Sierra Nevada, and the Alps.
- Excessive numbers of grazing animals in the Mediterranean region and elsewhere threaten many rare plants with extinction.
- Amateur botanists and, more seriously, the horticultural trade dig up mountain flowers and various bulbous plants. Species under particular pressure are saxifrages, bellflowers, Dianthus, and Cyclamen.
- The bulb trade between Turkey and western Europe is a peculiar scandal. A combination of the need of poor local people to make a living and the unscrupulous behavior of some bulb dealers has denuded large areas of bulbs, particularly crocuses, Snowdrop, and Cyclamen. One should always ascertain from dealers the precise source of their stocks.

famous Mt Parnassus, have a rich endemic flora. Mount Iti Speedwell, found in a few wet places on Mount Iti and nowhere else in the world, is in immediate danger of extinction due to nearby bauxite mining, despite the fact that its mountain home has been designated a nature reserve.

Over the past few decades there has been an unprecedented growth in personal wealth and leisure time among sections of the region's population, and people in many parts of Europe and Asia are now flocking to their mountains for recreation often damaging mountain habitats in the process.

--------- **Wetlands: in constant danger** ---------

Wetlands may be great expanses of water such as Lake Baikal in Siberia, large enough to have developed a whole suite of endemic wildlife, or regions such as the Camargue or the Volga delta, or they may just be small ponds or even damp hollows in an arable field. Whatever their size, they are perhaps the most threatened of all habitats. In Ireland, vast areas of bogland have been dug out to provide peat for domestic and industrial fuel, and its reserves of peat will be exhausted early in the next century. Elsewhere, wetlands have been drained on a huge scale for building or agriculture or because they harboured malaria. They are also susceptible to environmental pollution by acid rain or the runoff of fertilizer from farmland. More recently, recreational use has put pressure on inland areas of open water.

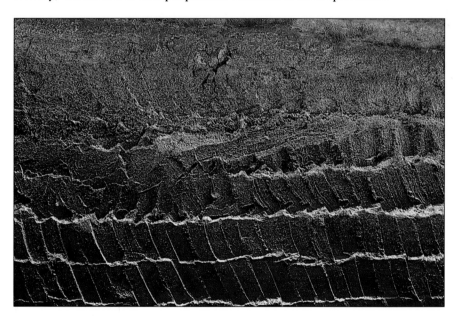

A growing problem in many areas has been the extraction of water to supply the human population, which has gradually lowered the watertables. Much of lowland Britain, for example, has become increasingly dry since the nineteenth century, when there were raised bogs even in southern England and wild Cranberries could be harvested around London. A dramatic example of threatened wetland is the enormous delta of the river Guadalquivir in southeastern Spain, forming the massive marsh and sand-dune systems of the Coto Doñana. These have a remarkable vegetation, dominated by woodland of Umbrella Pine and Cork Oak interspersed with impenetrable marshes and tidal lagoons. In the spring, a variety of rock roses and other shrubs give a blaze of color, and Wild Daffodils bloom under the pines. The area is famous for its bird life and is one of the last havens of the European Lynx. Alas, hoteliers and property developers have built indiscriminately around the reserve, and

the area is now drying out through extraction of water to serve the tourists.

The threat to wetlands is reflected in the large numbers of species that have declined in recent years. All over Europe, for example, the tiny Bog Orchid which grows on hummocks of moss in raised bogs has gradually disappeared.

The Mediterranean area: a very special case

The lands that surround the Mediterranean sea are subject to four months or more of hot and rainless summer. The vegetation is consequently dominated by trees and shrubs with drought-resistant, often small and leathery leaves, such as evergreen oaks, Carob, and Wild Olive. Many are aromatic, and familiar garden herbs such as Rosemary, Sage, and Thyme have their origin here. Thousands of years of felling, burning, and grazing have reduced the forests to a remnant. However, there are still great areas of scrubland, the maquis or macchie, and an even more degraded vegetation of often spiny hummocks less than a yard tall, the garigue. These areas of formerly wooded land have a rich flora, but it is too often dominated by alien plants, and several of the rarer species are threatened with extinction. This area has been affected by human activity for so long because of the great antiquity of the civilizations around the shores of the Mediterranean and in adjacent parts of the Middle East. These civilizations grew up as a result of the richness of the area's flora, which included the ancestors of many of our modern crops. The basic crops were wheat, olives and grapes, but people also made use of local cabbages, lettuces, chicories, onions and cresses, and fruits such as figs, dates, plums, and cherries. The wild populations of crop plants that survive in the Mediterranean region are a valuable reservoir of material for the plant breeder – and some of them are now rare or threatened. The Egadi Cabbage, a close relative of our garden cabbages, grows only on the small Egadi islands off the western coast of Sicily, which are facing increasing tourism and building. A related cabbage grows on one tiny island between Spain and North Africa and may already be extinct in the wild.

Far left *An Irish peat bog after cutting. Peat has been cut as a source of fuel for centuries, but in recent years an enormous market has developed for horticultural peat and this has destroyed many peat bogs. Efforts are now being made by the peat industry in Ireland not to exploit the biologically important bogs.*

Above *The Coto Doñana National Park relies on water that has its source outside the park. In recent years developments around the park have threatened its water supply, which could damage it irreparably.*

WILDLIFE

Tony Hutson left the Natural History Museum, London to spend six years as Conservation Officer on a project set up by the Flora and Fauna Preservation Society. He is currently Secretary of The Bat Conservation Trust and Secretary to the IUCN's Chiroptera Specialist Group.

Spotlight

- Pheasants (Phasianidae). Nine of the 15 Palearctic species are threatened by collecting for their plumage or for keeping in capitivity or through loss of habitat.
- Wolf *(Canis lupus)*. In Europe, the Gray Wolf has been subjected to unremitting persecution, resulting in a much fragmented relict population still undergoing local extinction. The Scandinavian population, for example, stands at seven.
- Capercaillie *(Tetrao urogallus)*. Hunting, habitat loss, and other human pressures have reduced most of Europe's population to isolated pockets. Eighty per cent of Scottish woods holding capercaillie recorded a decrease over the last five years to a population of 1,000–2,000 birds.
- Giant Panda *(Ailuropoda melanoleuca)*. Despite the most concentrated efforts in diverse ways, the Giant Panda continues to decline due to disturbance to it and its habitat, and natural factors. According to current estimates there are fewer than 1,000 in three main populations.

Elephants, large cats, hippopotamuses, rhinoceroses and other animals that are now regarded as essentially tropical once roamed the Palearctic region. The evidence of this early fauna can be found in fossil and subfossil remains, which reveal not just these big vertebrates, but also invertebrates, including insects and molluscs. Changes in climate and land connections have considerably altered this fauna. Some of the changes came in waves, most were slow, but in recent millennia the changes have been considerably influenced by the activities of one species – humankind. People affected the environment in a wide range of ways from utilization of forest timber to management of land for agriculture, settlement and transportation. The killing of wildlife for food or as "pests" or competitors – and, more recently, for "sport" – has also had a major influence, particularly on the larger animals.

It is possible to identify only about five Palearctic mammals that have become extinct in historical times, but many have been reduced to severely threatened relict populations in isolated areas, or persist only as domestic animals or through captive breeding. Other species have lost their Palearctic populations, but persist elsewhere in the world. The African Elephant may have survived in northwest Africa until about AD 100. The Lion is believed to have been present in Greece until about the same time, and occurred in Morocco until about 1920 and in Iran until 1942.

The western Palearctic and Japan have seen the most dramatic reductions in range of many species. Small remnant populations of, for instance, the Gray Wolf and the Brown Bear only survive at all through intensive conservation effort. However,

Right *The European Bison or Wisent* (Bison bonasus), *once extinct in the wild, is now thriving having been bred from captive animals and released into several east European forest reserves from the main herd in the Bialowieza forest, Poland.*

Left *The European Brown Bear* (Ursus arctos) *once occurred throughout Europe, surviving in Scotland until the Middle Ages. Only isolated remnant populations survive in western Europe, but there are healthier populations in Yugoslavia and other parts of eastern Europe.*

Below *In the Palearctic, the Gray or Timber Wolf* (Canis lupus) *survives in only a few places in Italy, Iberia, and eastern Europe after centuries of persecution. Continuing prejudice means that populations are still threatened with local extinction.*

even considerable effort and protection failed to save the European populations of the Bald Ibis, which became effectively extinct in Europe in 1990. The species survives as a few, small, isolated populations in Morocco. The Wisent (European Bison), once widespread from southern Sweden to the Caucasus, persisted only in captivity until wild populations were re-established in the Bialowieza forest of Poland and Lithuania, and subsequently in other isolated areas east to the Caucasus. The Arabian Oryx was destined for extinction, but some of the remaining wild animals were trapped and taken for captive breeding. The wild population did become extinct, but the captive-bred population allowed a later successful reintroduction program in Oman. Père David's Deer, from the lowlands of north China, was similarly extinct in the wild but widely kept in zoos and parks from a herd established in Woburn, England. It, too, has recently been re-established in the wild.

Forests

The land habitat that has probably been most reduced in area in historical times is forest. Huge tracts of forest were lost in exactly the same way as we are currently losing tropical forest: by extraction of the largest trees and by clearfelling for timber, for agriculture and for other development. Large programs of afforestation or reafforestation have occurred, but these have usually been with monocultures of introduced trees and frequently at the expense of other valued habitats, particularly heaths and moors.

The deforestation started in prehistoric times and was the cause of the demise of many larger mammals. In historical times, fragmentation continued and helped many local extinctions, for example of boars in Britain, but sufficient forest remains to maintain populations of these animals elsewhere in the Palearctic. However, European populations of European Lynx, Brown Bear and Gray Wolf are in a precarious state and their long-term survival relies on protected areas, since elsewhere they are still subject to persecution as pests, to hunting for sport and to loss

Right *A male Capercaillie* (Tetrao urogallus) *displaying in a Swedish forest. This large, extremely palatable game bird was exterminated in Scotland but successfully reintroduced from Scandinavia.*

Spotlight

- Bustards (Otitidae). The two European and the two other Palearctic bustards are all threatened by hunting and habitat loss. In Britain, for example, their low dry grassland habitat has been reduced by 95 per cent.
- Butterflies. Of Europe's 380 butterfly species; 96 are threatened and 15 endangered, particularly in western Europe, due to land drainage, agrochemicals and mechanization of agriculture.
- Tortoises *(Testudo)*. The three European species have been threatened by trade and even where this is controlled they still suffer from habitat loss.
- Cranes (Gruidae). Five of the seven Palearctic crane species are threatened by drainage of wetlands and hunting for food, sport, and their plumage.

of habitat. Small mammals may not often suffer persecution but they are vulnerable to habitat change, and the Bavarian Pine Vole, first described as recently as 1962, is probably already extinct.

The great Palearctic taiga, a forest of conifers, birch and aspen, lies south of the arctic tundra. With its equivalent in North America, it once constituted a third of the world's forested area. At its western end, in Scandinavia and the Baltic countries, it has been seriously eroded, and there is concern about a proposed forestry industry that could affect 1.6 million square kilometers (600,000 square miles) of unspoiled taiga west of the Urals. But further east in the vast and sparsely populated region of Siberia, extensive tracts persist. These maintain forest species that have suffered in the west, and also provide some shelter in the winter for many of the tundra animals. Thus the famed Sable, prized for its fur, no longer exists in Scandinavia, Finland, and western Russia, giving the Soviet Union total control over the trade in its fur. While the geese, ducks, waders, and many of the passerines of the arctic tundra migrate as winter approaches, other animals follow the Reindeer south to winter in the great northern taiga. There the Capercaillie, the most forest-loving of the grouse, is found in greatly reduced populations. It became extinct in Britain, Ireland and Belgium, but has been reintroduced to Scotland.

Moving south, the forests become more deciduous and diverse, until in the drier areas around the Mediterranean there is a return to a more restricted tree flora. The Mediterranean forests are very diverse in other plant and animal life. Those in northern Greece provide the last European strongholds of European Lynx, Gray Wolf and Brown Bear, but large areas have been lost and further losses are planned.

A different kind of forest altogether is found in China. Extensive high-altitude bamboo forests occur around central and southern China and up into the foothills of the Himalayas. In small remnant parts of this forest lives the Giant Panda. Taxonomists and systematists still debate this enigmatic creature's relationship to other animals. Its rarity and popularity have led to its being a prized diplomatic gift and it is both an emblem and a millstone of conservation. Despite vast resources devoted to attempts to conserve the species and increase its populations, there remain

Left *The Giant Panda* (Ailuropoda melanoleuca) *has come to symbolize endangered species, being used as the logo for WWF. Its requirements are extremely specialized and unless extensive areas of its bamboo forest home are protected, it may be doomed to extinction.*

serious doubts about its long-term future. In the wild it has nearly every protection people can offer, although severe disruption to its habitat continues. There have been concerted efforts to develop captive-breeding programs, but the animal remains uncooperative.

—————— Grasslands to deserts... ——————

Forest loss has been spread over such a long period that it is difficult to measure the declines of its fauna. In comparison, the conversion of grassland for agriculture, particularly for arable farming, has been rapid. Europe has lost about 90 per cent of its dry grassland in the last 100 years, and as a result some 30 bird species are now considered vulnerable. Several recent initiatives have been developed to help protect this habitat and its fauna. Many of these initiatives have come through European Community (EC) directives or recommendations coupled with local effort, often aimed particularly at flagship species such as the Great Bustard, Montagu's Harrier, and the Stone Curlew. But many of the steppic birds are dispersive, due to an erratic and thinly distributed food supply, and so local protection may not be enough. The grasslands may be one of the most important areas for international co-operation through, for example, EC and non-EC international treaties. While the major aims must be prevention of further losses of grasslands and even their re-creation, there is also the realization that sympathetically managed, pesticide-free cereal crops can provide good cover and feeding areas for some species.

The Arabian Bustard is probably now extinct in the Palearctic and the other three western Palearctic bustards (the Great, Little, and Houbara Bustards) are all considered endangered or threatened, with hunting being as responsible as habitat loss in some areas. The Corncrake is still widespread, but in very fragmented populations due to pressure of agriculture. The mixture of forest and grassland is particularly important for a number of mammals, including deer, Wisent, Wolverine, and wild horses. Przewalski's Horse was once widespread around the northern and western borders of the Gobi desert. Discovered in the 1870s, it is now only known from captive-bred stock and has been reintroduced to a number of places within its

DISTRIBUTION
GREAT BUSTARD

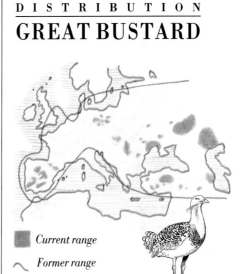

  Current range

  Former range

Great Bustard (Otis tarda). *Toward the end of the 18th century the Great Bustard reached the maximum extent of its range, encouraged by clearance of forest areas in central and western Europe. However, as steppes and dry meadows were replaced by arable land its range diminished. Hunting pressures, pesticides and further habitat changes mean that its current range is severely fragmented.*

former range. Another wild horse, the Tarpan, occurred throughout much of Europe and eastward, probably to China. It was last seen in Europe in about 1850 and is now also extinct. The Tarpan is the origin of the domestic horse and efforts have been made to recreate it by selective breeding, with some recent success in Poland.

The wild ass of Asiatic lowlands, the Onager, includes the Syrian Wild Ass, the smallest and most distinctive form. Only 1 meter (3¼ feet) high, this was the wild ass of the Bible, but it, too, is extinct. Its range took it into the deserts shared with gazelle, antelope, camel, oryx, and Arabian Tahr. Despite living in habitats that are apparently inhospitable to people, most of the Palearctic populations of these animals are at least threatened, with the Arabian Oryx only existing in the wild as a result of the reintroduction of captive-bred animals. Dromedary (one-humped) Camels only survive as domestic animals – indeed, the largest wild population is now in Australia! – while the wild population of the Bactrian (two-humped) Camel is reduced to a few hundred in protected areas of the Gobi desert. The bustards and the larger mammals have long been hunters' prey but, in some instances, human activity has helped species. The "greening" of Israel for food production has encouraged one gazelle species to the extent that it is now regarded as a pest and controlled by culling.

The large cats – Caracal, leopards, and Cheetah – are found from southwest Asia through Arabia to Africa. They are principally arid zone species, but the first two at least do occur in forests. Although they have a wide distribution and versatility of

Above *Domesticated Bactrian or Two-humped Camels* (Camelus bactrianus). *Their wild ancestors roamed the deserts of central Asia. They are now confined to a small area of the Gobi desert, but are strictly protected and may be increasing in number.*

Above right *The Snow Leopard* (Panthera uncia) *is found only at high altitudes in and around the Himalayas. Although it is probably the rarest of the big cats, its skins are still regularly seen on sale in Kashmir.*

behavior, their Palearctic populations are nowhere healthy and some of the more eastern ones are seriously threatened. The Snow Leopard occurs from western Mongolia down to the Himalayas and eastwards. Mongolia is the only country within its range that is not party to an international treaty to protect the species, and it allows foreign hunters to stalk and kill in exchange for very high trophy fees. The Caucasian race of the Tiger is extinct, and the population of the Amur or Siberian Tiger is only a few hundred. It has been suggested that there is now not enough wild game to sustain even this limited population and that the Tigers should be culled to prevent them turning to domestic animals.

Changes to the arid zones pose an equal threat to smaller birds and mammals. Various partridges and some of the larger birds of prey that soar over the plains in search of food are affected, and so is their prey, including some of the variety of snakes, lizards, and tortoises that are adapted to the dry regions. Europe is surprisingly rich in reptiles and some, such as the Meadow Viper, have been identified as species of international importance in the conservation of European grasslands. The status of tortoises has also excited interest, leading to the establishment of a tortoise "village" in the Massif des Maures of southern France. This is developing programs for tortoise breeding and rehabilitation, and forms a center for research and education, especially for the endangered Hermann's Tortoise of southern Europe. Rodents are a large and diverse group of mammals with their stronghold in the dry and arid zones, so it is pleasing to note that only one species from this habitat is threatened – Menzbier's Marmot, from southeast Kazakhstan, USSR, a poorly known rodent with an extremely limited population.

The dry grasslands also support many invertebrates. A quarter of Europe's 380 butterfly species are regarded as threatened, including 15 in danger of extinction. The Alcon Large Blue Butterfly is the most endangered in a genus of eight species, all threatened, and including the Large Blue, which was the most recent loss to the British butterfly fauna.

Swallowtail (Papilio machaon)

Apollo (Parnassius apollo)

Large Blue (Maculinea arion)

...and wetlands

In some areas the plains give way to desert, in some to wetlands, another habitat so threatened that an international convention has been established for its conservation. Overall the greatest problems are peat digging for fuel, and drainage. Grazing, hunting, and over-exploitation are also significant, while afforestation, as proposed for the unique flow country of northern Scotland, is being resisted by a determined conservation lobby. There are still spectacular freshwater wetlands, coastal wetlands, and salt marshes scattered through the Palearctic, but few do not face some threats.

Of particular concern are birds such as pelicans, herons, storks, and cranes, while wildfowl, waders and other birds are also threatened. For many species, the wetlands are only temporary homes – not their breeding grounds. But studies of birds using wetlands as wintering areas or stopover points on migration may give the first indications of population problems. The Slender-billed Curlew is regarded as Europe's rarest migrant and major efforts are being made to study it both on its wintering grounds in Europe and North Africa, and on its breeding grounds in the vast marshes of southwest Siberia. It is hoped that the wide-ranging international effort will establish the reasons for this bird's decline and improve its status.

Interest in the more spectacular cranes was also provoked by declines noted at migration points or wintering grounds. The two species of the western Palearctic, the Crane and the Demoiselle Crane, have disappeared from considerable parts of their former range, but are in no immediate danger. However, four species in the eastern Palearctic are giving grave cause for concern, with populations now limited and fragmented, and their habitats threatened. At least for the beautiful Siberian White Crane, an outstanding international conservation effort has resulted in a major success story. It is now protected at its known breeding grounds and along its migration routes, wild populations have been bolstered by captive-breeding programs and significant previously unknown populations have been discovered. As mentioned earlier, the Bald Ibis was not so fortunate and became extinct in Europe. Strenuous efforts are being made to monitor, study, and protect the few remaining wild Japanese Crested Ibis, backed up by a captive-breeding program.

One of Europe's rarest birds, the Greenland White-fronted Goose, faces major problems in its wintering grounds. It is being monitored with concern in Ireland, where it is hunted, Wales, and Scotland, including the island of Islay.

Right *Japanese Cranes* (Grus japonensis) *displaying. The elegant "dancing" displays of cranes have inspired many Japanese artists.*

Although the bird is protected by an EC directive, the UK government gave permission for peat digging of the raised bogs of Duich Moss on Islay and the birds are also persecuted on crop fields there. Despite massive public outcry, threats of action against the UK government and offers of compensation to farmers, the long-term future of the goose on Islay remains uncertain.

While many coastal wetlands have been lost or spoiled, some good areas have been created. The new polder lands of the Netherlands include extensive marshland, providing an important haven for waders, wildfowl, and reedland birds. Many human-made reservoirs, gravel, and sand pits have also provided wonderful wildlife areas. For example, birdwatchers flock to near Riems, France, to see the migrant cranes, sea eagles, and a great number and variety of other birds at reservoirs that were completed only about 30 years ago.

Lakes and rivers

The extremes of the wetland habitats are, of course, the lakes and rivers. An indication of the scale of the conservation problems facing this habitat is the fact that over half of the 200 European freshwater fish species are endangered. This is mainly due to pollution and overfishing, although the problem of probably the most threatened European fish, the Valencia Toothcarp, is competition with alien species such as the Mosquito Fish, introduced (as its name suggests) to control mosquitoes. A campaign has recently been launched by the Council of Europe to recognize and address the threats to fish. There has also been a surge of interest in dragonflies with the realization that many species are in trouble.

Rivers are an obvious example of a habitat that does not recognize political boundaries, and there is continual complaint by one country of pollution of its rivers by another. Nevertheless, there is hardly a country through which they flow that cannot take part of the blame for the troubled state of some of Europe's greatest rivers, such as the Danube and the Rhine. Some rivers have improved, for example the River Thames has much higher levels of oxygen than 30 years ago and over 100 fish species, including the Salmon, have been recorded in its waters. But this is still a far cry from the distant days when dockworkers on the Thames went on strike, refusing to eat salmon and oysters every day! Even the most highly protected and best funded fishing, that for game fish such as Salmon, has its own lobby for conservation of stocks, which are declining due to its own activities and commercial, non-sporting, fishing in river mouths and at sea.

Lakes and rivers have also been affected by the increase in boating activities of various kinds, causing pollution, damage to banks and bankside vegetation, and considerably reducing the amount of undisturbed water available to birds. Of particular concern have been pelicans, the Pygmy Cormorant and ducks, such as the White-headed Duck, in the west, and inland gulls (Relict and Saunder's Gulls) in the east of the region. The establishment of spectacular reserves for the shooting of waterfowl has had the side effect of poisoning birds, for example swans, which take in the lead pellets during feeding. While there has been considerable success in getting fishermen to change lead weights for weights of more acceptable materials, finding an alternative to lead shot is proving more difficult. Steel shot has been tried but it seems to be less effective than lead shot at killing birds and so may not be the best answer.

The mammals arousing most concern in the aquatic environment have been the Eurasian River Otter and the Beaver. The Beaver has long disappeared from much of its former range, and forestry interests and fear of flooding caused by the dams it builds have frequently deterred its reintroduction. Its current decline in Norway has encouraged only limited activity to protect it, but it has been reintroduced recently to Sweden, Finland, Czechoslovakia, and the Netherlands. The decline of the River Otter, on the other hand, has been widely regretted and there are major conservation programs to meet a variety of causes. These include recovery plans, reintroductions, pressure to reduce pollution, provision of havens and the development of devices to avoid its accidental capture in nets and traps. The range and populations of the Pyrenean Desman are also declining. This is a remarkable little insectivore of montane streams in the Pyrenees and other areas of northwest

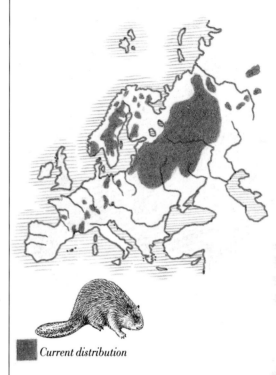

DISTRIBUTION
EUROPEAN BEAVER

■ Current distribution

Range of the European Beaver (Castor fiber). Formerly found throughout the forested areas of Eurasia, its current natural distribution is severely reduced. However, beavers have been reintroduced to France, Netherlands, Germany, Austria, Poland, Finland, Norway, and Sweden.

Left A Beaver (Castor fiber) lodge in Finland. Beavers are the only mammals that can modify the landscape on a large scale to suit their own specialized requirements. They do this by felling trees and damming rivers to form shallow swamps. The huge lodges are used for breeding and for storing supplies of food for the winter.

Spain and Portugal. Even in such mountain streams there is pollution, and afforestation causes shading and acidification of the waterways. The desman also suffers predation by feral American Mink, a scourge of European waterways which thrives even at the expense of indigenous European Mink.

The declines of some invertebrates have aroused considerable interest, such as that of the Medicinal Leech. Although no longer of much medical importance, the Medicinal Leech is a familiar, if not household, animal and its disappearance from much of its former range has led to high levels of protection for it. Many of the invertebrates are at least as sensitive to pollution as fish and ducks, and their diversity is being used increasingly as a biological indicator of pollution. This is important since even regular analysis of water samples can fail to detect major incidents of effluent pollution.

———— **Mountains** ————

As might be expected, the mountains are probably the least disturbed habitat. Apart from providing refuge for animals such as bear and wolf, they also have their own large mammal fauna, including the Ibex, Chamois, Mouflon, Markhor, and Goral. Nevertheless, forestry and farming have gradually encroached on wild territory, and the populations of these animals have become fragmented and reduced. The Pyrenean race of Spanish Ibex is almost extinct and the rest of its populations need continual support. The Mouflon and Chamois are experiencing mixed fortunes. Thought to be the origin of domestic sheep, the Mouflon is losing ground in some areas but increasing in, for instance, Poland. Until recently the Chamois population of Abruzzo National Park in northern Italy was considered endangered, while now it has recovered sufficiently for some animals to be used as founder stock for a

Above *A ram Mouflon* (Ovis musimon). *This animal may represent the wild form of an early domesticated sheep. Once endangered, it has been introduced in many parts of Europe as far north as Germany.*

Top *The Alpine Ibex* (Capra ibex ibex) *was nearly exterminated, having been extensively hunted in the nineteenth century for its horns, gallbladder, and other parts which were used in Europe as medicines and aphrodisiacs.*

reintroduction to another park. The Markhor, with its spectacular spiral horns, has been a much sought-after hunting trophy. It lives on lower slopes than the Ibex and, although still occupying most of its former range in central south USSR and further south, many populations are reduced or extinct.

For many of the larger birds of prey, which breed in the rocky mountaintops and range over large areas for food, persecution and disturbance are the main problems. In some areas, the placing of poisoned baits for pest species, such as foxes, or even for the birds themselves, has caused many deaths. The Lammergeier (or Bearded Vulture) hangs on in mountain areas of southern Europe and north Africa and has even been recently reintroduced to Austria, but its status is still precarious. The same is true for other vultures, such as the Griffon and Black, and eagles such as the Imperial Eagle. The Black Vulture is distributed from Spain to China but is believed to have a world population of fewer than 2,000 pairs, about 400 of which are in Spain. The largest colony occurs in an extensive hunting estate with a broadly sympathetic owner, and has recently survived a threat from a proposed airforce shooting range.

The mountain forests and bare tops also provide habitat for a range of pheasants, partridges, and grouse. Encroaching farmland can affect these birds by reducing feeding areas and forcing them into unsympathetic areas when they move down to lower altitudes in winter. The five species of snowcock are all restricted to small mountain areas and the Altai Snowcock is believed to be particularly at risk, as is the Caucasian Black Grouse. The spectacular pheasants of Asian mountain forests have been widely hunted for food, for sport, and for their beautiful plumage. Among the most threatened in the wild are Cabot's Tragopan, Chinese and Slater's Monals, and Brown-eared, Blue-eared, Elliot's, Reeve's, and Lady Amherst's Pheasants. Perhaps fortunately, their beauty makes them popular captive birds, but the genetic stock of some captive collections is unclear.

While afforestation may be a threat in some areas, deforestation is affecting the wildlife elsewhere. The growth of skiing has brought a range of problems, including the clearing of woodland that provided winter cover for a range of animals, compaction and scarification of heavily used ground leading to denuding of the soil, and increased disturbance. Extending the skiing season has a particularly bad effect on the flora upon which many special upland insects rely as well as on the breeding of birds and mammals.

Above *Earlier this century, the Black Vulture* (Aegypius monachus) *was widespread and abundant over most of southern Europe but it is now reduced to scattered isolated populations. Its future survival probably depends on the provision of "bird tables" where carcasses are put out for it.*

Caves

Caves provide an important refuge, notably for bats, but also for a range of other animals (including humans). While temperate caves do not contain the diversity of fauna found in tropical caves, a number of animals have become specialized for this type of environment.

Traditionally, certain species of bat, particularly horseshoe bats, some "mouse-eared" bats, and bent-winged bats, have used caves as their major breeding site, forming large summer colonies for the birth and rearing of their young. Northern European breeding colonies, especially those of horseshoe bats, have deserted underground sites and sought the extra warmth of surface structures, principally the roofs of buildings. It is speculated that this move followed disturbance and declines in populations, so that there were no longer sufficient numbers of these bats to maintain in caves the temperatures required for the successful rearing of young. In southern Europe, caves are still important for maternity colonies of bats. Throughout

Right *A cluster of roosting Greater Horseshoe Bats* (Rhinolophus ferrumequinum). *Many species of bat need to roost in large, closely packed clusters to conserve energy. When their populations become reduced they may have to use up energy maintaining the temperature of the cluster.*

Spotlight

- Horseshoe bats *(Rhinolophus)*. All five European species are threatened by disturbance of breeding sites and damage to feeding sites. The two most widespread species, the Greater and Lesser Horseshoe Bats, are disappearing in the north and west of their range, and the UK population of the former is estimated to have declined by over 95 per cent in the last 100 years.
- Bechstein's Bat *(Myotis bechsteinii)*. Cave deposits show that this bat was very common 3,000 to 10,000 years ago. It is now extremely rare throughout Europe, probably due to loss of forest for feeding and roost sites.
- Egyptian Fruit Bat *(Rousettus aegyptiacus)*. Having recently expanded in range following the increased cultivation of fruit, it is now under pressure from fruit growers and townspeople. Control campaigns in Israel resulted in the extinction of three insectivorous bat species and the near extinction of a further five species.
- Pond Bat *(Myotis dasycneme)*. This bat is still widespread through northern Europe to western Russia, but has only about three healthy centers of population. It has declined due to disturbance of its roost sites, particularly wood treatment of buildings housing summer roosts, and pollution of the waterways over which it feeds.

Europe, these underground structures provide hibernating sites – cool, undisturbed environments where bats can eke out reserves of fat through the winter period when their insect food is scarce.

To what extent the cave salamanders of Sardinia and of north and central Italy rely on this habitat is uncertain, but there are some exclusively cave-dwelling animals. The permanent association with the dark, stable environment of caves leads to adaptations, such as loss of color, loss of eyes and their replacement with the increased development of other sensory organs, such as antennae. One specialist, a salamander known as the Orm, has reduced eyes, is almost translucent, and retains its aquatic larval form (with gills) throughout its life. It occurs in caves in a small area around the north end of the Adriatic Sea. Fish of various groups have cave specialists, mainly in the tropics, but also in Iran, Iraq and Japan. There are also a number of invertebrate cave specialists, including freshwater crustaceans and insects – and certain fungi are specialist parasites of these insects.

Caves are like islands, where a restricted and specialized fauna can develop, frequently lacking a "normal" complement of species. Predators and decomposers are few, and pure herbivores are virtually absent. Whether the specialists have arisen separately for each cave system is unknown, but in some groups it is possible to differentiate between populations in individual caves, suggesting long isolation. Both the unique fauna of (perhaps even individual) caves and the other animals, such as bats, which rely on this stable environment, are particularly vulnerable to disturbance. Quarrying for minerals, blocking for safety purposes, tourism or sport, conversion to other uses (such as stores or dumps), and alterations in water tables, have all resulted in the loss of or damage to a vast number of caves and their specialist fauna. Unwarranted campaigns against fruit bats in Israel included the fumigation of large numbers of caves. While the fruit bats survived, this campaign resulted in the extinction or near extinction of many of Israel's insectivorous bat species.

Many caves also have intrinsic value as places of unusual beauty or historical interest, such as those with cave paintings. Careful management of use and observance of agreed codes of conduct is helping to preserve many important caves and their associated fauna.

Left *A Puffin* (Fratercula arctica) *with a beak full of sand eels. Seabirds once nested in vast colonies on most of the coasts of northwestern Europe. In addition to threats from oil spills and entanglement in fishing nets, they are now threatened by competition for declining fish resources. Even small fish such as sand eels are fished commercially.*

Below *Monk Seals* (Monachus monachus) *swimming off Mauretania. Once widespread in the Mediterranean, they are now among the most endangered mammals in the world, only breeding in sea caves or on remote beaches.*

The seas and oceans...

The fauna of this habitat suffers mainly from over-exploitation, dumping and spillage. Increasingly, limitations on pollution and exploitation are agreed, but quotas are hard won and difficult to enforce. Despite pressure through the International Whaling Commission and independent conservation bodies, Japan, Norway, and Iceland continue to hunt whales "for scientific purposes" and have increasingly turned to stocks of smaller whales. Even the small dolphins and porpoises are now being carefully monitored, having suffered from pollution, over-exploitation and accidental catch during tuna fishing. Subsistence hunting by Eskimos has also affected cetaceans particularly the Narwhal and Beluga. Efforts to stop the traditional rounding up and slaughter of Pilot Whales in the Faeroe Islands have met considerable resistance.

Steller's Sea Cow was barely known to science before it was wiped out in about 1770 through over-exploitation. Other large animals suffering over-exploitation or persecution include the Walrus, the Polar Bear, and Seals. Of three monk seal species, the Caribbean Monk Seal is thought to be extinct and the Hawaiian and Mediterranean Monk Seals are considered critically endangered. Once widespread in the Mediterranean and down part of the west African coast, hunting, disturbance, and pollution have drastically reduced populations of the Mediterranean Monk Seal. Even these reduced populations have been persecuted by fishermen for alleged damage to fishing nets, despite local protection and education campaigns about the seal and its habitat. In some areas compensation for net damage has replaced culling, but few viable populations remain. While not generally thought to have had a major impact on populations, culls of North Atlantic Gray Seals have been a very emotive issue. In contrast, a recent viral epidemic gave rise to major concern for Common or Harbor Seals around the North Sea. The virus killed over 17 000 seals and was similar to one that had already seriously affected the Baikal Seal. The recent epidemics have been linked with pollution, which has also seriously affected landlocked populations of Ringed Seal in Lake Saimaa, Finland, and Common Seal in the north Pacific Ocean.

Below *The seas of Europe are among the most polluted in the world. Oil pollution poses a major threat to marine life, killing millions of seabirds every year. The oil on this French beach is from the tanker* Bohlen. *In addition to the damage caused by the oil, many of the chemicals used to "clean" the beaches can be harmful to wildlife and the environment.*

Marine pollution, a particular problem in the Mediterranean, Baltic, and North Seas, also takes its toll on marine invertebrates. The most obvious pollutant is oil and wide coverage has been given to major accidents involving oil tankers. Starting with the *Torrey Canyon*, which sank off Cornwall in 1967, such incidents have been a frequent feature of recent years and have been responsible for the deaths of many thousands of seabirds, as well as otters and marine invertebrates. But, in fact, these major accidents contribute only a small proportion of the oil released through spillage and dumping. In addition, the importance of other pollutants, such as "waste" chemicals and sewage, is now beginning to be appreciated.

Over-exploitation of corals for trophies, and lobsters and sea urchins for food, has led to local extinctions. To reduce the harvesting of the Channel Islands

Left *People have had a dramatic impact on the natural vegetation and wildlife of islands such as Madeira, seen here in a view from the top of Pico Ruivo looking north. Recently tourism has posed an increasing threat, particularly in coastal areas where uncontrolled "development" has often destroyed the very features the tourists wish to enjoy.*

Ormer, benefactors were invited to "adopt" an Ormer and so raise money for a marine conservation area. The establishment of marine reserves has been slow, but the situation is improving and there are now major reserves in Mauritania, Madeira, and the Red Sea. Although a few have been set up in Britain and around the North Sea, it is hard to augment them in the face of serious pollution problems.

——— ...and their islands and coastlines ———

The islands of the Mediterranean Sea and the northern oceans carry their own unique fauna. Most of them offered limited opportunity for human settlement, but tourism has had profound impacts. In the North Atlantic, the Canary islands, Madeira, and, to a lesser extent, the Azores have all suffered from tourism and associated development. The Canary islands subspecies of the Black Oystercatcher is extinct, the Madeiran and Gon-gon Petrels, and land birds such as the Fuerteventura Stonechat, laurel pigeons, and the Blue (Canary Island) Chaffinch, have all been considered threatened, mostly by habitat loss and hunting. In some cases the problems have been or are being addressed, but certainly the Fuerteventura Stonechat and Madeiran Petrel (Freira) are endangered. The stonechat has healthy populations in some areas, and researchers have been investigating why it is present in such low densities in other apparently suitable areas. Conservation efforts for the petrel have concentrated on excluding from breeding areas the introduced rats which prey on eggs and young.

Most of the indigenous mammals on these islands are bats, none of which seems to be particularly threatened at present. Some endemic bats with limited populations need care, as do other mammals such as the Canaries White-toothed Shrew. The Hierro Giant Lizard of the Canaries is considered endangered, and Madeira has a threatened land nemertine worm and a number of endangered molluscs. Firmly including the fauna of these islands in European protective legislation could improve their conservation status.

Similar problems affect the fauna of Mediterranean islands, including land birds, such as the Barbary Falcon and Corsican Nuthatch, a range of reptiles, such as the Filfola Lizard of Malta, and possibly amphibians, such as the Mallorcan Midwife Toad. This toad was described only in 1977 from subfossil remains and it was not until 1980 that the first specimen was found alive. Mallorca lost several endemic

Spotlight
- Sea Turtles (Cheloniidae and Dermochelyiidae). Persecution and accidental trapping have taken their toll. Two nests of Loggerhead Turtle *(Caretta caretta)* were found along 250 kilometers (155 miles) of beach in Israel where 30 years ago it is estimated there were 15 nests per kilometer (24 nests per mile).
- Terns/gulls (Laridae). Many gulls and terns that nest on beaches and islands have declined due to disturbance and predation. The Arctic tern *(Sterna paradisea)* in Scotland has declined by 70 per cent since 1980 and the remaining birds are showing very poor breeding success. The British Roseate Tern *(S. dougalli)* population has declined by 85 per cent.
- Seals (Phocinidae). The Monk Seal *(Monachus monachus)* has retreated from nearly all its former breeding grounds, and the already depleted population of 40 years ago has been reduced by up to 90 per cent. Up to 70 per cent of many North Sea populations of Common Seal *(Phocina vitulina)* were killed by a virus in 1988.
- Fuerteventura Stonechat *(Saxicola dacotiae)*. The population of 50–150 pairs on Fuertaventura is threatened by introduced predators, development and long-term desiccation.

Right *Audouin's Gull* (Larus audouinii) *is one of the rarest gulls in the world. It breeds only on a few Mediterranean islands where competition from the much more adaptable Herring Gull is a major cause of its decline.*

Above *Half a century ago the Costa Brava in northeast Spain was still inhabited by wildlife. Uncontrolled development has destroyed all but a few of the most adaptable and tenacious species.*

species long ago and the evidence of subfossils suggests that the toad's distribution has been drastically reduced, probably through droughts and introduced predators. As a safety net, a captive-breeding program has been established.

Audouin's Gull, with only a few limited colonies on Mediterranean islands, is one of the world's rarest gulls. One of its major breeding sites is the Spanish possession of the Chafarinas islands, just off the Moroccan coast. The islands have been declared a national game reserve, but their protection status needs to be upgraded and enforced. Apart from current problems of human disturbance, Audouin's Gulls are affected by Herring Gulls, which compete for nesting space and prey on the smaller gull and its eggs.

Larger mammals often get preferential treatment in conservation nowadays. Although the Corsican Red Deer became extinct recently, the limited populations of Sardinian Red Deer and Sardinian and Cyprus Mouflon will probably survive, helped by captive breeding. Red Deer were reintroduced to Corsica from Sardinia in 1985 and this was supported by an education program, including a film shown to all schoolchildren. Less charismatic mammals, such as the endemic subspecies of the Genet on the Balearic islands, may not be so lucky. On the other hand, these islands can act as the last refuge for mainland animals – for example, a now extinct group of European rodents hung on until historic times only on Sardinia.

In the north Pacific, the Short-tailed or Steller's Albatross breeds on Japanese islands. It was brought to the verge of extinction by plume hunters in the late nineteenth and early twentieth centuries, with about 10 pairs left in 1953. Since then it has recovered but is still very rare. Also on Japan's islands is the rare Crested or Japanese Murrelet. With a small population and a very limited breeding distribution, it is a vulnerable species – and was especially so when the US Air Force began using one of its major breeding islands for bombing practice! Advised of the conservation problem, the Air Force quickly stopped its activities.

Gibraltar is famous for its Barbary Macaque (Barbary Ape), which was probably introduced from Morocco about 250 years ago. The relics of north African populations, which had dwindled to a few isolated colonies in Algeria and Morocco, have been supplemented from captive-bred animals. The population on Gibraltar is small but stable and well looked after. In view of the "ape's" popularity it has been proposed that at least one troop should be incorporated into a "monkey" park for education and fundraising.

Tourism has affected coasts as well as islands. Rocky coastlines still provide sanctuary for breeding seals and birds, including sea eagles, but the development of beach resorts has had an enormous impact. While this has been marked in northern Europe, it is nowhere more obvious than in the Mediterranean Sea. The rapid development of the coastlines of Spain, Portugal, and southern France continues apace. Now attention has turned to Greece and Turkey, and turtles are in the forefront of battles to save these beaches. Intense efforts are being made through national organizations, a pan-Mediterranean organization and other bodies, to conserve beaches important for Loggerhead and Green Turtles. The resultant clash of interests has been most apparent on the Greek island of Zakynthos, home to Europe's largest breeding population of Loggerhead Turtles. Tourism is deemed so important for the local economy that the efforts to restrict development have met strong local opposition and even violence.

Below *A Loggerhead Turtle* (Caretta caretta) *arriving at its nesting beaches. Many of the beaches in the Mediterranean have become holiday resorts, and turtles returning to nests have little chance of success.*

BUTTERFLIES

R. I. Vane-Wright started his career as a scientific assistant in the Entomology Department of The Natural History Museum, London. This led to a zoology degree and a consuming interest in systematics and evolutionary biology. Currently he is trying to establish a global program to combine his four main biological interests – butterflies, evolution, systematics and conservation – in the hope of contributing more effectively to international efforts to preserve as much as possible of the Earth's remaining biodiversity.

Above *Eastern Tailed Blue* (Everes comyntas), *from North and Central America. Many "blues" have complex ecological needs and are very vulnerable to change.*

Above *The Red Admiral* (Vanessa atalanta), *a familiar butterfly found throughout the Nearctic and Palearctic regions, is relatively adaptable to changing conditions.*

Right *This map of the Malay archipelago shows the number of butterfly species found on main islands. To set conservation priorities, we also need to know the distribution of every one.*

The total number of animal and plant species on Earth is between 5 million and 50 million, and each has special needs for its survival. We can try to conserve some, such as the Loggerhead Turtle or Channel Islands Ormer, by careful habitat management, or in zoos or gardens. But a significant proportion of the millions of species now seem to be at risk, and it would be impractical to make individual provision for them all. Instead, we need to plan how to save priority areas which between them will conserve the greatest possible variety of the planet's life. This section looks at the need for a plan, and how we might go about setting priorities, by examining the problems presented by one of the best-known groups – the butterflies.

Vulnerable butterflies

Of the 18,000 species of butterflies in the world, almost half are found in South and Central America. These include the brilliant *Morpho* butterflies with wings like blue mirrors – "little pieces of the sky come down" according to Amerindian folklore – which can be seen up to half a mile away. Africa accounts for another 3,000 butterflies, including many of the spectacular *Charaxes*. The Australasian region has more than 4,000 species, including all the birdwings, the largest butterflies on Earth. The whole of the Palearctic and North America are relatively poor, containing less than 2,000 species, including the Peacock and the Corsican Swallowtail.

The exotic-looking Peacock, with a color pattern like no other butterfly in the world, can be found throughout most of the Palearctic region, from Britain to Japan. Several hundred butterflies live only within the boundaries of this huge area. But, unlike the ubiquitous Peacock, many of them have very limited distributions, such as the Corsican Swallowtail. Found only on the Mediterranean islands of Corsica and Sardinia, this handsome insect is now considered to be endangered.

Many of the world's butterflies are known only from particular habitats, such as certain mountain ranges, forests, swamps, or islands, because they depend on particular plants for their caterpillars to feed on, or have other precise needs. Their

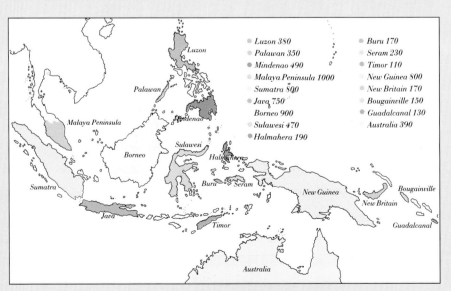

Luzon 380	Buru 170
Palawan 350	Seram 230
Mindenao 490	Timor 110
Malaya Peninsula 1000	New Guinea 800
Sumatra 800	New Britain 170
Java 750	Bougainville 150
Borneo 900	Guadalcanal 130
Sulawesi 470	Australia 390
Halmahera 190	

particular requirements make these butterflies very vulnerable to change. Draining the wetlands of East Anglia for agriculture wiped out most of the water dock and fenland habitat on which the English Large Copper depended, and this beautiful butterfly became extinct in Britain during the mid-nineteenth century.

Queen Alexandra's Birdwing, the largest butterfly in the world, is found only in northern Papua New Guinea, in one small area of lowland rainforest now extensively cleared for agriculture. Its caterpillars feed exclusively on one special type of vine. Such is the interest in this magnificent species that it is protected by international law – but its habitat is not. The Queen Alexandra's Birdwing could well become the first tropical insect to survive in captivity long after it has disappeared from the wild.

Because of their special appeal, this giant and a handful of other species may perhaps be preserved in insect zoos. But for the great majority of the 18,000 butterflies, let alone the many millions of other insects, it is inconceivable that individual care could be lavished on them. Those that remain to delight future generations will be those, like the Peacock, that can survive despite us – unless we make some provision for vulnerable species.

There are two major ways in which we can help butterflies on a global scale. The first is by managing agricultural, recreational and wastelands so as to maintain natural and semi-natural habitats within them. This would not only preserve species but also help to maintain a healthy enough environment for our own survival. The

Above *A male Rajah Brooke's Birdwing* (Trogonoptera brookiana). *The caterpillars of this spectacular insect, which lives only in parts of the Malay archipelago (including Malaysia, Sumatra and Borneo), can only feed on particular vines.*

Below *The Paris Peacock* (Papilio paris), *was once voted the most beautiful butterfly in the world. Many of its natural habitats in China, India, and Indonesia are vulnerable.*

*Two butterflies from the island of Sulawesi. Vindula dejone (**above**) is widespread, occurring throughout most of the Malay archipelago. In contrast, Moduza lyncides (**below**) is one of some 200 butterfly species only found on Sulawesi and small islands nearby.*

second method is to set up nature reserves in wilderness areas. Reserves must be safeguarded from interference and managed to ensure the survival of species within them. Funds to buy or set aside areas and manage them effectively are very limited, so the areas need to be carefully chosen. We must aim to identify a series of priority areas which will form a worldwide network of reserves, protecting as great a variety of living things as possible. Looking at butterflies which live on islands can give us ideas on how to set about this complex task.

Island butterflies

Throughout the world, islands vary remarkably in the number of native breeding butterflies they support. Hawaii has only two, New Zealand about a dozen, Great Britain less than 60, Hispaniola 196, Sri Lanka 242 and Trinidad over 600. Islands also vary in endemism – the proportion of species not found elsewhere. Both of the native butterflies of Hawaii and most of the native butterflies of New Zealand are endemics, while almost all of the Trinidadian species occur on the South American mainland and not one British butterfly is an endemic. Levels of endemism are of profound importance in identifying priority areas to preserve.

All the major islands of the Malay archipelago have a wealth of butterflies. The richest is Borneo, with an estimated 900 species, including the fabulous Rajah Brooke's Birdwing. This may seem to suggest that Borneo should be the top priority in the archipelago for conservation action. Yet only a handful of these species are restricted to Borneo, with Java, Sumatra, and the Malay Peninsula sharing much the

Right *Africa is home to nearly 200 species of Charaxes. Some of these fast-flying butterflies live in the savannas, but many are restricted to forests. This Black-bordered Charaxes (C. pollux) has just emerged from its chrysalis.*

same set of butterflies. In contrast, of the roughly 600 butterflies in the Philippine islands to the east of Borneo, more than 40 per cent cannot be found in any other country and many are restricted to particular islands within the Philippines. Similarly, 43 per cent of the 470 or so species on Sulawesi only occur on this curiously shaped island. A high proportion of the butterflies of New Guinea are also endemics, including the Queen Alexandra and a number of other remarkable birdwings.

To plan a network of reserves to protect as many of the butterflies of the archipelago as possible, it is essential to have accurate knowledge of all the species and their distributions. Such knowledge is now being assembled for this purpose. Inevitably, high on the list will come the major islands of the Philippines, Borneo, New Guinea, and Sulawesi. Regrettably, the plan may be too late to save many of the Philippine species because so many of the islands have been completely stripped of their native vegetation.

But the task cannot stop there. For example, not all the 470 species on Sulawesi occur throughout the entire island. Kuekenthal's Tiger is a striking

Below left *The Peacock* (Inachis io) *is closely related to the Red Admiral, Small Tortoiseshell and other familiar north-temperate species. From Britain to Japan, its unique color pattern is constant.*

Below *A female Archduke* (Lexias pardalis), *one of many species distributed from Assam through parts of the Malay archipelago. The male looks very different, but both sexes enjoy feeding from rotting fruit on the forest floor.*

primrose-tinted milkweed butterfly known only from montane areas near Manado, in the far north of the island. Bedford-Russell's Idea, a huge black and white milkweed butterfly discovered just a few years ago, is restricted to a few of the central mountains. The Bonthain Tiger, another endemic milkweed species, flies only on the volcanic peak of Mount Lompobatang, at the island's southern tip. Today these butterflies remain on sale by dealers and, unless their particular habitats are adequately protected, they will soon disappear forever.

They could be saved by identifying a set of sites that between them cater for all the butterflies of Sulawesi, in all their different habitats and communities. Similarly, we could identify priority islands or regions in other parts of the world, and then set up networks of well-managed reserves within each of these areas. In this way it would be possible to make provision for the majority of the world's butterflies – and, in a similar way, for the widest possible variety of other animals and plants.

It has taken 2,300 million years for butterflies, and all the other forms of life, to evolve on our planet. It will take about 10 years to make a plan to save most of the thousands and millions that still remain. If we devote the resources, the strength, and the will, we can put that plan into action. If we fail, the Earth will be forever impoverished.

Above *Bush-browns of the genus* Lohora *form the largest group of butterfly species entirely confined to the Sulawesi region. They will only survive if the dense forests survive too.*

ARCTIC

GREENLAND

BERING STRAIT

BROOKS RANGE

Banks Island

DAVIS STRAIT

Yukon

Victoria Island

Baffin Island

ALASKA RANGE MACKENZIE MOUNTAINS

Mount
McKinley

Mackenzie

Great Bear Lake

R
O
C
K
Y

Great Slave Lake

Southampton Island

HUDSON
BAY

LABRADOR

M
O
U
N
T
A
I
N
S

Churchill

Saskatchewan

Newfoundland

CASCADES RANGE

Lake Winnipeg

WHITE
MOUNTAINS

NOVA
SCOTIA

Mount Rainier
Mount St Helens

Columbia

Lake Superior

Lake Huron

Mt Washington

SIERRA NEVADA

Snake

Missouri

Lake Michigan

Lake Ontario

Lake Erie

Great Salt
Lake

Mount
Whitney

Platte

GREAT PLAINS

Ohio

APPALACHIAN MOUNTAINS

Colorado

OZARK
PLATEAUS

Arkansas

Mississippi

BLUE RIDGE MOUNTAINS

San Andreas

BLACK RANGE

Red River

Bermuda

VIZCAINO
DESERT

GULF OF CALIFORNIA

CHIHUAHUAN
DESERT

Rio Grande

EVERGLADES

Bahamas

GULF OF

WEST INDIES

MEXICO

MEXICO

CARIBBEAN SEA

P A C I F I C   O C E A N

SOUTH
AMERICA

THE NEARCTIC REGION

The Nearctic region (northern New World) embraces Canada, Greenland, the USA and parts of Mexico. Deciduous forests, swamplands, prairies, mountains, deserts, coniferous forests, and arctic tundra combine to form a wonderfully varied landscape, despite the extensive alterations brought about by the spread of European settlement.

Steller's Sea Lion (Eumetopias jubatus), *Vancouver Island, BC.*

HABITAT & PLANTS

Peter Alden graduated from the University of Arizona, Tucson. He led dozens of Mexican bird and nature trips in the 1960s and wrote *Finding Birds in Western Mexico*. From 1968 to 1982 he led birding tours worldwide for the Massachusetts Audubon Society and co-wrote (with John Gooders) *Finding Birds around the World*. From 1982 to 1989 Peter was a vice president and naturalist guide for Lindblad Travel. He wrote the *Peterson First Guide to Mammals* and has been a major contributor to field guides on birds of the USSR, Mexico, Colombia, Venezuela and Peterson's Western Birds. He has seen over 5,000 birds in travels to 100 countries on 7 continents.

This region encompasses Canada, the United States of America or the USA (minus Hawaii) and parts of Mexico north of the tropical zone. Flanked by the Atlantic and Pacific Oceans, it is a mosaic of extensive deciduous forests, swamplands, prairies, mountains, deserts and great coniferous forests, with arctic tundra to the north bordering the Arctic Ocean.

Settlers from Europe and elsewhere wrought major changes in these habitats, felling virgin forests, putting prairies to the plough and draining swamplands. Within only a few hundred years, vast areas of wilderness vanished and with them went countless animals and plants. A few of these extinctions were well publicized and public attitudes gradually started to shift. In the late 1800s, the first national parks were created and private nature groups began to form. Progress in setting aside reserves and protecting species by law continued into the 1900s. Then in the 1960s and 1970s, public outrage, provoked mainly by the effects of DDT and rampant pollution, resulted in various endangered species Acts. Inventories of long-neglected species began, and these took note not just of mammals, birds, and trees, but of the entire range of animals and plants. Even subspecies were studied, and the presence of one tiny fish or flower could stop a dam, move a highway or close an offending industrial plant. Many schools focus on endangered species, and as a result some rare creatures are better known than common everyday species. Yet pressures on vulnerable flora and fauna continue, and much work remains to be done.

While loss of habitat, over-exploitation, and collection are frequent threats, other diverse and sometimes subtle factors may affect species. Identifying these is essential if conservation work is to be effective. The following sections outline case histories of particular interest which, between them, illustrate a wide range of the problems being faced by plants and animals and how these are being tackled.

Nearctic plants

Among the first areas of the Nearctic region to receive settlers from Europe, eastern Canada and northeastern USA were covered with vast tracts of great virgin forests. These have long been felled and replaced by second-growth woodland. Along with the majestic trees went much of the smaller flora, virtually unremarked. The huge increase in awareness that has taken place since then is illustrated by the efforts made in recent times to conserve even tiny threatened plants.

The Dwarf (Robbin's) Cinquefoil of the rose family sports solitary yellow flowers at two sites in the alpine zone of New England's mountains. One of the sites straddled the Appalachian Trail near Mount Washington, New Hampshire and the plants were being trampled, so this famous trail was rerouted. Another tiny plant even helped stop a dam. Listed as endangered, the Furbish Lousewort is a perennial snapdragon with spikes of greenish yellow flowers. It once grew along terraces above the St. John river on the Maine-New Brunswick border. In 1976, a plan to build a huge dam which would flood a large area was being opposed by many people. Then the lousewort, last seen in 1943, was rediscovered in the area to be flooded – and was a factor in killing the plan.

Further south, most of the original trees were also cut, including the Bald

Left *Bald Cypress* (Taxodium distichum)
swamps such as this one in Illinois once
covered huge areas of the southeastern USA.
Although they have been extensively logged,
some are now protected including the
Okefenokee swamp in southern Georgia and
the Big Cypress swamp in southern Florida.

Venus fly trap

Pitcher plant

Cypress which once grew along the great rivers and swamplands of the southeastern USA. This deciduous conifer, with buttress roots and protruding "knees," dominated many swamps and anchored valuable wildlife habitat. Its wood is excellent, and nearly all the virgin stands were exploited. Ancient, massive specimens now only survive in a few preserves.

Areas of the southeast with impoverished soil are home to some of the region's most fascinating plants – the carnivorous (or insectivorous) plants, including sundews, bladderworts, Venus flytraps and pitcher plants. All have developed ways to lure and trap insects for food. In pitcher plants, leaves have been modified into long tubes full of trapped water and digestive enzymes. Colorful or scented hoods lure the insects while downward-pointing hairs help direct them into the deadly soup. The great Green Swamp area of North Carolina has been stripped of all its insect-eating plants, as have many other sites. The attractive pitcher plants have been particularly sought by collectors and, while all may be in trouble, some have suffered a drastic decline. The first to make the endangered species list was the Green Pitcher Plant which survived at just four sites. Then a commercial dealer made a wholesale raid at the DeSoto State Park in Alabama, and the number is now down to three.

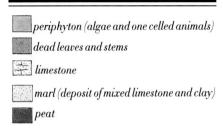

- periphyton (algae and one celled animals)
- dead leaves and stems
- limestone
- marl (deposit of mixed limestone and clay)
- peat

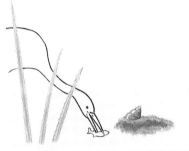

Above *Periphyton is the basis of the complex web of life in the Everglades. Not only is it the beginning of the many food chains in the marsh, it also removes calcium from water flowing over the limestone and converts it to marl. Sawgrass roots in the marl; dead sawgrass forms peat; other marsh plants grow in the peat; acid from the peat and from decaying plant matter dissolves some of the marl and bedrock – and the cycle is complete. Damage to any part of this cycle or to the many food chains – pollution, lowering the water table, elimination of a predator – could destroy the glades.*

Right *Florida Slash Pine* (Pinus elliottii) *and Saw Palmetto* (Serenoa repens) *in the Florida Everglades. The core of the Everglades is the shallow outflowing of Lake Okeechobee (the Sea of Grass). In the drier, slightly elevated areas, pines and tropical hardwood hummocks occur.*

Even rarer in the wild is a long-leaved tree with showy white flowers discovered by John and William Bartram in 1765 by the Altahama river in Georgia. It was last seen in the wild in 1803, but fortunately the Bartrams had cultivated some, and the Lost Franklinia is now grown in a number of gardens. Another tree with problems is the Virginia Roundleaf Birch, discovered in 1914 at an altitude of 850 meters (2,800 feet) near Sugar Grove Station, Virginia, growing among Sweet Birch. It was not found again until 1975, when a local biology teacher spent the whole summer searching for it and eventually found 12 trees and 16 seedlings. Although high fences were erected around the plants, in 1983 vandals destroyed all but five of them. Today, a few still survive in arboretums and at secret sites on national forest lands.

The Mountain Golden Heather, a dwarf rockrose which produces solitary yellow flowers in early summer, has also "reappeared." Described by Thomas Nuttall in 1818, it was thought to be extinct by the 1960s and then 2,000 individuals were recently found. Unfortunately, they grow in areas of the Blue Ridge Mountains of North Carolina attractive to campers – and one camper was noted building a fire on top of a colony of these threatened plants.

While rare plants often survive in an isolated area among commoner species, in northwest Florida there is a concentration of a dozen or so rare and endangered plants restricted to the vicinity of the Apalachicola river. Various members of the yew family are common ornamentals, but two small trees of this family are found only there, the Florida Torreya and Florida Yew. Chapman's Rhododendron grows at only three sites in this area and is the rarest member of its genus in North America. Clumps of it have been dug up for the nursery trade, and large areas of the bogs in which it lives have been "improved" for commercial pine plantations. Harper's Beauty is restricted to ten individuals at two sites by the river. This yellow-flowering lily and many other rare plants and animals depend on sound management of the Apalachicola National Forest and the efforts of the Nature Conservancy to save this river valley. Further south, the Everglades area of south Florida is partly protected by the Everglades National Park. However, the majority of its life-giving water flows down a wide river of grass and marsh from central Florida and much of this has been diverted to supply cities, industry, and agriculture, reducing the Everglades to a shadow of its former richness.

Extending from the Canadian Prairie provinces south to Texas is the area known as the Great Plains. Before cultivation, fencing and urbanization, there was a sea of grass from the eastern forests west to the Rockies. Over 99 per cent of the long-grass prairie growing in the eastern half of the Great Plains has been destroyed. Tiny plots have been found in Illinois and elsewhere, while somewhat larger tracts in the Flint hills of eastern Kansas and parts of northeastern Oklahoma may gain national park status. The larger remnants of the drier short-grass plains to the west are protected in a number of provincial and national parks. One of the most beautiful wildflowers of the southern plains area is the Texas Poppy Mallow, which produces showy wine-purple, cup-shaped flowers in May and June. Today its only known site is an area of deep sandy soil along the "other" Colorado river in Texas.

While cattle rustling in Texas has almost ceased, cactus rustling is booming. In a recent year, over 500,000 small, globular cacti were harvested by illegal aliens working for dealers who shipped the cacti out nationwide and around the world. Rarer species command high prices in the USA, Japan and Europe, and many buyers

The Antioch dunes, California
The first land to be bought by the US government from private landowners to protect habitat for endangered plants was a remnant of the Antioch dunes above the San Joaquin river in California. Once reaching 35 meters (115 feet) in height and stretching for miles, these dunes have been mined to supply pottery works, brickyards and mix for asphalt and concrete. The remaining 22 hectares (55 acres) with dunes only 9 meters (30 feet) tall were purchased in 1980. The dunes flora includes the Contra Costa Wallflower, a member of the mustard family with showy yellow flowers, and the Antioch Dunes Evening Primrose.

Above left *The tallgrass prairie is defined by a predominance of big bluestem grass. Tallgrass prairie used to cover more than 400,000 square miles over 12 states of the USA. Now only a few nature reserves and isolated pockets remain.*

Left Mammillaria pectinifera *cacti from the higher altitudes of Mexico's Sierra Madre. It is a relatively small species, less than 5 centimeters (2 inches) across, and like several other species with a restricted range, very easily wiped out by commercial collectors.*

insist on wild specimens. One of the smallest and rarest cacti in the world is the 25-millimeter (1-inch) Nellie Cory Cactus which usually grows under clubmoss. One of its two remaining colonies was wiped out by cactus rustlers in the 1960s. A small button cactus, *Epithelantha bokei,* has even been poached from the remotest corner of Big Bend National Park in southwest Texas.

To the southeast, the southern and western flanks of the Mexican plateau gradually rise up into the wetter forested Sierra Madre mountains. These were covered with great virgin forests of long-needled pines and short-needled firs mixed with oaks and many other hardwood trees, while vast freshwater lakes and marshes filled the valleys. Now, the old-growth trees are essentially gone and the swamps largely drained. Two trees there are considered endangered. The wood of the Guatemalan Fir or Pinabete is used for making hand looms, saplings were cut for Christmas trees, and seedlings are eaten by sheep. Then it became illegal to cut young conifers for Christmas trees. The Ayuque only grows to 7 meters (23 feet), and with

*Right Saguaro Cacti (*Carnegiea cereus gigantea*) seen here through Ocotillo flowers, are popular with gardeners in the southwest USA and have been dug up in large numbers in many areas. They are also frequently damaged by trigger-happy gunmen.*

Ancistrocactus tubuschii

Epithelantha micromeris *var. Bokei*

Coryphantha minima *Baird*

its pyramidal shape and brilliant red flowers in season, made a good substitute. The Ayuque has now been virtually eliminated from its home area in Michoacan state.

Two endangered wildflowers of New Mexico are linked with gypsum layers. The Gypsum Wild Buckwheat, with large clusters of bright yellow flowers, lives only on one limestone hill near Artesia. A proposed lake which would have covered its only home has been stopped, and it now only has to contend with cattle, off-road vehicles and botanists. Todsen's Pennyroyal, a mint with solitary red flowers, escapes these threats – all 750 individuals occur on steep gypsum slopes of the San Andreas mountains in the White Sands missile range.

The Channel islands off the coast of California are a botanical wonderland with 76 flowering plants not found on the mainland and 18 that are restricted to just one island. Many of these islands had no major herbivores and their flora has been devastated by introduced grazers, browsers and plants. On the relatively large San Clemente, the main problem is feral goats which have eaten most of the plants, causing erosion and wreaking ecological havoc. Four of the island's 14 endemic plants were the first plants to be listed as federally endangered – the San Clemente Broom, Bushmallow, Larkspur, and Paintbrush. The only way to save the island's plants and birds was to remove the goats. As many as possible were trapped and it was decided to shoot the rest. Then animal rights activists heard about it and took legal action to delay the killing. So the goats ate and bred, and entire species of plants came closer to being lost from the planet.

On the mainland, the west-facing slopes of the majestic Sierra Nevada south of Lake Tahoe are home to the largest living organism in the world – the Giant Sequoia, which can weigh up to 2,000 tons and live for thousands of years. Large numbers were cut, but national parks created in the 1890s, such as the Yosemite, saved many virgin stands from plunder. Until recently, it seemed that another great tree, the Coastal Redwood, would not be so fortunate. Growing from Santa Cruz to southwest Oregon, in the hills and valleys that absorb the coastal fogs, this redwood can reach 110 meters (360 feet) high and takes about 500 years to mature. Its lumber is straight-grained, free of knots, resistant to termites and easily worked – and so, of course, the trees were chopped down. After a messy battle, some of the last of the truly great virgin stands have been saved in the new Redwoods National Park in northwestern California.

Left *Giant Sequoias* (Sequoiadendron giganteum) *in Yosemite National Park, California. Large numbers were felled in the late nineteenth and early twentieth centuries and the majority of the survivors occur within national parks and other protected areas.*

WILDLIFE

In this overview of endangered and threatened Nearctic animals, the region is divided into twelve areas. Some species range (or used to range) over several areas and these are described in just one major part of their range.

———— Eastern Canada and the northeast USA ————

When Europeans began whaling off these shores in the late 1400s, numerous North Atlantic Right Whales lived near the coast. These slow surface swimmers were so-named because they floated rather than sank when harpooned and so were the "right" whales to catch. While all whales are protected off North America today, only about 350 of these carry on the ancient ritual of summering off New England and the Maritimes and swimming to Florida for the winter. This area is also the summer home of the Humpback Whale, which is viewed by thousands of people on the popular

Right *Throughout the early exploration and colonization of North America by Europeans, the Canadian (or American) Beaver* (Castor canadensis) *was one of the most important exports and was systematically exterminated over much of the continent. Under conservation and management programs it has now recolonized or been reintroduced to much of its former range.*

whale-watching day cruises. Once numbering in the hundreds of thousands worldwide, it became the prime target for whalers in the early 1900s and its numbers dropped to 4000.

On land, the American (or Canadian) Beaver lured the early explorers into every stream in every quarter throughout North America. Beaver pelts had a market that never dropped and the animals were hunted and trapped ruthlessly, causing them to vanish from much of their range. In recent years they have been reintroduced in many areas for their value in creating wetlands and increasing the diversity of plant life within the forests.

Fiercer mammals were persecuted through fear or because they were viewed as competitors. Wolves are long extinct in the US part of this area, while the Newfoundland White Wolf continued to hunt caribou (reindeer) until the last of these wolves was shot in 1911. The eastern race of the Cougar (or Puma or Mountain Lion) was also killed on sight, being the subject of bounties. The last American bounty was paid in 1890 in the Adirondacks of New York. About 25 managed to survive in northern New Brunswick, however, and today these animals appear to be quietly re-occupying their range, feeding on healthy numbers of White-tailed Deer.

Birds as well as mammals were decimated by the settlers. A race of the Prairie "Grouse" called the Heath Hen was abundant on salt marshes and open heathland from New England to the Carolinas. It was a major source of food for European colonists and by 1791, had become rare. Then its heaths were turned into farms, cats and rats raided its nests, and it succumbed to diseases spread from chickens. By 1830 it was extinct on the mainland, and by 1896 there were only 100 left on its last stronghold of Martha's Vineyard Island, Massachusetts. A reserve was established there, and its numbers rebounded to 2,000. Then in 1916, fire swept the island, burning the birds' cover, an influx of hawks arrived and a turkey disease swept

Below left *The Piping Plover* (Charadrius melodus) *is a small shore bird that breeds on sandy beaches, where it and its eggs are extremely well camouflaged. Its populations have suffered from human disturbance and off-road vehicles.*

Below *After dramatic declines in the 1950s and 1960s due to pesticide poisonings, the Peregrine Falcon* (Falco peregrinus) *has made a remarkable comeback and can even be seen in some city centers where it preys on feral pigeons.*

through the population. In 1927, 13 survived and on 11 March, 1932, the last one died. This shows the vulnerability of a healthy population reduced to just one locality.

A newcomer to the endangered species list, the Piping Plover, nearly suffered a similar fate. Like so many shorebirds, it was a target of market gunners in the late 1800s but recovered after 1900 when the hunting of it was banned. It nests only on beaches, both inland in the Great Lakes and Plains, and on Atlantic beaches from Virginia to Newfoundland. There the ever-increasing numbers of beach users and off-road vehicles caused serious disturbance and many eggs and young were crushed under oversized wheels. By 1987 there were only 17 pairs in the Great Lakes and 475 pairs on its US Atlantic coast range. Eventually the bird was listed and government agencies had to close many prime beaches during the early summer. This resulted in great cries of protest from beach users and marked improvements in the numbers of plovers fledged.

The Peregrine Falcon had to contend with rather different threats. It is the

Above *The Bald Eagle* (Haliaeetus leucocephalus), *despite being the national bird and depicted on the great seal of the USA, was once widely persecuted. Populations also crashed during the 1950s and 1960s due to pesticide poisoning. However, their recovery is another success story and they are now widespread and locally abundant.*

world's fastest bird, reaching nearly 320 kilometers an hour (200 miles per hour) as it dives on prey, usually a flying bird. A local race of this falcon bred on many cliffs in the forested mountains of the area and northwest to Alaska south of the tundra. At one time, it suffered from capture by falconers, but more recently it was severely affected by the widespread use of DDT on crops. This insecticide, accumulated in the falcon's prey, caused the falcon's eggshells to become so thin they broke easily. The resultant extinction of the bird in the US and its great decline in Canada were instrumental in getting DDT banned. Today the public watches with great interest the reintroduction of captive-bred Peregrine Falcons into many cities and reserves.

Lost in all the commotion over the rare bigger creatures is the story of many a small invertebrate. The Giant Carrion Beetles are fascinating insects that look after their young as carefully as many "higher" animals. They locate a small dead rodent or bird, bury it, lay their eggs on the carcass, and then cover it up. The parents communicate with the larvae by buzzing sounds and tend them until they pupate. The Giant Carrion Beetle lived in virgin forests from Nova Scotia to Louisiana and was once found in 33 states and provinces. Today it is known only in Rhode Island – one of the largest reductions in an insect's range ever recorded.

The southeast USA and Bermuda

Bermuda, a British colony off the Carolinas, has many endangered animals and plants, but none is more famous than the Cahow or Bermuda Petrel. Vast numbers of these shearwaters used to nest there free of humans and their animals. Shakespeare described the birds in *The Tempest* as millions of shrieking, winged shapes swirling round the masts of a Spanish galleon riding out a storm in the lee of one of these islands in 1603. The Spanish sailors left pigs as a source of meat for the next ship and by the time English settlers arrived in 1612, there were few Cahows left on the main island. Cats, dogs, and accidentally introduced rats killed the rest. In 1616, the Cahows received protection from the first game law in the New World but they never recovered. A few must have returned secretly to uninhabited rocks over the centuries, because they were rediscovered there in 1951. This led to a rescue attempt by David Wingate, which included building baffles around each burrow. Despite losses due to DDT in the 1960s and disturbance from the nearby NASA station and airport, 36 pairs had fledged 22 young by 1982.

One of the characteristic sights along the shores of the Gulf of Mexico and the Atlantic coast is the huge aerial diving Eastern Brown Pelican. It nested by the thousands in coastal Texas and Louisiana, but by 1968 it had vanished from both states. As with the Peregrine Falcon, the main culprit was DDT. After the banning of this pesticide, 50 birds taken from healthy Florida colonies were placed on Grand Terre Island, Louisiana, and did well. Then in 1975, 300 died from Endrin, a pesticide used on boll weevils and sugar cane borers, which had washed down the rivers from hundreds of miles away. Fortunately the birds recovered from this setback and by 1987, there were 6,000 pelicans in Louisiana, and 300 pairs in Texas raised 500 young.

Another success story is provided by the American Alligator, once found from New Jersey south to Texas. Trade in its skin became so lucrative that it declined in most areas and had to be protected in the 1960s. This allowed its numbers to increase so much that it is no longer considered endangered, although commerce in its skin is still strictly regulated.

In the cypress swamps of the southeast, the American Ivory-billed Woodpecker once lived. Many were killed for sport, food, and to supply private collections of birds but the systematic logging of virtually all the old-growth timber doomed it. Its last major stronghold, the Singer tract in Louisiana, was logged and turned into soybean fields in 1934. Now another southeastern woodpecker is in trouble. The Red-cockaded Woodpecker lives in fire-climax pines, and requires trees at least 65 years old for nesting. Modern forestry practices on 90 per cent of its range include cutting trees of age 30–45 years, and the woodpecker's population has become very scattered and is declining rapidly. When some land-developers heard that these endangered woodpeckers were inhabiting an area due for development, they instructed employees to chop down all nesting trees and shoot the woodpeckers! But word got out, and the developers were prosecuted and fined hundreds of thousands of dollars.

The most endangered of the southeastern mammals is the Red Wolf. Weighing up to 34 kilograms (75 pounds), it is smaller than the Gray Wolf, with a narrower face, longer ears and longer legs. It occurred from Pennsylvania to Texas in the southern swamps and woods until people started killing it off. By the early 1970s, pure-blooded individuals existed only at a few spots from southwest Louisiana west to southeast Texas. With this species virtually exterminated, Coyotes moved east and interbred with the scattered remaining Red Wolves. In an extensive program to rescue the species, the few surviving pure Red Wolves were captured and bred. By 1977 the species was extinct in the wild, but radio-collared individuals have since been released at Coyote-free sites in North and South Carolina, Florida and Mississippi. A pair released at Horn Island, Mississippi, produced a litter of seven, and

Below *The American Alligator* (Alligator mississippiensis) *was exterminated over a large part of its range by hide-hunters. Fortunately, protection enabled a rapid recovery and in most areas where suitable habitat occurs, populations are increasing.*

the Red Wolf became one of the first mammal species, extinct in the wild, to raise young in the wild again. Despite the fact that these animals hunt alone and seldom prey on large mammals, there is local opposition at release sites.

Among the endangered reptiles of the southeast is the Gopher Tortoise. Formerly very common, it inhabits sunny sand ridges with pine and oak, and digs deep burrows of great value to many other animals. Commercial forestry practices have excluded fire from its homes, and the herbs it feeds on cannot grow in the shade of the heavy brush. In addition, people have killed many for food, it is frequently run over on highways and farms, and housing and agriculture have taken over much of its habitat.

In the rivers of the southeast, 14 of the 18 freshwater mussels are endangered due to coal mining in the basins of the Cumberland and Tennessee rivers. Silt containing coal particles has washed into many streams, and chemical pollutants have added to the damage. Fish have suffered as well, including the darters. While the Snail Darter became famous for stopping a dam in the 1970s, the Sharphead and the Trispot Darters have been lost due to reservoirs, and the Niangua Darter is in trouble.

Florida

This state has truly tropical habitats and a number of unique animals of concern. Most of the thousand or so remaining West Indian Manatees live there, swimming slowly at the surface, clearing vegetation from the waterways. They once occurred from the Carolinas to Texas, but hunting, and pollution, dredging and filling in of waterways have greatly restricted their range. The propellers of the rapidly

Below *A Florida Keys White-tailed Deer* (Odocoileus virginianus clavium) *being followed by a Cattle Egret. The Key Deer is exceptionally small and its population is considered to be endangered.*

increasing motorboats have caused many deaths and injuries among the survivors. Boat speeds are now regulated in many manatee areas in Florida, and the whole state has been declared a manatee refuge. Many of these animals congregate during cold spells at the warm-water outflows of power plants – the same plants that are fuelling the loss of the manatee's habitat.

The Key Deer (a subspecies of the White-tailed Deer) used to occur over much of the state, but today it is only found in the Florida Keys. The size of a large dog with small antlers, it has a low birthrate like most animals in the tropics (other than humans). By 1947, numbers had dropped to 30 and the deer were given a refuge. Although they have since increased to 600 and inhabit 18 islands, the Key Deer still face threats. In dry spells they have to swim back to Big Pine and No-Name Keys to find permanent fresh water. Development continues rapidly in their range, stray dogs and poachers still hunt them and many are killed by traffic.

Key Largo, the largest of the Florida Keys is the only home of the Key Largo (Eastern) Woodrat and a race of the Cotton Mouse. It is also one of the last homes of the Schaus' Swallowtail Butterfly, which is at risk due to urbanization, aerial mosquito spraying and overcollecting. The state of Florida is trying to protect parts of Key Largo in the face of land developers.

Among the reptiles, only a few hundred American Crocodiles survive in the Florida Keys and the Everglades coastal fringe, having been shot for their valuable skin, for sport, and as nuisances around marinas. Sea Turtles have also suffered greatly, sought after for their meat and shells, while their eggs are considered a delicacy. Now the turtles face new dangers. It is estimated that 11,000 drown annually in shrimp nets off Florida and the southeastern states. Hatchling turtles, instead of crossing the sand to the sea, are attracted to lights of nearby highways and hotels, often fatally. The increase in offshore oil drilling and tanker traffic has led to more turtles eating tarballs – and eating plastic bags that resemble the jellyfish they feed on. Efforts are now underway to force shrimpers to use turtle-excluding devices in their nets, and massive publicity campaigns have resulted in urban lights being turned down on hatching nights.

Much of the water which used to flow to the famous Everglades area of south Florida has been diverted, and this has shrunk the marshes where Apple Snails live. The Florida Everglade (Snail) Kite feeds chiefly on these snails, and its numbers now average about 500. Special nest baskets for the kite have been introduced into prime breeding areas with good results. Water drainage and diversion have also affected the

Famous extinctions

- The flightless Great Auk, which stood 80 centimeters (30 inches) tall. Clubbed for food and feathers, it was extinct in the USA by 1841.
- The Sea Mink hunted for its fur, which was even more luxuriant and valuable than that of the American Mink. The last was killed near Jonesport, Maine, in 1880.
- The Eastern Wapiti (Elk), doomed by the demand for its canines from every member of the fraternal Order of the Elks. It was extinct by 1877.
- The Labrador Duck, the first purely North American bird to became extinct in historical times. The last was shot in 1878 by a young boy and served by his family for dinner.

Below left *The Florida Panther* (Felis concolor coryi) *is a small race of the Mountain Lion. It is critically endangered, and, due to the many killed by vehicles, it may not recover.*

Below *The Green Turtle* (Chelonia mydas) *has fewer than 1,000 breeding females in Florida today, although it formerly nested in much larger numbers.*

Above *American Bison* (Bison bison) *in Yellowstone National Park, Wyoming. Once occurring in herds numbering millions, by the end of the nineteenth century they were virtually extinct. Thanks to farsighted conservation measures introduced by a few enthusiasts, a small herd was protected in Yellowstone and this has been used to found herds elsewhere.*

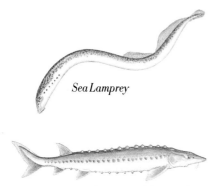

Sea Lamprey

Lake Sturgeon (Acipenser fulvescens)

Florida population of the Wood Stork. So few young could be fledged that the population declined from 20,000 to 6,000 pairs, and the bird was declared endangered in 1984.

By this time, the Dusky Seaside Sparrow was virtually extinct through habitat destruction. In the years prior to 1956, this heavily black-striped saltmarsh sparrow lived by the thousands around Merritt Island on Florida's east coast. Much of the bunchgrass-dominated saltmarsh that the sparrow lived in was altered to control mosquitoes and enhance the area for waterfowl. Then drainage of land for housing, pastures and highways wiped out the last of its habitat in the shadow of America's space center. In 1979, the five survivors were captured and all turned out to be males. These were bred in captivity with females of other races, but the last Dusky died on 16 June, 1987 in a modest cage beside the glitz and glitter of Disney World.

The Great Lakes and the Midwest

Overfishing, massive pollution, and the completion of the St. Lawrence Seaway doomed the Great Lakes fishery. The seaway allowed some ocean fish to get above Niagara Falls, in particular Sea Lampreys. These invaded the lakes and attached themselves to many fish that had no strategies to thwart them. Three ciscos were major components of the Great Lakes fisheries until the invasion of Sea Lampreys, and fish competing for food, such as the Alewife and Small Bloater. The Deepwater Cisco was last taken in 1951, the Blackfin Cisco was last seen in 1955, while the Longjaw Cisco was declared extinct in 1983.

The Lake Sturgeon is the largest fish in the Great Lakes, exceeding 2.1 meters (7 feet) and 130 kilograms (300 pounds). As far back as 1885, millions of kilograms of this fish were sold commercially. Today it is greatly reduced in numbers and range, its last stronghold being Lake Winnebego, Wisconsin. Before its swift decline in the 1950s, the Blue Pike produced catches of 9 million kilograms (20 million pounds) a year from Lake Erie and a fraction of this a year from Lake Ontario. Now it is virtually absent from both lakes. In an attempt to save the species, a pair was captured and 9,000 fry were placed in isolated clean lakes.

Over-exploitation and alteration to habitat have also devastated species on land. In the great forests of the Midwest (and eastwards) there once lived the commonest bird in the world, the Passenger Pigeon. This large blue pigeon with a long pointed tail easily numbered five billion. Vast flocks roamed the forests, nesting together in areas with heavy crops of nuts. Extensive lumbering destroyed their habitat in many areas, and they were shot by local residents for food, but it was the coming of the railroads and the telegraph that wiped them out. Railroads pushed into most corners of the pigeon's range in the mid-1800s and through these and the telegraph lines joining towns, news of mass nesting sites was sent out far and wide. Professional market gunners came every year along with amateur sportsmen to

capture the prized fat nestlings, and to trap and shoot the adults. By the mid 1880s, only a few scattered lonely groups remained. The Passenger Pigeon has not been seen in the wild since 1906, and the last captive bird died at the Cincinnati zoo in 1914.

Today, the Midwest is the only breeding area of the endangered Kirtland's Warbler, the entire world population of which would fit in a suitcase. A gray and yellow warbler with black streaks, it breeds only in young jack-pine areas in central Michigan, ignoring other similar territory around the Great Lakes. Never common, its numbers dropped from 500 pairs in 1951 to 167 in 1974 and this provoked major conservation efforts. Attempts were made to improve the quality and size of its habitat. The Brown-headed Cowbird, which has increased enormously in recent decades and parasitizes the warbler's nests, was trapped and removed from breeding areas. Birders can only see the warblers on strictly regulated tours, and are not allowed to take tape-recordings or other devices to lure them closer. Despite all these steps, there were only 212 pairs in 1989 and it is thought that the bird might be experiencing problems in its wintering grounds in the Bahamas.

Many larger mammals, such as the Bison, Wapiti (Elk) and Cougar have lost their Midwest populations. The Gray (or Timber) Wolf continues to hang on at Michigan's Isle Royale National Park in Lake Superior, and there are a number of

D I S T R I B U T I O N
BISON

■ Extent in 1850

American Bison (Bison bison). *The vast expanse of the North American plains was once the migration route for huge herds of buffalo. Although buffalo numbers have slowly rebuilt, the plains are now plowed, built on and crisscrossed with roads, making it unlikely that buffalo will ever again roam in a truly wild state.*

packs in the north woods of Minnesota. A smaller mammal, the Indiana Bat, illustrates the damage that can be caused by even well-intentioned humans. The bat's population has dropped from 900,000 to 450,000 in recent years. The bats hibernate chiefly in seven cold caves in Indiana, Kentucky, and Missouri, and human disturbance in just one of them caused 60,000 to die. The entrance to another cave was blocked to keep people out. This also prevented cold air from entering and 80,000 bats died as the temperature mounted.

The Great Plains

Before humans arrived this area was home to an aggregation of large mammals that would rival today's Serengeti plains in Tanzania. Most were killed off by the early hunters and gatherers that streamed south from the Bering Strait landbridge. But the Plains Bison still numbered around 75 million when European settlers arrived. Then in about 1830, the US government urged the extermination of this animal as a way to decimate the native Americans of the plains, who stood between the colonizers and the Pacific Ocean. The coming of the railroads, waves of settlers and their constantly improving firearms led to a great slaughter, and only about 800 animals remained by the late 1880s. A rescue attempt saved them from extinction, and today about 30,000 live on private ranches and in various parks and reserves.

The Great Plains Wolf, often called the Buffalo Runner, lived with the vast herds of plains animals. As the big game vanished, the incoming ranchers of sheep and cattle shot and poisoned the wolves, the last one perishing in 1926. Coyotes were also persecuted but remain widespread. Unfortunately, the poisoned bait put down for them was often taken by Swift Foxes and the northern race of this species may be extinct in the Canadian praries. Restrictions on poisons in the 1970s have revived populations, at least in the southern part of their range.

A much smaller animal brought to the brink by poisons is Wiest's Sphinx Moth. This small, diurnal moth was badly affected by sprays used to kill grasshoppers. In its last home in Weld County in the plains of eastern Colorado 300 were counted in 1979, and only 25 in 1981 after a spraying program in 1980. County officials, scientists and landowners have agreed to try using parasitic protozoans to kill grasshoppers instead of insecticide sprays.

Texas

This enormous state harbors more birds than any other in North America. The endangered Whooping Crane winters only in the middle of the Texan Gulf coast and the Red-cockaded Woodpecker inhabits the eastern pinewoods. The colorful Golden-cheeked Warbler breeds only on the Edward's Plateau, and the Black-capped Vireo breeds there and northwards into central Oklahoma. Both the warbler and vireo are declining fast due to habitat destruction in Texas and on their wintering grounds in Mexico.

In the 1800s, the coastal prairies of Texas and Louisiana resounded with the booming calls of millions of Attwater's Prairie Chickens (a subspecies of the Greater Prairie Chicken). Since then, much of their prairie home has been converted into fields of crops, rice paddies, and pasture for cattle, and the birds have been heavily hunted. Their decline was evident in 1903, when the state of Texas established a bag limit of 25 birds a day. Today only 500 remain, scattered over a few refuges between Houston and Corpus Christi.

Two cats which also occur in Latin America are endangered in south Texas, the only US part of their ranges. The Texas Ocelot is a beautiful spotted nocturnal cat that was once found as far as Arkansas. It has suffered from habitat clearance, and has been trapped for its pelt and for its meat and blood, which were said to aid stamina. The small dark weasel-like Jaguarundi formerly inhabited the bottomland forests of the lower Rio Grande valley and 99 per cent of these forests have been destroyed. A recent survey of 1,500 trappers revealed that none had caught or seen a Jaguarundi recently – and with so many trappers around a comeback seems unlikely!

Texas is also home to some endemic animals with very restricted distributions. The Houston Toad, for example, is found in just a few areas of Loblolly Pine in east Texas. Alterations to its habitat have brought it into contact with other toads, and it is being genetically swamped by them. The Texas Blind Salamander occurs in

caves and underground streams in Hayes County. In one cave, it ate invertebrates which were nourished by guano from roosting bats. When a door was put on the cave, the trapped bats starved and the rest went elsewhere. Although the door was later removed the bats have not returned and with no new bat guano, the salamanders have dropped in numbers.

Some species of small fish live only in certain springs in west Texas. All these fish have suffered due to water being pumped away for use in agriculture, which lowered water tables, and from the introduction of exotic competitors. The Comanche Springs Pupfish and the Pecos Gambusia survive only at Phantom Lake spring near Toyahvale, while the Leon Springs Pupfish was last seen in 1851. The struggle of another fish, the Big Bend Gambusia, illustrates how active intervention can pay off. This tiny fish with orange and yellow pigments was discovered in 1928 at Boquillas springs. When these dried up, the fish was feared extinct. Then in 1954 more were found at another spring, but they were threatened by competition from the closely related *Gambusia affinis*. So the 19 surviving Big Bend Gambusias were removed, their relatives were killed off and the Big Bends were returned to the springs. They did well until *G. affinis* somehow re-infested Boquillas springs. The four surviving Big Bends were then placed in a specially created new pool where they thrived free from competition. They have since been placed in Croton springs in Big Bend National Park, and their numbers have reached 1,000.

Above left *Attwater's Prairie Chicken* (Tympanuchus cupido attwateri) *is another animal that once numbered in millions. By 1989 it had been reduced to about 500 and there seems little hope for the species unless sufficient unmodified prairie can be protected in Texas.*

Above *The Jaguarundi* (Felis yagouaroudi) *is a small cat whose coat may be one of several colors. It is rare in the USA, which is on the extreme north of a range that extends through Central America and most of South America.*

Right *The Mexican Axolotl* (Ambystoma mexicanum) *is a popular aquarium pet, often bred from an albino strain. It can remain in its larval form with gills throughout its life. This salamander used to be common in highland lakes of Mexico, but has been hunted for food and eaten by introduced trout.*

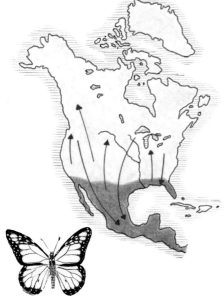

DISTRIBUTION
MONARCH BUTTERFLY

The Monarch (Danaus plexippus) *is the only butterfly that makes birdlike migrations on a regular basis. Although they migrate both north and south, no single individual makes the entire round-trip. In spring the butterflies head north and breed along the way. Their offspring return south in the autumn.*

Mexico

The Nearctic region includes the non-tropical areas of northern and plateau Mexico. There, as in other parts of Mexico, a handful of dedicated scientists and government agencies are involved in conservation, but they are not backed up by the powerful private organizations and millions of amateur naturalists that are active in the north. This is partly due to the paucity of field guides on the area. However, the government can and does call on the help of the military!

Since 1967, military units have been protecting the nesting females and eggs of the Kemp's Ridley Sea-turtle at Rancho Nuevo on the Gulf of Mexico in Tamaulipas. In the 1940s, tens of thousands of the turtles came ashore each year on a single day, attracting locals who slaughtered them for meat and leather, and gathered all the eggs. By 1963, only a few thousand were coming ashore, and in the 1970s, sometimes only a few hundred. It is hoped that the protection, and the hatchery programs that have been initiated, will show good results when the youngsters are old enough to return to their ancestral beaches. Unfortunately in the meantime many are being killed in shrimp nets, because the turtles feed on crabs near the sea bottom where shrimp congregate.

Inland, in the mountains of Nuevo León and Coahuila states, pressure from logging and other human activities is increasing. The removal of the trees on which they feed has reduced the number of cliff-nesting Maroon-fronted Parrots to 2,000. Below these mountains stretches a vast desert containing scattered springs. Many of these harbor fish, turtles and invertebrates that are endangered due to the use of these springs by industry, and for recreation and washing clothes. The Parras Pupfish and the Sharptooth Minnow are already extinct, while the Mexican Blindcat and the Checkered Killifish are each restricted to single springs and may soon follow them. The Aquatic Box-turtle lives only in marshes of the Cuatrociénagas basin in Coahuila. In addition to overuse of its marshes and waters, this turtle is being over-collected by amateur naturalists.

The future of the largest surviving ground-living reptile in North America, the Bolson Tortoise, also looked bleak. It occurs on the gentle slopes above the seasonal flood plains in the Bolson de Mapini in the Chihuahuan desert. The Tobosa Grass on which it feeds was severely overgrazed by cattle, and the tortoise was overcollected for food and the pet trade. Now a major campaign has been instituted and the tortoise is protected by law and given refuge by concerned ranchers and in the new Mapimi biosphere reserve.

Further south, the mountain forests of Michoacan and Mexico states are the winter home of most of the Monarch Butterflies of North America. Some 15 million come here from all over eastern and central North America, beating their orange and black wings to accomplish the most notable migration of any insect. The threats to these butterflies include logging, cattle which eat them attracted by their massive winter roosts, and insensitive tourists who flush them to enjoy the spectacle they create – and force them to use up their precious fat reserves. A private Mexican organization has now been formed to save the Monarchs and it pays local people to guard them, helping the local economy.

Three aquatic salamanders are in trouble in the remnants of the highland lakes of the area. The famous Mexican Axolotl, which can retain its larval form throughout its life, is commonly bred in laboratories around the world. In its home, though, in Lake Xochimilco east of Mexico City, it is rare and threatened by introduced predatory fish and pollution. The Lake Lerma Salamander is prized as food, and its lake has been largely drained. Michoacan's Lake Patzcuaro Salamander is another local delicacy, and is suffering from the introduction of bass, silting, pollution, and the pumping of water for agriculture.

The Sierra Madre Occidental along the western side of the Mexican mainland

Below *American Monarch Butterflies* (Danaus plexippus) *migrate to Mexico and coastal California where they hibernate in huge clusters which may number several million. The butterflies accumulate poisons from their food plants and these ward off most birds that prey on insects.*

Above *The Gulf Porpoise (Phocoena sinus) is the smallest of its kind and may be the smallest of all cetaceans. It is very like the Common Porpoise (bottom) in shape but, on average, is about 30 centimeters (12 inches) shorter and 5 kilograms (10 pounds) lighter.*

is a lightly populated wonderland of deep canyons, cliffs and vast pine-oak forests. Nevertheless, loggers, trappers, and hunters penetrated the remotest areas, wiping out the silver-colored race of the Grizzly, the Mexican Grizzly Bear. The Mexican Gray Wolf was also persecuted but a few survive in remote areas and may be saved by a captive breeding program near Tucson.

The peninsula of Baja California, separated from the mainland by the Gulf of California, is home to the Baja California Pronghorn. It has been driven by local and North American hunters out of most of its former range and less than 100 now roam the Vizcaino desert near Scammon's Lagoon. These few survivors have to compete for forage with domestic animals, and fences restrict their movements.

Surrounded by dry deserts and lonely mountains, the Gulf of California's waters are rich in marine life. A large fish of the Gulf, the Totoaba, has been so overexploited that it was declared endangered in 1975. Gill nets set for this fish also killed many of the endemic Gulf of California Porpoise. Only discovered in 1958, this is the smallest and rarest cetacean in the world. Unfortunately, illegal gill-netting continues and reports of these porpoises are decreasing.

In contrast, healthy Gray Whale populations now calve in the quiet warm lagoons around this gulf and on the west side of Baja. Once numbering up to 50,000, they had been reduced by hunting to only 100 by 1937, when they were protected. Mexico set up the world's first whale sanctuary at Scammon's Lagoon, and the Gray Whale's numbers have increased to about 11,000.

California

Flying into Los Angeles airport on the Pacific Ocean, you might notice a small area of sand dunes and brush among the vast urban sprawl. This is the El Segundo sand dunes, the last remnants of many miles of dunes, and the last home of the El Segundo Blue Butterfly and many other specialized insects. Elsewhere along southern California's famous beaches, human activities have affected wildlife. The formerly widespread California Least Tern, for example, was forced to abandon most of its nesting colonies, and its numbers sank to about 600 pairs. Since being listed as endangered, its nesting sites have been fenced and new ones created, with papier

Right *A Gray Whale* (Eschrichtius robustus) *surfacing to breathe off the coast of British Columbia, Canada. Under strict protection its numbers are slowly increasing, and a major industry has developed taking tourists whale watching.*

Left *The California Condor* (Gymnogyps
californianus) *became extinct in the wild in
1987 when the last one was captured to join 26
others in a captive breeding program. Andean
Condors* (Vultur gryphus) *have been released
into the wild in the USA as part of long-term
research before reintroducing California
Condors.*

DISTRIBUTION
CALIFORNIA CONDOR

▨ *Principal location from 1805 to 1934*

California Condor (Gymnogyps californianus)
*By the time Europeans reached California and
Oregon, the California Condor was already a
rare bird. Collecting for museums, as well as
poisoning, played a part in their demise.
Although extinct in the wild, there are plans for
their reintroduction.*

mâché decoys placed to attract the terns. Spirits rose when an early arriving male
offered a fish to one of these decoys!

The coastal salt marshes of southern California have been largely filled in for
marinas and housing. As a result, a small, dark race of Clapper Rail, the Light-footed
Clapper Rail, only survives in disjunct populations. Some marshes have only males,
some only females, and 65 per cent of apparently suitable marshes have no rails at all.
In 1986, only 143 pairs bred in six marshes, and half the birds were restricted to
Upper Newport Bay in heavily populated Orange County.

Mountains soar above the coastal cities of California. Unfortunately the
California Condor no longer soars above the mountains. These giant birds once
ranged east to the Great Plains and Florida, and in historical times they flew from
British Columbia down to Baja California. When the gold rush began, their last
strongholds in California were overrun with people who shot them and most of the
larger mammals on which they relied. In later decades they ingested the poisons left
for Coyotes by ranchers, and the lead left in deer by hunters. By the mid-1970s, only
about 50 remained in the wild and many of them unhealthy and not fledging young.
So it was decided to capture the remaining birds, and all are now in the San Diego and

Los Angeles zoos. In 1989, four healthy young hatched, and the population stood at 32. It is hoped that in the coming decades some can be released.

The little gray and white Least Bell's Vireo is also under severe threat. Once common in streamside willows throughout much of California, this bird is down to about 355 pairs, most of them in San Diego County. Everyone wants to take water from the streams – farmers, municipalities, industry – and many of the waterways have been channeled, diverted, or gone dry. The vast increase in farmland, feed lots and cattle has greatly benefited the parasitic Brown-headed Cowbird, and a distressing number of vireo nests are now full of cowbird eggs.

The cold waters of central California are well known for the richness and variety of their marine life. One of the most sought-after animals there was the Southern Sea Otter, valued for its pelt. This southern race of the Sea Otter ranged from Washington state to Baja California before Russian and American sealers began harvesting them. By 1910, the southern race was thought extinct, but in 1914, a group of 14 was located near Monterey. To protect them, their existence was kept secret until 1938 when they numbered 100. Although the population is now nearing 2,000, their habitat is sliced by oil tankers and they are being killed by people harvesting abalone, so a new colony is being started elsewhere.

Above *The largest herds of the Tule Wapiti or Elk* (Cervus canadensis nannodes) *occur in the Owens Valley of California. Other herds have been established south of San Francisco. Under protection, most of these are slowly increasing.*

Above right *The San Joaquin Kit Fox* (Vulpes macrotis mutica) *survives in only a few relict populations in central California. Intensive agriculture in the San Joaquin Valley has reduced the available habitat.*

A greater recovery has taken place among Northern Elephant Seals. So many were slaughtered for oil on the beaches of California and Baja that by 1892 only 100 survived at their last stronghold on Guadalupe Island. Protected in Mexico, these 3-ton deep-sea divers staged a comeback. By the 1930s, they had recolonized some of the Channel islands, and in 1979, they started a mainland colony at Ano Nuevo Point near Santa Cruz in California. Today they number 65,000, and are proving a major tourist attraction for Santa Cruz.

Less of an attraction is the Santa Cruz Long-toed Salamander which lives nearby in an area of ponds and woods. Unfortunately its rarity has caused it to be heavily collected by amateur biologists. To try to save the salamander, its breeding ponds have been made into reserves and additional ponds have been created for it.

To the north, San Bruno mountain divides San Francisco from its peninsula communities and between the mountain's two ridges lies an industrial park. While it is protected to some degree, exotic plants, recreational activities, and fire suppression are altering the natural vegetation. This is the last home of two grassland butterflies, the Mission Blue Butterfly and the Calliope Silverspot, while the endangered Bay Checkerspot, a black butterfly with red and yellow markings, is found here and at a few other sites down the peninsula. Another vividly colored creature, the yellow, red, and black striped San Francisco Garter Snake, survives in just a few reservoir and pond edges from San Bruno mountain southward on the peninsula.

At least three-quarters of the saltmarshes around San Francisco and San Pablo bays have been filled in and dyked. As a result, the docile, cinnamon-colored Salt Marsh Harvest Mouse has been "on the list" since 1970. The vulnerable California Clapper Rail and two subspecies of the Song Sparrow (*Melospiza melodia pusilla* and *samuelis*) also rely on the remaining bits of marsh.

The great central valleys of California, once covered in vast forests, grasslands and marshes, are now under the plough. Half a million of the smallest race of Wapiti (Elk), the Tule Wapiti, used to roam these valleys and the coastal hills from Santa Barbara to the Russian River. They were slaughtered for meat until only one herd remained, in the tule swamps of Kern County. There they were, at last, protected and have since been released at new sites in the Owens valley, Cache creek in the coast range, and elsewhere. Today they number over 2,000.

Rivers in the valley once hosted the abundant Thicktail Chub, last seen in 1957. Other fish barely hang on in undrained areas where pools collect in the spring. These pools have a hardpan of compacted clay underneath preventing winter rain water from seeping away. To add to the problems of conserving fish species, fishermen seem to care little about the purity of stock of fish grown and released from hatcheries. Two trout subspecies of the Sierra Nevada are endangered due to these sloppy practices. All the rivers of the Kern Rainbow Trout, a race with golden-yellow sides and orange on the ventral regions, have been invaded by hatchery hybrids and the last pure-bloods occur only in the Little Kern river. The Paiute Cut-throat Trout, which lacks spots, has probably been wiped out by the introduction of the wrong trout stock into its last home on Silver King creek.

The American Southwest

The dominant plant in southern Arizona is the tallest cactus in the world, the Saguaro Cactus, and one of its most important pollinators, Sanborn's Long-nosed Bat, has disappeared from most of its roosts. The 20,000 that once roosted in Colossal cave near Tucson are gone and the other caves these bats rely on are subject to destruction, disturbance and vandalism. In addition, locals in Mexico kill all bats in an attempt to eradicate the Vampire Bats which do cause losses in cattle. The related Mexican Long-nosed Bat has dropped in numbers from over 10,000 in 1967 to about 1,000 in 1983 at its chief US roost in Big Bend National Park in Texas, and it is also crashing in Mexico. As these long-tongued bats decline, the reproductive success of the Saguaro, other cacti and the night-blooming agaves could suffer, sending these plants into a related downward spiral.

These deserts are home to many reptiles, including the sought-after Gila Monster and Desert Tortoise. A large poisonous lizard covered with black and orange beads, the Gila Monster is vulnerable through overcollecting for sale in Europe and elsewhere. The Desert Tortoise is threatened by habitat degradation, capture for the pet trade, and off-road vehicles which cause its dens to collapse. State laws made it illegal to catch or kill the tortoise and it now receives national protection.

Above *The Gila Monster* (Heloderma suspectum) *is the only poisonous lizard found in the USA. Although its poison is rarely fatal to humans, it has been persecuted and is also collected for the pet trade.*

DISTRIBUTION
DESERTS IN THE USA

DISTRIBUTION
DESERTS IN THE USA

■ Great Basin Desert

☐ Sonoran Desert

■ Mohave Desert

■ Chihuahuan Desert

Mammals of the desert have also suffered. The Arizona Jaguar used to live from California east to Arkansas and southward into Mexico. The last Californian individual was killed near Palm Springs in 1860, and New Mexico's last one in 1905. But some still wander north from Mexico, including one sighted in Arizona in 1971. Another overhunted animal, the Sonoran Pronghorn, has in addition to compete with domestic animals for forage. Perhaps 1,000 now survive in the deserts of northwest Sonora and southwest Arizona.

A luxuriant grassland covered wide valleys at the edges of the Sonoran desert northwards into Arizona. Massive herds of cattle were driven there to feed in the late 1800s, and a drought in 1892 forced them to devour every last blade of grass. The soil turned to cement, and deep-rooted mesquite bushes took over the grasslands. This greatly reduced the range of a very distinct race of the Bobwhite quail. Well isolated from other races to the east, the Masked Bobwhite has a black head and an entirely orange breast. By the mid 1900s only one good population of this quail could be found, in the Benjamin Hill-Carbo area. Some birds were taken to Arizona but the reintroduction attempt failed and the Masked Bobwhite's survival rests on keeping cattle out of large enough reserves in Sonora.

Many people think of Arizona as an area of deserts and canyons, not realizing that the mountains in the center and southeast are verdant with forests and flowers nurtured by over 100 millimeters (40 inches) of rain in the summer and winter months. Naturalists flock there to see many animals from the Sierra Madre that occur virtually nowhere else in the US.

While birders enjoyed views of trogons, Painted Whitestarts (Redstarts), and a dozen kinds of hummingbirds, the cone-eating Thick-billed Parrot was absent for many years. These huge green parrots, with red forehead and yellow stripes under the wing, were shot by early miners and loggers, and disappeared from the Chiricahua

Right *The Masked Bobwhite* (Colinus virginianus ridgwayi) *is a distinctive subspecies of the Northern Bobwhite. It is confined to the Mexican state of Sonora, where it occurs in thickly grassed desert among shrubs and cacti.*

mountains in the 1930s. In the Sierra Madre Occidental of Mexico, their numbers are dropping, partly due to capture for the cage-bird trade. In the 1980s, 30 Thick-billed Parrots being illegally imported into the US were confiscated. Since they are threatened in Mexico, it was decided to attempt a reintroduction into their former range in the Chiricahuas. Some dispersed up to the Tonto National Forest in central Arizona, where they bred in the wild, and the parrots can now be seen regularly in the Chiricahuas in southeast Arizona. If the birds continue to do well, some could be reintroduced to Mexico when needed.

The Chiricahuas are also home to the Arizona Ridge-nosed Rattlesnake. This small species is at risk due to an active trade in live specimens by private collectors.

The removal of areas of forest has silted up the rivers of two forms of trout, the Gila and Apache Trouts. These fish have also suffered from having exotic trout released in their waters. The last strongholds of the Gila Trout were in the Black Range of New Mexico, while the Apache Trout may still survive in streams of the White Mountains of Arizona.

The Rocky Mountains and Great Basin

This vast area of snow-capped peaks, wide valleys and sculptured rocks has not escaped the ravages of humans. The Wood Bison is now gone and the Plains Bison is a shadow of its former self. The Southern Rocky Mountain Wolf was last seen in 1940, and the Northern Rocky Mountain Wolf, once abundant from Oregon to the Dakotas, is down to about 35 individuals around Glacier National Park in Montana. Formerly found across many of the northern states, the Selkirk herd of the Woodland Caribou barely hangs on as loggers invade its last home in the old-growth coniferous forests of northern Idaho.

A brighter story can be told of the Northern Pronghorn. Its numbers had dropped to about 20,000 in 1900 due to hunting and fencing of its range. Now fences are used which restrict the movements of sheep but not Pronghorns. This and good management have raised its numbers to more than 500,000. The Utah Prairiedog has also bounced back from 3,000 in 1979 to 10,000 today. While other species of prairiedogs continue to be shot, gassed, and poisoned, the persecution of the Utah Prairiedog has been stopped. To overcome the additional problem of habitat loss caused by overgrazing and farming, colonies were started at new sites where artificial holes had been dug and some predators removed to help them get started.

Some of the animals that depend on the waters of the Colorado river basin

Below left *The Thick-billed Parrot* (**Rhynchopsitta pachyrhyncha**) *only occurs in the Sierra Madre Occidental, Mexico, where it is endangered through trapping for the caged bird trade and destruction of the old growth pine forest. A population has recently been established in Arizona.*

Below *The Ridge-nosed Rattlesnake* (Crotalus willardi) *is confined to the extreme south of Arizona, New Mexico and adjacent Mexico. It lives in scattered populations in pine-oak woodlands at altitudes of over 1,700 meters (5,500 feet).*

Right *The Pronghorn "Antelope"* (Antilocapra americana) *is one of the fastest animals on land. The sub-species resident in Baja, California, Sonora, and Arizona have become very rare.*

are in trouble. The demands on this water made by farmers and water authorities in Mexico, Los Angeles, and Phoenix increase daily. Dams have been built for hydroelectricity, canals divert the water, and overgrazing, logging, and agricultural runoff cause pollution and siltation. The poor native fish have experienced blockage of their migration routes, massive changes in stream flow and temperatures, and the stocking of new lakes with exotic fish that compete for food and prey on them. The Colorado River Squawfish used to reach 35 kilograms (80 pounds) and was a major source of food for native Americans and early settlers throughout the basin down to Mexico. Today it survives in just a few reaches of the upper Green and Colorado rivers. The Humpback Chub, a minnow highly specialized for life in fast streams, is gone from all areas below the dams and reservoirs. It is too early yet to tell whether a recovery agreement on the native fish of the basin signed in 1988 will revive these and other inhabitants.

The growth of Las Vegas in Nevada caused local water authorities to take over springs and seepages in the area. Along with the introduction of Bull Frogs, this action caused the first known extinction of an amphibian in historical times in North America – the Vegas Valley Leopard Frog, last seen in 1942. Water usage and competition from introduced fish killed the last of the Pahrangat Spinedace in 1959.

A now-protected area to the west of Las Vegas, Ash Meadows, is the only home of many plants and fish which are endangered due to earlier habitat disturbance and introduced predatory fish. One of the endangered fish, the Devil's Hole Pupfish, may have the most restricted range of any vertebrate on Earth, being found at only one pool in Ash Meadows. The 125 adults there are protected by a high fence and a locked gate.

The Pacific northwest

Vast virgin coniferous forest once blanketed the Cascades and the Pacific slope of the northwest. Today perhaps 75 per cent of it has been cut, and younger trees, farms and scrubland cover the land. Over 200 species of wildlife live in the old forests, including Marbled Murrelets nesting on the mossy limbs of the great trees, Black-tailed Deer and Roosevelt Wapiti (Elk) grazing below, and many species of salamanders inhabiting the forest floor. But most of the native wildlife is doing poorly

Left *Trumpeter Swans* (Cygnus buccinator) *in the National Elk Refuge, Wyoming. Heavily hunted, they were protected only at Red Rock Lakes, Montana in the "lower 48". Stock from there was transplanted to other lakes in the west in recent years.*

in the managed plantations that sprang up in place of the old-growth forests.

The Cascade Wolf, a brown race of the Gray Wolf, is gone from this area and survives only in coastal British Columbia. Oregon Giant Earthworms grow up to 58 centimeters (23 inches) long in the deep soil of little disturbed old-growth forests. Such forests in the Wilmette valley of Oregon have been cut down to such an extent that these giants are now found in only four scattered patches of forest. However, the animal that has become the central figure in the heated battle between loggers and environmentalists is the Northern Spotted Owl. This endangered subspecies needs large areas of old-growth forest to survive, and is suffering from competition with other owls in the forest fragments that remain.

The first areas cleared for farms were the willow thickets and meadows by the Columbia river. This was the habitat of the Columbian race of the White-tailed Deer and only a few hundred now survive along the lower Columbia river. They can no longer be hunted and a reserve protects some of them.

———— Western Canada and Alaska ————

This huge area has extensive boreal forests, great mountain ranges, most of North America's tundra, and cold ocean waters teeming with life. Extending from northeast Alberta into Northwest Territories lies Wood "Buffalo" National Park, named for its resident population of Wood Bison. This differs from Plains Bison in being larger and having a longer neck, longer hair on the forehead, hairy horns, darker color, and a square hump. It was once found in meadows and forests of the Rocky mountains, but was killed off virtually everywhere. Now animals from this park have been used to start new herds in a number of other Canadian parks.

The Wood "Buffalo" park is the only nesting ground of the Whooping Crane. This huge white crane with bare red skin on the head once lived over much of the continent. A long decline due to overhunting, nest disturbance and habitat clearance brought the population down to only 15 birds in 1941, and their last breeding grounds were discovered in this park in 1954. The birds had to pass an army of hunters in the Great Plains on migration to their wintering grounds in Texas. A massive education campaign reduced this threat and the crane's numbers reached 43 in 1964. The Whooping Crane lays two eggs, but only the stronger one survives.

DISTRIBUTION
TRUMPETER SWAN

~ *Former breeding range*

▨ *Former wintering range*

Trumpeter Swans (Cygnus buccinator). *These birds used to winter on both the west and east coasts and bred as far east as the Great Lakes. By the turn of the century they were confined to the Rockies, but are now once more spreading.*

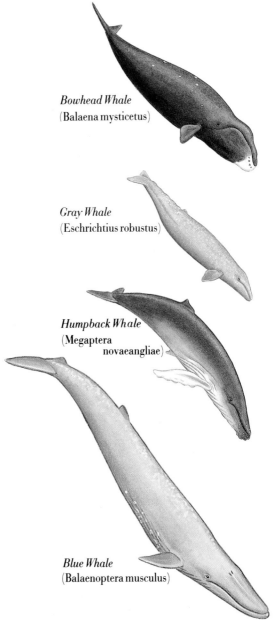

Bowhead Whale
(Balaena mysticetus)

Gray Whale
(Eschrichtius robustus)

Humpback Whale
(Megaptera
    novaeangliae)

Blue Whale
(Balaenoptera musculus)

Starting in 1964, spare eggs from many nests were removed in the hope of building a captive flock. This succeeded and there are now about 130 wild birds and about 70 in captivity. In the 1970s, some Whooping Crane eggs were placed in the nests of foster-parent Sandhill Cranes in Idaho. The young followed their "parents" to their wintering grounds in New Mexico, but they have not done well and have not bred on their own. Efforts now focus on starting a non-migratory flock in Florida or in Georgia using resident Sandhill Cranes as foster parents.

The Copper river delta near Cordova, Alaska, is the main breeding ground of a more numerous but still threatened creature, the Dusky Canada Goose. This dark, medium-sized race numbered about 25,000 before an earthquake in 1964. The quake uplifted the delta and much of the marshland became a dry bluff. The goose's numbers increased at first as there was less flood damage to nests, but alder and willow thickets soon took root providing bears and other nest predators with good cover. The geese winter in Oregon's Wilmette valley, and hunters there funded a program to remove bears from Alaska. Despite this, the Dusky Canada Goose population has dropped to 12,000 and it is in trouble.

An emergency decree in 1990 focused attention on the huge Steller's (or Northern) Sea Lion. In the late 1950s, there were 140,000 in southwest Alaska, but a census in 1989 found only 25,000. The decline is thought to be due to the reduction in its favorite fish prey caused by commercial fishing, and many thousands being killed in trawls or dying tangled in marine debris. This sea lion is now being studied closely, and people are being kept well away from all known breeding grounds.

Alaska is a major summering area for many endangered whales including the California Gray, the Blue and the Humpback, viewed by tourists from dozens of cruise ships. Less often seen are the Bowhead Whales of the Arctic Ocean. These whales help the Arctic seals and smaller cetaceans by breaking a way through thick ice. They have been hunted by the Inuit for centuries, but suffered a steep decline when commercial whalers arrived in the late 1800s. By 1977, only 3,000 survived and populations are being monitored while the Inuit continue to hunt them.

The vast tundra is the breeding ground of many of the New World's shore-birds and waterfowl. Huge numbers of Eskimo Curlew used to breed there before flying south to winter in Argentina. Market gunners turned their sights onto migrating shorebirds and the Eskimo Curlew was thought to have been shot to extinction. Recently, though, it has been spotted occasionally on migration and may be nesting somewhere in the Northwest Territories. Another migratory bird, the Tundra Peregrine Falcon, is suffering from a very different threat. Although its far northern breeding grounds are relatively free of DDT, this chemical is still in use in its Latin American wintering grounds.

Some of the larger mammals of the tundra and further north remain at risk from hunters. With the arrival of the rifle, the Musk Ox was exterminated from much of its high Arctic range, and was extinct in Alaska by 1865. It has been reintroduced to protected islands in the Bering Sea, such as Nunivak Island where descendants of 31 pioneers now number about 750. Some of these have been placed elsewhere in Alaska. Only about 500 Barren-ground Grizzly Bears are thought to survive and, although they are protected, illegal kills may number 30 or more a year. The Polar Bear is not yet endangered but is being watched closely. It is absent or reduced in many areas, shot for the high price of its hide by hunters in their new snowmobiles or from small planes and boats.

However, in the long-term the wildlife of the far north and the Canadian islands is probably less threatened by hunters than by impending global warming and the effects of haze and soot from industrial centers far away.

DISTRIBUTION
ESKIMO CURLEW

- - - *Migration route*

Breeding

Wintering

The Eskimo Curlew (Numenius borealis). *Once one of the most abundant birds in North America, it now teeters on the brink of extinction. The map shows the migration routes between its arctic breeding grounds and its wintering grounds in South America.*

Left *Ross's Gull* (Larus rosea) *near Churchill, Manitoba. The world population of this gull is probably low but its status is uncertain because its main breeding colonies are in remote parts of Siberia. However, small colonies have recently been found near Churchill, and other parts of the Canadian Arctic.*

MIGRATING BIRDS

Tobias Salathé studied biology at Basle University, Switzerland. He then worked for six years on the ecology and conservation of waterbirds at the biological station of Tour du Valat in the Camargue, southern France. Back in Switzerland he acted as freelance conservation consultant for governmental offices and private conservation organizations. Tobias is currently the coordinator of the Migratory Birds Conservation Program of the International Council for Bird Preservation, focusing on the conservation problems of migratory birds in the West Palearctic-African flyways.

The annual migration of millions of birds has fascinated people since the beginning of history, being first recorded in magnificent paintings in 4,000-year-old Egyptian tombs. Weird theories to account for these movements, such as swallows vanishing in the muddy bottom of lakes and cuckoos turning into sparrowhawks in winter, persisted until recently. They have now disappeared, thanks to modern research including records from bird-ringing stations, and direct and radar observations of migrating birds.

As days in higher latitudes become shorter, heralding a harsh season with scant food supplies, migrants leave their breeding sites in temperate regions to spend the winter in milder climates. Longdistance migrants may have to fly over large inhospitable areas with little or no suitable food. There are ecological barriers several hundred miles across, such as the Gulf of Mexico (traversed by the globally threatened Blackburnian Warbler), the Mediterranean Sea, the Sahara desert, and the western Pacific. So the birds have to start their journey well prepared.

Migrants deposit fat reserves mainly under their skin by increasing their food intake up to 40 per cent prior to departure. Small warblers like Kirtland's Warbler, now nearly extinct, may accumulate deposits up to half of their lean body weight, which they can restore by only a few days' stopover in an area with abundant food. Such refueling sites at either end of ecological barriers along international flyways are of great strategic importance. Outstanding among these are the wetlands in northern Africa situated between the sea and the desert like El Kala in Algeria or Lake Ichkeul in Tunisia, while the Waddensee mudflats of Germany, Denmark, and the Netherlands are also significant.

Whooping Crane (Grus americana)

Right *A female Arctic Tern* (Sterna paradisaea) *begs food from the male on an ice floe in Churchill, Canada. After breeding in the Arctic, they will journey to the Antarctic, undertaking the longest annual migration of any bird.*

Far right *This map shows the main migration routes for birds.*

The journey of long-distance migrants may be many thousand miles –up to 30,000 kilometers (18,600 miles) or more for some waders and the Arctic Tern, migrating back and forth between the Arctic circle and the Antarctic pack ice. Bad weather, storms, predators, and competition for scarce food and shelter encountered during migration may levy a heavy toll. What percentage of the migrants that set off accomplish their journey is largely unknown.

The flyways

The phenomenon of bird migration involves movements between northern and southern continents, and also shorter journeys within single continents and regions. The current routes or flyways evolved some 10,000 years ago after the retreat of ice age glaciers. Since then, some birds originating in the tropics have migrated to breed in temperate regions where they can take advantage of abundant food supplies during the summer months.

For example, the Mexican tropical forests harbor an extreme variety of migratory warblers breeding in the eastern USA. In the Americas, there are four important flyways used by birds breeding in North America and wintering mainly in Central America and northern South America, with some species migrating as far as Tierra del Fuego at the southern tip of the South American continent. The most eastern, the Atlantic flyway, follows the east coast south to Florida. Birds breeding further west in Canada and Alaska use the Mississippi flyway with its many wetlands, on which some 8 million ducks, geese, swans and coots spend the winter, among them the endangered Piping Plover. The Central flyway runs east of the Rocky Mountains to the coastal wetlands of Texas and Louisiana. The Pacific flyway leads birds along the Rocky Mountains and the Pacifice east coast to Central America.

Migrants cross the European continent flying south and southwest on a wide front. Many Siberian birds start migrating westwards to Europe and then partly follow a southsouthwesterly route. The Slender-billed Curlew, of which only a

Above *Waterfowl, including large numbers of Snow Geese* (Anser caerulescens), *wintering in the Tule Lake National Wildlife Refuge in northern California.*

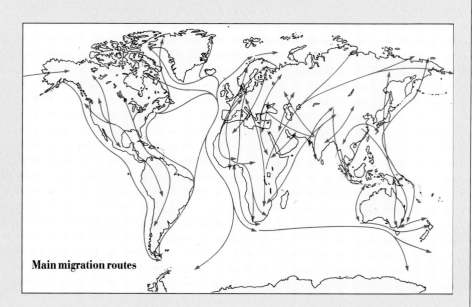

Main migration routes

Flyways and the hunters' toll
The fixed routes followed by migrating birds (see map, **left**) make them extremely vulnerable. Along many of the Mediterranean, Caribbean and south-east Asian flyways in particular, bottleneck areas enable people to shoot and catch migratory birds with decoys, nets and limesticks. With the widespread availability of shotguns and mistnets, this "sport" has been taken up by many who cannot claim "tradition" as an excuse for their destructive pastime. It is estimated that in the Mediterranean region alone, 1,000 million birds are killed annually by 10 million shooters and an additional 1 million trappers. This means that up to a fifth of all birds crossing the Mediterranean may be falling prey to humans. A detailed analysis of birds ringed in Europe and later found dead reveals that the chances of a bird population surviving decrease significantly with increasing hunting pressure. Hunting is believed to be one of the main reasons for the near extinction of the Eskimo and Slender-billed Curlews in America and the Mediterranean respectively.

Barn Swallow (Hirundo rustica)

hundred or so may survive, breeds in Siberia and crosses southeastern Europe to winter in North Africa. Important concentrations occur during fall migration and throughout winter on the northern coast of the Mediterranean at wetlands and maquis with abundant food sources in the Camargue (France), Coto Doñana (Spanish Atlantic coast), the Evros delta (Greece), and the Danube delta (Romanian Black Sea coast). Some soaring species like storks, pelicans (including the endangered Dalmatian Pelican), and many raptors choose narrow sea crossings at the Straits of Gibraltar and Messina, or follow the eastern Mediterranean flyway over the Bosphorus and along the Levant coast. Birds taking the western Mediterranean flyway cross the western Sahara and tend to winter in the Sahel countries, some going as far south as Angola. Birds using the eastern Mediterranean flyway follow the Nile valley or the Red Sea coast and the Rift valley, and winter in eastern and southern Africa. The White Stork is the most conspicuous bird on this route. Many breeding birds from Siberia and central Asia migrate instead over the Arab peninsula to southeastern Africa.

Important wintering areas of Palearctic birds in Asia, including the threatened Siberian Crane, are located south of the Caspian Sea, on the Indian subcontinent, in Japan, and in the Asian tropics. Some species migrate west of the central Asian mountains, others on the eastern side. But a large number cross the Himalayas over a wide front. Important flyways follow the Asian Pacific coast, through eastern Indonesia and the Philippines to Australia. The Mekong delta in Vietnam and the Sumatran coastal swamps are the most important refueling stops.

Below *The Dalmatian Pelican* (Pelecanus crispus) *breeds from Yugoslavia east to China, wintering in Greece, Turkey, the Middle East, and India. Over the past century it has declined dramatically and there may be less than 2,500 pairs in the world.*

Below right *The Red Kite* (Milvus milvus), *still widespread in some parts of mainland Europe, has declined dramatically in the British Isles and now only a small population survives in Wales. Recently a reintroduction program was initiated.*

Stopover and wintering sites

Migrants concentrate at favorable stopover and wintering sites in enormous numbers. Hawk mountain in the USA, the Bosphorus near Istanbul, and the Sinai peninsula in Egypt are famous places for gatherings of thousands of raptors. Refueling and wintering sites for several million waders and other waterbirds include the Banc d'Arguin in Mauritania, the Copper river delta in Alaska, and the Waddensee in Europe. At such bottlenecks, migrants have traditionally been captured in large numbers for human consumption. Quails and, to a lesser extent, Corncrakes are netted by the thousands when they arrive exhausted at the north coast of Sinai after crossing the Mediterranean. With the advent of shotguns the numbers of hunters and birds killed increased drastically. The largescale netting or capture

with lime sticks, clapnets, and blinded decoys of thrushes, warblers, robins, and other migrating birds has become a pastime in many areas of the Mediterranean, Caribbean and southeast Asia.

Habitat destruction

But the most important threats which face migrants are the alteration and destruction of the habitats they visit in the course of their annual cycle. In the highly industrialized and populated northern countries, traditionally used farmland, natural grassland, woodland, and many wetlands are disappearing because of urban, industrial and agricultural developments. Consequently Whooping Crane, Red Kite, and Marbled Teal have shown marked declines. The widespread fragmentation of forests in North America poses a particular threat to species like the Worm-eating Warbler, adapted to the conditions of the interior of large unbroken stretches of boreal forest. Habitat destruction is no less a conservation problem in the wintering areas. Wetland drainage, landslides on cleared forest slopes, and deforestation of primary and secondary tropical forests in Central America and southeast Asia directly affect many migrants. Recent extreme drought conditions in the African savannas have substantially contributed to the decline of many Palearctic migrants. The droughts also led to overgrazing, overuse of firewoods and overfishing of remaining wetlands, such as in the Senegal valley and the inner Niger delta in Mali. This increased human pressure on the fragile lands degraded the migrants' habitats even more. Key stopover and wintering sites are being lost through tourist developments, such as those along the coasts of Amvrakikos gulf in Greece and Chesapeake bay in the USA. Large-scale water management schemes, including huge dams and reservoirs, are destroying important wintering sites in South America, Sahelian Africa, and south and southeast Asia.

A few countries alone cannot avert these threats. Migratory birds are the common property and responsibility of many nations and, as such, they act as flagships for wider conservation issues. They form bonds of interest between countries, emphasizing the need for international cooperation, and establishing major educational and institutional connections through which many other kinds of conservation can follow. Since its foundation in 1922, the International Council for Bird Preservation (ICBP) has been particularly active in promoting the conservation of migrants through its Migratory Birds Program.

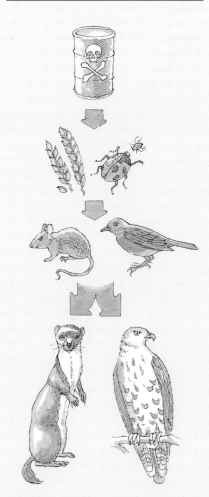

Above *At each stage in the food chain, pesticides accumulate and become more and more concentrated. Predators, such as hawks and stoats, are more likely to eat contaminated prey, because poison makes animals weaker and easier to kill.*

Left *The Barn Swallow* (Hirundo rustica), *found in both the Old and New Worlds, is perhaps the best known of all migrants. Until the eighteenth century it was widely believed that swallows spent the winter at the bottom of a pond.*

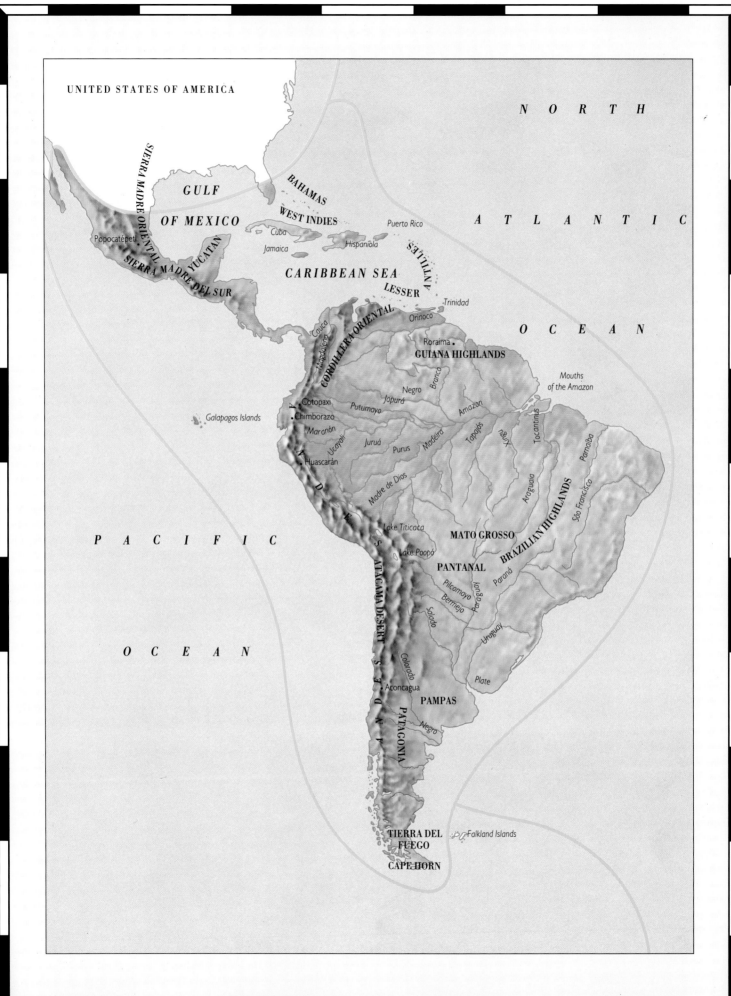

UNITED STATES OF AMERICA

SIERRA MADRE ORIENTAL

GULF
OF MEXICO

BAHAMAS

WEST INDIES

Popocatépetl

YUCATAN

SIERRA MADRE DEL SUR

Cuba

Jamaica

Hispaniola

Puerto Rico

CARIBBEAN SEA

LESSER ANTILLES

Trinidad

NORTH

ATLANTIC

OCEAN

Cauca

Magdalena

CORDILLERA ORIENTAL

Orinoco

Roraima

GUIANA HIGHLANDS

Branco

Mouths
of the Amazon

Galapagos Islands

Cotopaxi

Chimborazo

Marañón

Negro

Japurá

Putumayo

Amazon

Tapajós

Xingu

Tocantins

Parnaíba

Huascarán

Ucayali

Juruá

Purus

Madeira

Madre de Dios

São Francisco

Araguaia

PACIFIC

Lake Titicaca

Lake Poopó

MATO GROSSO

BRAZILIAN HIGHLANDS

PANTANAL

OCEAN

ATACAMA DESERT

A N D E S

Pilcomayo

Iguaçu

Paraná

Bermejo

Salado

Uruguay

Colorado

Plate

Aconcagua

PAMPAS

PATAGONIA

Negro

TIERRA DEL
FUEGO

Falkland Islands

CAPE HORN

THE NEOTROPIC REGION

The Neotropic region is all of South America and Central America as far north as coastal Mexico, and the Caribbean. The two dominant physical features of the region – the massive ridge of the Andes mountains and the vast Amazon river – have dramatic effects on the climate, vegetation and wildlife. Landscapes vary from tropical forest to the wastes of Patagonia.

Monkey Puzzles (Araucaria araucania), *Chile.*

HABITAT & PLANTS

Sabina Knees is a botanical consultant and writer with a special interest in the floras and vegetation of Central and South America. After reading botany at University College North Wales, Bangor, and the University of Reading, she was appointed assistant botanist to the Royal Horticultural Society, Wisley. Sabina then moved to Kew as conservation officer, dealing with international conservation legislation and research into the effects of trade on endangered or vulnerable species of plants. She is currently working mainly as a research associate on the European Garden Flora project at the Royal Botanic Garden, Edinburgh.

The countries of Central and South America contain a variety of biogeographical areas, from the very wet to the very dry. The climate ranges from tropical in the north, where the equator passes through the continent, to subarctic at the southern tip. Two massive physical features have dramatic effects on climate and conditions. The long ridge of the Andes mountains runs along almost the entire length of the western (Pacific) coast, influencing climate and wildlife in seven countries, while the mighty River Amazon and its many tributaries dominate an area in the north that includes much of Brazil and parts of five other countries.

Away from the Andes and Amazonia, vast tracts of tropical grasslands (or savanna), and tropical deciduous forest, cover the hotter northern regions, giving way to treeless temperate grassland (the pampas) further south. As the climate becomes cooler in southern Argentina, the pampas changes to a scrub of thorn and parched grasses, with the vegetation dwindling through Patagonia to the cold, windy wastes of Tierra del Fuego.

DISTRIBUTION
FLORISTIC REGIONS

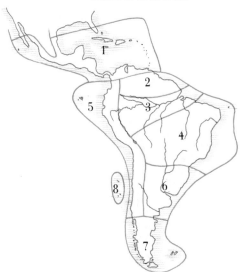

1 Caribbean
2 Venezuela and Guiana
3 Amazon
4 South Brazilian
5 Andean
6 Pampas
7 Patagonian
8 Juan Fernandez

The eastern coast receives moist winds from the Atlantic Ocean, supplying rain to a strip of tropical forest that follows much of Brazil's coast. Although no more than a few miles wide in places, this region supports a rich flora and fauna. The western coast from Ecuador to Santiago in Chile is a virtual desert, since the rain that comes from Amazonia to the northeast is extracted by the Andes and returned to the Amazon system. Further south, prevailing winds from the Pacific Ocean bring moisture to support a temperate deciduous woodland, until the bitter winters of the far south impose their own limitations on the landscape.

Within the Neotropic region, then, are many distinctly different types of landscape. Each main type contains a number of variations, depending on latitude and topography, in some places giving rise to virtually unique habitats, where precisely adapted plants and animals occupy narrowly defined niches. Some of the endangered species of the region inhabit such places. Other more widely distributed species are threatened by large-scale alterations made by people.

Left *Rainforest in the Serra dos Carajas, Pará State, Brazil, shrouded in early morning mist. The tree in the center has a termite's nest hanging from it.*

Above *Patagonian pampas near Valdez, Argentina. Like many temperate habitats it lacks the rich diversity of tropical areas.*

——— Tropical rainforest ———

The Neotropic region is divided into eight regions of flora (floristic regions): the Caribbean, Venezuela and Guiana, Amazon, South Brazilian, Andean, Juan Fernandez, Pampas, and Patagonian. The first four of these are largely covered by rainforest, giving the Neotropics probably the greatest species diversity in the world.

Unlike its counterparts in Africa and southeast Asia, the extensive area of tropical rainforest covering much of Brazil and adjacent countries in South America had remained more or less intact until the rapid destruction in the latter part of the twentieth century. The greater the area of tropical rainforest, the greater the number of species likely to be found inhabiting it. The Amazonian rainforest is no exception with an estimated 80,000 species of seed-bearing plants, about one third of the world's total, making it the most species-rich area in the world. By comparison, the rainforests of Africa and southeast Asia each contain about 30,000 seed-bearing plant species. It is mainly their favorable climates that allow rainforests to support such a great number of species and, for comparison, Britain has just 1,800 while the states of North and South Carolina combined contain some 3,360 species.

Much of the area covered with tropical rainforest in the Neotropics is flat or

Above *A mahogany tree* (Swietenia) *shrouded with climbers in the botanic gardens on the island of St. Vincent. Throughout Central America and the Caribbean, large mahoganies are now found only in protected or remote areas.*

Above right *The dense cover of creepers and epiphytes in a Costa Rican tropical forest. The rich flora at the canopy level is almost invisible from the ground, except when an occasional plant or flowerhead falls to the forest floor.*

rolling, with mountainous areas rarely exceeding 1,200 meters (4,000 feet). Annual rainfall varies from 2–4 meters (80–160 inches) per year, and the temperature is relatively high and uniform, usually around 24–26°C (75–79°F). There is no regular seasonal change affecting the whole vegetation as in temperate parts of the world. The component plants may lose their foliage on an annual basis, but the timing varies from species to species, and flowering and fruiting is a year-round event.

Forest trees are the most obvious structural component of the rainforest, forming the canopy or "roof" of the forest. Some familiar and everyday as well as fine cabinet woods come from the Amazonian forests, including rubber (*Hevea brasiliensis*) and mahoganies. Among the endangered trees of the Ecuadorian lowland rainforest is the Caoba (*Persea theobromifolia*). Described as new to science as recently as 1977, this tree is a relative of the Avocado and has commercially important lumber with properties similar to mahogany. The main cause of the Caoba's demise is the rapid conversion of forests to banana and oil palm plantations.

With so many species concentrated together in the rainforest, it may seem surprising that the forest floor is often no more colorful than that of a northern beech or pine forest. This is because in undisturbed or primeval rainforest, little light reaches the ground except in clearings where a tree has fallen. All the color and much of the life and activity of a tropical rainforest are concentrated in the canopy.

The herbaceous plants, including gingers, ferns, grasses and sedges, only occur where sufficient light penetrates the tree strata. There they may become large, often growing to 5 meters (16 feet) or more.

Unlike the trees and herbaceous plants, the lianas, vines and other climbers are dependent on external mechanical support. With the support of large trees, climbers can grow to 200 meters (650 feet) or more. The larger climbing palms and rattans are prominent examples of climbers greatly exploited by humans. *Dicliptera dodsonii*, an orangeflowered vine of lowland forest is, like the Caoba, a recently described species threatened with extinction through forest conversion.

Epiphytes and collectors

On tree trunks and branches, and on the climbers, grow the epiphytes, well known outside their natural habitat as house or conservatory plants. It is probably this group which contains the greatest number of endangered or vulnerable plants. Among the epiphytes often collected for specialist growers around the world are the air plants or bromeliads. Many of the 411 species of the genus *Tillandsia* are endangered through overcollecting. *Glomeropitcairnia erectiflora* is vulnerable in the cloud forests of Trinidad because of disturbance by visitors climbing to the summit of Mount Tucuche. Many of the rainforest orchids are epiphytes and these highly specialized plants occur in greatest numbers in the tropical rainforests. Ecuador, for example, boasts 2,670 species out of a world total of about 25,000. In contrast, the whole of the USA has a mere 200. Sadly, there is now only 6 per cent of the original coastal rainforest left in Ecuador, the rest having been converted into farmland since 1970.

The Andean floristic region

Much of western South America is included in the Andean floristic region. Traveling south from Colombia on the western side of the Andes, the tropical rainforest soon gives way to dry forest, then to a Mediterranean-type vegetation and eventually to true desert, with less than 2 millimeters (0.08 inch) annual rainfall in the Atacama

Bromelia serra

Vriesea hieroglyphica

Orthophytum burle-marxi

Left *An air plant or epiphyte* (Tillandsia) *from Mexico. Several species of these bromeliads are extremely rare and yet are collected for the houseplant trade.*

Right *The Chilean False Larch* (Fitzroya cupressoides) *may take up to 500 years to mature and live for over 4,000 years. Only a few forests now survive, the rest having fallen to loggers or been consumed by fire.*

Below *The Monkey Puzzle Tree* (Araucaria araucana) *in its natural habitat in the Chilean Andes looks very different from the familiar straggling garden specimens.*

region of Chile. Among the most vulnerable plants there are the succulents, particularly the Chilean barrel cacti. The threat to these is overcollecting for commercial purposes rather than habitat destruction.

Chile is the longest country in the world, spanning some 4,000 kilometers (2600 miles) from the Atacama desert to Tierra del Fuego and encompassing many vegetation types. At latitudes greater than about 38 degrees south, the annual rainfall is actually higher than in tropical South America, the average often exceeding 5 meters (200 inches) per annum. Chile does not include any tropical rainforest, but an equally valuable temperate rainforest has developed over thousands of years on the windward side of the Andes. Covering a much smaller area than its tropical equivalent, this unique forest is very vulnerable.

Rare conifers such as the Chilean False Larch *(Fitzroya cupressoides)* and the curious Monkey Puzzle *(Araucaria araucana)* are characteristic of the temperate rainforest. The False Larch has been described by the Chileans as a cornerstone of their culture and civilization, needed throughout life from the cradle to the grave. Large tracts of native forest have been felled to obtain its lumber, which is used in building and construction as well as in smaller items, such as musical instruments. The threat to this remarkable tree is heightened by the fact that it is extremely slow growing, often taking up to 500 years to reach maturity. Nearly all the really fine specimens, believed to be up to 4,000 years old, have been removed. Even if replanting programs were to be considered, who would invest in an afforestation program with a 500-year cycle? Furthermore, once felled, temperate and tropical rainforests cannot be recreated and, like the tropical mahoganies, the False Larch is unable to grow in monocultural stands. Despite CITES listing, which bans international trade, and internal protection, the trees are still being felled.

The Monkey Puzzle is also threatened, mainly because of the central role it has played in the lives of the original inhabitants of the Andes, the Araucarian Indians. They traditionally used the tree's seeds as a source of food and now also use it to make buttons and other artefacts to supplement their basic income. As a result, the Monkey Puzzle's gene pool has been severely depleted. More recently, large areas of the forests have succumbed to the chainsaw in a futile attempt to clear land either for cattle ranching or, even worse, reforestation with alien species.

Juan Fernandez

Juan Fernandez is a small group of Pacific islands, lying some 640 kilometers (400 miles) west of Santiago, Chile (see also p.210). They form a separate floristic region because they are even more isolated botanically than the Galapagos islands. Their endemic flora includes about 98 flowering plants and 17 ferns, the vast majority of which are threatened by forest destruction caused by introduced grazing animals. Crusoe's Mayu-monte *(Sophora fernandeziana)*, scattered through the montane forests of Isla Robinson Crusoe, is described as vulnerable. Another species of the same genus, Selkirk's Mayu-monte *(Sophora masafuerana)*, is considered to be endangered. It occurs only on the neighboring Isla Alejandro Selkirk, where it is found on cliff ledges and in the forest covering the walls of deep canyons. These two species are particularly important as they represent a vital link between other species of the genus found in Easter Island, New Zealand, Hawaii, and Chile.

Pampas and Patagonia

The floristic region described as Pampas covers a large area in temperate South America, including Uruguay, southeastern Brazil, western Argentina, and the Argentine pampas. Large parts of this region have been modified by humans over many centuries, and cattle ranching maintains the area in a way comparable with the savannas of east Africa, where grazing by herds of large herbivores and natural fires prevent the growth of secondary forest.

The Patagonian region comprises Patagonia and Tierra del Fuego, the southern Andes and the Falkland islands. These areas have not suffered the phenomenal population explosions experienced in the tropical north and so the threats to their native flora and fauna are much less significant. However, tourist development since the 1980s could have an adverse effect on the wildlife of the Falkland islands. Felton's Flower is now considered extinct in the wild, although it survives in cultivation close to its original locality on West Point Island. Three other species are considered rare and another *(Arabis macloviana)* is endangered, all as a result of overgrazing.

Below *The steppes of Patagonia are bleak and inhospitable, rendering them fairly safe from most forms of exploitation. However, overgrazing by sheep has occurred in some areas.*

WILDLIFE

Chris Madsen is a professional writer and editor. She read zoology at Oxford University, taught, worked in natural history and science publishing, and eventually went freelance. Chris has written four books and contributed to books, magazines, and periodicals. Her main interests are mammals, particularly carnivores, and ecosystems.

Much of South America's wildlife is unique. Whole families of birds, such as ovenbirds, antbirds, cotingas, manakins, tinamous, and toucans, live nowhere else on earth. Guinea pigs, hutias, pacas and agoutis, spiny rats, leaf-nosed bats, and the prehensile-tailed woolly monkeys and spider monkeys are all totally neotropic families, as are marmosets and tamarins. This is mainly because, after South America separated from Africa, about 100 million years ago, its wildlife evolved in isolation until the Panama land bridge joined South America to North America about 2 million years ago. The many marsupial mammals then occupying South America were outclassed by invading placental mammals from the north, and are now represented only by opossums. Anteaters, armadillos, sloths, and the New World monkeys are also relics of pre-Panama fauna. Parrots go even further back, to the days – perhaps 200 million years ago – when South America, Africa, India, and Australia were all connected.

Tropical rainforest

Tropical moist forest contains the richest and most varied flora and fauna in the world. The perfect combination of warmth and moisture favors the growth of vegetation without any seasonal check, and the gigantic forest trees themselves confer even more stability on the climate in which they live and prosper. In sheer quantity

Below *Despite the amazing color, variety and richness of life in a tropical forest most tropical soils are relatively shallow and often poor in nutrients. If the forest is cleared, the soil quickly deteriorates. This makes it unsuitable for farming and means that the forest has little capacity for regrowth.*

of material, or biomass, the world's tropical moist forests account for four-fifths of the planet's terrestrial vegetation, although they occupy barely 7 per cent of the land's surface.

Some Central American countries have little rainforest left. Mexico, for example, has lost 92 per cent of the 22 million hectares (54 million acres) it once contained. Rainforest is exploited for the timber it contains, often by crudely demolishing whole tracts of trees in order to pick out the few commercially valuable trunks from among the heaps of felled giants. Alternatively, the forest may be flattened and bulldozed clear to provide pasturage for beef cattle, or burned to open up a patch of ground for cultivation. The land thus obtained is of astonishingly low fertility, and new patches have to be cleared every few years. Poor soil fertility is a characteristic of tropical moist forest, where practically all the available resources are locked up in the living trees. Organic material circulates rapidly in the moist tropical climate: leaves and fruits are quickly snapped up by millions of animals, themselves falling prey to other species, and anything that lands on the ground is either eaten by scavengers or decays in a matter of days. Little penetrates to fertilize the soil, which tends to be light and sandy. Cleared forest has only a small capacity for regrowth, especially if all the timber is bulldozed away, and it soon loses what little soil it had to erosion by wind and water. The forest is a self-maintaining system that, once broken, cannot be put back together again.

Throughout Central America, animals are in danger from forest clearance. Troops of Central American Squirrel Monkeys once flourished in the forests of Panama and Costa Rica, feeding on fruit and insects in their small home ranges. Most of their home has now been cleared for growing rice, sugar cane, and bananas, and their only chance of survival may be a single reserve in Costa Rica. The islands, too,

Above left *The Vinaceous Amazon* (Amazona vinacea) *formerly occurred in forests from southeast Brazil through Paraguay to northeastern Argentina. It has suffered a dramatic decline through loss of habitat and an isolated population in Misiones, Argentina, is particularly at risk.*

Above *The Resplendent Trogon or Quetzal* (Pharomachrus mocino) *is confined to cloud forests of Central America. Although still locally abundant in more remote areas, it has disappeared over much of its range, which remains unprotected. The Quetzal is both the national bird of Guatemala and the name of its currency.*

are losing rainforests. Puerto Rico and Dominica have some left, but it is rapidly diminishing. The Puerto Rican Amazon Parrot has been on the verge of extinction for at least a quarter of a century. A population of 200 in 1950 fell to just 24 by 1968, due to a shortage of trees in which to nest. Two birds died in 1974 from injuries received while fighting over nest sites, and this problem continues to thwart efforts to save the species.

Black-handed Spider Monkeys, though more widely spread from Mexico to Panama, are vulnerable to forest clearance, and face the added problems of being killed for food or captured as pets. Spider monkeys take about four years to reach maturity, and then only produce a single offspring once in two or three years. Four of the five species are on the danger list and the status of the fifth is not known. A related species, the Yellow-tailed Woolly Monkey of Peruvian montane rainforest, is also endangered by hunting and habitat destruction. Forest is being cut on the slopes where these monkeys find most figs to eat. The deforestation is partly due to roadbuilding, and as road construction crews also need food, the monkeys suffer further losses. In the north of Colombia, the little Cotton-top Tamarin is endangered because of its popularity as a pet. Between 1960 and 1975 as many as 40,000 were exported to the USA, the survivors of perhaps 60,000 that had been caught. Deforestation is adding to the pressure on this creature, and on the vulnerable, closely-related White-footed Tamarin from the same region.

The hoofed mammals, tapirs, live near water in lowland and montane forests, foraging on the ground for leaves and fruits. They have only one offspring after a gestation period of over a year. Although the striped and spotted baby can travel with its mother almost as soon as it is born, it must suckle for another year before it becomes independent. Tapirs are extremely shy and secretive, and very easily disturbed. They are also very good to eat, and it is no surprise to find their numbers are rapidly declining. The Central American Tapir is probably already extinct from Mexico and El Salvador, and practically extinct in Panama.

The forest cats are also hunted, but in their case it is for the fur trade. In 1975, nearly 77,000 skins from spotted cats went from the region to Britain alone. Ten

Below *The Cotton-top Tamarin* (Saguinus oedipus), *once widespread in Panama and Colombia, was collected extensively for use in biomedical research. Trade in wild specimens is now controlled and it is being bred in captivity.*

Below right *Baird's Tapir* (Tapirus bairdii) *has extremely palatable flesh and has consequently been hunted to extinction over much of its range in Central and northern South America.*

years later, legislation and falling demand had reduced this annual number by more than half, but this still means that 34,500 skins went to Britain in 1985. Jaguars, the largest neotropical cats with the most prized fur, have been ruthlessly hunted – often with traps baited with "protected" species of monkeys. They were once fairly common from California to Argentina, but are now extinct from all of North and most of Central America, with the notable exception of Belize, where unspoiled rainforest has survived and is being actively conserved. Although not yet classified as endangered, Jaguars are rapidly declining in numbers throughout the region. Smaller cats like the Margay and Tiger Cat, also vulnerable to forest clearance and under pressure from fur hunters, are becoming scarcer. Ironically, information about the status of a species is much easier to obtain when the species is consistently hunted. The number of Jaguarundi still surviving in the rainforest is not known, and even the habits of this exotic cat are a mystery, as it is neither good to eat nor the possessor of a desirable skin.

We are ignorant of much of the flora and fauna of the tropical forest, particularly species for which no "use" has been found. "New" species are constantly being discovered, sometimes on the brink of extinction in a rapidly dwindling patch of forest. One such new-to-science species is a lion tamarin that was recently found on a small island off the Paraná coast of Brazil. No more than 200 individuals of this beautiful primate remain. It has been named the Black-faced Lion Tamarin just in time to join the list of lion tamarins already known to be endangered in Brazil's dwindling Atlantic forest. Three other species, the Golden, Golden-headed, and Golden-rumped Lion Tamarins exist in distinct areas of this coastal rainforest, with populations of under 100, under 200, and about 100, respectively. All four species of lion tamarins like to live in the privacy of tangled vines between 3 and 10 meters (10–30 feet) above ground level in dense primary forest, where they feed in small groups on fruit and insects. They have probably always been rare, and it has been their misfortune to have evolved in a region destined to become one of the most densely populated in Brazil, close to the conurbation of Rio de Janeiro.

Brazil's Atlantic coastal forest has been reduced to no more than 2 per cent of

Jaguar

Margay

Mountain Cat

Tiger Cat

Above *The beautiful skins of the spotted cats have made them vulnerable to hunting for the fur trade. Despite legislation and reduced demand, skins are still being exported to the developed world. As a result, all species are becoming increasingly rare.*

Left *A young male Jaguar* (Panthera onca). *Jaguars once ranged from the southern states of the USA south over almost the entire South American continent, but are now extinct in almost all areas close to human settlements.*

Above *The Seven-colored Tanager* (Tangara fastuosa) *now has an extremely limited range in forest and secondary growth of northeastern Brazil. It has declined due to habitat destruction and collection for the caged bird trade.*

Above right *Like most other curassows and guans, the turkey-sized Red-billed Curassow* (Crax blumenbachii) *is threatened by hunting and habitat loss. It is now restricted to a few areas of primary forest in southeast Brazil.*

Below *Natterer's Longwing* (Heliconius nattereri) *from Espírito Santo, Brazil, is one of many threatened species in this area.*

its original area. Plantations of sugar cane, cocoa, coffee, rubber and bananas have replaced the giant forest trees, driving out an unknown number of endemic species. Besides the lion tamarins, primates now known to be in danger there include the Buffy-headed Marmoset, the Buffy Tufted-eared Marmoset (a subspecies of the Common Marmoset), Masked Titi, and the Woolly Spider Monkey. The endemic Three-toed Sloth must be in serious decline after losing so much territory, as must the Thin-spined Porcupine.

Birds endangered in the Atlantic coast forest range from the little Hook-billed Hermit Hummingbird to the White-necked Hawk. Most of the 115 species that live there are in trouble, and 94 of them exist nowhere else on Earth. Spix Little Blue Macaw has reached the brink of extinction due to hunting and trapping for the pet trade. There may be 20 individuals left in captivity around the world, but attempts to breed them have not been successful. Another bird that has all but disappeared is the Alagoas Curassow, a grouse-like game bird that may only exist now in a private zoo. About 40 species of related game birds – curassows, guans, and chacalacas – live in woods, forests and grasslands, even on mountainsides, throughout the Neotropics, and 16 of these are considered to be in danger. Loss of habitat has added extra pressure to the intense hunting with which these tasty birds already have to cope. They have never been domesticated, but will happily associate with domestic fowl and breed well in zoos. Perhaps, instead of being annihilated from the wild, this group might be exploited in captivity to provide a valuable source of food in the future.

Amazonia

In the forests of Amazonia, as elsewhere, the species known to be at risk are those that are actively sought. Vulnerable primates include two marmosets, the White (or Silvery) and the Tassel-eared. Already much depleted by the pet trade, their home ranges are being lost to ranching and road building. The Bearded (or Red-backed)

Saki is endangered by two highways cutting through its home range, as well as a hydroelectric plant. This small primate has the added misfortune of owning a tail that is traditionally used as a duster. Woolly monkeys and spider monkeys are hunted for meat, as well as being captured for the pet trade. They live high in the tree canopy, which makes capture difficult. The most common method is to shoot a mother carrying a baby on her back and then hope that, when they both fall to the ground, the baby is not killed by the fall. If it survives the baby is sold, and if it dies it is eaten; the mother is eaten in any case. The Black Spider Monkey is endangered, and the Long-haired Spider Monkey and Woolly Monkey are also vulnerable. Like all woolly and spider monkeys, they breed very slowly, maturing at four to five years and producing a single infant only once in two or three years.

Among the few large animals living on the ground in the deep forest are two dogs. The Small-eared Dog, a middle-sized, short-legged animal, is extremely shy

DISTRIBUTION
NEOTROPIC FORESTS

Extent in late 1980s

Forest destroyed since early 1940s

Left *A woolly monkey on the edge of the Amazon. Like most South American primates, it has a prehensile tail that can act as a fifth limb.*

Right *Although the Harpy Eagle* (Harpia harpyja) *has a vast range, extending from southern Mexico to northern Argentina, it is extremely rare, surviving only in large areas of undisturbed forest.*

Amazonian variety

- At least 50,000 flowering plants, amounting to possibly half of all the flowering plants in the Neotropics, are found here.
- One acre may contain 235 species of trees, supporting 100,000 species of insects.
- An adjoining acre may contain 100 tree varieties not found in the first acre.
- A temperate forest may only have 25 different tree species in one acre, and an adjoining acre may not differ at all.
- Some trees are so rare that single specimens found over 50 years ago are still the only ones of their kind known to science.
- Many tree species still have no scientific name.
- Nearly a quarter of all medicines known to the West have been derived from tropical rainforest plants.
- The Amerindians utilize many of the plants and animals of the forest, such as this male arrow poison frog *(Dendrobates pumilo)*. As its name suggests, they tip their arrows in the poisons the frogs secrete to protect themselves against predators.

and so secretive that it is hardly ever seen. While little is known of its lifestyle and less still of its numbers, it must be seriously disturbed by any encroachment on deep forest, such as roadbuilding. The smaller Bush Dogs are found in many forested regions, but are rare everywhere. They have an ambivalent relationship with people, sometimes being kept as pets and often shot on sight by hunters.

Another carnivore that is vulnerable to human activity is the Giant Otter. These charming animals are goliaths among otters, measuring about 2 meters (6½ feet) including the tail and weighing up to 40 kilograms (88 pounds). They live in sociable family groups, playing and hunting by day in the lakes and rivers of the Amazon basin. Like the spotted cats, these otters are hunted for their fur and, being tied to water, are less able to escape. Unfortunately, they are also easy to locate and approach because they are very noisy, constantly calling to one another as they swim along, practically fearless (even hunting small caimans) and insatiably curious. They are rare or extinct wherever they have been disturbed and only survive in remote or protected areas.

The rivers of the region contain even larger mammals: two species of dolphin and the Amazonian Manatee (see also p.218). Manatees are entirely aquatic and live in enormous herds, floating lazily in the warm water and browsing on underwater vegetation. They breed slowly, cows probably only having one calf in about four years, and taking seven to ten years to mature. They give birth to a single calf in the water after a gestation period of about a year, and float on their back as it suckles at a mammary gland under the front flipper. When water levels fall in the dry season towards November, manatees migrate to lakes, where vegetation is sparse, and virtually fast until the rainy season begins in May or June. Then they go with the floodwater into the forest and feast on flooded vegetation. Manatees are very vulnerable creatures, easy prey to hunters and threatened by any disturbance to the waters where they live. The main cause of their decline in numbers was the demand for hard-wearing manatee leather which has been superseded by synthetic materials.

Left *The White Uakari* (Cacajao calvus calvus) *is restricted to the* varzea – *the area of the Amazon forest which floods regularly. It is very similar to the closely related Red Uakari, differing only in the color of its fur.*

Above *A male arrow poison frog* (Dendrobates pumilo). *As its name suggests, the poisons secreted by this and related frogs to protect themselves against predators were used by the Amerindians to tip their arrows. Some species have been popular in the pet trade.*

The manatee is now officially protected, but it still remains a valuable source of food for local people and is likely to become more important as other sources of meat become scarcer.

Highly sociable animals such as the manatees probably need a higher level of population to ensure their survival than solitary animals would. On the other hand, solitary creatures may require a large territorial range and so be more vulnerable to habitat loss over a wide area. Eagles and hawks need a large territory, and none is more vulnerable to loss of hunting-ground than the magnificent Harpy Eagle. This huge bird needs vast tracts of tall primary forest in order to survive. Its relative, the Crested Eagle, has similar requirements. In the Neotropics, 13 species of birds of prey are considered to be threatened, and four more may be about to join the list.

Where broad rivers cut through the forest, light and air flood in to produce a ribbon development and a further variation in conditions is provided when the rivers flood in the rainy season. Forest regions that are seasonally inundated by small lowland blackwater rivers are called igapo. The floodplains of large whitewater rivers, running swiftly down from the Andes, are called varzea. Floodplain forest is the home of a rare primate, the Uakari. White uakaris live in varzea forest, and Red ones in the igapo forest. Both subspecies feed on nuts and seeds, specializing in cracking really hard shells, like Brazil nuts, and foraging over a wide area. They reproduce only slowly and are clearly dependent on the contrasting seasons of the flood cycle – like so many other animals and plants whose existence we are only now beginning to notice, and whose ways of life are still a mystery.

Deciduous forests

Not all the forests of the Neotropics, or even of the equatorial region, are evergreen rainforest. Outside the tropical belt, and on higher ground within it, are many other types of forest – deciduous broad-leaved, coniferous, and bamboo. These have also been exploited to some degree for timber and for fuel, or encroached on by

Forest fish
- There are possibly as many as 2,000 indigenous species of freshwater fishes in the Amazon system, compared with about 300 species in the whole of Europe.
- During floods, millions of fishes are carried into the igapo forest to feed on fallen leaves and fruits, returning to the rivers when the waters subside.
- Specializations include a species with teeth and jaws capable of cracking rock-hard rubber-tree seeds, while another leaps into tree branches to glean insects, and even hummingbirds.

agriculture, roads or mines. Although deciduous forests do not reach the degree of concentration and biological diversity of the tropical moist forests of Amazonia, they contain much endemic fauna.

The endangered parrots of the Neotropics – macaws, parakeets, parrotlets and the amazons – occupy a variety of niches in tropical and subtropical forests. Hunting for export to the pet trade has been the major factor in bringing so many near extinction. The largest parrot (aside from the flightless Kakapo of New Zealand) in the world is the Hyacinth Macaw, which lives in dry forests and on the edges of wet forests in Brazil, Bolivia and Paraguay. Total numbers of surviving Hyacinth Macaws are now estimated at under 5,000 (and may be as low as 2,500), with very few outside Brazil. A related species, the Glaucous Macaw, is probably extinct, and the Indigo Macaw is down to 60 individuals hanging on in a patch of thorn scrub next to a sandstone cliff in Bahia State, northeast Brazil. Additional pressures on parrots come from habitat loss and being shot to protect crops. Pearly Parakeets are losing their home forests in northeast Brazil, and many other species of parakeets have been reduced to estimated populations as small as 2,000. Since as many as 20,000

Above *The large and spectacularly colored Hyacinth Macaw* (Anodorhynchus hyacinthinus) *is extremely popular in the zoo and pet trade. By the late 1980s, it was estimated that there were fewer than 5,000 left in the wild.*

Right *The Red Siskin* (Carduelis cucullata) *once ranged across northern Venezuela to Colombia with isolated populations elsewhere. It produces red-plumaged hybrids with domestic canaries, and so has been extensively exploited.*

Far right *The Purple-winged Ground Dove* (Claravis godefrida) *is confined to wooded country in southeastern Brazil and Paraguay where it is dependent on flowering bamboo, and consequently vulnerable to any change in its habitat.*

Gray-cheeked Parakeets have been exported from Peru in a single year, such small populations are clearly in grave danger.

Forest birds with very different requirements are the hummingbirds, each occupying a narrow niche that must contain a particular food plant, nest site, and climate. These birds are found almost anywhere there are trees, and some even manage to live high above the treeline in the Andes. Almost incessantly active during the day, hummingbirds have a high energy turnover and need a great deal of carbohydrate food. At night, their body temperature falls, thus enabling them to survive without food while they roost. Being so specialized, they are very vulnerable to disturbance, and the relationship between a hummingbird and its foodplant can be so close that loss of the hummingbird causes the plant's pollination system to fail. These jewel-like creatures attract a great deal of attention from the pet trade. Of Neotropic hummingbirds, 29 species are in danger, and a further 21 may be heading that way, making 50 species known to be at risk out of a total of about 320.

Ovenbirds and antbirds are also very specialized, requiring particular nest sites and specific types of insects on which to feed. About 50 birds in these two groups

Splendid Parakeet
(Neophema splendida)

are thought to be threatened due to habitat disturbance. Other endemic bird families with members at risk include the cotingas, a group that contains many extraordinarily eccentric species; tyrant flycatchers, a large group with species in every habitat where there are insects to be caught; and three out of five known species of potoos. Also called wood nightjars, potoos are secretive nocturnal birds that are hardly ever seen but emit horrible screams in the forest at night which sound like somebody being murdered. Grounddoves are vulnerable to disturbance, too, and several species in various regions are becoming very scarce, for example the Purple-winged Ground Dove which is dependent on flowering bamboo.

Two species of woodpecker have been hit especially hard by habitat loss: the Mexican Imperial Woodpecker and the Helmeted Woodpecker of south Brazil, Paraguay, and Argentina. The Imperial Woodpecker, which may in fact be extinct, once occurred in high pine forests that have been extensively felled. Helmeted Woodpeckers are known to survive in a single national park, but seem to have disappeared from all the other places they once inhabited.

Vinaceous-breasted Parrot
(Amazonia vinacea)

Trade in birds
The pet trade has taken its pick of South American parrots for many years. Captured and crammed into crates, birds with brightly-colored plumage are exported around the world. Only a fraction survive the journey and, of these, many more die within weeks of arriving at their destination. Between May 1980 and August 1981, 33,000 wild parrots passed through Schipohl Airport in the Netherlands, and half of these came from Latin America.

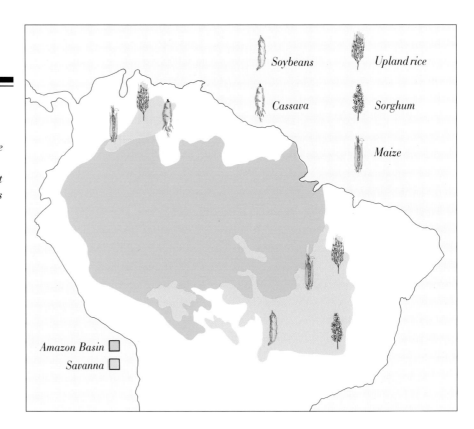

Soybeans   Upland rice

Cassava   Sorghum

Maize

Amazon Basin ☐
Savanna ☐

Above *Although protected by law, the Chilean Huemul or Southern Andean Deer* (Hippocamelus bisulcus) *is still hunted. By the early 1980s it was thought to number less than 2,000 and was confined to the southern Andes and possibly some islands.*

Throughout the forests of the region, large mammals such as the Ocelot are becoming rarer. The fur hunters have taken their toll, and this beautiful cat is further threatened by habitat loss. It is adaptable, however, both in the type of country it can cope with and in the prey it will take, and could recover if hunting were properly controlled. Unfortunately, as with many furrier's favorites, the price of Ocelot skins invites illicit trading. In 1980, for example, forged permits were found to have been used by a single trader to authorize the export of 40,000 Ocelot skins from Paraguay. The level of hunting that these and other cats could safely sustain is not established, so that even the numbers "properly" authorized are arbitrarily set.

The only South American bear is the Spectacled Bear and this is probably the only Neotropic bear, since no Mexican Grizzly has been seen since 1962. Spectacled Bears are catholic in diet, though mainly vegetarian, and inhabit forest, mountain, desert and scrub from Venezuela to Bolivia. From the little that is known, they seem only to be prospering in remote regions or reserves. Disturbance, habitat loss and hunting all pose a threat and, since captive breeding has so far largely failed, this bear's future depends on proper protection being afforded now.

Grasslands

Large tracts of natural grassland occur in parts of the region. The highlands of eastern Brazil, as they rise from the Amazon basin, grow deciduous forest on their lower slopes and hot, dry savanna higher up. Grassland of a different sort – temperate and fertile – is found around Uruguay. The plateau of the Mato Grosso, between the Amazon and Plata river systems, provides pasture for cattle, and poorer scrubby grassland extends southwards into Argentina. The natural wildlife of grasslands tends to be rich in numbers but less rich in species, and the Neotropics are no exception to this general rule. The chief enemy of the natural fauna is the cattle ranch.

There are no endemic sheep, goats, antelope, or gazelles in the Neotropics. The native grazers are deer, Llamas and their kin, peccaries, tapirs, and various rodents. Some large rodents like the Mara and Capybara fit into niches that might be occupied by hoofed mammals in the Old World. Rodents have a talent for breeding that helps them to survive heavy losses, but many other grazers have difficulty competing with humans and their domestic stock.

The native deer of South America are vulnerable to the diseases and parasites of domestic cattle. In the temperate forest and open country of the southern Andes in Chile and Argentina, the South Andean Huemul has probably always been hunted for food. Now its habitat is shrinking, and it is ravaged by foot-and-mouth disease, coccidiosis, nematodes and tapeworms from domestic cattle, together with bladder-worms from the dogs that also harass it. There are probably fewer than 2,000 of these huemuls left. North Andean huemuls face a different assortment of problems. In Bolivia, they are killed to make dried salt meat called charque; in Chile they are killed because they like to eat crops of lucerne, and are losing their tree cover to charcoal burners; in Peru, mining brings hungry people and charcoal burners to encroach on their territory. Almost everywhere, cattle, sheep and Llamas compete for forage.

Argentinian Pampas Deer, once abundant throughout 647,000 square kilometers (250,000 square miles) of pampas from the Andes to the Atlantic coast, are now reduced to two small populations on the Argentinian coast, plus a few scattered groups in San Luis Province. Hunted mercilessly for skins and for sport during the eighteenth and nineteenth centuries, they lost ground to ranching as well

Below *The 1-meter (3¼-foot) long Pampas Deer* (Ozotoceros bezoarticus) *lives in small herds in open habitats from Brazil to central Argentina. It has declined through loss of habitat and uncontrolled hunting.*

and, by 1980, practically no stretch of pampas large enough to support deer remained. Diseases of cattle have added to their problem, and the future existence of these deer is seriously in doubt.

Wolves are traditionally persecuted almost everywhere in the world, and the Maned Wolf of Brazilian open forest and grassland is no exception. Although much of its savanna home has been turned into agricultural and grazing land, it seems to have survived this conversion quite well. But in farming regions, where the wolf's usual mixed diet of wild birds, rodents, lizards and small armadillos is supplemented with chickens, it is shot on sight. The annual burning of grass to improve pastures probably kills wolf pups, as well as many other breeding mammals and birds.

The Giant Anteater and Giant Armadillo are very widely distributed but have highly specialized feeding requirements. Solitary and secretive animals, both species dig for ants and termites in open woodland and savanna. Armadillos are good to eat and have been hunted for food, while anteaters, though of little value as game, are occasionally killed out of curiosity. Both species are losing ground to plantations, ranching and other alterations of natural grass and scrub. The Three-banded Armadillo of Brazil and the Fairy Armadillo of Argentina may also be in some danger, although no estimates of the numbers of these shy creatures have been made.

Some grassland birds have been badly affected by human activities, and four species of tinamous are thought to be threatened. These birds nest on the ground and their chief means of defence is to keep very still and rely on camouflage. If this fails, they will fly up explosively at the last possible moment. Nothing a tinamou can do will keep it safe from machines or fire. Nightjars, too, must be at risk from agriculture, but they are such secretive birds that their numbers are virtually impossible to estimate.

The Andes

The Andes system runs for about 7,200 kilometers (4,500 miles) from the isthmus of Panama to Cape Horn, reaching nearly 7,000 meters (23,000 feet) at the highest peak. Rising from tropical land in the north and extending southwards into the subarctic, the system encompasses an enormous variety of habitats and conditions, from desert to cloud forest. The main human activities there are mining and herding

Below *Giant Anteaters* (Myrmecophaga tridactyla) *are found mostly in open grassy areas, where they use their powerful claws to tear open termite mounds in order to feed on the grubs.*

Below right *The long legs of the Maned Wolf* (Chrysocyon brachyurus) *may give it a better view in the tall grass of its swamp and savanna habitat. While its numbers have declined, its range has extended in the west.*

animals. Mining brings roads, people, and machinery, together with increased demand for fuel wood and meat. Domestic animals compete with wild ones for forage and space, and may pass parasites and diseases to related wild species.

Four species of camels once lived wild in the Andes. Two – Llamas and Alpacas – have been domesticated, and probably do not exist any longer in the wild. The other two have lost ground for contrasting reasons. Guanacos are the largest animals of the group, and are of little value to people except as food. They range along the western side of the mountains, from the coastal desert up to 4,000 meters (13,000 feet) in small herds of females led by a male, who will fiercely defend his harem against young males or any other threat. Their actual numbers are not known, though there can be little doubt that habitat loss, competition from domestic animals, and hunting are reducing their numbers. Vicuñas are the smallest animals of the group. Their pale golden-brown wool, which keeps them warm in the high, cold lands where they live, is considered to be the finest in the world, and has always been prized. Among the Incas, it was forbidden for anyone other than royalty to wear Vicuña-wool robes. Vicuña proved impossible to domesticate, and the Incas rounded up wild herds every three to five years to shear them. There were probably more than 2 million

Above *A herd of Vicuña* (Vicugna vicugna) *in the High Andes of Peru. Once threatened by overhunting for their exceptionally fine and valuable wool, they have increased dramatically and have even been reintroduced into areas from which they had been extirpated.*

Right *The Longtailed Chinchilla (Chinchilla laniger) from the Andes of northern Chile was brought to the brink of extinction by hunting for the fur trade. Since the 1920s, the fur industry has depended on captive-bred Chinchillas, and very little is known of the animal's current status in the wild.*

DISTRIBUTION
VICUNA

Former distribution

Current distribution

Vicuña (Vecugna vicugna). *It is estimated that during the Inca period there were up to 2 million vicuna. By 1965 there were around 6,000. Strict conservation methods have allowed numbers to rebuild to approximately 80,000 in the wild.*

roaming the flat rangeland (puna zone) of the Andes in Inca times. Then, during the 500 years after the Spanish conquest, Vicuña were simply killed for their wool. Tens of thousands a year were slaughtered until, by 1965, only 6,000 animals remained. Strict regulation and protection pulled them back from the brink of extinction, and now their numbers have risen to over 80,000. The Vicuña is an extremely valuable resource, especially in Peru where the majority of the animals are found, but the best method of management has not yet been established. Since most of the surviving animals are concentrated in reserves, where drought, overgrazing, or epidemic could cause disaster, the Vicuña's future is by no means secure.

Two rodents are also protected from the chill of the high Andes by wonderfully soft, warm coats. Chinchillas have been mercilessly hunted for their fur and hardly any now survive in the wild. But for the establishment of chinchilla farms in the 1920s, they would probably have become extinct. The better-known Long-tailed Chinchillas live sociably in dens among rocks on shrubby north-facing slopes, feeding on leaves, seeds and fruits. They are not as prolific as many rodents, producing two young once (sometimes twice) a year, and are only known to survive in the wild in a small area of Chile's coastal cordillera. Short-tailed Chinchillas are even more scarce – they are believed to exist in the wild but none has been located. Living higher in the mountains than the long-tailed species, they were kept in semi-captivity by the Incas and are still bred in captivity today. Although their long-tailed relatives are bred in North America, it has proved impossible to keep short-tailed chinchillas outside their natural high-altitude range. Chinchillas have been protected

Left *The Andean Flamingo* (Phoenicoparrus andinus) *is confined to the Altiplano of southern Peru, northern Chile, western Bolivia, and northwestern Argentina, where it nests in only one or two high-altitude salt lakes. With a population possibly as low as 50,000, it may be the rarest flamingo in the world.*

Llama

Alpaca

Guanaco

in Chile since 1929. Despite this and captive breeding, the commercial value of wild pelts is so high that poaching still occurs and chinchillas may not have much time left as wild creatures of the Andes.

The demand for firewood and grazing land is rapidly reducing tree cover and scrub in the mountains, driving away shy creatures like the Northern Pudu and Mountain Tapir. Neither of these animals is normally abundant, and both are hunted for meat. Where mines are in operation, the quest for firewood and food intensifies and such species are put under even more pressure. The Tamarugo Conebill, a warbler of the high shrub zone of south Peru and north Chile, is another species whose habitat is going up in smoke. *Prosopis* trees make good firewood for mines, and it is thought that this bird depends on the trees in some way. In addition, it is only known to breed in scrub containing a particular combination of plants. Like many other small species with no great commercial value, little is known about this bird's numbers, and by the time its ecology and behavior are understood it may have ceased to exist.

Other birds have been decimated by the abstraction of water from lakes for piping to towns and cities. High, remote lakes in the Andes were once utterly private places where many species could live and develop in glorious isolation. They are home to the Andean Flamingo and the Puna Flamingo of Peru, Bolivia, Chile, and Argentina, both very rare species. Other rare waterbirds that are being lost from mountain lakes include the Colombian Grebe, the Junin Grebe, the Horned Coot and the Atitlan Grebe, which has completely lost the power of flight. This last bird may have become extinct due to breeding with (or being ousted by) the closely-related Pied-billed Grebe, while no Colombian Grebes have been seen since 1977.

——— Wetlands ———

The Pantanal is an area of seasonally flooded wetland, outstanding in its size and importance to wildlife. Its name is Spanish for "large swamp" and it covers 130,000 square kilometers (50 000 square miles) of western Brazil, on the borders with Bolivia and Uruguay. The Pantanal provides a refuge for the Marsh (or Swamp) Deer, which has become scarce and scattered throughout the rest of the region. A solitary creature, this deer likes to have its feet wet while it browses and grazes on swamp vegetation. It has been seriously affected by hunting, by loss of habitat through drainage of marshes for pasture and cultivation, and by competition with domestic cattle during the rainy season, when deer and cattle are driven together onto limited patches of high ground above the floodwaters. Within the Pantanal, disease is probably the greatest threat. The Marsh Deer is susceptible to brucellosis, foot-and-mouth disease and other ailments carried by domestic cattle, and the virtually captive population is very vulnerable to an epidemic.

Whether the Pantanal continues to offer sanctuary to these deer and other beleaguered wetland animals depends on future plans for the area. There is already concern about raised levels of mercury due to goldmining. Forest destruction higher up the Paraguay river, where much of the Pantanal's water comes from, is causing erosion that may reduce water flow to the swamps. Another problem highlights the

Below *The Orinoco Crocodile* (Crocodylus intermedius) *is an endangered freshwater species restricted to Venezuela and eastern Colombia. It was hunted excessively for its skin from the 1920s, and since the 1950s has been too rare to be regularly used by the hide trade.*

Above *The Warbling Antbird* (Hypocnemis cantator) *is characteristic of the Amazonian region, where it is usually seen in dense undergrowth.*

Above left *The Swamp Deer or Guasupucu* (Blastocerus dichotomus) *is the largest South American deer, weighing up to 150 kilograms (330 pounds). Its numbers have declined drastically due to loss of habitat to agriculture and through drainage, as well as hunting.*

interdependence of different species: piranhas are increasing in number dramatically because the caimans, which normally eat them, have been reduced by hunting. Drainage to improve pastures in the savanna of the region also threatens the swamp.

Other, more localized wetlands are being steadily lost to drainage and pollution. A warbler called the Altamira Yellowthroat draws attention to the loss of marshes in Mexico. Two species of rails, *Rallus antarcticus* of southern Chile and Argentina and *Rallus semiplumbeus* of the Bogota savanna of Colombia, have become very rare indeed.

Swamps offer some protection from humans, but rivers have always provided highways through remote and sparsely populated regions, making aquatic creatures vulnerable to local hunters. Even some of the crocodiles of the region, in spite of (or perhaps because of) being apparently well able to defend themselves, are now under threat. The large Black Caiman is considered so dangerous to livestock that it has been regularly slaughtered on the island of Marajo at the mouth of the Amazon, and its numbers are alarmingly low. Two other crocodiles, the Broad-nosed Caiman of eastern Brazil and the Orinoco Crocodile, a large creature that lives only in the Orinoco river, are also endangered.

Turtles, on the other hand, have no defence. The South American River Turtle gathers on a few islands in the Amazon and Orinoco rivers each year to lay its eggs. The eggs have traditionally been gathered by local people to be turned into turtle-egg oil, while many adult turtles were killed as they returned to the water. In the mid-nineteenth century, an estimated 48 million eggs a year were being destroyed. Even then, it was apparent that the turtles could not sustain such losses. Today, the few turtles that miraculously remain have, in addition, to contend with habitat loss and dams flooding their egg-laying islets.

Trade in animal skins

Spotted cats are not the only animals endangered by the trade in skins. Reptiles are also hunted mercilessly, the Black Caiman, Spectacled Caiman, and Yacare Caiman all being pursued for their desirable skin. Manatees were once hunted for their skins, which made thick, hard-wearing leather. Now they are killed for meat.

Above *The Argentine Pearl Fish* (Cynolebias
nigripinnis) *is a killifish, many species of which
are popular with aquarists. It breeds in
temporary pools and puddles and is
particularly susceptible to habitat changes
and to pollution from pesticides in the run-off.*

Hydroelectric developments also threaten one of South America's rarest
ducks. The Brazilian Merganser is a parochial tree-nesting duck, spending the whole
of its life in a small section of a small stream. It was thought to be nearly extinct until
a colony was found in the province of Misiones in Argentina – and this colony is now
in the path of a hydroelectric project. Two colonies also exist in national parks in
Brazil and Paraguay, but such a localized species remains very vulnerable.

Species with habitat requirements so exact that they have always been rare
are easily swept away. Annual fishes (*Cynolebias*) are tiny topminnows which hatch
and breed in the puddles and streams that collect during the rainy season. When the
waters dry up the adult fishes die, leaving their eggs buried in the ground waiting to
hatch with the coming of the next rainy season. Wherever land reclamation improves
drainage, these little fishes and their precise lifestyles are lost. The deserts of Mexico
are an even more unlikely environment for fishes, yet tiny topminnows have survived
there in underground springs since before the desert became dry. After hanging on
for so long against all the odds the Desert Pupfish is now facing extinction due to
human interference.

Desert and shore

The two main areas of desert in the region lie in Mexico and along the Pacific coast of
Peru and northern Chile. Although there tends to be less human activity in desert
lands, species that manage to live there are already so close to the limits of survival
that the smallest extra pressure can tip them into extinction. In semidesert areas,
tortoises are not only threatened by the pet trade, but lose their habitat to agriculture

Left *The largest colonies of Kemps Ridley Turtle (*Lepidochelys kempii*) are in the Gulf of Mexico. These have been reduced from an estimated 40,000 seen nesting in a single day in 1947 to around 500 per season in the 1970s.*

and have their burrows damaged by off-road vehicles. The Bolson Tortoise of Mexico has the added burden of being hunted for food.

Along the shore, turtles are also heavily exploited for food, and Kemp's Ridley is gradually succumbing to extra pressures from pollution and shrimp trawl nets in the Gulf of Mexico (see p.70). Prawn fisheries on the coast of Peru threaten very different animals – Marine Otters, very like the Sea Otters of North America, and similarly vulnerable to sustained hunting. The otters are perceived as competitors for shellfish stocks and hunted as pests. Southward along the Chile coast, they are not seen as pests but as possessors of a marketable skin, a distinction that makes little difference to their fate.

It is important to bear in mind that not all the losses suffered by wild animals and plants come from human activities. Natural events can have devastating effects on an entire ecosystem or a single species. The Peruvian Penguin, which has been declining for over a century along the coasts of Peru and Chile, lost over half its population to an aberration of El Niño in 1982/1983. Hurricanes are fairly regular events in some regions of Central America, and, when Hurricane Joan swept across Nicaragua in 1988, it cut down one of the last untouched rainforests of Central America in an area only recently marked for preservation. A year later, Hurricane Hugo so damaged the breeding area of the endangered Puerto Rican Amazon Parrot that the handful of remaining wild birds had to be taken into protective custody in the hope that they can be kept going until the forest regenerates. Disasters such as these serve to remind us that pushing survival to the limits is a dreadful risk to take with so much of the world's wildlife at stake in the Neotropic region.

Sue Wells has a zoology degree from Cambridge University and is a freelance consultant, specializing in tropical marine conservation. She worked at IUCN for ten years, initially as co-author of the IUCN Invertebrate Red Data Book and subsequently as compiler and editor of a three-volume reference work *Coral Reefs of the World*. Sue is currently involved in the Greenpeace Pacific Campaign; the work of the Coral Reef Team of the UK-based Marine Conservation Society, and various marine projects with IUCN.

MANGROVES

Sometimes referred to as "forests of the sea," mangroves are marine tidal forests, growing in areas periodically flushed by salt and freshwater. As well as the black mangroves (*Avicennia*) and the red mangroves (*Rhizophora*), these forests contain other bushes and trees, such as the palm-like Nypa, creepers and vines, ferns, lichens, and even orchids.

The mangroves have special adaptations to help them survive in their harsh tidal environment. They grow best in sheltered areas where the waves and winds do not uproot seedlings, but their unusual root systems help them to cope with strong currents and tides. Shallow "cable" roots spread out over a wide area just below the surface of the mud, while smaller vertical roots descend deeper. The muddy soils lack oxygen but chimney-like roots protruding from the soil or descending from higher up the trunk are covered with pores through which oxygen can enter.

Animals of the mangrove forest

Some 400 species of fish and many more invertebrates are dependent on mangroves for all or part of their life cycles. Other animals spend some time in the forest, feeding, roosting, or breeding, particularly birds and reptiles. Fallen mangrove leaves are the basis of the food chain that supports all these animals. The leaves, partially broken down by fungi and bacteria, are an ideal food for small animals which in turn provide food for fish, birds, and other vertebrates, including humans.

Enormous numbers of molluscs, such as oysters and ark shells, and crabs live in the mangroves, and are harvested by local people. But it is as a nursery habitat for prawns, shrimps, and fish that the forests are most important to commercial fisheries. The densities of fish and prawns may be up to an order of magnitude greater in mangroves than in other adjacent nearshore habitats.

Mangroves harbor reptiles and amphibians, although these are not generally dependent on them. The threatened and increasingly rare Gharial, Mugger Crocodile

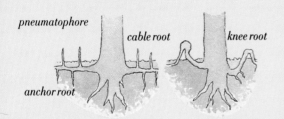

pneumatophore

cable root

knee root

anchor root

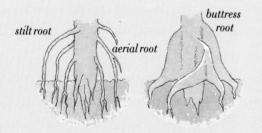

stilt root

aerial root

buttress root

Above *Types of mangrove root.*

Right *Mudskippers are characteristic fish of mangroves. When the tide retreats they are able to survive in the muddy creeks and some species even clamber among the trees. Out of water, they hold water and air in their gill chambers and also breathe through their skin and fins. They move by levering themselves forward on their pectoral fins. The different species have very different diets, ranging from algae to crabs.*

Left *Mangrove forest in the Sundarbans Tiger Reserve, West Bengal, India. Soil accumulates around the mangroves* (Bruguiera gymnorhiza) *eventually allowing other species such as the palm* (Phoenix paludosa) *to colonize.*

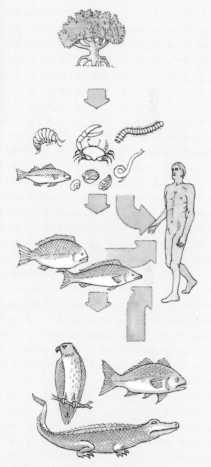

and Estuarine Crocodile can be found in mangroves in Asia. Several turtles and terrapins, such as the endangered River Terrapin, known only from one river system in the Bangladesh Sundarbans, seek the shelter provided by mangroves.

A variety of birds use mangroves, such as the beautiful Scarlet Ibis and other migratory and resident waterfowl and waders, including herons, egrets, and spoonbills viewed by thousands of tourists at the Caroni Swamp in Trinidad. The threatened Mangrove Hummingbird is found only on the Caribbean coast of Costa Rica. The Masked Finfoot, a strange coot-like bird dependent on secluded streams in mangrove forest, and a stork, the Lesser Adjutant, are threatened throughout their southeast Asian ranges.

Rather fewer mammals are found in mangroves, but these are becoming of increasing concern as their habitat shrinks. While the Crab-eating Macaque (*Macaca fascicularis*) is still common throughout much of coastal South Asia, some populations are under threat. The Bengal Tiger, a subspecies of the Tiger, is found only in the Sundarban mangroves and its presence there has ensured protection for these mangroves at least. Some estuarine and river dolphins spend time in the river

Above *Often disparaged as swamps and wastelands, mangroves are among the richest habitats in the world. At the bottom of the food chain are fish and invertebrates, which in turn provide nourishment for birds and reptiles. Humans can either benefit from or destroy this interdependence.*

and creek systems of mangroves, and populations of Ganges River Dolphin have been drastically reduced by the same dams and irrigation schemes that are damaging the mangroves of India and Bangladesh.

Above *A boatload of mangrove wood cut for fuel in Brazil. The value of mangroves for fuel, lumber, and the woodchip industry has led to over-exploitation.*

Right *Mangroves are most luxuriant around the mouths of large rivers and in sheltered bays, in regions where rainfall is at least 1,500 millimeters (60 inches) a year and the temperature does not fall below 20° Centigrade (68° Fahrenheit).*

Threats

Mangroves are now seriously at risk throughout much of their range. In developed countries, their destruction to build marinas, ports, factories, and houses is perhaps the major problem. In developing countries, where the major stands of mangroves remain, many factors contribute. The most damaging may be clearfelling for lumber and wood chips. For example, this is affecting about half the existing mangrove area in southeast Asia. In addition, uncontrolled exploitation of mangroves for firewood and charcoal is a widespread practice in southeast Asia, India, and Africa. Diversion of rivers or reduction in flow arising from irrigation schemes or dam construction is probably the second most serious threat. A drop in freshwater inflow has caused the decline of the commercial mangrove tree *Heritiera fomes* in the Ganges delta. In the Indus delta, the mangroves are sparse and stunted because dams upstream cut off fresh water for nine months of the year.

Culture of fish and prawns in ponds has affected vast areas, including about 1.2 million hectares (3 million acres) of mangroves in the Indo-Pacific. Such aquaculture is also often counterproductive. In Ecuador, nearly all the mangrove has been converted into shrimp ponds. This almost certainly caused the decline in wild shrimp larvae that has forced shrimp farmers to go to Peru in search of larvae to stock their ponds. Since the Peruvians are now also destroying their mangroves in order to start shrimp farms, the Ecuadorean farmers may have to set up expensive hatchery operations to produce the larvae. Similarly, the clearing of mangroves for agriculture, practiced in many parts of the world, is rarely successful in the long term. In the Rufiji delta in Tanzania, for example, the yield in areas converted to rice cultivation drops rapidly and farmers have to move on and clear new areas.

Mangroves are also vulnerable to pollution. Oil spills kill the trees by smothering the roots, and cause high mortalities in the molluscs attached to them. A year after a spill of more than 8 million liters (1.8 million gallons) of crude oil on the Caribbean coast of Panama in 1986, mangroves had died along 27 kilometers (17 miles) of coast, along with their associated invertebrates.

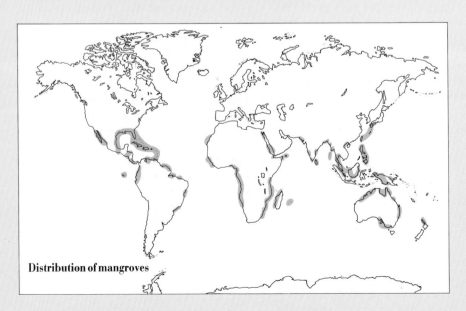

Distribution of mangroves

Left *Mangroves have evolved several different rooting systems to help support them in their unstable environment and to enable them to breathe. The* Rhizophora *species have stilt-like roots.*

Below *Mangrove seedlings are being planted in many countries, as here in Vietnam, either to encourage and speed recovery of damaged mangrove forest or even to recreate forest that has been totally destroyed.*

Conservation

Although long viewed as wastelands, mangroves have an enormous commercial value and this provides a strong incentive for their wise management. In several countries, such as Thailand, Venezuela, and Malaysia, some of the large mangrove forests have been managed for many years, with trees cut in rotation and regeneration encouraged by the planting of seedlings. In Indonesia, mangroves are managed simultaneously for forestry and fishery by villagers under a system known as *tumpang-sari*.

In many developing countries, regulating the exploitation of mangroves is difficult because of their economic importance locally. Efforts are therefore being made to involve local people in management and to return to traditional systems of sustainable multiple use. Replanting schemes are being initiated in many countries. This can be done on mudflats, in abandoned aquaculture areas and in degraded forests. An added incentive for reafforestation is the fact that mangroves stabilize shorelines and protect them from erosion and storms. In India and Bangladesh, loss of life and property from cyclones has been found to be noticeably lower in the Ganges-Brahmaputra delta behind the mangroves than in the unprotected areas to the east and west. This role of mangroves will become increasingly significant if sea levels rise in response to global warming.

In most management schemes, the emphasis is on exploitation rather than protection, and over time exploited mangroves may lose some of their associated wildlife. It is therefore very important to retain some areas of undisturbed mangroves in national parks and wildlife reserves. One of the largest fully protected areas is the 100,000 hectares (250,000 acres) of mangrove in the Everglades National Park in Florida. Several of the most important mangroves are protected under the Convention on Wetlands of International Importance or Ramsar Convention, an international treaty which encourages countries to cooperate over issues such as the management of shared water systems.

The economic value of mangroves

- Subsistence fisheries in the mangroves yield each year an estimated 9 tons per 0.4 square mile.
- Honey production in Florida's *Avicennia germanis* forest is estimated at 7½–20 ounces per 2½ acres.
- In the Chanthaburi mangroves of Thailand, charcoal, fish and shrimp production bring in an estimated 160 dollars per 2½ acres.

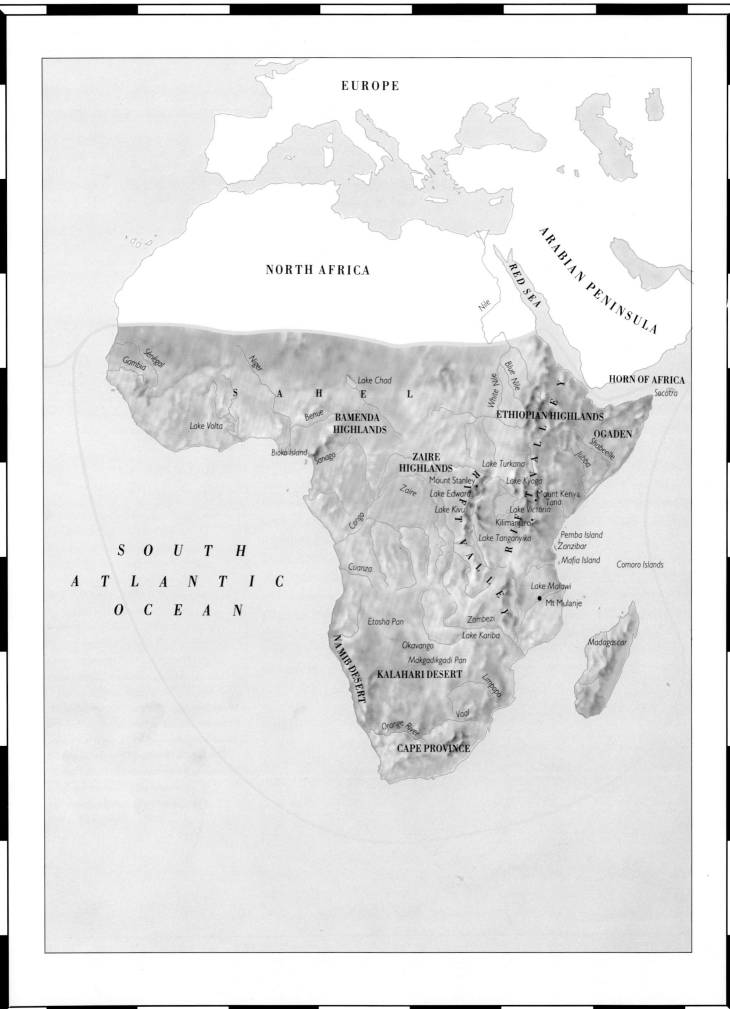

EUROPE

NORTH AFRICA

ARABIAN PENINSULA

RED SEA

Nile

HORN OF AFRICA

Socotra

Sénégal

Gambia

Niger

Lake Chad

White Nile

Blue Nile

S   A   H   E   L

Benue

Lake Volta

BAMENDA
HIGHLANDS

ETHIOPIAN HIGHLANDS

OGADEN

Shabeelle

Bioko Island

Sanaga

ZAIRE
HIGHLANDS

Lake Turkana

Jubba

Zaire

Mount Stanley

Lake Kyoga

Mount Kenya

Lake Edward

Tana

Congo

Lake Kivu

Lake Victoria

Kilimanjaro

Pemba Island

Zanzibar

Lake Tanganyika

Mafia Island

Comoro Islands

Cuanza

R   I   F   T   V   A   L   L   E   Y

S   O   U   T   H

A   T   L   A   N   T   I   C

O   C   E   A   N

Lake Malawi

Mt Mulanje

Etosha Pan

Zambezi

Madagascar

Okavango

Lake Kariba

Makgadikgadi Pan

NAMIB DESERT

KALAHARI DESERT

Limpopo

Vaal

Orange River

CAPE PROVINCE

THE ETHIOPIAN REGION

The Afro-tropical or Ethiopian region consists of Africa south of the Sahara, and Madagascar. From savannas and grasslands to tropical forests and from thorny thickets to deserts and glaciers, the main threat to this region is the fast-growing human populations and their exploitation of the land for crops, livestock and firewood.

African Elephant (Loxodonta africana), *Tanzania.*

HABITAT & PLANTS

Stephen Droop is a consultant botanist and conservationist some of the time, and a publishing and design consultant the rest. After training as a plant taxonomist, he worked at the IUCN Conservation Monitoring Centre, Kew, where he collected information on threatened plants and habitats of Africa and its associated islands. He has contributed to IUCN's *Plants in Danger: What do We Know?* and Anthony Huxley's *Green Inheritance*.

The vast herds of wildebeest, antelope, and zebra of the African savanna are world famous, yet the backdrop of grass and scattered trees that make up their habitat receives little attention. To take plants for granted is to be blind to an immense variety of form and lifestyle, and sheer breathtaking beauty. In addition, of course, the savanna herds – and virtually all the animals on our planet – are dependent on plants for the air they breathe and the food they eat.

As well as the familiar savannas and grasslands, Africa's habitats range from rain-drenched forests and impenetrable thickets to deserts and glaciers. Almost everywhere, the plants have found some way of making a living – until human actions led to the destruction of huge areas of Africa's wilderness. As the diversity of habitats is lost, so too are large numbers of the species living within them, many disappearing even before they have been discovered. The cause of much of this destruction is a lack of foresight on the part of developers, miners, and so on. But by far the largest losses are due to the use of the land for collecting firewood, grazing livestock and growing crops needed by the region's fast-growing human populations. And so the loss has been described as the tragedy without a villain.

The plants of Africa are well-known compared with those in some other parts of the tropics, but most of the knowledge comes from collections made up to 250 years ago. Information is available on the present status of some groups of special interest

Right *By 1967 the Socotran Fig* (Dorstenia gigas) *was confined to an area inaccessible to goats on the island of Socotra. The particular cliff where it survived was also home to a number of other endangered plants. Socotra, which is part of the Yemen Republic, has been visited only rarely by botanists. When last investigated it had an enormous number of endemics, most of which were threatened.*

to horticulturists and others, such as succulents, bulbs, cycads, timber species and palms, and most of the ericaceous species from South Africa. But no one is really sure how well many of the rest of the plants are surviving in the face of such massive loss of habitat. In particular, little is known about the status or even the botany of the "lower" plants in tropical Africa.

We can get to know habitats better, since there are fewer of them and they are much bigger. Most scientists now agree that the key to species conservation is the protection of as wide a range of habitats as possible. If a habitat is protected, then so too are all the species that live within it – plants and animals – whether or not we know them all by name.

Forest

The tropical rainforests of the world have received a lot of attention recently, and many people are now aware of the great diversity of life which exists within them. People are also aware of the pressing need to protect them, both to conserve species and to maintain the overall health of the planet and its weather systems.

The forests of tropical Africa are somewhat less rich in flora than their Amazonian counterparts, but nevertheless harbor an enormous variety of wildlife. There are two main areas where rainforests are the natural habitat: the huge Congo basin in central Africa around Gabon and Congo and extending into Cameroon, and a broad coastal band in west Africa extending from Ghana westward to Senegal. The central African forests are the more intact, being very much less accessible. The west African forests have almost completely disappeared as a result of logging and shifting agriculture, and most of what remains is in the Ivory Coast.

One species at risk is *Prunus africana*, a relative of the Cherry. Its bark has been found to contain chemicals which help in the treatment of certain ailments of the prostate gland. Huge quantities of bark are shipped to Europe each year, resulting in

Below *The bark of* Prunus africana *contains chemicals which are used for certain ailments of the prostate gland. As a result, Europe imports huge amounts of bark and, without some kind of management program, this formerly common species could easily face rapid extinction.*

Below left Thonningia sanguinea *is a root parasite from the Cameroon. Because it is totally dependent on its host and cannot be cultivated, its survival is inextricably linked to that of its rainforest habitat.*

Above Strophanthus thollonii *from Korup forest in Cameroon has been found to contain cardiac glycosides used in Western heart drugs. However, it is doubtful whether its discovery will contribute to the economy of the Cameroon or the preservation of the forest where it was found.*

the death of thousands of trees. If the demand continues and no control is exercised, this formerly common species could soon face extinction.

Thonningia sanguinea is a root parasite found in the rainforests of Cameroon. It has no photosynthetic tissue of its own, and therefore is totally dependent on its host. If the forests go, so will this plant for it cannot survive in cultivation. Rainforest is also the home of *Strophanthus thollonii*. The chemicals it contains are used as an arrow poison in Cameroon, and as heart drugs in Western medicine. Its habitat is now threatened.

—— Woodland and grassland ——

By far the greatest part of Africa south of the Sahara is occupied by deciduous woodland or grassland, either naturally or as a result of degradation of forest. The vegetation ranges from the moist *miombo* woodland covering huge parts of southern tropical Africa, to the very dry, near-desert steppes south of the Sahara. In between is a range of drier woodland types including the *mopane* woodland named after the dominant species, *Colophospermum mopane*. *Mopane* is the Bantu word for butterfly, and this tree's leaves look rather like butterflies.

Loss of habitat due mainly to population pressure and burning is so severe that widespread extinctions can be expected in the foreseeable future. There is no

Right *Desertification in Africa commenced tens of thousands of years ago, but since the introduction of agriculture it has been steadily accelerating. The Sahara desert spread rapidly following the introduction of grain crops by the Romans, and elsewhere overgrazing by introduced cattle, sheep, and goats over the past 2,000 years has caused desertification. However, deserts and arid environments are not devoid of wildlife and many species are adapted to survive in these harsh habitats.*

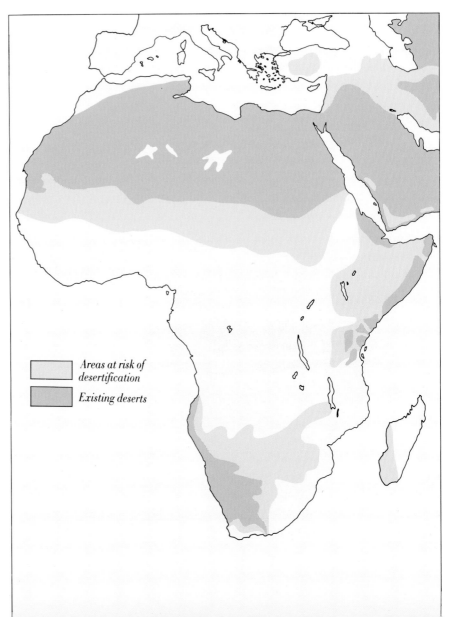

Areas at risk of desertification

Existing deserts

easy way to halt this as the population is growing quickly and people need firewood and land on which to grow crops. Long-term investments and survival strategies mean nothing when you have to feed your family this week and next.

Among the species suffering is the African Blackwood, highly sought after for making musical instruments. This tree is also very prone to fire, and so most of the specimens left are small, rather contorted – and of no use for clarinets.

Desert

There are two main areas of desert or semidesert in mainland Africa apart from the great Sahara desert: parts of lowland Ethiopia and Somalia in the northeast, and the Namib and Kalahari deserts in the southwest.

The northeastern desert, which stretches across the Red Sea to the Arabian peninsula, is quite separate from the Sahara, and the plants it contains are related to those from tropical Africa rather than the Mediterranean. The vegetation is mostly deciduous bushland and thicket, with large areas of semidesert. Many of the species are succulents, and a good proportion are found nowhere else. The problem facing these plants is desertification and its associated climatic changes. The local population needs firewood and grazing for its flocks, and the resulting denudation and erosion lead to a change in the rainfall pattern and desert.

The Yeheb Nut is a valuable food crop in arid lands because of its ability to survive in very low-rainfall areas. Uncontrolled exploitation combined with habitat deterioration and overgrazing have reduced the plant to seriously low numbers in the wild. Trials are underway to cultivate it, but it remains to be seen if these will be successful. The Nubian Dragon Tree, a relative of Sisal, has been exploited, probably beyond redemption, for firewood and for its fibrous leaves which are woven into mats and baskets. Also on the verge of extinction is the Socotran Pomegranate, the demise of which would be an enormous loss to plant breeders. It grows only on the island of Socotra off the Horn of Africa, where possibly fewer than 20 specimens survive and there are no signs of regeneration.

Spotlight
- The Madagascan Periwinkle *(Catharanthus roseus)*. This plant has been found to contain many chemicals that are important to the treatment of some forms of cancer. Its close relative *Catharanthus coriaceus*, which almost certainly contains many such useful chemicals, is critically endangered in its Madagascan home and may already be extinct.
- The African Violet *(Saintpaulia ionantha)*. One of the progenitors of all African Violets in the horticultural trade, it is almost extinct in the wild.
- The Yeheb Nut *(Cordeauxia edulis)*. Potentially a very valuable source of food in low-rainfall areas susceptible to famine, it has been overexploited in the wild.
- The Socotran Pomegranate *(Punica protopunica)*. It is of enormous potential importance to plant breeders, but is reduced to less than 20 individuals and there are no signs of regeneration.

Right Senecio dendrosenecio. *There are several species of giant senecio growing near the tops of east Africa's highest peaks. Related to grounsels, they have huge rosettes of leaves at the ends of branches which help to protect its buds and stems from temperature extremes.*

Socotra

The island of Socotra off the horn of Africa has about 680 species of flowering plants, of which 215 are found nowhere else. Of these, all but 81 are believed to be threatened with extinction and one is already extinct. The climate is predominantly dry, and so many of the species are succulent. The main problem facing them seems to be overgrazing by introduced goats – a common problem on islands. Many of the rare plants only survive at all because they can grow on inaccessible cliffs.

The desert areas in the southwest cover much of Namibia and extend east to northern South Africa and Botswana. Their isolation from other areas of low rainfall means that many of their plants are unique. The largest single threat to the flora seems to be the same as that facing the South American pampas: huge areas of Botswana are being used for the ranching of cattle to supply the beefburger trade.

Parts of this region are so dry that they only receive rain once every 10 or 20 years. When rain does come the plants must make full use of it, resulting in the formation of single-age stands. One plant which continues to grow between the rains is *Welwitschia bainesii*. A relative of the conifers, it inhabits the Namib desert and is among the oddest plants in the world. It has no trunk to speak of, and bears only two leaves which keep on growing for hundreds of years. Although not in immediate danger, it cannot be cultivated and so we would lose it forever if anything damaged or destroyed its desert home.

Mountains

The mountains in the west and south are of great botanical interest. But it is in the east that most of Africa's highest mountains occur, associated with a rift valley system created by great Earth movements over millions of years. The chain of high ground they form is almost like an archipelago of islands in the sea.

The climate on a mountain is so different from that of the surrounding lowlands that its species are as isolated as on an island, often not found anywhere else or only on other mountains. The combination of high altitude and low latitude means that the ground gets very hot during the day and very cold at night. The plants that have succeeded in adapting to this problem include several species of giant senecio

(*Dendrosenecio*) growing near the top of east Africa's highest peaks. Huge rosettes of leaves at the ends of the branches, and a thick layer of decaying leaves over the rest of the plant protect the vulnerable buds and stem from temperature extremes. Other mountain plants have come up with different solutions, some so bizarre that plants like them are found virtually nowhere else on Earth with the exception of the Andes in South America.

Species on the upper slopes of mountains are relatively safe from human interference – except, perhaps, from overenthusiastic botanists! Unfortunately, the highest numbers of species are found on the lower slopes, where the montane habitats merge into lower-altitude woodlands and grasslands, and where species are subject to the pressures of human populations and habitat loss.

The very attractive Spiral Aloe of the Drakensberg mountains in Lesotho has been decimated by uprooting for the horticulture trade. It is now officially protected, but will undoubtedly continue to suffer at the hands of poachers. This is particularly silly since it almost never survives transplanting, and has to be grown from seed.

The well-known African Violets of the horticulture trade are all derived from *Saintpaulia ionantha* from Tanzania. This grows only on limestone cliffs shaded by dry evergreen forest, and there are no more than a handful of specimens left. The forest is threatened by encroaching agriculture and when it goes, so too will the Violets, leaving as their only memorial a multimillion pound houseplant trade.

The Cape

The Cape of South Africa is rather like a florist's – only it is outdoors! It harbors an incredible number of species crammed into a small area, including 8,500 or so flowering plant species. This is nearly as many as can be found in the whole of Argentina, which is about 30 times as large, or nearly five times as many as in Britain, which is nearly three times the size. About three quarters of the Cape's flowering plants grow nowhere else.

Below *The Mulanje Cedar* (Widdringtonia cupressoides) *grows in South Africa as well as Malawi, but reaches its greatest size only on Mt. Mulanje, Malawi.*

Right *The Giant Protea* (Protea cynaroides) *has the largest flowerhead of the protea family – up to 30 centimeters (11 inches). It became South Africa's national emblem in 1976 – official endorsement for the growing public awareness of the country's unique flora.*

Far right *Erica* verticillata *is extinct in the wild, and is now found only in cultivation.*

extent of fynbos

Fynbos

The southernmost tip of Africa has one of the world's highest concentrations of plant species, with 8,550 vascular plant species, occupying an area of only 89,000 square kilometers (34,000 square miles). Of these plants, 73 per cent grow nowhere else.

The natural vegetation of most of the area is a type of scrub called *fynbos*. The area is highly populated and already about a third of all the fynbos has been destroyed. This has put many species at risk: 36 are already known to be extinct, another 98 on the very verge of extinction and a further 1487 are threatened. Scientists fear that the greatest numbers of plant species extinctions could occur in this area.

Such richness is remarkable because the Cape does not contain any tropical forest habitat, where the highest levels of diversity are usually expected. Whereas most of Africa south of the Sahara has rain in the summer months, the summers in the southwest corner of Cape Province are very dry and windy and rain falls only in the winter. The main natural vegetation is *fynbos*, a shrubby habitat containing mainly plants with small, hard leaves, such as heathers and proteas, and also a lot of bulbs.

Unfortunately, the Cape is highly populated, and the natural vegetation is rapidly being eroded by agriculture and other development, and by the uncontrolled spread of alien species. For example, one of the main areas of *fynbos* is threatened by the planned construction of a missile range by the government's Armaments Corporation. Another problem is that many of the plants are very showy and so are attractive to the horticulture trade. The combination of high species diversity and high human population in the Cape has led scientists to predict that the greatest numbers of plant species extinctions could occur there. Thirty-six of its species are already known to be extinct.

Official endorsement for the growing public awareness of the Cape's unique flora came in 1976 when the Giant Protea became the country's national emblem. One of the most famous Cape species, it is a highly sought-after garden plant. In contrast, the Bluebearded Iris was only discovered in 1973, restricted to a small granite hill. It was nearly wiped out a few years later by a quarrying company, and dynamiting was stopped just in time to save the species. The shrub *Erica verticillata* was not so fortunate. It became extinct in the wild and is now found only in cultivation.

—————— Madagascar ——————

Almost as amazing is the island of Madagascar with between 10,000 and 12,000 species of flowering plants, of which perhaps as many as 80 per cent grow nowhere else on Earth. It contains three main types of vegetation: rainforest in the east, dry deciduous forest in the west, and spiny thicket in the south of the island. Sadly only about one-fifth of the island's original vegetation survives, much of the remainder having been converted to a uniform grassland through slash-and-burn farming. Very

little rainforest is now left in the east where about three-quarters of Madagascar's plant species occur – or occurred.

The spiny thicket in the south must be one of the oddest-looking habitats in the world. Most of the plants are adapted to keep in as much water as they can, and have developed some very unusual shapes to achieve this. As with succulent species around the world, their unusual and attractive life forms have made them targets for the horticulture trade. This has, in some cases, been a threat to their continued existence in the wild. No plants or seeds may be exported without permission, but this is freely granted for the removal of thousands of rare succulents each year.

The recently discovered and bizarre *Didierea trollii* is very rare in its spiny Madagascan home. Its whole family is unique to Madagascar. The distinctive palm *Marojejya darienii* is close to extinction in the northeast of Madagascar. It only occurs in two small populations anyway, and is subject to the unscrupulous collection of its seeds for the horticulture trade in California and Australia, and to destruction for "palm hearts."

The Madagascan Periwinkle, commonly cultivated around the world, is known to produce about 70 chemicals of great medicinal value, including some used in treatments for cancer. Its close relative, *Catharanthus coriaceus*, is critically endangered in the dry forests of Madagascar, and is so rare that no one has been able to collect enough of it to assess its undoubted chemical and medicinal importance.

WILDLIFE

Martin Jenkins worked at the World Conservation Monitoring Centre for ten years after graduating in zoology from Cambridge University. He co-authored Part 1 of the IUCN Mammal Red Data Book, and went on to produce an Environmental Profile of Madagascar covering all aspects of its ecology and conservation. He has also worked on a variety of other topics, including the wildlife of the Sahel and Ethiopia, and the Pacific Ocean Coral Reefs. He is now a freelance writer and researcher in conservation and wildlife issues.

Below *Although superbly adapted to life in the desert and able to survive without drinking water, the Addax* (Addax nasomaculatus) *tires easily when pursued. People hunting with high velocity rifles from cars were easily able to kill them, and in the past half century have reduced herds numbering thousands to the brink of extinction.*

For many people, Africa is *the* wildlife continent, full of teeming herds of "big game." In fact, these occur mainly on the eastern and southern savannas and spectacular as they are, form only a small fraction of the biological riches of this vast continent. Africa is a land of many parts, and each has its own complement of unique and distinctive species, as well as a share of the continent's more widespread fauna. Each of these parts is also subject to pressure from human activities and the degree of this pressure is reflected in the status of the animals found there. In some areas, environmental destruction and disturbance are as yet so limited that most species are still relatively secure. In others, human impact has been far-reaching and a high proportion of the fauna is under some degree of threat, or (as in some Indian Ocean islands) has already been exterminated. Sadly, in most parts of the continent, the loss of natural habitats is proceeding at an ever-accelerating pace and the number of species being driven toward extinction is bound to increase. This is true even in apparently inhospitable areas, such as the Sahara desert and the high Ethiopian mountains.

The Sahara and the Sahel

The great Sahara desert and the arid semidesert Sahel area to the south harbor some of the most critically endangered of all African animals, notably several species of desert antelopes. The two largest, the spiral-horned Addax and the elegant Scimitar-horned Oryx were formerly abundant in the dry steppe-lands of the Sahel, the oryx also occurring in semidesert regions north of the Sahara proper. Competition with domestic livestock, especially in periods of drought, progressive desertification and hunting with rifles from desert-ranging vehicles have brought them both to the very brink of extinction in the wild. It is possible that a few Scimitar-horned Oryx survive in the vast Ouadi Rime–Ouadi Achim Reserve in Chad – a stronghold where conservation activities ceased in the late 1970s owing to civil disturbance – but even if they do, their long-term prospects are poor. Similarly, although a very few Addax may persist in the Air and Ténéré region of Niger, it is unlikely that the population there is viable. Fortunately both species breed well in captivity and reintroductions have been planned in some of the countries within their former range. Also reduced in numbers and range, although less imminently endangered, is the Dama Gazelle, the largest true gazelle. Several hundred survive in the wild, mainly in Chad, and the species breeds well in zoos.

Least known of all the desert antelopes is undoubtedly the Slender-horned Gazelle. This rarely seen species is the most desert-going of all the region's antelopes, and has specially adapted splayed hooves to enable it to walk over the soft desert sand without sinking in to it. Its population density will be naturally low in such an inhospitable habitat, making it vulnerable to hunting and other pressures. However, living in some of the least visited parts of the whole African continent may also protect it to some extent from humans.

The mountain massifs of the Sahara are home to the Aoudad or Barbary Sheep. Despite its name, this animal is thought to be halfway between the sheep and the goats. It has been heavily hunted and suffers from competition with domestic

Left *The Barbary Sheep or Aoudad* (Ammotragus lervia) *formerly occurred extensively in and around the Sahara. Although flourishing in captivity, they are now extinct in their natural range. They have been introduced into the USA and Mexico for hunting and are locally abundant there.*

Spotlight

- Scimitar-horned Oryx *(Oryx dammah).* This oryx, once widespread, is now virtually extinct in the wild. A few dozen may survive in Chad.

- Addax *(Addax nasomaculatus).* It has been reduced from a population of tens of thousands spread across north Africa to a few dozen at most in Niger.

- Dama Gazelle *(Gazella dama).* Only a few hundred Dama survive in Niger and Chad, having declined drastically in the last few years.

- Slender-horned Gazelle *(Gazella leptoceros).* This is one of the least known of all antelope. Possibly only a few hundred survive in remote parts of the Sahara desert.

---

sheep and goats, but the harshness of its terrain affords it a measure of protection.

The Sahel is, paradoxically, inhabited by a distinctly un-desert like species. The vast inland delta of the Niger river in Mali in the heart of the Sahel harbors an important population of the wholly aquatic West African Manatee. This placid, sluggish creature also occurs in rivers through much of the rest of western Africa as far south as northern Angola. Reputed to make very good eating, it is widely hunted and its very low reproductive rate means that populations are slow to recover from overhunting. So despite still being widespread, it is vulnerable.

North of the Sahara desert is found one of the most threatened and, to many eyes, one of the ugliest of all birds, the Waldrapp or Northern Bald Ibis. Once widespread in central Europe, North Africa and the Middle East, the population has

Right *A Bald Ibis* (Geronticus eremita) *at one of its last surviving breeding station at Birecik, Turkey. Attempts are being made to boost the population by captive breeding.*

Spotlight
- Walia Ibex *(Capra walie)*. Its population has been reduced from several thousand in the nineteenth century to a few hundred now, all found in a small part of the Simēn mountains.
- Simēn Jackal *(Canis simensis)*. This is the rarest member of the dog family. It occurs only in the Simēn and Bale mountains, where well under 1,000 survive.
- Mountain Nyala *(Tragelaphus buxtoni)*. A few thousand exist in the Bale mountains, where the population is relatively stable but remains permanently at risk.
- Prince Ruspoli's Turaco *(Tauraco ruspolii)*. Probably only a few hundred survive in juniper forests in southwest Ethiopia where they are increasingly threatened by deforestation.

plummeted, for reasons that are not fully understood, to a few dozen birds in scattered colonies in Morocco and one small colony in Turkey. The decline is apparently continuing and the only real hope for the survival of the species seems to rest with captive breeding, which has luckily proved uncomplicated.

The Ethiopian highlands

This is by far the largest high montane area in Africa, with some of the most spectacular scenery anywhere in the world. The mountains support a rich and varied wildlife, much of which is found nowhere else. They also support an ever-growing human population, and each year people clear more and more of the mid-altitude forest for cultivation and firewood, and graze increasing numbers of livestock in the high alpine moorlands and grasslands. The resultant erosion and progressive shrinkage of habitat threatens species whose entire world range is already perilously small. One of the most spectacular and rarest of these is the Walia Ibex, which leads a precipitous existence on some of the steepest and highest crags of the Simēn mountains, north of the great Rift valley.

Formerly quite widespread, the Walia Ibex has been drastically reduced over the past century by hunting and human encroachment on its habitat. It is now confined to a mere 30-kilometer (19-mile) stretch of cliffs at around 3,000 meters (9,000 feet) where it numbers perhaps 300-500 individuals. The entire range of the Walia lies within the Simēn National Park, which should theoretically help safeguard its future. Indeed, by the late 1970s, poaching and habitat destruction in the park had been brought under control and prospects seemed good. Since then, however, political unrest in the region has led to the cessation of conservation activities there and the future of the Walia would seem to lie once again in the balance.

The Walia shares its range with the world's most terrestrial monkey, the shaggy, herbivorous Gelada Baboon. Similarly confined to mountains north of the Rift valley, the Gelada is much more widespread and abundant than the Walia and is not considered immediately endangered. But it, too, suffers from progressive encroachment of its habitat by human settlers and is certainly declining in numbers.

The Simēn mountains have given their name to what is probably the rarest living member of the dog family, the Simēn Jackal or Fox. This stocky, tawny-colored animal lives in the high-altitude moorlands and grasslands where it feeds mainly on small mammals, in particular the abundant molerats of the family Spalacidae, several of which are themselves endemic to Ethiopia. As well as occurring in the Simēn mountains, the Simēn Jackal is found in the much smaller Bale mountains in the southeast of the highland region. The existence of two separate populations is a safeguard for the species, reducing the chances of a single catastrophe, such as an outbreak of disease, wiping it out. The Jackal also benefits from the fact that 2200 square kilometers (850 square miles) of the Bale mountains are well-protected in a national park. This park is home to virtually the entire world population of the Mountain Nyala, one of the most attractive of African antelopes. It holds the distinction of being the most recent large African mammal to be made known to science, having been described only in 1919. Although locally common and not apparently declining rapidly in numbers, its total world population and range are very small for such a large animal, and, as a result, it must be considered permanently under threat.

The Ethiopian highlands are inhabited by around 30 endemic bird species. Fortunately most are widespread and not considered threatened at present, but some have a very limited range and are definitely at risk. For ornithologists, the most remarkable is certainly the Ethiopian Bush Crow, a species not discovered until 1938. It has proven almost impossible to classify – it may be related to the crows, the starlings or neither. Whatever its affinities, it is known to be confined to a very small area of about 6,000 square kilometers (2,300 square miles) in southern Ethiopia. Although none of its habitat is formally protected, this bird does not appear to be under immediate threat. The situation may be worse for another restricted species,

Below left *A male Gelada Baboon* (Theropithecus gelada). *This baboon is confined to northeast Africa at altitudes of up to 5,000 meters (16,500 feet) where it lives in rocky gorges, alpine meadows and other largely treeless areas. An old male leads the troops, which sometimes gather into packs of up to 600.*

Below *The Walia Ibex* (Capra walie) *is found only in the Simēn mountains of Ethiopia at altitudes of 2,500–4,500 meters (7,600–13,000 feet). Reduced to perhaps 300–500 individuals its future is precarious.*

Prince Ruspoli's Turaco. This also occurs in southern Ethiopia in a few scattered localities in juniper forests (at around 1,800 meters/5,900 feet), which were largely undisturbed until recently. It now appears that these forests are being cleared rapidly by settlers from drought-affected parts of Ethiopia and their future, and the Turaco's, looks far from secure.

The Somali-Masai

Apart from the Ethiopian highlands, most of the Horn of Africa is taken up by an area known as the Somali-Masai which includes much of lowland Ethiopia, all of Djibouti and Somalia, and northern Kenya. The area supports a large number of arid land species, including a wide diversity of antelopes. Least known, and almost certainly one of the rarest, is the diminutive, rock-haunting Beira of the hills of northern Somalia and adjacent Ethiopia. It is very seldom recorded and its total world population remains unknown but is undoubtedly small. This species is believed to have declined as a result of drought and competition for food with domestic livestock, particularly goats. An antelope which is definitely known to have decreased in number and is now thought to be seriously endangered is Hunter's Antelope. In the late 1970s there were an estimated 18,000 surviving in a small range on the Somali-Kenya border, while recent surveys could find no more than 1,700. If this alarming decline continues, the species will soon become extinct. Grevy's Zebra is rather more widespread, but is still declining rapidly in numbers. The most elegant of all the zebras, it has suffered markedly from droughts, competition for grazing with

Below *Grevy's Zebra* (Equus grevyii) *in the Samburu, northern Kenya. This zebra is thought to have particularly attractive striping, and so it has been hunted for its hide. There may be as few as 15,000 left in the wild.*

domestic livestock and, formerly, hunting for its beautiful skin. Unlike Hunter's Antelope, which does not occur in any protected area, Grevy's Zebra is found in at least one game reserve, Samburu in northern Kenya, but is still regarded as seriously threatened. Closely related to Grevy's Zebra, and at least as endangered, is the African Wild Ass. Once widespread in the Somali-Masai and Sahel, it is now confined to northern Ethiopia and possibly Sudan. Less immediately endangered but, nevertheless, still threatened are Speke's Gazelle and the Dibatag or Clarke's Gazelle. The former is confined to coastal lowland Somalia and northeastern Ethiopia, and, although still locally common, is declining rapidly. The elegant, long-necked Dibatag is mainly found in the low-lying Ogaden region of eastern Ethiopia and adjacent Somalia. Its overall population remains unknown, but it is undoubtedly rare and decreasing in number.

Several bird species are also confined to the Somali-Masai. The most threatened of these is the Djibouti Francolin, restricted to two small areas of juniper forest in Djibouti. These forests are being cleared for firewood and pasture at such a rate that they, and the francolin, will certainly have disappeared by the turn of the century unless action is soon taken.

The west African rainforests

Rainforests are the richest habitats on Earth, with an astonishing variety of animal and plant species. The African rainforests are no exception, although they generally have slightly fewer species than equivalent areas in South America and Asia. There are two major blocks: the vast central African forests and the much less extensive west African forests, now largely confined to the Ivory Coast, Liberia, Guinea, and Sierra Leone. The two blocks have many species in common, and each also has its own complement of unique plants and animals.

Many of the west African species are considered threatened to some degree, mainly because the forests themselves are seriously threatened. A large and growing human population has cleared so much forest for logging, agriculture, and mining that undisturbed rainforest now only occupies a tiny, and decreasing, fraction of the area it once covered. While some rainforest species can survive in disturbed or logged-over habitats, others seem dependent on primary or virtually undisturbed forests. Moreover, forest animals are a major source of protein in most west African countries and many species are under intense hunting pressure.

One of the most sought-after animals is the Pygmy Hippopotamus. This retiring, pig-sized cousin of the widespread Hippopotamus is found near watercourses and lakes in lowland rainforest. Its solitary habits and secretive nature make it very hard to estimate numbers, but it is thought that several thousand still survive. However, Pygmy Hippo populations invariably decline as human population levels rise and it is undoubtedly becoming rarer.

Scarcer and less well known even than the Pygmy Hippo is the strikingly colored gray and chestnut Jentink's Duiker, one of the largest of this widespread genus of forest antelopes. Previously only known from a few specimens in Liberia and the Ivory Coast, it has recently been discovered on the Freetown peninsula in Sierra Leone. There, as elsewhere in its range, it is hunted for its meat and skin and it is unclear how long populations will be able to survive. Also under threat, although apparently rather more numerous at present, is the closely related but smaller Zebra Duiker. The Liberian Mongoose, the least known of all mongooses, occupies a very similar range to these two antelopes. A specialist feeder on earthworms, it is also

Above *Hunter's Hartebeest* (Damaliscus hunteri) *is confined to a 100-kilometer (60-mile) wide strip north of the Tana River, Kenya, where it is declining due to competition from cattle.*

intensively hunted for its meat and is reported by villagers to be declining in numbers.

DISTRIBUTION
GORILLA

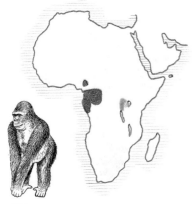

■ *Western Lowland Gorilla*

■ *Eastern Lowland Gorilla*

■ *Mountain Gorilla*

Gorilla (Gorilla gorilla). Three distinct populations survive. The western lowland form is still relatively abundant, numbering around 40,000; the eastern lowland form is much rarer with only 3,000–5,000 surviving; and the highland race is rarer still with a population of around 400 in the central African highlands.

Right *A Pygmy Hippopotamus* (Choeropsis liberiensis) *with its young. They are normally solitary and nocturnal, and are found in wet forests and swamps in a small area of west Africa. They have probably always been thinly populated, but are becoming increasingly rare due to hunting and destruction of their habitat.*

intensively hunted for its meat and is reported by villagers to be declining in numbers.

Relatively few primates are confined to these forests, exceptions being the attractive Diana Monkey and the Olive Colobus. Both are subject to the twin threats of hunting and habitat loss, but appear more resistant to these than many of the larger terrestrial mammals. So, although both give cause for concern, neither is regarded as imminently endangered.

This is far from the case for some of the birds, such as the White-breasted Guineafowl. This species is regarded as one of the most endangered birds in the whole of Africa because of its very limited range, its complete dependence on primary rainforest, and the intensity with which it is hunted. Fortunately, populations of the White-breasted Guineafowl, and of much of the rest of the threatened fauna of the west African rainforests, are present in protected areas. Most notable of these are the Tai National Park in the Ivory Coast, and the Sapo National Park in Liberia. Both parks are, however, subject to encroachment and poaching, and whether they will be adequate to conserve populations in the long-term remains to be seen.

The central African rainforests

These are far more extensive than the west African rainforests and are under less immediate threat. Many of their inhabitants are still widespread and relatively abundant, and are considered reasonably secure, at least in the short or medium term. There are, however, notable exceptions to this, including several primates. The most endangered is probably the Drill, an imposing, gregarious relative of the baboons. This species occupies a small range in lowland rainforest in Cameroon, extreme southeastern Nigeria, the island of Bioko and possibly part of Gabon. It is hunted extensively for its meat and as a crop pest, and its noisy and social nature make it easy for hunters to track groups down and kill large numbers at once. In addition, the forests it depends on are being rapidly cleared. The only protected population is that in Korup National Park in Cameroon, and it is not known whether the numbers there are large enough to enable the species to survive in the long-term.

Closely related to the Drill is the Mandrill, the males of which are among the most flamboyant of all monkeys, with multicolored faces and hind quarters. Although it is subject to the same threats as the Drill and is declining rapidly in numbers, it is regarded as less immediately threatened. The Mandrill occupies a range to the south of the Drill's and is rather more widespread. Occupying a similar

Left *Only the male Mandrill* (Mandrillus sphinx) *has the spectacular facial coloration. They live in groups of up to 250, each of which ranges over an area of 5,000 hectares (12,400 acres). Due to extensive hunting and trapping, they are now among the rarest monkeys in Africa.*

Below *The White-necked Picathartes* (Picathartes gymnocephalus) *nests in small colonies in rock clefts and caves. It is confined to forests in west Africa where it is seriously threatened by habitat destruction. In the past it was collected extensively for exhibition in zoos.*

range to the Mandrill is the highly arboreal Black Colobus. This species was regarded as rare in much of its range as long ago as the 1930s and appears to be especially vulnerable because it reportedly cannot survive in disturbed or logged-over forests.

The forests of Cameroon and neighboring Nigeria and Gabon are very important for bird species. The mountain forests of the Cameroon highlands, for example, harbor no fewer than 22 species found nowhere else, seven of which are definitely threatened with extinction. Most mysterious, and undoubtedly the rarest, is the Mount Kupe Bush-shrike. Known only from Mount Kupe, it has not been seen since 1951 despite recent extensive searches. Two other critically endangered species are the Banded Wattle-eye and Bannerman's Turaco. Both these birds seem destined soon to disappear unless the last few remnants of their forest home on Mount Oku in the Bamenda highlands are preserved.

Also giving cause for concern is the extraordinary, bare-headed, Gray-necked Rockfowl or Picathartes, an inhabitant of lowland rainforests of southern Cameroon and northeast Gabon. Like the similarly threatened west African White-necked Picathartes, the bird has very precise habitat requirements – caves and rocky cliffs under a rainforest canopy. This makes it naturally rare and particularly vulnerable to habitat destruction. These forests are also home to the world's largest frog, the Goliath Frog, which is avidly hunted for food and considered vulnerable.

Further east lie the forests of the great Zaire river basin and the eastern Zaire highlands. Notable species found here include the remarkable, velvet-skinned Okapi. This close relative of the Giraffe was first discovered by Westerners only in 1900. It is not regarded as immediately endangered, but it has a relatively limited range in eastern Zaire, occurring particularly in the Ituri forest east of the Zaire river. Similarly confined entirely to Zaire is the Dwarf Chimpanzee or Bonobo. Although extensive tracts of forest persist within its range, Bonobo populations seem to be very scattered and it is absent from many apparently suitable areas. No sizable population is protected in a national park or reserve at present.

The most noteworthy avian inhabitant of these forests is undoubtedly the Congo Peacock. The only true pheasant found in Africa, this spectacular bird was not described until the 1930s. Like the Dwarf Chimpanzee, it occurs over a wide area but is nowhere common. It is extensively hunted and seems to have disappeared from the vicinity of most villages and settlements within its range.

Two of the Dwarf Chimpanzee's larger and better-known relatives are considered under some degree of threat, despite both being still widespread and relatively numerous. These are the Gorilla, largest of all primates, and the Chimpanzee. Three separate populations of Gorillas exist, all within the general area of the central African rainforests. The western population is the most abundant, with per-haps 35,000-40,000 surviving, the majority in Gabon. A population estimated at 3,000-5,000 inhabits lowland eastern Zaire, where it is highly threatened by forest clearance. A further 300-400 Mountain Gorillas are found in the Virunga volcano region of Rwanda and Zaire and in the Bwindi forest in Uganda. The Mountain Gorilla population is fairly stable at present but a few are lost to poaching, and both it and its habitat will have to be subject to constant vigilance if they are to survive.

The Chimpanzee is considerably more abundant than the Gorilla, with

Below *An old male Chimpanzee* (Pan troglodytes) *photographed in Liberia. In addition to loss of habitat, Chimpanzees have been seriously threatened by the trade for biomedical research. Captive breeding programs are now partially satisfying this demand.*

perhaps 200,000 surviving. It ranges through the west African forests as well as much of the central African rainforests and is also found in a variety of more open, wooded habitats. It remains under threat, however, from hunting for food and habitat loss. In west Africa, it also suffers from hunting for export, particularly for biomedical research, although this has decreased considerably in recent years.

Also found in both the west African and central African forests is one of the smallest of crocodilians, the African Dwarf Crocodile. This inoffensive reptile has been heavily hunted for its hide and has declined in many parts of its range, although reasonable populations may survive in remote areas. The African Giant Swallowtail Butterfly has not been persecuted but appears to be naturally rare throughout its range in central and west Africa, and to be vulnerable to loss of its forest habitat.

Above left *A captive Broadfronted or African Dwarf Crocodile* (Osteolaemus tetraspis). *Little is known about the status of this species in the wild, but small numbers are being bred in captivity.*

Above *The Pancake Tortoise* (Malachochersus tornieri) *lives in rocky areas of southern Kenya and northeast Tanzania. It is a slow breeder, laying a single egg once or twice a year.*

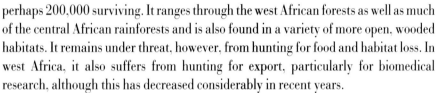

The east African forests

While less rich than the rainforests further west, the forests of Kenya and Tanzania – particularly those of the Kenyan coast and the scattered low mountain ranges of Tanzania – support a significant number of rare and localized species, especially birds. Six threatened bird species occur in the 100-square kilometer (40-square mile) Sokoke forest in Kenya and two of these, the Sokoke Scops Owl and Clarke's Weaver, are found nowhere else. Around 1,000 pairs of the owl are estimated to survive in the forest, which is decreasing in size every year because of logging for the lumber trade. Another threatened species there, the Amani Sunbird, is slightly more secure since it occurs as well in a similar sized area of forest in the East Usambara mountains, some 320 kilometers (200 miles) south of Sokoke. However, this forest, which supports several other threatened birds, is also shrinking and is in urgent need of increased conservation efforts.

A reptile causing concern is the appropriately-named Pancake Tortoise which looks as if it has been flattened by a steamroller. A small rock-dwelling tortoise, it is less dependent on the forests than the birds. But it has been seriously affected by collection for the pet trade and is generally rare with no population known to be protected in a national park or reserve.

Spotlight
- Drill *(Mandrillus leucophaeus)*. The total population is unknown, but is certainly declining rapidly in its small range of less than 10,000 square kilometers (3,900 square miles) in western central Africa.
- Okapi *(Okapia johnstoni)*. A few thousand Okapis survive in a small area of the eastern Zairean rainforests, where they remain at risk from habitat destruction.
- Congo Peacock *(Afropavo congensis)*. This pheasant is widely but patchily distributed in the Zairean rainforest. Its total numbers are unknown, but it has certainly become progressively rarer over the past few decades.

Right *The Brown Hyena* (Hyaena brunnea) *is confined to southern Africa. It is extinct over much of the Cape, but is still widespread in Botswana and Namibia, particularly in the Kalahari and Gemsbok National Parks.*

Far right *A Black Rhinoceros* (Diceros bicornis) *in Amboseli National Park. In the 1950s this animal was still found over most suitable habitats in Africa south of the Sahara. By the 1970s, poaching had reduced its population to about 30,000 and by the late 1980s, there were possibly less than 5,000.*

DISTRIBUTION

AFRICAN ELEPHANT

▨ Probable range 1600
▨ Range in 1987

African Elephant (Loxodonta africana). *An original population of several million had been reduced to just over 1200,000 by the early 1980s and now stands at under 700,000.*

———— Southern Africa ————

The varied habitats of southern Africa support an equally varied assemblage of species, many of them unique to the area. Much of the area has been heavily settled for many years and some habitats have been drastically reduced in extent by intensive agriculture and urbanization. The only two large mammals to have become extinct in sub-Saharan Africa in the past 200 years – the Quagga and Blaubok – lived in this area. The last surviving Quagga, a partially-striped zebra, died in the Amsterdam Zoo in 1874. The Blaubok, an antelope of the veld region of Cape Province in South Africa, was exterminated around 1800. In more recent times, concerted conservation efforts have prevented several other species following suit.

The Mountain Zebra of Namibia, southern Angola and the southern part of Cape Province in South Africa at one time looked likely to suffer the same fate as its cousin, the Quagga. It was ruthlessly persecuted by farmers as an alleged competitor with livestock, and the population plummeted from an estimated 50,000 to 70,000 in the early 1950s to fewer than 7,000 by the late 1960s. Most of these are now protected in game reserves and national parks, and the population is relatively stable. Also unjustly persecuted, this time as a stock-killer, is the carrion-eating Brown Hyena, an inhabitant of the arid semidesert parts of southern Africa. Like the Mountain Zebra, reasonable numbers of Brown Hyenas are protected in national parks and reserves, but outside these areas it has become very scarce. The White Rhinoceros was also decimated by hunters and the 4,000-odd remaining are now well-protected in a number of areas in southern Africa. In addition to this relatively stable southern population, the last vestiges of a once-common northern population cling on in Garamba National Park in northern Zaire, but their prospects are poor.

Some southern African species are threatened particularly by habitat destruction in their already tiny ranges. This is the case for the Giant Golden Mole, confined to small, and rapidly disappearing, forest patches in eastern Cape Province. Similarly the tiny, star-patterned Geometric Tortoise has had its range reduced by an estimated 90 per cent to a few square miles in southwest Cape Province and numbers at most a few thousand individuals. The Cape Platana Frog is found in the same area and has been similarly depleted as the ponds it inhabits have been polluted or drained and filled-in for building and farm land. The only known protected populations are in three small ponds in the Cape of Good Hope Nature Reserve.

——— Widespread species ———

Some of the best known of all African threatened species have ranges which span – or spanned – a large proportion of the continent. Many of these suffer primarily from persecution by people. The Black Rhinoceros is perhaps the most notable example. Formerly widespread in woodlands and savannas in sub-Saharan Africa, the population has plunged from an estimated 20,000-30,000 in the early 1970s to around 3000 today. This decline can be virtually entirely ascribed to poaching for the rhino's horn, which is used in medicines in the Far East and for dagger handles in Yemen. The only hope of halting the decline lies in the vigorous protection of the last few viable populations, such as that in the Zambesi valley in Zimbabwe.

Although the African Elephant is still far more numerous and widespread than the Black Rhino, it is evidently declining at almost as fast a rate. It is notoriously difficult to count elephants, particularly those in the dense central and west African rainforests, but the best estimates indicate that the population has dropped from around 1,200,000 in 1981 to 600,000-700,000 today. The major cause of this has been hunting for ivory. Also, as more land is converted to agriculture, elephants inevitably destroy crops in their constant search for food, bringing them into conflict with people. The long-term survival of elephants outside a few well-protected reserves will depend not only on control of the ivory trade, but also on the full involvement of local people in management plans.

Never abundant, and apparently declining as rapidly as the elephant and

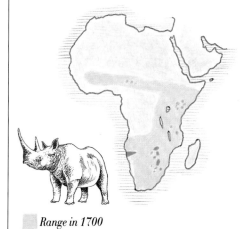

DISTRIBUTION
BLACK RHINO

Range in 1700
Range in 1987

Range of Black Rhinoceros (Diceros bicornis). Fewer than 4,000 now exist compared with at least 25,000 in the early 1970s.

DISTRIBUTION

MADAGASCAN FORESTS

Original extent

Extent in 1985

Madagascar

- Of the island's 106 endemic breeding birds, 27 are threatened with extinction and one is extinct.
- It has 30 surviving lemur species of which 28 are found only on Madagascar, the other two also occurring on the Comoros. Ten of these lemurs are considered endangered.
- Madagascar is home to 260 reptiles, including two-thirds of the world's chameleons. Around 90 per cent of the reptiles are endemic and among these are four threatened tortoises, including the Angonoka *(Geochelone yniphora)*, one of the world's rarest.

Black Rhinoceros, is the nomadic African Hunting Dog. It was previously found in open plains and savannas in most of sub-Saharan Africa, but has died out in much of its former range. This is largely due to persecution as an alleged predator of livestock and diseases, such as canine distemper, anthrax and rabies, to which it appears to be particularly susceptible. Conservation of this species is problematic because few existing protected areas are large enough to hold viable populations. The Cheetah is less threatened than the Hunting Dog but is still declining in many areas. Like the Hunting Dog, this cat requires very large areas of suitable habitat if it is to thrive.

Africa's expanses of wetlands, such as the vast Sudd swampland in southern Sudan and the inland Okavango delta in Botswana, house a number of distinctive species which will become increasingly threatened as these areas are drained and developed. One of the most aquatic of all antelope, the Lechwe, is found in marshes and floodplains in southern central Africa, mostly in Zambia and Botswana. It has been heavily hunted and some populations have been badly affected by hydroelectric schemes. The striking Wattled Crane occupies much the same range as the Lechwe, with an outlying population far north of this, in Ethiopia. The population densities of this bird are always very low and it appears to be particularly susceptible to disturbance, so it is likely to be threatened by any development of its habitat. The same is true of one of the most extraordinary of all birds, the Shoebill Stork, which inhabits marshes and swamps from Sudan and Ethiopia south to Zambia.

Madagascar

Although it is included in the Afrotropical realm, Madagascar truly is a world apart. This enormous island, roughly the size of France, has been separated from the mainland for at least 100 million years, allowing a unique flora and fauna to evolve. Such is the richness and diversity of wildlife on the island that it has been described as a paradise for naturalists. Sadly it is a paradise very much under threat as its forests are being destroyed at a terrifying rate, mostly for slash-and-burn cultivation, and to produce pasture for cattle in the west and on the central highlands.

The best known of all Madagascar's animals are surely the lemurs, a group of primates which evolved on the island. They are found nowhere else in the world, except for the nearby Comoro islands where the highly threatened Mongoose Lemur and the commoner Brown Lemur occur. These two species were almost certainly introduced to the Comoros by people some time in the past few hundred years. When humans first arrived on Madagascar, between 1,500 and 2,000 years ago, there were at least 45 species of lemur. The largest, *Megaladapis edwardsi*, was roughly the size of an adult male Orang Utan. This and 14 other species of lemur, including all the largest ones, are now extinct. Some of the remaining 30 or so species are hanging on so precariously that it is unlikely to be long before they follow their larger cousins.

One of the more threatened is the largest surviving lemur, the Indri. This splendid beast looks like a cross between a gibbon and a piebald teddy bear. Like all Madagascar's forest species, its habitat is inexorably shrinking, and it is now confined to a stretch of around 500 kilometers (300 miles) of the north and central eastern rainforests of Madagascar – a much smaller area than it was found in even a few decades ago. In addition it has a slow reproductive rate, with females not breeding until they are at least seven years old. Its large size and diurnal habitats make it very vulnerable to hunting but, fortunately, in many areas Indris are protected by local taboos as they are thought to represent the ghosts of departed ancestors.

In contrast, the extraordinary Aye-aye, with its pop eyes, shaggy coat, rodent-like teeth, long, bony fingers, and nocturnal habits, is often regarded by the Malagasy people with suspicion. In some areas it is considered a harbinger of evil and is killed on sight. This, and the infrequency with which it was recorded, led many people to conclude that it was on the very brink of extinction. So in 1966/67, nine Aye-ayes were released on the island of Nosy Mangabe, off the eastern coast of Madagascar, in a last ditch attempt to save the species. Although Aye-ayes certainly still survive on this island, in fact the species is now known to be much more widely distributed on the Madagascan mainland than was previously thought. They are extremely elusive, and certainly not common anywhere, but may be no more threatened than many other Madagascan species. Similarly the Hairy-eared Dwarf Lemur may be commoner than has been thought. This diminutive creature had not been seen since the 1960s until 1989, when a population was discovered in northeast Madagascar near the original collecting site. Its size and arboreal habits mean that it is easy to overlook.

Two species which are definitely threatened are the Greater Bamboo Lemur and the recently discovered Golden Bamboo Lemur. As their names suggest, both

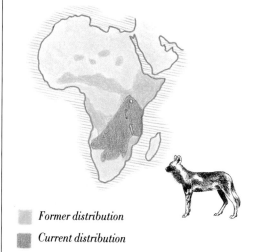

AFRICAN WILD DOG

Former distribution

Current distribution

Range of African Wild Dog (Lycaon pictus). Total numbers are unknown but there are probably no more than a couple of thousand, and it is thought likely that this dog will become extinct in 20–40 years if present trends continue.

Opposite *A pack of Hunting Dogs (Lycaon pictus), each one of which has its own unique pattern and coloring. Earlier this century they were killed as vermin even in national parks and game reserves. They are now one of the most endangered mammals in Africa.*

Far left *The Cheetah (Acinonyx jubatus) once occurred in the more open habitats of eastern and southern Africa, and in southern Asia. Its range is now fragmented and it is only numerous in Namibia and a few areas of adjacent South Africa.*

Left *The Mongoose Lemur (Lemur mongoz) inhabits a wide variety of mostly forested habitats on Madagascar, where it is declining with the destruction of the forests. It also occurs on the Comoro islands.*

Right *The Aldabra Tortoise* (Geochelone gigantea) *is restricted to the atoll of Aldabra in the Indian Ocean. Although they number well over 150,000 at present, their dependence on a single island leaves them vulnerable to both human-made and natural disasters.*

Below *The Madagascar Boa* (Sanzinia madagascariensis). *Like the majority of the island's fauna, this snake is only found there. It lives in trees, where it is particularly well camouflaged.*

species are specialized feeders on bamboo and are apparently confined to the same small area of southeastern Madagascar. The populations of each are unlikely to exceed 400 individuals and are certainly declining. It is estimated that if the current rate of habitat destruction in their range continues, neither species will exist in 20 years time. Some hope is offered by the fact that 500 square kilometers (190 square miles) of their range, near the village of Ranomafana, has been proposed as a national park. If this is set up, it will also offer a refuge to a variety of other threatened lemurs, including the beautiful Diademed Sifaka, the Red-bellied Lemur and the striking Ruffed Lemur. The Fossa, the largest of Madagascar's unique carnivores, is also found there.

Madagascar's 250 or so bird species include over 100 that are unique to the island. Unfortunately, at least 30 birds are currently considered threatened, some of them seriously so. In addition, the Snail-eating Coua, a relative of the Cuckoos, is almost certainly extinct, having last been seen in 1834 on the island of Nosy Borah off the eastern coast of Madagascar. There is a faint possibility that it survives deep in rainforest somewhere on the mainland.

The spectacular Madagascar Serpent Eagle was, until recently, also feared extinct. This bird of deep forest had not been seen for 58 years when, in 1988, one was found in the mountainous, inaccessible Marojejy Reserve in the northern part of the island. Although evidently surviving, it must be very rare and, like most tropical forest birds of prey, is likely to require large areas of undisturbed habitat to feed and breed in, so its future seems bleak. Somewhat better known, but also apparently on the brink of extinction, is the Madagascar Fish Eagle. Fewer than 100 of these are believed to survive along the coast of northwest Madagascar where they breed mainly on small offshore islands. The extraordinary, ground-dwelling Long-tailed Ground Roller is another bird of very restricted range. Its entire population in southwest Madagascar probably numbers less than 1,000. The species seems stable at present but with none of its habitat protected it remains permanently at risk.

Madagascar is also home to an astonishing variety of reptiles, including two-thirds of the world's chameleons and the world's rarest tortoise – the Angonoka. This tortoise is found in one small area of northwest Madagascar where fewer than 400 are believed to survive. While attempts are being made to establish captive breeding colonies, progress to date has been slow. More widespread but still threatened is the beautiful Radiated Tortoise of southwest Madagascar. This species has been extensively collected for the pet trade and its habitat is being rapidly cleared for crop cultivation and charcoal production. The Madagascar Boa mainly inhabits the moist forests of the north and east where it is at risk from habitat loss.

The Mascarenes and Seychelles

The Mascarene islands – Réunion, Rodrigues and Mauritius – lie to the east of Madagascar, and the Seychelles to the north. While far less rich in species than Madagascar or mainland Africa, their fauna is bizarre and exotic. Sadly, it has also been thoroughly devastated by humans. Since the first Europeans visited these islands in the sixteenth century, more species (mainly of birds and reptiles) have become extinct here than in the whole of mainland Africa and Madagascar combined. Those that have gone include probably the most famous of all extinct animals, the Dodo of Mauritius. This giant, flightless relative of the pigeons was exterminated by 1665, a few decades after its discovery. The Rodrigues and Réunion equivalents of the Dodo, the solitaires, survived into the eighteenth century. Also gone are at least eight species of giant tortoise (*Cylindraspis*), and only one species from another genus remains in the Indian Ocean to remind us of what we have lost. The Aldabra Giant Tortoise, whose shell may be over 1 meter (3¼ feet) long, exists in good numbers on the Aldabra atoll in the Seychelles group. The species seems reasonably secure at present but is permanently at risk from natural disasters affecting the atoll.

The catalogue of extinctions on the Indian Ocean islands is probably far from complete (see p.210). Several of the surviving species exist in critically low numbers, although concerted efforts are being made to rescue some of them. The Pink Pigeon of Mauritius has been reduced to fewer than 20 birds in the wild, all breeding in a single unprotected grove of trees. Fortunately the species breeds well in captivity and the zoo population numbers over 100 birds. Although still in a precarious position, the wild population of the Mauritius Kestrel has been increased, mainly by release of captive-bred birds, from 6 in 1974 to around 25 at present. One of the few native mammals of the Mascarenes, the Rodrigues Flying Fox, may not survive for much longer in the wild. Like the Pink Pigeon on Mauritius, it is now confined to a single grove of trees and numbers fewer than 100.

The fate of the Mascarene fauna – with many species already extinct and others keeping a precarious toehold on survival in the wild, or reduced entirely to captive populations – provides a sobering warning of the possible, or even probable, future for much of the fauna of Madagascar and continental Africa. Many of the species discussed above are confined to small patches of suitable habitat which are the continental equivalent of islands like the Mascarenes. However, these habitat "islands" are shrinking in size year by year. Local conservation activities have sometimes helped slow down, or even halt for a while, the tide of destruction. But the long-term future for most of these species, and many others not yet considered threatened, will only fully be assured when we realize that our future wellbeing depends on the maintenance of a healthy biosphere, and that the conservation of natural habitats and the wildlife they contain is an integral part of this.

Above *The Mauritius Kestrel* (Falco punctatus) *was once one of the rarest birds in the world, with only 6 surviving in 1974. It has been rescued from the brink of extinction by a combination of protection in the wild and captive breeding.*

Sara Oldfield graduated in botany and
geography at London University. Since
then she has worked for various
conservation organizations, including the
Nature Conservancy Council and the
World Conservation Monitoring Centre in
Cambridge, UK. Her knowledge of rare
plants around the world developed while
she was employed by the Royal Botanic
Gardens, Kew, working on international
conservation issues. Sara has been involved
in research into trade in rare tropical
timbers for the past three years and is
currently preparing a report on the
conservation status of tropical timbers in
trade, commissioned by the International
Tropical Timber Organisation.

TROPICAL TIMBERS

Tropical forests harbor the greatest diversity of plant and animal species in the
world, including plants of great economic value which occur only there. Hardwood
timber is the main economic product derived from this rich and rapidly disappearing
habitat. The current volume of the trade is approximately 80 million cubic yards with
an annual value of over 6 billion Dollars. If the tropical forests were properly
managed they could provide a much needed and sustainable source of income for
developing countries. At present, however, only a tiny fraction of the forests are
managed successfully for lumber production. Selective felling of tropical hardwoods
has damaged the forests over the centuries and is leading to scarcity of many valuable
species.

Exploitation in historical times led to the virtual disappearance of certain
island timbers, *Diospyros hemiteles*, a species of ebony found only on Mauritius, has
been reduced to a single tree remaining in the wild. Two endemic species of St.
Helena, the St. Helena Ebony and Redwood are on the brink of extinction. By the end
of the seventeenth century these trees were already becoming rare and the British
East India Company, which controlled the island, banned the sale of St. Helena
Redwood for private use. Valuable species of ebony, highly sought after for their
decorative wood, include the true Ebony (*Diospyros ebenum*) which is now very rare
in Sri Lanka and *Diospyros quaesita* which is virtually extinct on the same island.
Diospyros celebica found on the Indonesian islands of Sulawesi and the Philippine
Ebony (*D. philippinensis*) are other threatened species.

The pace of destruction has increased dramatically during the present
century, with many more tropical timbers becoming threatened by international
trade. Export of the socalled African mahoganies (species of *Khaya* and *Entandrophragma*) began in Ghana about 100 years ago, while the French developed an
interest in the mahoganies of the Ivory Coast around the same time. Malaysia's wood
export industry developed to supply Britain's demand for timber early in the present
century. In west Africa, Malaysia, and other parts of the tropics, exploitation for the

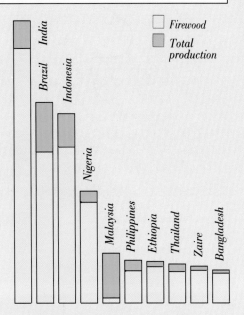

Above and right *Most tropical timber is
produced for use as firewood, as can be seen in
this analysis of the ten largest producers.
Tropical timbers are also a valuable source of
income and foreign exchange for many
developing countries. However, as the two
maps on this page demonstrate, in fact only a
handful of countries account for most tropical
wood exports.*

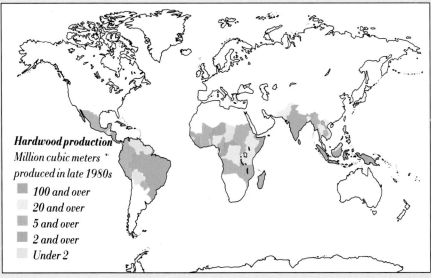

Hardwood production
*Million cubic meters
produced in late 1980s*
- 100 and over
- 20 and over
- 5 and over
- 2 and over
- Under 2

export market has concentrated on a very limited number of species, leading to their depletion, and has ignored the wide range of other timbers which could be brought into commercial use.

African timbers

African "mahoganies" are still highly sought after and in west Africa supplies are now very restricted. In the Ivory Coast, for example, a recent survey carried out by the World Conservation Monitoring Center for the International Tropical Timber Organization has shown that two species of *Khaya* and four of *Entandrophragma* are vulnerable. This means that they are likely to become extinct there unless positive conservation measures are taken to stop their decline. One of the trees, Acajou (*Khaya ivorensis*) was the most exploited species within the country until 1952, and it is now included in a list of protected species. The Acajou has also suffered from over-logging in Ghana. A ban on the export of its logs from Ghana was introduced in 1979, but 10 463 cubic meters (13 685 cubic yards) were still exported in 1989.

The main commercial timbers of *Entandrophragma* are Tiama (*E. angolense*) Sapele (*E. cylindricum*) and Sipo (*E. utile*). As stocks of these species have declined in west Africa, the timber is being increasingly sought from central African countries. Sapele is one of the most important commercial timbers of Cameroon and is one of the few species logged for export from the remote eastern forests of the country. It is also logged in the northern forests of the Congo which have remained relatively intact.

Along with Sapele, Afrormosia is one of the very few timbers exploited commercially in the virgin forests of northern Congo and eastern Cameroon. One of the world's most valuable hardwoods, it was little known to the trade before the Second World War but over the past 50 years its decline in the wild has been rapid. It also occurs in pockets of forest in Ghana and the Ivory Coast. In both countries it is under threat and, although still exported from Ghana, it is considered to be on the point of commercial extinction there. Congo and Zaire are now major suppliers of this

Below and below left *This graph of selected major importers of tropical timber demonstrates that currently most exports come from Asian countries. However, Latin American exports are expected to increase as Asian forests are denuded. The focus is on the largest sources of tropical timber; most countries import smaller amounts from other areas.*

From Asia

From Africa

From Latin America

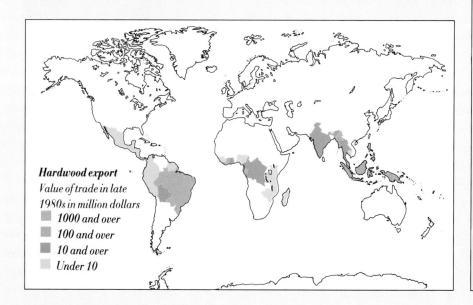

Hardwood export
Value of trade in late 1980s in million dollars
- 1000 and over
- 100 and over
- 10 and over
- Under 10

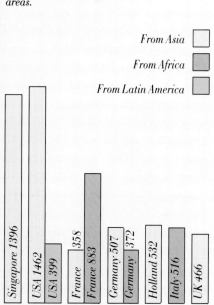

Japan 15 677
Singapore 1396
USA 1462
USA 399
France 358
France 883
Germany 507
Germany 372
Holland 532
Italy 516
UK 466

Above *Mahoganies have been severely depleted worldwide for their very valuable lumber.*

species. Afrormosia is similar in appearance to teak and is used for ship decking, furniture, joinery, and decorative veneers. Unfortunately, unlike teak, it has not been developed as a plantation timber.

In total, Africa exports around 35 principal timber species. In southeast Asia logging concentrates on just under 100 species, with members of the dipterocarp family accounting for around 60 per cent of the trade. There are about 500 species within this family and their wood is marketed under broad trade names on the basis of timber characteristics. The main commercial groups are Meranti (species of *Shorea*), Keruing (species of *Dipterocarpus*), and Kapur (species of *Dryobalanops*). Many trees within these groups are threatened by logging and other processes of forest destruction.

Crisis in the Philippines

The situation is particularly acute in the Philippines where around 40 dipterocarp species occur. Commercial exploitation of the dipterocarp forests has reduced their area from 27 million acres to less than 2.4 million acres over the past 50 years. The most important commercial timber is Philippine "mahogany" (species of *Shorea* and *Parashorea*) and Britain is one of the main importers of this wood. Large-scale logging of the Philippines' forests expanded after the Second World War, mainly to supply the US market. Japanese demand starting in 1961 led to a dramatic increase in destructive logging and deforestation. The timber boom of the 1960s was a time of vast profits for logging companies, and the government was unable to enforce effective logging regulations. The decline of the forests and improved conservation

Right *Mature dipterocarp trees growing along a riverbank in the Taman Negara National Park, Malaysia. In the past, areas such as this were particularly vulnerable. Most logging was done within easy reach of rivers because they were the main form of transport to the sea.*

Left *The remnants of tropical forest in the Bicol region of the island of Luzon in the Philippines. Many of the forest's endemic animals and plants have already disappeared from most of their range and, with current rates of forest destruction, are doomed to extinction.*

Below *Logs being bulldozed into a sawmill in southern Bahia state, Brazil. Like most logging operations, this one is extremely wasteful, taking only part of the tree and destroying much other wildlife in the process. The rate of destruction could be reduced by simply making practices less wasteful.*

measures have reduced logging by 90 per cent over the past 20 years and the Philippines now bans the export of logs and lumber. Some species of dipterocarp are, however, already believed to be extinct and most others are vulnerable.

Latin American timber

In Latin America, high-value timbers are also under pressure from logging. Trees of true mahogany (species of *Swietenia*) are felled wherever they are found. *Swietenia mahogani*, native to Central America and the Caribbean, has been traded around the world since the sixteenth century. Stocks are now severely depleted and *Swietenia macrophylla* has become the main source of the true mahogany. This species is widespread in South America but is endangered in parts of its range, for example through illegal felling in the Brazilian states of Acre and Rondonia, where even Indian reserves and nature reserves have been pillaged. Most Brazilian mahogany is destined for the US market, and Britain is also a major importer.

Selective logging or "mining" of valuable species does not in itself lead to total deforestation and some wildlife can survive in the forests that remain. But commercial logging operations are often the first step in the process of forest loss. Roads built to bring out the selected timbers provide access for land-hungry settlers who remove all the trees for agriculture. Such clearfelling obviously causes much greater species loss.

The demand for tropical wood and wood-based products is enormous, and at present the raw materials are undervalued and squandered. New wood-processing technology has generally led to increased forest destruction rather than more efficient use of tropical timbers. In the 1960s a method was devised to make paper pulp from woodchips of tropical hardwoods and this led to clearfelling, for example, in Papua New Guinea and Colombia. Now the tide may be starting to turn, with timber consumers increasingly demanding wood from sustainably managed forests, and countries, such as Thailand, introducing a ban on all logging. But concerted, sustained international efforts will be necessary if the centuries of destruction are to be reversed.

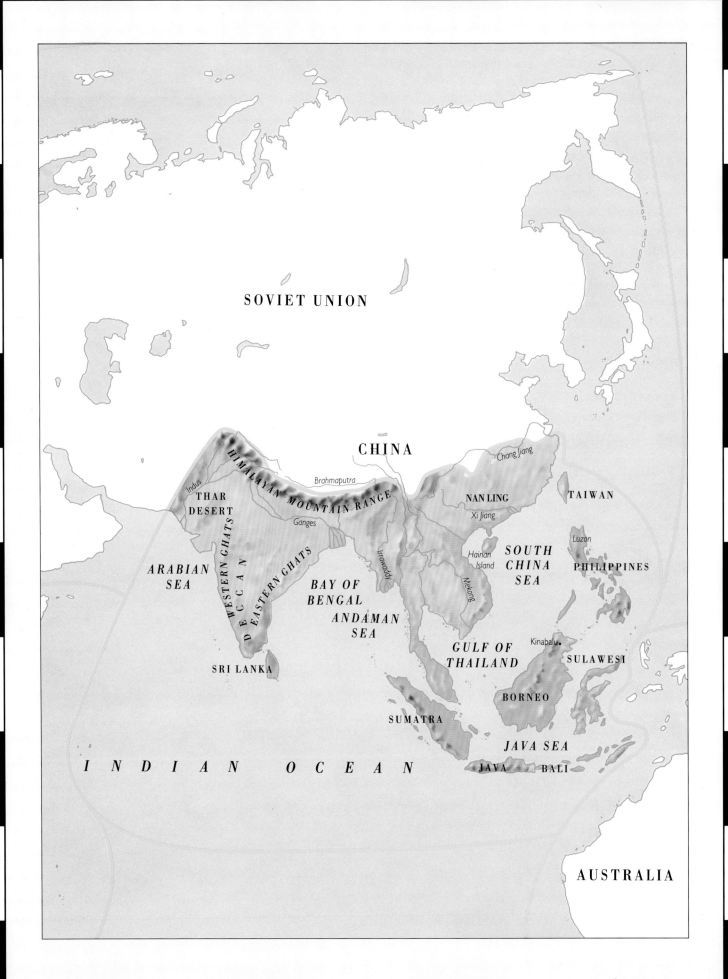

THE
INDIAN & ORIENTAL
REGION

The Indian and Oriental region covers the lands south of the Himalayas, through Indochina and the Malay peninsula to the islands of southeast Asia. Its southeastern boundary has been the subject of much debate among biogeographers, and in this book is taken as being between Sulawesi (Celebes) and New Guinea.

Marsh Mugger (Crocodylus palustris), *Sri Lanka.*

HABITAT & PLANTS

Ruth Taylor graduated from the University of Durham with a degree in biology/ecology. She worked for the conservation unit at the Royal Botanic Gardens, Kew, followed by fieldwork with the Nature Conservancy Council and a project with the Hertfordshire and Middlesex Trust for Nature Conservation. Six years spent teaching in London has given her considerable experience for her present position as education officer at the Chelsea Physic Garden, London. She has traveled widely and been involved in conservation projects in Mexico.

This vast and diverse region stretches from the Baluchistan mountains of Pakistan and the Indus valley in the west to the hills of Yunnan and southern China and Taiwan in the east. The Himalayan chain forms the region's northern boundary. To the southeast and east lie the Philippines, the islands of Sulawesi, the Lesser Sundas and the Moluccas which comprise an important transition zone between the faunas of Asia and Australasia. These islands are included in this section. The region contains a wide range of vegetation types, and a number of floristic zones. These include the Indian zone, the southern part of the Sino-Japanese zone, the continental southeast Asiatic zone, and the Malaysian zone.

Indian zone

This zone can be divided latitudinally into three distinct parts – the sub-tropical flanks of the Himalayas, the Indian peninsula, and Sri Lanka. Essentially a meeting place of floras from the west, the north and the east, it includes an estimated 15,000 vascular plant species and about 140 endemic genera. The natural vegetation cover over much of India between the Himalayas, the Thar Desert and Western Ghats is tropical moist deciduous forest. On the Himalayan foothills of Assam and in the Western Ghats below 1,500 meters (4,900 feet) tropical semi-evergreen forests and subtropical broadleaved hill forests are found. The northeast of India up to 1,200 meters (3,900 feet), and the seaward side of the Western Ghats are covered in tropical evergreen rainforest, although it is mostly cleared below 500 meters (1,600 feet). In northern and central India at lower levels there is tropical dry deciduous forest with Teak and tropical moist deciduous forest with Sal. Sal is one of the most important lumber trees in India and Nepal, being used for buildings and in temples for carvings and decorative beams. Much of this forest is becoming depleted, although in some places in the Terai there are areas of pure Sal forest; cool attractive forests, devoid of

Right *When forests are cut in mountainous areas, such as in this Chaipur ridge region of eastern Nepal, erosion is often rapid and dramatic. The soil washed away impoverishes the mountainsides, and the excessive loads of silt carried by the rivers and streams can damage aquatic life.*

Left *Rice, seen here drying, is an important crop in many parts of the world. Throughout southern Asia, wetlands have been converted into rice paddies, and even steep hillsides are cleared and terraced to increase production. However, the deforestation may reduce the annual rainfall, and adequate water supplies are essential for rice cultivation.*

undergrowth and pleasant to walk in. In the south of India large areas of bamboo forest are found. Along the south coast of West Bengal and Bangladesh, particularly in the Sundarban region at the mouth of the Ganges, mangrove forests are extensive, covering 6,000 square kilometers (2,316 square miles).

Much of India's natural vegetation has been greatly modified by various forms of agriculture, forestry, and urbanization, although certain plant species are also threatened by natural causes such as landslides, floods, and droughts. Over half of the land area is cultivated, with rice being the principal crop. The estimated rate of deforestation of closed broadleaved tropical forests is 1,320 square kilometers (510 square miles) per annum out of a total of 460,440 square kilometers (177,740 square miles) although only just over half of this can be considered adequately stocked forest lands. All forests, particularly moist forest types, are being degraded rapidly as a result of population pressure and shifting cultivation. The widespread effects of this degradation include reduction in rainfall in some areas and flooding in others. For instance, at Mahabeleshwar south of Bombay, where the surrounding hills have been logged, annual rainfall has decreased from 1,000 centimeters (390 inches) a year to just over 600 centimeters (240 inches).

The more fertile parts of India have been so long and so densely inhabited by people that there is probably little of the original vegetation left. But overall, the Indian flora is an important and characteristic one. It contains many plants of commercial value, including important medicinal plants and a number of these are becoming rare through over-exploitation. The root of Kuth yields an essential oil on steam distillation, and resinoids on extraction with solvents. Both these products are highly priced, being in great demand in Western countries for blending high-class perfumes. The plant grows wild in Jammu and Kashmir states, mainly occurring in the Kishanganca valley and higher elevations of the Chenab valley. Because of the

Spotlight

- *Paphiopedilum druryi.* This orchid survives in cultivation but is endangered or extinct in the wild, not having been seen there since 1972. The causes of its decline have been forest fires, and excessive collecting.

- *Dendrobium pauciflorum.* Again endangered or possibly extinct, this orchid was recorded in the last century from two localities but a search in 1970 only revealed a single plant. At that time attempts to bring the plant into cultivation were unsuccessful.

- Indian Podophyllum *(Podophyllum hexandrum).* Formerly fairly widespread in India at an altitude of 2,000–3,000 meters (6,500–10,000 feet), this perennial is now under threat from commercial exploitation of its root for use in medicine.

- Rauwolfia *(Rauvolfia serpentina).* Once widely distributed in the sub-Himalayan tract from Hamachal Pradesh eastward to Sikkim and Bhutan, the plant is now under threat due to over-exploitation to obtain reserpine, a substance used in medicine.

Spotlight
- Blue Vanda *(Vanda coerulea)*. A victim of its own beauty, this orchid used to be widespread in the humid evergreen forests of northeastern India and northern parts of Burma and Thailand. Massive deforestation and commercial exploitation have brought it to the brink of extinction.
- *Merrillia caloxylon*. This plant has a restricted distribution, only occurring naturally in primary evergreen rainforest below 400 meters (1,300 feet), often in riparian forest. It has been exploited for its wood and is now facing extinction in the wild. First collected from southern Thailand in 1896, it is being cultivated successfully.
- *Ailanthus fordii*. This tree is rare in the wild, being originally known from only 10 specimens in one locality. Recent research has found further trees in nine localities.
- *Camellia crapnelliana*. A single specimen of this endangered tree was discovered in 1903 and was cut down. The species was then thought to be extinct until it was rediscovered in 1965 at the same locality.

threat to its survival in the wild from commercial exploitation, it is listed on appendix I of CITES, which means export cannot take place unless the plants are artificially propagated specimens. Indian Podophyllum is found in the Himalayas from Himachal Pradesh to Sikkim, and is also reported from Nepal, Afghanistan, Bhutan and China. The root was used in the past to treat intestinal worms and constipation. Now a semi-synthetic derivative from the root, Etoposide, has been found to be a first-class cytotoxic (cell-poisoning) agent and is used to treat cancer. Podophyllum plants in the wild are threatened by exploitation and growth of the species is slow, so export of the plant or roots is banned under Indian law. Another very important medicinal plant under threat is *Rauvolfia serpentina*, an age-old remedy in India for mental disorders. The alkaloid reserpine was isolated from it in 1952 and this is now used internationally as an effective remedy for hypertension and as a sedative or tranquillizing agent. The wild plants are protected in India by an order prohibiting export of live specimens and roots, and by listing on appendix II of CITES.

Indian plants are also threatened by over-collecting for horticulture; the orchids being particularly vulnerable. *Paphiopedilum druryi* was originally only known from a single locality in the state of Kerala and has been collected to extinction in southern India. It has not been seen in the wild since 1972, when collecting was particularly severe, but it is just possible that some rhizomes or seedlings may still remain. The orchid *Dendrobium pauciflorum*, an epiphyte reportedly found in riverine jungles, was recorded in the last century from two sites open to felling in West Bengal and Sikkim. It has not been seen in the wild since 1970 and is thought to be extinct, due to habitat destruction.

The flora of Sri Lanka has a high degree of endemism, about a third of native species being endemic. Most of Sri Lanka's best known plants are also found in India or elsewhere, but among the endemics are the Ebony, an important timber tree, and *Areca concinna*, a threatened palm. The palm occurs in a low swamp-like woodland along a backwater and there are only about 1,000 individuals in the population. The tree is at risk from changes in the drainage pattern that have occurred since the surrounding slopes were cleared of vegetation for agriculture.

Right *Mangroves, seen here in the Samunsan Reserve in Sarawak, Malaysia, are among the most productive habitats in the world. The network of roots and stems traps the falling leaves and silt, providing nutrients for the fish and other wildlife sheltering there.*

Far left Paphiopedilum druryi *is an orchid which survives in cultivation, but is almost certainly extinct in its native habitat in southern India. A re-introduction program is now planned.*

Left Paphiopedilum micranthum *was first described in 1951. Taken from its restricted habitat in south-east Yunnan and illegally exported from China, plants sold for up to 500 dollars a growth. By mid-1985 they were widely available for a few dollars a plant and had been exploited to the verge of extinction in the wild.*

Sino-Japanese zone

This includes the elevated area of the Sino-Himalayan-Tibetan mountains and the rest of China, except the south. Its flora is almost certainly the richest in the whole of the northern temperate zone and is especially abundant in trees. The total number of endemic genera is probably 300 or more. The Sino-Himalayan mountain system is the native land of many garden plants highly prized throughout the world. Their introduction to cultivation in the West took place mainly during the first few decades of the present century. Notable garden plants originating in this region include *Anemone japonica, Paulownia tomentosa, Jasminum nudiflorum, Kerria japonica, Lonicera nitida,* and *Morus alba.* The debt which the horticulturist owes to the plants of the Himalayas is well shown by *Cotoneaster frigidus, Gentiana farreri, Magnolia campbellii,* and *Meconopsis betonicifolia.*

Continental southeast Asiatic zone

This includes the Andaman and Nicobar islands, Burma, southern coastal China including Hainan and Taiwan, Thailand, and the northern part of the Malay peninsula. Its flora is comparable in luxuriance to that of Malaysia. Most of the important crop plants, rice, tea, and various citrus fruits, are believed to be natives of this region. The Nicobar islands have tropical broadleaved evergreen rainforest. Other vegetation on the Nicobars and on the Andaman islands consists of tropical evergreen rainforest, rich in *Dipterocarpus* and *Pterocarpus* species, tropical semi-evergreen rain forest and tropical moist deciduous forest. The remaining areas of rainforest are under severe pressure from logging and agriculture, particularly on the Andamans. The coastal areas of both support mangrove forests.

Over 40 per cent of Burma is covered by forest, mostly evergreen rainforest with some mixed deciduous forest containing teaks and dry dipterocarp forest in central Burma. These forests are under increasing pressure, especially in the lowlands. Southern coastal China is also rich in forest. Tropical evergreen rainforest covers the lowland parts of Yunnan and Guangdong provinces and the eastern side of Hainan island. Mangrove forests are found along the southern coasts, with temperate

Jasminum nudiflorum

Kerria japonica

Paulownia tomentosa

deciduous forests and subtropical evergreen and monsoon forest in the south. Evergreen, semi-evergreen, and mixed broadleaved deciduous forests occur on limestone in the tropical and subtropical areas of the south. The most extensive tracts of natural forest are in the northeast and southwest provinces of Sichuan and Yunnan. Probably more land has been recently afforested in China than in any other country in the world. Taiwan contains subtropical evergreen forests in the lowlands and broad-leaved evergreen forests at medium altitudes. There are mixed forests, coniferous forests and extensive grasslands at higher altitudes.

The tropical lowland evergreen rainforest which originally covered much of central and southern Thailand is now reduced to fragments in south peninsular Thailand. Mangroves are extensive along the western coast. Semi-evergreen forests dominated by the dipterocarp family are found in the interior and north of Thailand and below 1,000 meters (3,300 feet). On hills grow evergreen forests, but the largest area is covered by dry dipterocarp forest with bamboo, and mixed deciduous forests with teak. The teak forests are extensively logged or burned.

Malaysian zone

Probably nowhere else in the world, with the possible exception of parts of tropical America, do flowering plants attain such richness and luxuriance as in Malaysia, where conditions favor their fullest development in almost every way. The flora also

Below Rafflesia arnoldii *bears the largest flower in the world. It is a rainforest parasite and this one is growing on a Teliastigma vine. Its distribution is dependent on the distribution of the lianas which it parasitizes.*

contains many plants which are of value to people – indeed, the "Spice Islands," as part of the archipelago was called in earlier days, played a significant part in the history of many nations. The economic plants thought to have originated somewhere in Malaysia include Breadfruit, Nutmeg, and Ginger.

Climatic conditions throughout the Malay archipelago are in general constant. Nearly all the islands are heavily forested, tropical evergreen rainforest being the main natural vegetation. These forests are teeming with plant and animal species, being particularly rich in climbers, palms, and epiphytes, notably orchids. A major threat to the rainforests is the insatiable world hunger for wood, and forest loss is most severe in the countries with the finest lumber trees.

Other vegetation types include lowland dipterocarp forest, hill dipterocarp forest, and montane rainforest above, while semi-evergreen rainforest occurs in the far northwest of peninsular Malaysia. The rugged limestone hilltops of western Malaysia are relicts of an ancient calcareous mantle and have an extremely varied flora with numerous orchids. Many of the species are endemics with restricted distribution and are hence at great risk from habitat destruction. *Maxburretia rupicola* is a small palm confined to three limestone hilltops within 40 kilometers (25 miles) of Kuala Lumpur. It is threatened on one hand by quarrying and at risk on another from fires lit by climbers.

As the forests disappear, so too does a vast potential wealth of biological resources. On the Lesser Sunda islands, much of the original forest has been destroyed and valuable trees such as the East Indian Sandalwood have come close to extinction in the wild. Sandalwood has been used for 4,000 years to provide an aromatic oil, but with the increase in the European trade over the last century, the wild populations have become seriously threatened. Today, most of the oil to supply the perfume, cosmetic, and soap industries has to come from plantations.

The rattans are very important to the rural economy of southeast Asia, providing employment and a supplement to income from agriculture. These climbing palms with long flexible stems ascend the rainforest canopy using barbed whip-like growths on the ends of leaves. The best-quality canes for commercial use come from the genera *Calamus* and *Daemonorops*, mainly found in Malaysia and Indonesia. Rattans are usually harvested from the wild and are the second most important commercial product of the rainforest, after timber. After processing, they are made into furniture and other goods for export. If harvesting is well planned, rattans can be a renewable resource. However, over-harvesting of the highest quality long canes, particularly in the Indonesian forests, is damaging their long-term survival.

One of the most spectacular plants of Indonesia and Sumatra is *Rafflesia arnoldii*, which has the largest flower in the world, up to 1 meter (3¼ feet) or more in diameter when open. A parasitic plant, dependent on a climbing vine, it is found in mixed dipterocarp forests on moist valley bottoms or on steep but moist slopes. This plant is under threat from the destruction of nearby rainforest, collecting by novelty hunters and for use in medicine. Nature reserves have been created to protect it.

There are believed to be 3,000 to 4,000 species of orchid – twice the number of species in the whole of Britain's flora – in the area from mainland Malaysia to New Guinea. Many of these species are vulnerable due to deafforestation and over-collecting. The *Corybas* orchids are naturally rare because they have unusual habitat requirements. *Corybas fornicatus*, for example, is found only on sharply drained, mor humus banks on ridge tops in very humid montane forest, usually among mosses. It is now seriously endangered by the illegal cutting of firewood, and forest fires.

Spotlight

- *Abies densa*. This fir has a restricted distribution in Nepal, Bhutan, Assam, and Sikkim. It is threatened in Nepal by removal of forest for firewood and grazing land.

- Indian Gentian *(Gentiana kurro)*. Found in India and the northwest Himalayas, its population is scarce and declining due to the roots of the plants being collected for use in traditional medicine.

- Dove Tree *(Davidia involucrata)*. This plant is now widely cultivated but is becoming rare in the wild.

- Kuth *(Saussurea lappa)*. The distribution of this species ranges over Indian and Sino-Japanese zones with small populations in the northwest Himalayan region. It is threatened due to collection in the wild for its roots, from which essential oils are extracted.

- *Rafflesia arnoldii*. This rafflesia is endangered in the wild by destruction of the rainforest and collection of the plant for medicine and as a novelty.

- Rajah Pitcher Plant *(Nepenthes rajah)*. This was once so abundant at Pinasok in the Kinabalu reserve that the area was called Rajah kingdom. Now there are no pitcher plants to be seen.

- *Maxburretia rupicola*. A vulnerable palm confined to three limestone hilltops, its total population is probably below 1,000 individuals.

- *Corybas fornicatus*. The only known extant population is seriously endangered by fire and the cutting of firewood.

WILDLIFE

Tim and Carol Inskipp Tim monitors wildlife trade at the World Conservation Monitoring Centre in Cambridge, UK. Carol is a freelance writer and nature conservationist. They have a special interest in birds of Nepal and the Oriental region, and have visited a number of countries in the Orient studying birds and other wildlife. Together they have written a book on the distribution of birds in Nepal and Carol has written books on other aspects of Nepalese ornithology.

Below *A young female Tiger* (Panthera tigris) *which has just emerged from a swim. Although the tiger's decline, which was dramatic between the 1940s and 1960s, has slowed down or halted, its range is now fragmented and it is largely confined to isolated reserves and national parks.*

This region is characterized by its high species richness, Indonesia, for example, supporting 17 per cent of the world's bird species. This is partly due to the Himalayas, which have acted as an effective barrier between the Orient and Palearctic for the last 10 million years, encouraging speciation. Also, the tropical climate has provided ideal conditions for the evolution of a large number of endemic species.

Oriental animals and their habitats are now under severe pressure. In 1988, for instance, the International Council for Bird Preservation identified over 300 Oriental bird species which are globally threatened. The human population is rapidly increasing through almost the entire region. The consequent forest losses and deterioration are major threats as many animals are entirely dependent on this habitat for their survival. Other serious problems are wetland drainage, overgrazing by domestic stock, hunting for food and the live animal trade, and pollution.

The Oriental region is divided into the Indian subcontinent, the Indochinese subregion, the Sundaic subregion and islands between the Orient and Australasia.

The Indian subcontinent

A major factor helping to maintain the subcontinent's wealth of animal life is the influence of culture and religion. Most people in India, Nepal, Bhutan, and Sri Lanka are Hindus or Buddhists. Those who adhere strictly to these religions do no deliberate harm to any living creature. Animals are closely associated with Hindu gods, such as

the Naga or snake with Shiva and Vishnu, and the elephant which forms the head of Ganesh, the god of wisdom. Buddhist stories frequently describe the noble qualities of animals, such as the elephant, as examples to people. Cows are sacred to Hindus and huge numbers of them live in every habitat in India, being allowed to forage wherever they like unharmed and consuming vast amounts of vegetation. In addition, concern for the environment and an appreciation of the value of wildlife as a natural heritage are growing. In India, the Chipko Andolan movement protects natural forests and encourages the planting of native trees. This grassroots movement is led by women of the Chipko community and has gained widespread support.

There are numerous protected areas covering 3 per cent of India, 7 per cent of Nepal, and as much as 20 per cent of Bhutan. Conflicts between local people and park staff are, however, increasing and now pose serious threats to many reserves. In India, almost every protected area is surrounded by hostile people living at subsistence level. Many depend on forests for their vital daily needs, for example obtaining their food by hunting game and collecting roots, wild fruits, vegetables, and honey, or practicing shifting cultivation. It has recently been widely recognized that the long-term future of protected areas can only be assured if the people around have a vested interest in them. The history of Project Tiger in India illustrates the conflicts between parks and people, and the attempts being made to resolve them.

The Tiger is the national animal of both India and Bangladesh. This magnificent predator occurs in most Oriental countries but the main population is in the Indian subcontinent. Aptly called "the spirit of the jungle," the Tiger inhabits all types of forest and was formerly found almost throughout India. In 1970, a census revealed that the Indian population of the species had fallen alarmingly from an estimated 40,000 in 1930 to about 1,800 animals. The causes were loss of forest, excessive hunting and the soaring prices of skins on the international market. Counts in other countries also showed serious declines with evidence of only about 5,000 Tigers throughout its huge range. To meet this crisis, Project Tiger was launched in 1972, leading to the banning of Tiger hunting and the establishment of Tiger reserves throughout the subcontinent.

Recent surveys in India have produced estimates that the population has more than doubled since 1970, although some experts believe these figures are exaggerated by as much as 25 per cent. In any case, the future of the Tiger is still very uncertain. The destruction of its forest habitat outside reserves is accelerating. Zoologists believe that a contiguous population of at least 500 Tigers is necessary to maintain an adequate gene pool but, with the exception of that in the Sundarbans in northeast India and Bangladesh, all known populations are less than this. The smaller reserves now hold the maximum number of Tigers they can support, forcing some animals to hunt outside reserves, where they come into conflict with surrounding villagers. At the same time acute lack of fodder and firewood have increasingly forced local people to enter reserves illegally. Violent incidents have occurred, such as at Ranthambhore where people illegally grazing stock stoned a forest patrol, causing the death of a forester in 1984. A non-governmental foundation has since been set up there to improve the conditions of the local people. This has provided, for example, a mobile

Above *A Golden Langur* (Presbytis geei) *high in a Flame of the Forest tree in the Manas Reserve, Bhutan. This langur was first discovered in 1953, and its range is restricted to Bhutan and adjacent Assam, India.*

clinic and a forestry farm. Similar projects are being developed to help people who live around other protected areas that are under pressure.

The Tiger reserves created have also helped to protect many other threatened animals, such as the beautiful Golden Langur at Manas. Amazingly, this large diurnal primate was not described until 1956. It has a very restricted range in the mixed deciduous forests of northwest Assam and Bhutan.

Another Assamese speciality at risk is the Great Indian Rhinoceros, the main population of which occurs in the tall grasslands of Kaziranga National Park. Since ancient times, rhinos have been highly prized as sources of medicines. Rhino horn sells at huge prices on the international market and is still found in some Far Eastern pharmacies. Rhino numbers were severely reduced earlier this century by excessive hunting, but with protection and the creation of national parks, they have now increased substantially. They are even exceeding the carrying capacity of

Right *The Great Indian or One-horned Rhinoceros* (Rhinoceros unicornis) *was widespread from northern Pakistan to Thailand in the Middle Ages. By the 1950s the world population had fallen to around 400, but with protection it has risen to over 1,000, mostly in India.*

some parks. For example, at the Royal Chitwan National Park in central Nepal, rhinos frequently leave the park at night to maraud the crops of local villagers. To try and overcome the problem of overcrowding and to create new centers of population, a small number of rhinos have been transferred from Assam to Dudhwa National Park in Uttar Pradesh, northern India, and from Chitwan to the Royal Bardia National Park in far west Nepal. Whether the rhino will become established at these new sites remains to be seen.

Assam's grasslands are a stronghold for the Bengal Florican, one of the world's most endangered bustards. This florican is also recorded in Nepal, Bangladesh, and Cambodia, and has recently been rediscovered in Vietnam. Its reputation of being one of the most delicious game birds in India must have contributed to its early decline. Also, much of its habitat has been claimed for agriculture and most of the remaining grasslands are burned annually to encourage the growth of a new flush of grass for grazing herbivores and for thatching. Another inhabitant of these grasslands, Finn's Baya Weaver, is now extremely local with disjunct populations in northwest India and Assam.

To the north of Assam's lowland grasslands lie the Himalayas, the highest and youngest mountain chain in the world. The Himalayas are rich in species of

DISTRIBUTION
TIGER

Range 100 years ago

Range today

Range of Tiger (Panthera tigris). *Formerly Tigers were very common. We do not know exactly how many there were, but 40,000 were estimated to occur in the Indian subcontinent in the early part of this century. By 1989 there were only 4,300 in India and the world population totalled between 6,500 and 9,000 Tigers.*

pheasants, including the gorgeously plumed Western Tragopan and the extremely skulking Cheer Pheasant. These species frequent temperate forests in the western part of the range, and both are endangered by deforestation and hunting. The Lesser or Red Panda is another seriously threatened inhabitant of temperate Himalayan forests. Little is known of this charming animal, mainly because of its nocturnal habits. A recent study in Langtang National Park in Nepal revealed that it is particularly susceptible to human disturbance as well as to loss of its forest habitat.

Invertebrates in the Himalayas are also suffering from deforestation. These include a dragonfly *Epiophlebia laidlawi*, a species surviving from the Mesozoic era and now known only from the eastern Himalayas in India and Nepal. One of the most spectacular of the butterflies is the Kaiser-I-Hind which has been recorded in Nepal over thickly wooded hills in the temperate zone. It also occurs in Sikkim, Arunachal Pradesh, and Burma.

The Snow Leopard (see p.36) occurs mainly north of the Himalayan range, but many people associate it with these mountains. Despite protection, it is widely hunted for its beautiful pelt. However, the reduction in the population of its natural prey, mainly wild sheep, is considered to be a much larger threat to its survival.

The great Indian or Thar desert in northwest India and Pakistan is home to the Blackbuck. Regarded as sacred by Indians, this attractive antelope is widely illustrated in Indian paintings and sculptures and its skin is used in religious ceremonies. It was formerly common in the desert, but hunting, competition for grazing from the constantly increasing population of domestic cattle, and the spread of cultivation have reduced its population to disjunct pockets. The most outstanding bird on the Thar desert is the stately Great Indian Bustard, the males of which stand more than a meter (3¼ feet) tall and weigh up to 14 kilograms (31 pounds). It is confined to the Indian subcontinent and is now rare. Hunting, egg collecting, loss of thorn scrub and the extension of agriculture have all contributed to its decline. Considerable efforts are being made to save the bird and by 1989, eight sanctuaries and several conservation areas had been set up for its protection.

Wildlife is abundant in the less-populated areas of the Deccan, the great plateau in peninsular India, notably at Kanha National Park. The park's speciality is

Above left *The Lesser or Red Panda* (Ailurus fulgens) *is found in temperate forests of the Himalayas above 1,500 meters (5,000 feet). They spend the day asleep high in the trees, descending at dusk to feed. They have been sought after for their rich soft pelt and were also popular as pets.*

Above *A Swamp Deer or Barasingha* (Cervus duvauceli) *with a Black Drongo on its rump. The Swamp Deer has large splaying hooves to enable it to walk in its swampy habitat. There are probably fewer than 4,000 in the wild, but there are substantial populations breeding in zoos.*

Right *A male Lion-tailed Macaque or Wanderoo* (Macaca silenus). *Around 400 survive in the tropical forests of the Western Ghats of southern India. Their habitat has been drastically reduced by encroaching agriculture and attempts have been made to build hydroelectric dams in the Silent valley, one of their remaining strongholds.*

DISTRIBUTION
MUGGER

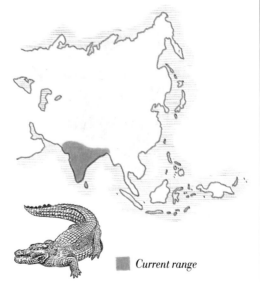

■ *Current range*

Range of Mugger (Crocodylus palustris). *Although the range of this crocodile has not substantially changed, its numbers have been heavily depleted in most areas and it has disappeared from many of its former haunts.*

the Swamp Deer or Barasingha which has suffered drastic declines, mainly because of losses of its tall, swampy grassland habitat. The Barasingha is confined to India and Nepal, and the central Indian subspecies is almost entirely restricted to Kanha. In recent years grasslands have been increased in the park through the relocation of villages and the Barasingha is now steadily increasing there.

In Andhra Pradesh on the eastern side occurred perhaps the most exciting ornithological event in India in recent times – the rediscovery of Jerdon's Courser. This bird had been recorded only rarely since its discovery and not at all in this century. Then, after intensive searching, a specimen was spotted one night in 1986 in a headlight. Virtually nothing is known about the bird's ecology, chiefly because of its nocturnal behavior.

The humid, dense forests of the Western Ghats and the other south Indian hills support a richer fauna than the adjoining dry Deccan, including some species which are restricted to them, such as the handsome Lion-tailed Macaque. Once widely traded for zoos, this macaque is now considered endangered and given full protection. Another endemic mammal of the southern Indian hills is the Nilgiri Tahr, a wild goat restricted to rock and grass-covered slopes above the tree line. Like the Lion-tailed Macaque, it is suffering from fragmentation and reduction of its habitat.

The island of Sri Lanka has as many as 21 endemic bird species, eight of which are considered at risk. Many of the endemic species, including the endangered Ashy-headed Laughing-thrush, are dependent on undisturbed dense forests.

The drainage of wetlands and pollution are threatening many birds in the subcontinent. The majestic Siberian Crane has only two remaining widely separated breeding areas. The great majority of the western population now winters at the Keoladeo Ghana National Park in northern India. The crane undergoes a very long hazardous migration of over 6,000 kilometers (3,700 miles) and, in addition, faces the dangers of shooting or trapping by professional crane-hunters in Pakistan.

Several species of storks have markedly declined, notably the Greater Adjutant, the largest of India's storks. It occurred widely from India east to Vietnam but it has either disappeared or become extremely rare over much of its former range. The only known breeding population of the species now seems to be in Assam. Similarly, the Spot-billed Pelican was once widespread in Asia, but has suffered severe declines and now breeds only in southeast India and Sri Lanka. Pallas's Fish Eagle may be found at large heronries, such as Keoladeo Ghana where it feeds on waterbirds and fish. It, too, is now thinly distributed and declining.

In large rivers in the north of the subcontinent, such as the Ganges and Brahmaputra, lives the Ganges Susu, a small dolphin about 2 meters (6½ feet) long. It is vulnerable to the construction of dams which have fragmented populations and to accidental trapping in fishing nets. Two other threatened aquatic predators are the crocodiles, the Mugger and the Gharial. The Mugger is virtually confined to the subcontinent and can live in all types of freshwater habitats from large rivers to pools. It was once common, but hunting has reduced it to a few protected areas and rivers. The Gharial is restricted to rivers of the subcontinent where it feeds almost entirely on fish. The combined pressures of hunting and the damming of rivers nearly caused the Gharial's extinction. Fortunately, both species breed well in captivity and many hundreds have been released back into the wild.

The most extraordinary endangered species of the region must be the Sacred Mud Turtle. The entire population of up to 200 turtles lives in one large artificial

Left *The Siberian Crane* (Grus leucogeranus) *has only two known breeding grounds, both in the USSR. It migrates to Bharatpur, India, where these were photographed, Iran and China. The population in China was discovered comparatively recently and numbers nearly 2,000.*

Below *The Gharial* (Gavialis gangeticus) *is a highly specialized fish-eating crocodilian. Once on the brink of extinction, it has been saved by a comprehensive captive breeding program followed by reintroductions.*

pond associated with an Islamic shrine near Chittagong in southeast Bangladesh.

A number of reptiles and amphibians have suffered because of their commercial value. The Six-fingered Frog is one of several large frogs, millions of which have been caught in the subcontinent so that their legs can be severed and exported to Europe as a delicacy. A recent export ban in India may have removed the main threat to the species. India also exported a huge number of snakeskins for many years, and this export was banned in 1976. However, the internal trade continues and skins are still illegally exported. Populations of several species have been depleted as a result, including the Indian Python, the Oriental Rat Snake, and the Asian Cobra.

Indochinese subregion

This area extends from Burma through southern China east to Taiwan and south to Thailand, Cambodia, and Vietnam. In addition to habitat damage and losses, successive wars and hunting pressures encouraged by a proliferation of firearms have devastated wildlife in parts of Indochina.

One of the best known animals in the Orient is the now-endangered Asian Elephant, closely linked there with mythology, religion, and culture. It once had a huge range, extending as far west as the Tigris and Euphrates, north in China to the Chang Jiang river and south to Sumatra. Unlike its African counterpart, the Asian Elephant has been used extensively by people over the centuries for any jobs requiring enormous strength, such as the felling of trees and the transportation of

Below *An Asiatic or Indian Elephant* (Elephas maximus) *in the Galoya National Park, Sri Lanka. The Asiatic Elephant's tusks are small or absent, probably as a result of selection by human hunters over thousands of years.*

logs. The earliest records of tame elephants in the Indian subcontinent date back to the third millenium BC. Although once abundant, its numbers are now severely reduced and all populations are fragmented to some degree. Habitat loss is the most serious threat and poaching for ivory is also a major problem.

The Leopard is another very widespread Oriental species at risk. Formerly it ranged throughout much of Africa and from the Near and Middle East to Siberia and south to Java. A highly adaptable animal, the Leopard will inhabit high mountains and coasts, tropical forests and deserts. Despite this, most of the Leopard's Asian populations are now endangered as a result of persecution over centuries for its valuable skin.

The major factor causing the decline of the Asiatic Black Bear is forest destruction. Other threats are the persecution of bears as pests, over-hunting for sport and the capture of live bears for trade. The Asiatic Black Bear had a wide range in

Asia's forested hills and mountains, from the Soviet Far East south to Thailand, Vietnam, and Cambodia, and west to Pakistan. Its numbers are now greatly reduced and it no longer occurs in many parts of its former range.

The Musk Deer is also widely distributed in the montane forests of Asia. This deer is intensively hunted for musk, a secretion produced by glands of the male, and used in perfume and Chinese medicine. As a result the species is rapidly diminishing, and musk has become one of the most valuable animal products in the world. Musk can, however, be extracted without killing the deer and farms have been set up in China for this purpose. Another animal of the forested mountains is the Common Goral, a goat antelope with short horns. It occurs from the Himalayas east to Burma, northern Thailand and north through eastern China to southeast Siberia, but is declining in many areas because of hunting for sport.

The three Asian species of pangolins (scaly anteaters) are threatened by heavy trapping for their scales and for their flesh, which is considered a delicacy. All occur in Indochina: the Chinese Pangolin in forested mountains from Nepal east to southern China and Hainan, the Indian Pangolin in the Indian subcontinent and China, and the Malayan Pangolin with a range extending into the Sundaic subregion.

Deforestation is the chief threat to numerous montane forest bird species in

Left *The Indian Pangolin* (Manis crassicaudata) *is hunted extensively for its scales, which consist of compressed hair and are similar in structure to the horn of rhinos. The scales are used in Oriental medicine, as is the pangolin's blood which is believed to cure internal bleeding.*

DISTRIBUTION
ASIAN ELEPHANT

■ *Present distribution*

□ *Former distribution*

Range of Asian or Indian Elephant (Elephas maximas). *No early estimates were made of the population of the Asian Elephant, but it has undoubtedly suffered a dramatic decline. Only 34,000 to 54,000 Asian Elephants now survive, a significantly lower figure than the total number of African Elephants.*

Indochina. For example, the Giant Nuthatch, the largest of a family of small birds, now has a very restricted range. It is rare and local in Thailand, its status in Burma is unknown, and there is only a single record from China.

Below and to the south of the subregion's montane forests lie luxuriant, species-rich tropical rainforests. Hornbills are characteristic birds of these forests. They are particularly vulnerable to deforestation because they feed on fruit and small animals in the canopy and so require mature trees. Also, their relatively large size makes them susceptible to hunting. The Rufous-necked Hornbill which used to occur from Nepal east to Vietnam is one of the most threatened. It is now probably extinct in Nepal, declining in India, and vulnerable in the rest of its range.

One of the most impressive animals of the tropical forests is the Gaur, huge wild cattle which may have horns as long as a meter (3¼ feet) and weigh up to 1,000 kilograms (2,200 pounds). The Gaur was once found from India east to southern China and south to peninsular Malaysia but now it only survives in disjunct populations. Its numbers have been seriously diminished by extensive forest losses, indiscriminate hunting and diseases caught from domestic cattle. Another Indochinese species of wild cattle is the Kouprey, one of the world's rarest and least known mammals. The Kouprey's range is centred on Cambodia and extends into southern Laos, eastern Thailand and Vietnam. Its numbers are unknown but are believed to be very low. Prolonged warfare in much of its range, hunting for food and its horns, and a naturally low reproductive rate have all contributed to its decline.

The wetlands of Indochina harbor some fascinating endangered species. The

Below *A young male Gaur* (Bos gaurus) *in India. This cattle has been domesticated and there are feral as well as wild populations, including around 50,000 in Arunachal Pradesh, India. The gaur is threatened by habitat loss and hunting, and also by cattle diseases.*

Baiji is a river dolphin restricted to limited sections of the Chang Jiang river and its tributaries. Accidental drowning in fishing nets, collisions with ships' propellers, and water pollution are the chief causes of its decline. The same river is home to another endangered Chinese endemic, the Chinese Alligator. Local people persecute the alligator because it eats their fish and domestic fowl. In addition, land reclamation and irrigation works seriously damage its habitat. In order to try and save the alligator a breeding center has been set up, and this has already succeeded in artificially rearing significant numbers.

Also confined to China is the Chinese Giant Salamander, which frequents mountain streams at over 1,000 meters (3,300 feet) in the center and southwest. The world's largest living salamander, growing up to 180 centimeters (71 inches) long, is considered a great delicacy and so has become highly endangered.

The Giant Catfish is one of the world's largest catfish, reaching a length of about 3 meters (10 feet) and a weight of 300 miles (660 pounds). It reportedly migrates several thousand miles from Cambodia to spawning grounds in southern China and is thus seriously affected by dams which prevent it from moving upstream. In addition, it is valued for its size and high-quality flesh and so is threatened by overfishing.

Hunting also threatens the enigmatic White-eyed River Martin and may have already caused this bird's demise. It has not been recorded since 1980, despite intensive searching at its only known locality, Bung Boraphet, the largest freshwater marsh in Thailand. The roosting Barn Swallows, with which it associated in winter, have reduced in number from hundreds of thousands to fewer than 10,000 as a result of bird trapping and reed-harvesting.

Sundaic subregion

This comprises the Malay peninsula and the islands of Borneo, Bali, Java and Sumatra, and overlaps with the Indochinese subregion to the north in southern Thailand, Cambodia and Vietnam. All of these territories stand on a shallow continental shelf that once formed a large peninsula known as Sundaland which had a characteristic fauna. Much of Sundaland is now flooded, but many of its animals are still confined to the remaining land masses. Unlike in India and Indochina, there have been no long-term feelings of sympathy for wildlife based on religious beliefs. So in some of these countries animals are suffering from even more severe persecution, as well as habitat loss.

One of the animals restricted to the area is the endangered Orang Utan, Asia's great ape. It now only occurs in Sumatra and Borneo, but historically it ranged through lowland forests north to China. The gibbons, close relatives of the Orang Utan, are confined to the forests of the Orient, and all gibbon species are declining. Among those most at risk is the Siamang, a denizen of montane forests in Malaysia and Sumatra. The numbers of both it and the Orang Utan have been drastically reduced by logging and shifting cultivation. Hunting for food and, formerly, collection of live animals for trade also contributed to the decline of the Orang Utan. These apes are superbly adapted to life in trees, the gibbons swinging on their long arms and the Orang Utan climbing adeptly using its flexible toes.

Another threatened primate is the Slow Loris, which occurs from India south to Java. It spends all its time in the trees, but has adapted to a variety of habitats including tropical forests, secondary forest growth and plantations. Loss of cover and, in Indonesia, hunting for use in medicines are causing problems for this species.

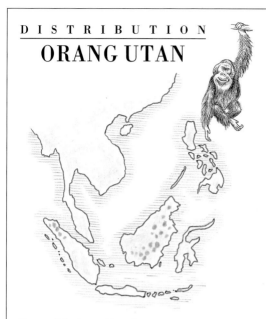

DISTRIBUTION
ORANG UTAN

Range of the Orang Utan (Pongo pygmaeus). *Once found throughout Indo-China, Malaysia and north to China, the Orang Utan is now confined to Sumatra and Borneo where its range is contining.*

Above *An old male Orang Utan* (Pongo pygmaeus) *in Kalimantan, Borneo. They also occur on Sumatra and were once more widespread, ranging north to China. Their decline may be due to malaria.*

Right *The Slow Loris* (Nycticebus coucang) *is a nocturnal primate found in forests over much of southeast Asia. They are threatened mainly by habitat destruction and are also hunted locally for use in traditional medicine.*

DISTRIBUTION
SUMATRAN RHINO

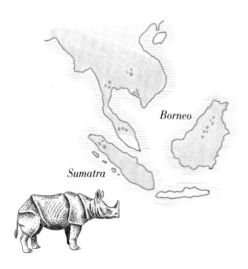

Borneo

Sumatra

■ *19th century distribution*

■ *Current distribution*

Range of Sumatran Rhinoceros (Didermocerus sumatrensis). *The numbers of the Sumatran Rhinoceros have been drastically reduced to several hundred animals in total, occurring in scattered and isolated populations.*

The giant squirrels (*Ratufa*) are all confined to the Orient. They leap from tree to tree, hardly ever coming to the ground, and so are dependent on tall trees which are often selectively logged. Other animals are particularly vulnerable to deforestation because they require primary rainforest. One such, the Asian Tapir, is now reduced to isolated populations throughout its historical range which extends from this region into Indochina. Over-hunting and capture of live animals for trade have had additional impacts on the species. The Clouded Leopard is also vulnerable to the loss of primary forest, and hunting for its beautiful skin. It is now thought to be rare throughout its wide range which extends from Sumatra to Nepal. Little is known about this very secretive cat.

The White-winged Wood Duck lives in primary evergreen forest ranging from lowland swamps to hill forests. However, it can survive in other forests if remnant patches of primary or old dense secondary forest are allowed to remain. It is now rare and restricted to northeast India, Bangladesh, southwest Thailand, probably Burma, and Sumatra. The largest surviving population is likely to occur in Sumatra, but much of the bird's habitat there is being converted to agriculture and settlements.

The wildlife of lowland rainforests is especially at risk because these forests are the most accessible to people and so are the first to be cleared. Gurney's Pitta, one of the rarest birds in the Orient, is probably confined to tiny pockets of lowland forest in peninsular Thailand. In addition the pittas are threatened by trapping for the cage-bird trade. Some localities are now being actively protected to try and guarantee the survival of this beautiful bird.

The highly endangered Javan Rhinoceros has suffered from the extensive clearance of lowland forests combined with relentless hunting. Once it was widespread and often common, occurring from northeast India east through Indochina and south to Java. Now there are only two known populations, in Java and Vietnam, and both are too small to be sustainable. Its relative, the Sumatran Rhinoceros (Asiatic Two-horned Rhinoceros) is threatened chiefly by the high demand for its horn and other organs. Only disjunct populations survive in this rhino's original large range from Assam east to Vietnam and south to Sumatra. Sadly, much suitable habitat remains unoccupied in protected areas.

Wetland habitats are also very vulnerable to destruction. Overfishing. river dredging and clearance of swamp forest severely threaten the Asian Arowana. a primitive fish confined to tropical freshwaters of the Orient. It apparently no longer occurs in Thailand, but still occurs in Vietnam, Cambodia, Malaya, and Sumatra. Chinese people consider that it brings good luck to their homes and large specimens are extremely valuable. Hunting for hides and live specimens is largely responsible for the decline of the Siamese Freshwater Crocodile. Formerly it occurred in Java. Borneo and southern Indochina, but now there is only one known surviving wild population, at Bung Boraphet in central Thailand, and that is small and decreasing.

The spectacular Milky Stork inhabits coastal mangroves in Cambodia. the Malay peninsula, Sumatra, Java, and Sulawesi. Very little was known about its status until 1984, when surveys revealed that it is suffering seriously from mangrove destruction, hunting, and disturbance at its nesting colonies.

The chief threat to the Bali Starling. the only bird endemic to Bali. is trapping for trade. In 1987 the captive population totalled about 10,000 birds. but less than 20 survived in the wild in 1990. Although captive-bred Bali Starlings are now being reintroduced, this will require a long-term effort.

Below left Until 1986, Gurney's Pitta (Pitta gurneyi) was believed to be extinct. A small population was then discovered in southern Thailand but it is critically endangered by deforestation.

Below Forest destruction and hunting have drastically reduced the numbers of the Green Peafowl (Pavo muticus). Once a common bird extending as far as northeast India, it is now rare or locally extinct throughout its range. It is similar in appearance to the more familiar Indian Peafowl but is generally green instead of blue and occurs in more dense forest.

At the southern extremity of the subregion lies Christmas Island. the breeding site of two threatened seabirds. Abbott's Booby and the Christmas Frigatebird. Mining for phosphate has destroyed much of the rainforest used by the booby for nesting, while its low reproductive rate is also a problem. A national park which encompasses 30 per cent of the nesting sites has been created. but whether the reduced population will be viable in the long term is not known. None of the breeding colonies of the Christmas Frigatebird is protected, so these birds remain vulnerable to harvesting for food, disturbance, and habitat loss.

The transition zone

This includes a large number of islands, in Indonesia from Lombok east to the Kai islands, and north to the Talaud islands. The Philippines are also in this account. People have had devastating effects on the big game animals in many areas, particularly in recent years when firearms have been more readily available.

Sulawesi has a fairly high percentage of forests remaining and a reasonable system of protected areas. However, in the Philippines and the Lesser Sundas 80 per

Sulawesi

Sulawesi has an exceptionally high level of endemism. Of the 130 mammal species, comprising 70 bats and 40 rodents, around 60 per cent are confined to the area. An additional 13 mammal species have yet to be described for science. There are 265 resident bird species of which 28 per cent are endemic, including eight parrots, eight doves, six owls, six kingfishers, and a flightless rail. At least 120 species of reptiles occur there, of which about 30 are endemic, including 17 snakes and 13 lizards. There are only 25 indigenous species of amphibians but 19 of them are endemic.

Below *The Maleo* (Macrocephalon maleo) *is confined to Sulawesi. It breeds communally, laying its eggs in forest clearings heated by geothermal activity. The main threats are egg collectors in local villages and predation by dogs.*

Below right *The Nicobar Pigeon* (Caloenas nicobarica) *occurs from the Indian Nicobar and Andaman islands east through Indonesia and the Philippines to Papua New Guinea and the Solomon islands. Little is known about its status, since most of these islands are little studied, but it is believed to have declined dramatically in many parts of its range.*

cent of the natural vegetation has been destroyed, mainly for agricultural purposes, and many forest species are now threatened by fragmentation or complete loss of their habitat. Some of the islands that are particularly rich in endemic species, such as Sumba, have little forest remaining and virtually no protected areas. This island, in common with most islands in the Lesser Sundas, suffers frequent human-made fires and is now mainly covered by species-poor grassy hills.

The Philippines have an exceptionally high number of endemic animals, including about 60 per cent of the mammals and about 40 per cent of the resident birds. Illegal logging and hunting are the main threats throughout the majority of the inhabited islands. Most of the endemic mammals are poorly known rodents and bats. The larger species include the Tamaraw, a water buffalo confined to three montane areas in Mindoro and severely reduced by hunting and destruction of its forest habitat. Protection in recent years has allowed it to increase in numbers but habitat loss is still a threat. It has potential for domestication which could benefit the local people. The Calamian Deer, restricted mainly to Busuanga and Culion in the south-west Philippines, has also been over-hunted despite complete protection.

The best known endemic bird and also one of the most threatened is the Philippine Eagle. This huge powerful bird requires extensive tracts of forest to survive and such habitat has now almost disappeared within its range. Its best hope lies in an education program which is slowly changing the local people's prejudice against birds of prey. Other threatened birds include the Philippine Cockatoo, once widespread throughout the archipelago but now rarely seen anywhere because of over-collection for the pet trade; and the brightly colored Whiskered Pitta, which has perhaps always been rare in its steep oak forest habitat in northern Luzon. Little is known about the status of other Philippine vertebrates, apart from the Sailfin Lizard and Gray's Monitor which are threatened by habitat loss and trapping.

Two swallowtail butterflies are listed as threatened, including the Luzon Peacock Swallowtail, a fairly large greenish-black species, the hindwings of which are margined with a striking pattern of red, purple and blue. It was first described as recently as 1965, and occurs only in a restricted montane area of northern Luzon where it is threatened by collectors. At one time it was so valuable that the sale of a few specimens in Japan paid for the costs of a return trip to Luzon!

Sulawesi also has a high level of endemism, with about 60 per cent of the mammal species, about 28 per cent of the resident birds, and approximately 30 per

Left *Komodo Dragons* (Varanus komodoensis) *in the national park on the island of Komodo, Indonesia. They are the largest lizards in the world, growing to nearly 4 meters (12 feet), and feed on animals up to the size of pigs and deer. Because they are confined to Komodo and a few adjacent areas, they are vulnerable to hunting, collecting and other threats.*

cent of the reptiles restricted to the area. Two of the mammal species are anoas or dwarf water buffalo. Both the Highland and Lowland Anoas are suffering from hunting pressures except in some well-protected reserves. The curious-looking Babirusa is a fairly large pig that has declined in many areas because of hunting. The Sulawesi Palm Civet inhabits primary forests, feeding mainly on palm fruits and small mammals. Once considered extremely rare it has recently been found to occur more widely, and its prospects are considered reasonable given proper management.

The Maleo is an unusual bird that buries its eggs in warm sand and leaves them to hatch in the sun's heat. The large eggs are a delicacy sought after by people and dogs, and the species can now only survive with active management of its breeding areas. The Satanic Nightjar is known only from one specimen. Its name is due to a frequently heard nocturnal "plip-plop" call, believed by the local people to be the sound of the bird taking out a person's eyes.

The Lesser Sundas have fewer endemic species than Sulawesi and fewer species that are considered to be threatened. Of its 23 species of threatened birds, the six that occur on Timor are perhaps most at risk as they all seem to be confined to small pockets of highly disturbed lowland forest. One of these, the attractive Orange-banded Thrush, also occurs on Wetar, which has apparently not been visited by an ornithologist for over 70 years! The status there of this species and two endemic honeyeaters is completely unknown. The Komodo Monitor (or Dragon), mainly restricted to the island of Komodo, is the most spectacular threatened animal of the area. It is the world's largest lizard at about 3 meters (10 feet) long and it regularly attacks animals up to the size of water buffalo, but is not averse to carrion. It was threatened by capture for zoos until it received increased protection. The main problem remaining is fire in its savanna habitat.

Animals of the Moluccas causing concern include some of the 69 endemic birds. The majority of the nine parrots there have been heavily exploited for the pet trade. The cockatoos, particularly the Salmon-crested, are especially vulnerable because of their low reproductive rates. Up to 10,000 Salmon-crested Cockatoos have been exported annually from Seram in recent years, despite the bird's extremely small range. International trade was banned in January 1990. The Purple-naped Lory is a small, brightly colored parrot restricted to a narrow altitudinal band on Seram and Ambon. It has been totally protected for some years but still appears in the trade in small numbers.

Spotlight

● The Bengal Florican *(Houbaropsis bengalensis)* is the rarest bustard in the world with a current population of only 350 to 400 birds. Once fairly common over much of its range from northwest Uttar Pradesh in India, east through the lowlands of Nepal and northeast India to Bangladesh and in Cambodia and Vietnam, it is now confined to a few isolated pockets.

● In the past, the Bali Starling *(Leucopsar rothschildi)* had a restricted distribution, only occurring on the 300-square kilometer (116-square mile) island of Bali in Indonesia. Now this has diminished to less than 50 square kilometers (19 square miles) encompassed by the Bali Barat National Park and its wild population was less than 20 in 1990.

● The Musk Deer *(Moschus)* was originally widespread throughout the forested mountains of Asia including those of the USSR, Korea, China, the Himalayas, and northern Vietnam. Although its overall range is little changed, the population is reduced to disjunct pockets.

CORAL REEFS

Sue Wells has a zoology degree from Cambridge University and is a freelance consultant, specializing in tropical marine conservation. She worked at IUCN for ten years, initially as co-author of the IUCN Invertebrate Red Data Book and subsequently as compiler and editor of a three-volume reference work *Coral Reefs of the World*. Sue is currently involved in the Greenpeace Pacific Campaign; the work of the Coral Reef Team of the UK-based Marine Conservation Society, and various marine projects with IUCN.

Coral reefs are among the most productive ecosystems on Earth and can be thought of as the marine equivalents of tropical rainforests. They are also among the oldest ecosystems, having existed for some 450 million years. Reefs are unique in having their basic framework constructed by animals. Each tiny coral animal, called a polyp, secretes a stony cup around itself. The polyps grow and divide to form colonies, some rounded as in brain corals, others branching as in staghorn corals. The living coral colonies form a veneer on the accumulated skeletons of dead coral and so gradually build up into reefs.

Fringing reefs are the youngest type of reef, and develop along the edges of continents and islands, such as those along the coast of east Africa. When changes in sea level separate a fringing reef from the coast, it may form a barrier reef, such as the Great Barrier Reef of Australia which is so large that it is visible from the Moon. If an island "sinks", its fringing reef may evolve into an atoll reef forming a circle with a lagoon in the center. The word "atoll" originated in the Maldives of the Indian Ocean, which are made up entirely of atolls with some of the richest coral reefs in the world.

Essential to the reefs are tiny algae (plants) which live within the coral tissues and use the sun's energy to manufacture food for themselves and for the coral. The algae are responsible for the colors of many corals, but also contribute to the vulnerability of reefs. Algae need plentiful sunlight, so silty or polluted water is

Above *When exposed by the tide, as in Upolu, western Samoa, coral reefs look dull and stony yet they teem with life beneath the sea.*

Right *Reefs are one of the most colorful ecosystems in the world, as can be seen in this general view of a reef in the Red Sea.*

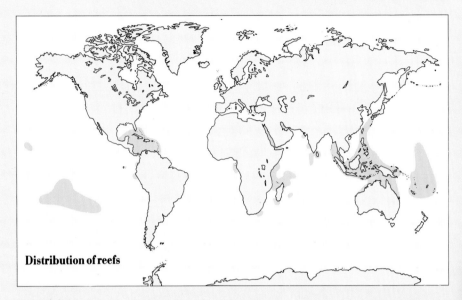

Distribution of reefs

Left *Reefs cover an estimated minimum area of 230,000 square miles (600,000 square kilometers), extending out of the tropics only where there are warm currents.*

Below *The Copper Band Butterfly Fish* (Chelmon rostratus), *has the bright colors typical of many coral reef fish. Its gill covers are raised as an invitation to the cleaner shrimp* (Hippolysmata grabhami) *to inspect its gills and remove any parasites within them. Several species of fish are cleaned by shrimps while others have a similar relationship with smaller cleaner fish.*

potentially lethal. They are also very susceptible to changes in temperature and a rise or fall of only a few degrees can cause the algae to die and be ejected from the coral.

Corals grow very slowly and if they die, or are broken or removed, it may be decades before a reef recovers. Hurricanes often devastate reefs, a particularly serious problem in the Caribbean. Corals also suffer from disease, are eaten by Crown of Thorns Starfish and other predators, and are eroded by burrowing sea urchins.

Life on the reef

The complex, three-dimensional structure of reefs provides food and shelter for a huge range of plants and animals, the most diverse communities being found in southeast Asia and northern Australia. After corals, fish are the most conspicuous animals on a reef. There are more species of fish on a coral reef than in any other habitat in the sea, and there is no terrestrial habitat, not even a rainforest, which has a greater variety of vertebrates. Reefs are home to the smallest known vertebrate, a goby, and are visited by some of the fiercest predators, the sharks. The Hawksbill Turtle feeds on sponges and other invertebrates on the reef, while the Green Turtle is often seen near reefs, and feeds in adjacent sea-grass beds. Seabirds congregate near reefs and atolls, and remote small coral islands provide undisturbed breeding sites for boobies, frigate birds, gulls, and terns.

The reef is also home to a vast array of invertebrates, with almost all major groups represented. Molluscs occur in even greater variety than fish. Some 4,000 species are known from the Great Barrier Reef, including cowries, conchs, Giant Tritons and many others popular as marine curios. Other reef inhabitants include sponges, fan and tube worms, crustaceans, such as the valuable spiny lobster, starfish, and sea urchins.

This enormous variety and productivity mean that many people around the world can make their livelihoods from reefs through, for example, subsistence and commercial fisheries, and the tourist industry. Like rainforests, reefs are also proving

The costs of reef loss
The beauty of reefs and their diverse community are priceless, but the following give some idea of their economic significance.
- The potential world yield of fish, crustaceans and molluscs from reefs is estimated at 9 million tons a year.
- Tourism and recreation on the Great Barrier Reef bring in each year an estimated 117 million Australian dollars, and reefs in Florida an estimated 30–50 dollars.
- Destruction of the reef around Male in the Maldives necessitated the building of a 2½ mile seawall at a cost of 12 million dollars. So as a natural breakwater alone, the original reef was worth 8000 dollars a yard.

to be a significant source of medicinal compounds, such as potential anti-cancer drugs, prostaglandins, and even an ultraviolet blocker, found in the tissues of corals, which acts as a "suncream" for the polyps and could be similarly useful for humans.

--------- **Threats** ---------

The reef is constantly worn away by the action of waves and the thousands of burrowing animals that live in it. Normally, the growth of a reef keeps pace with erosion and it recovers given sufficient time. But in many areas reefs appear not be regenerating and it looks as if humans may be to blame. There is growing concern that the widespread bleaching of corals in the Caribbean and elsewhere may be a symptom of the "greenhouse" effect. On the Great Barrier Reef, the Crown of Thorns Starfish has caused serious damage to corals, while in Kenya and Mauritius, plagues of sea urchins are eroding reefs faster than they are growing. Although neither of these problems is fully understood, some theories suggest that they are due to overfishing by people of the natural predators of the starfish and urchins.

Damage as a result of human activities has been reported in over 90 of the 109 countries with significant coral communities and reefs. Deforestation, resulting in soil erosion and siltation, is affecting reefs in over 50 countries. For example, silt deposited by the Sabaki river in Kenya is killing corals in the reefs of Malindi Marine Park. Coastal development, including dredging, reclamation, destruction of mangroves, and the construction of harbors, airports, roads, and hotels, has affected reefs in nearly 70 countries. Such activities also smother the remaining corals in silt

Exploitation of reefs

Coral provide us with, for example:

- fish, molluscs and crustaceans for food
- mother of pearl and ornamental shells
- aquarium fish
- sites for tourism and recreation
- coastline protection
- sheltered harbors
- white sandy beaches.

Below *The Crown of Thorns Starfish* (Acanthaster planci) *eats coral and has caused extensive damage when its numbers have increased dramatically. The reasons for such population explosions are not fully understood, but may be due to overfishing of some of the starfish's predators.*

and are often followed by high levels of sewage and other pollution.

Long appreciated as one of the most beautiful ecosystems on Earth, the reefs and the white sandy beaches formed by their erosion are major tourist attractions. Yet the tourist industry is now threatening the reefs on which it depends in nearly 60 countries. In Florida, for example, there has been a dramatic decrease in live coral cover over the last ten years, and boat groundings, anchors, and divers are clearly implicated.

The reef corals, fish, turtles, molluscs and crustaceans are also being over-exploited. Giant Clams, the largest bivalve molluscs in the world reaching up to 137 centimeters (54 inches) in length, have been fished almost to extinction in Fiji and the Philippines. The trade in ornamental corals is increasing, while coral mining for building materials is stripping reefs bare. It has been calculated that in North Malé atoll in the Maldives, all shallow submerged reefs could be damaged by the year 2014 if coral mining continues at the current rate. The methods used to exploit reefs are themselves often damaging. Dynamite or other explosives are used to stun reef fish in at least 40 countries, and a beer-bottle sized bomb can destroy a 7-square meter (75-square foot) patch of reef. Aquarium fish are often collected using sodium cyanide, a poison that temporarily paralyses the fish – and kills much of the other life.

Conservation

There are now nearly 300 protected areas covering reefs in about 65 countries and a further 600 reefs have been recommended for protection. The largest marine park in the world covers nearly 2,000 kilometers (1,250 miles) of the Great Barrier Reef. A system of zones allows one part to be strictly protected, while others are used for research, education, recreation and commercial fishing. However, marine parks alone will not stop the deterioration of reefs: it will never be possible to fence the Crown of Thorns Starfish out of the Great Barrier Reef, or the erosion-induced silt out of Malindi Marine Park. The coast has to be treated as one unit, with the shore, inland catchment area, mangroves, estuaries, and reefs being managed together.

New technology to reduce reef damage is available. Silt "curtains" erected around dredging and mining sites can prevent sediment spreading onto reefs. Sewage can be piped out into deep water or, preferably, treated fully. Artificial reefs, built out of materials as diverse as bamboo, old tires or concrete blocks, can increase fish populations. Species such as Giant Clams can be farmed in tanks or in shallow parts of the reef. The economic importance of reefs provides enormous incentives for these and other methods of protection to be put into practice.

As with all conservation, though, success will depend on improving public understanding of the value of reefs and involving local people in their management. In many Pacific islands, traditional ways of managing reefs are being resuscitated and used in the development of marine parks and reef programs. In the Philippines, numerous small reserves are being set up by fishing villages, with the assistance of local marine scientists and government officers. These reserves usually have a central sanctuary where fishing is prohibited, within a larger area in which traditional ecologically sound fishing methods are permitted. The villagers themselves devise the regulations and are responsible for their enforcement. They often build a small visitors' center and encourage low-level tourism as an additional source of income. In the longer-established reserves, fish populations and damaged corals are starting to recover and fish catches have gone up. This sort of positive feedback will, in the long run, provide the key to the future survival of reefs.

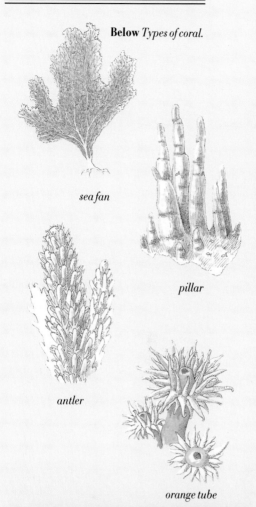

Below *Types of coral.*

sea fan

pillar

antler

orange tube

Above *A snorkeler in the Indian ocean with a table coral. Although generally a harmless pastime, snorkeling can damage a reef, particularly if the visitor handles the coral or kicks it with swimming fins.*

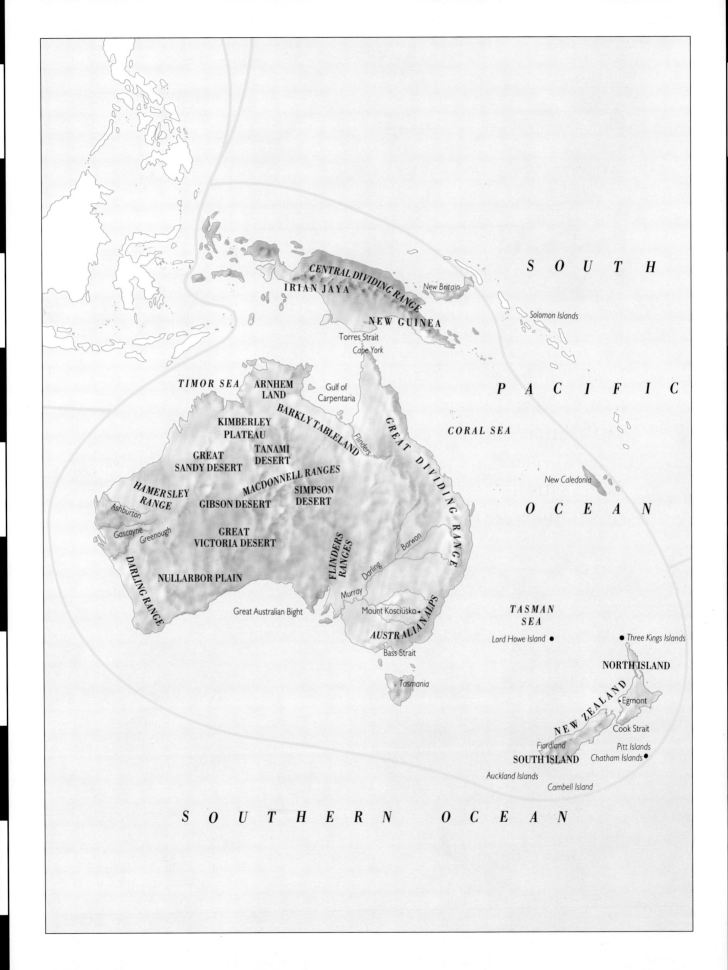

CENTRAL DIVIDING RANGE

IRIAN JAYA

NEW GUINEA

New Britain

S O U T H

P A C I F I C

O C E A N

Solomon Islands

Torres Strait

Cape York

TIMOR SEA

ARNHEM LAND

Gulf of Carpentaria

CORAL SEA

KIMBERLEY PLATEAU

BARKLY TABLELAND

TANAMI DESERT

GREAT SANDY DESERT

Flinders

GREAT DIVIDING RANGE

New Caledonia

MACDONNELL RANGES

HAMERSLEY RANGE

GIBSON DESERT

SIMPSON DESERT

Ashburton

Gascoyne

Greenough

Barwon

GREAT VICTORIA DESERT

FLINDERS RANGES

Darling

DARLING RANGE

NULLARBOR PLAIN

Murray

Great Australian Bight

Mount Kosciusko

AUSTRALIAN ALPS

TASMAN SEA

Lord Howe Island ●

● Three Kings Islands

Bass Strait

NORTH ISLAND

Tasmania

● Egmont

NEW ZEALAND

Cook Strait

Fiordland

Pitt Islands

SOUTH ISLAND

Chatham Islands ●

Auckland Islands

Cambell Island

S O U T H E R N   O C E A N

THE AUSTRALASIAN REGION

The Australasian region includes New Guinea (Irian Jaya and Papua New Guinea), Australia and New Zealand. Some classifications put New Zealand in with Antarctica, and New Guinea in Oceania. Habitats range from rainforest to the arid areas of Australia's interior. The diversity of the region's fauna is due to millions of years of undisturbed evolutionary processes.

Erosion on Philip Island caused by rabbits.

HABITAT & PLANTS

Australasia encompasses Australia. New Guinea (Irian Jaya. and Papua New Guinea) and New Zealand. (In this book. islands such as Sulawesi. the Moluccas and the Lesser Sundas are included in the Indian and Oriental section. pages 148–169.) It is one of the richest areas in the world for plants. with New Guinea alone probably having up to 20.000 vascular plant species. although only about half of these have so far been discovered and named. The habitats range from the luxuriant evergreen and semi-evergreen rainforests of New Guinea. and the Queensland coast of Australia. to the extremely arid deserts of Australia's interior.

There are strong resemblances between the floras and faunas of New Guinea. Australia. and New Zealand. These can be traced back to around 135 million years ago. when the supercontinent. Gondwanaland. comprised these three island complexes with Antarctica. Madagascar. India. Africa. and South America. Between 40 and 50 million years ago. Australia and New Guinea. called the Sahul. finally broke away from Antarctica. Australia and New Guinea are now separated only by a shallow sea over the Sahul shelf. New Zealand and the Sahul continued their long. slow evolutionary development. in what was to prove to be rather splendid zoological and botanical isolation. Reminders of those very early links. however. still remain. For example. the southern beeches have a proven poor seed dispersal ability. Yet different species of southern beech (of the genus *Nothofagus)* dominate tropical montane forests in New Guinea and New Caledonia. as well as cool temperate rainforests in places as far apart as Australia. New Zealand. and Chile.

New Guinea

The richest communities of the region are the tropical evergreen rainforests. which are most extensive on New Guinea. About 70 per cent of the island is still under forest cover of one sort or another. In Irian Jaya (the western part of New Guinea) the figure approaches 92 per cent. giving it the largest tract of tropical evergreen forest

Stephen Davis is a senior research botanist for IUCN. Until recently, he worked within the Threatened Plants Unit at Kew and was responsible for developing and maintaining the computer database on threatened plants for the Asia and Pacific regions. In 1986 Stephen co-authored *Plants in Danger: What do We Know?* and has recently completed work on the *World Plant Conservation Bibliography*, a compendium volume of over 10,000 references, jointly published in 1990 by the World Conservation Monitoring Centre, and the Royal Botanic Gardens, Kew, UK. He is currently working on a project which will result in a major IUCN-WWF publication on the world's centers of plant diversity and endemism.

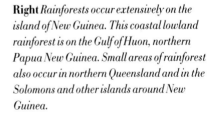

Right *Rainforests occur extensively on the island of New Guinea. This coastal lowland rainforest is on the Gulf of Huon, northern Papua New Guinea. Small areas of rainforest also occur in northern Queensland and in the Solomons and other islands around New Guinea.*

remaining in Indonesia. Coastal mangroves and vast lowland swamps are replaced on drier ground and on alluvial plains by lowland evergreen rainforest. Some of the trees have enormous canopies of 50 meters (160 feet) or more, and *Anisoptera thurifera*, one of New Guinea's most important timber trees, reaches 60 meters (200 feet) tall with a girth of 3.6 meters (12 feet). In the forest understory are a host of tree ferns, palms, gingers, marantas, screw pines, epiphytic orchids, and ferns, together with an intertwining network of woody lianas. Rainfall patterns play an important part in governing the natural distribution of this type of forest. For example, in the drier parts of southeastern Papua New Guinea, where there is a marked dry season and annual rainfall of less than 1800 mm (70 inches), rainforest gives way to woodlands containing eucalyptus species different from those found in Australia.

Mountains are a dominant feature of the New Guinea landscape, and include the highest peaks in all of southeast Asia. The backbone of the island is the Central Dividing Range, stretching for more than 650 kilometers (400 miles) and including, in the west, the four highest, permanently snow-capped peaks. A climb up the mountains is a journey through distinct vegetation zones. On mountain slopes, oaks, southern beech and conifers such as the Hoop Pine and the endemic *Papuacedrus papuanus* are predominant. At around 3,000 meters (9,800 feet) one enters the

Left *Tree ferns are attractive and decorative plants. This species,* Cyathea contaminans, *is characteristic of the montane flora of New Guinea.*

Medicinal plants

Plants provide us with numerous drugs for the cure and prevention of illness. About 80 per cent of the population of developing countries relies on traditional medicine, 85 per cent of which involves the use of plant extracts. In modern Western medicine, one in four medications prescribed by doctors is likely to contain one or more plant products. It is thought that as many as 1,400 tropical rainforest plants have anti-cancer properties, but less than one per cent of the rainforest flora has been screened. Recent research on the Moreton Bay Chestnut *(Castanospermum australe)*, a tree found only in the rainforests of Queensland and New South Wales, has revealed that it contains a compound, castanospermine, that reduces the infectivity of the AIDS virus.

subalpine zone or mossy forest, in which brightly colored rhododendrons and other ericaceous plants form dense thickets, and trees take on a stunted appearance, often draped in mosses and orchids. On the Kemabu Plateau of Irian Jaya, strange-looking giant ant-house plants (*Myrmecodia brassii*) with swollen stem bases provide a home for hundreds, and sometimes thousands, of ants. There, too, grow several species of carnivorous pitcher plants, a group which is highly sought after by commercial collectors and "hobbyists" throughout south-east Asia. In other parts of the region, some species of pitcher plants have been brought close to extinction by collecting from the wild. Further up, a landscape of tree ferns and grasslands occurs on some of the high mountains. These tree fern savannas thrive in areas which have been burned, or which experience periods of drought.

Above the tree limit (at around 3,900 meters/13,000 feet) are montane grasslands and alpine communities, where plants such as buttercups, gentians, and potentillas are found. Although close relatives of these plants are familiar to temperate botanists, most of the species found in the mountains are unique to New Guinea. In fact, around 90 per cent of all the flowering plants of New Guinea may be endemic. This extraordinarily high level of endemism is a reflection of New Guinea's long isolation.

The tropical swamps and exceptionally rich rainforests of New Guinea have sustained indigenous coastal dwellers, shifting cultivators, and hunter-gatherers for thousands of years. The majority of people still rely on the forests for food, medicines, fibers and fuel. Among existing staple foods are sago (a palm of tropical Asian swamps), yams, sweet potato, taro, and breadfruit, an extremely important fruit tree occurring widely in the lowlands. A host of plants provide valuable medical treatments, including an aroid lily (*Amorphophallus campanulatus*) whose sap is used as an infusion to treat stomachaches, and a fig (*Ficus sceptica*) used for treating fever.

Few plants from the rich rainforests of New Guinea have as yet been screened for their potential value in western medicine. The chance to do so may be slipping away as the pressures to clear the forests continue to grow. Even in remote Irian Jaya, large tracts of forest are being cleared for logging or for the resettlement of thousands of people from the overcrowded island of Java. Commercial logging and clearance for oil palm and other plantation crops is also taking place in Papua New Guinea (the eastern part of New Guinea).

In Papua New Guinea, especially, shifting cultivation accounts for significant forest losses each year. When practiced on a small scale this system of agriculture mimics the natural openings created in the forest by tree falls. Patches of forest are cleared by the cultivators on a rotational basis to grow a range of crops, and then the cultivators move on to new areas after a few years. Plants gradually invade the once-cultivated land, replenishing the soil nutrients, and a forest similar to the original develops. But as the human population increases, more land has to be cleared more often, and the forest does not have time to regenerate. With repeated burning and clearance over larger and larger areas, forests are converted to grasslands. Today in Papua New Guinea there are approximately 1.5 million people (over half the population) engaged in shifting cultivation, and vast areas which once supported rich tropical rainforest are now dominated by a single species – the Kunai Grass.

Australia

In Queensland and New South Wales, tropical and subtropical rainforests have been severely reduced by logging and clearance for dairy cattle, sugar cane, and maize. The Cape York peninsula of Queensland alone has the highest number of rare or threatened plants of any region in Australia – 633 species out of a total of 3,329 for all of Australia (including Tasmania). These forests include *Idiospermum australiense*, a curious tree with primitive characteristics known only to occur in two small areas in northern Queensland. Already one population has almost been destroyed by clearfelling, while the other survives within a protected area. Further south, and in the uplands of New South Wales, Victoria, and Tasmania, are cool temperate

Below left *Rainforest in Lamington National Park, Queensland, Australia. In addition to the oft-cited value of rainforest as a source of important medicinal, timber and other plants, it has a less tangible but nonetheless important aesthetic value, as this scene demonstrates.*

Below *Despite the fact that Australia is a wealthy nation with numerous natural resources, remnants of tropical rainforest outside of protected areas are still being destroyed and fragmented through the expansion of agriculture, building developments and road schemes. Even a road as wide as this one can be a barrier to dispersal for some rainforest plants.*

rainforests dominated by southern beech, and including trees such as the Giant Gum Tree (or Mountain Ash), the world's tallest flowering plant reaching up to 100 meters (330 feet).

The forests of Australia are remnants of the original closed forests of Gondwanaland from which most of the present-day Australian flora has evolved. Due to the continent's isolation over the last 45 million years (since Australia separated from Africa and South America), 80 per cent of the species are endemic and there are over 500 endemic genera. As Australia slowly drifted to the north, plants from southeast Asia were able to spread into Australia. The original temperate flora was gradually replaced by one which was adapted to the arid conditions of Australia's interior, and the tropical zone of the north. Today, the forest remnants are regarded as extremely important. Their protection was firmly placed on Australia's political agenda by vigorous national and international campaigns over the proposed damming of the Franklin river, which threatened Tasmanian temperate rainforests, and the destruction of tropical forest at Daintree River in Queensland caused by road building.

Tropical and subtropical closed forests are not the only ones under threat in Australia. Open forests and dry woodlands of acacia and eucalypts have also been extensively cleared, mainly for sheep or cattle grazing. Today, there are over 150 species of eucalypts and 160 species of acacia listed as either rare, threatened or insufficiently known. Heathlands, too, particularly in the southwestern part of

Below *There are more than 500 species of Eucalyptus, a genus of gum trees, ironbarks, and stringybarks, almost all of which are restricted to Australia. Although some species dominate Australia's forests and woodlands, there are over 120 species currently at risk, mainly as a result of forest clearance, grazing, and urban expansion.*

Western Australia, continue to be cleared for agriculture. There, 46 species out of a total heathland flora of 3,700 species are critically endangered, including orchids, such as *Drakaea jeanensis* and *Diuris purdiei*, and a number of banksias, such as *Banksia goodii*, which are also highly sought after by collectors. An orchid in Western Australia that eludes collectors (but not land developers) is *Rhizanthella gardneri*, one of two amazing Australian species with flowers below ground level. Unfortunately, the distribution of this underground orchid coincides with Western Australia's wheatbelt. Providing some areas of heathland are saved as reserves, the future of this extraordinary plant, along with other endemic heathland plants, can be secured.

New Zealand

When the first Europeans began to settle in New Zealand during the early nineteenth century, they found a land of mountains and forests. Now only 23 per cent of New Zealand is covered by forests, mainly montane remnants of the primeval indigenous forests. The changes, which began with the arrival of the Polynesians some 12,000 years ago, have accelerated in the last 200 years, as forests have been cleared for agriculture, grazing, and settlements. The once extensive Kauri forests of the northern part of North Island have been logged for valuable timber. Further south, much of the podocarp-hardwood forest has met with a similar fate. Today, about 10 per cent of New Zealand's 2,000 native vascular plants are rare or threatened in the

Below left *Heathlands similar to this one near Mount Chudilup, Western Australia are still being cleared for agriculture. As in Britain and the rest of Europe, they are considered wastelands. The rich and diverse flora of Australia's heathlands includes the famous underground orchid (*Rhizanthella gardneri*).*

Below *The Philip Island Hibiscus (*Hibiscus insularis*) is confined to Philip Island between New Zealand and Australia, where its continuing survival depends on the effective control of rabbits.*

Right *A Tanemahuta Kauri tree* (Agathis australis) *in Waipoua forest, New Zealand. The massive kauris, growing up to 55 meters (180 feet) and with a wide girth, were ruthlessly exploited until 1974.*

Tecomanthe speciosa

Hebe speciosa

wild. either through habitat loss or introduced grazing animals and competition from introduced plants. For example, at least seven species of shrub known as Australian laurel (*Pittosporum*) are threatened by the loss of their forest and scrub habitats. one species (*P. pimelioides*) being reduced to less than 100 individuals.

New Zealand's flora, like that of Australia and New Guinea, has evolved for millions of years in isolation and about 80 per cent of New Zealand's flowering plants are unique to the two main islands. The main threat to the flora is grazing by domesticated and feral animals. Goats and pigs (first introduced by Captain Cook as a food source for later seamen) together with sheep, deer, chamois, and Australian possums, have all had a bad effect on native plants. Even *Hebe speciosa*, a shrub well known in cultivation, has become reduced in the wild. The removal of native vegetation by grazing animals may also have caused increased erosion of the coastal cliff habitat.

Some of New Zealand's offshore islands have their own unique species and these are also threatened by grazers. There are 12 endemic species on the Three Kings islands. of which *Tecomanthe speciosa*, a woody vine, was reduced to just one individual in the wild until recently. On Chatham islands. there are about 30 endemic plants out of a total flora of around 300 species. The vegetation. which originally included swamp forests, upland bogs, and rushlands, has been drastically affected by grazing and by draining. burning and peat-digging. More than half the endemic species on the islands are now at risk, including the attractive Chatham Island (or Giant) Forget-me-not. This succulent herb, with a rosette of fleshy leaves up to 1 meter (3¼ feet) in diameter. was said to have formed an unbroken line along the shores of Chatham. Pitt and the Mangere islands. but grazing and trampling by pigs.

sheep and cattle have reduced the wild population to around 1,000 plants. On Chatham, it is now only found at a few sites.

In the alpine zones of New Zealand, where nearly all the plants are endemic, goats, deer, and chamois are a particular threat. Mountain recreation, tourism, road construction, and up-rooting of plants by collectors can also have profound impacts on habitats and plants. Alpines at risk include several species of alpine daisies, such as *Celmisia adamsii* which is restricted to only a few sites on the Coromandel peninsula of North Island.

All, however, is not lost. Today, over 5,000 square kilometers (1,900 square miles) of land are included within reserves administered by the New Zealand Department of Lands and Survey, and over double this area lies within reserves administered by the Forest Service. In addition, quite a number of New Zealand's threatened plants, like those of Australia, are horticulturally desirable, offering the hope that the numbers of at least some may be boosted by cultivation in botanic gardens and reintroduction to the wild.

As elsewhere, the long-term survival of the diverse flora of the Australasian region depends upon the identification and protection of areas and habitats that have important concentrations of plant species and endemics. Wherever possible, land needs to be used in a way that maintains plant resources at a sustainable level. The monitoring of rare plant populations allows effective conservation measures to be implemented. As a safeguard against total extinction, some plants can be rescued and cultivated within botanic gardens or gene banks. Gardens and nature reserves also provide important opportunities for educating the public and generating the public support that is so vital to the success of conservation efforts.

Clianthus puniceus

Celmisia adamsii

Left *Of the 150 species of* Hebe, *a genus of shrubs related to speedwell, about half occur in New Zealand. A number of species, such as* Hebe salicifolia, *are well-known temperate garden shrubs, but wild populations are being reduced by livestock grazing, trampling, and erosion.*

WILDLIFE

Michael Kennedy became the Co-ordinator of Friends of the Earth New South Wales in 1978 and in 1981 took up the position of Campaign Director for The Fund For Animals Ltd., Australia, one of the country's largest membership conservation organizations. Michael also jointly established a TRAFFIC office in Australia in 1983, and in 1986 became personal environmental adviser to the Australian Federal Minister for the Environment. He is currently Senior Project Officer for World Wide Fund for Nature Australia and coordinates the National Threatened Species Networks. He has been published widely on the issue of threatened species conservation.

The diversity and beauty of wildlife species to be found in the Australasian region are immense. Australia, for example, has the most desert reptiles of any nation in the world, and its overall national reptile count of some 700 species is second only to Mexico's (with an estimated 717 species).

The diversity of the region's fauna is due to both millions of years of undisturbed evolutionary processes, and the extremely broad range of ecosystems and habitat types that still exist today. Vast tracts of tropical rainforests, thousands of square miles of perhaps the most inhospitable deserts known to humankind, untouched expanses of precious wetland and mangrove stands, alpine habitats, temperate forests resplendent with numerous wild and untamed rivers, grasslands, heathlands, and many other discrete biogeographic provinces provide a species variety to please the most ardent wildlife watcher.

The risks that face these ecosystems and species are unfortunately significant. As the following pages will show, Australasia has suffered more than, or at least as much as, any other region of the globe. The process of halting such a loss of biological diversity has become one of the most urgent issues of our time.

——————— **New Guinea's tropical wilderness** ———————

The island of New Guinea, comprising Irian Jaya in the west and Papua New Guinea in the east, has been described as one of the six major tropical wilderness areas left on

AUSTRALIA

Below *This graphic representation of the status of Australasia's extinct and threatened wildlife does not include whales, dolphins, or marine turtles. It is also important to remember that it only represents species whose status is known; question marks indicate that the status of a particular group is still to be determined.*

Extinct
Endangered
Vulnerable
Potentially vulnerable
? Unknown
+ Probably more

NEW ZEALAND

Mammals   Birds   Reptiles   Invertebrates   Fish   Amphibians

NEW GUINEA (Sulawesi)

Invertebrates   Fish   Amphibians   Reptiles   Birds   Mammals

Mammals   Birds   Reptiles   Fish   Invertebrates   Amphibians

Earth. It is a "good news" area according to one well-known scientist. where unusual species concentrations exist and where the threats are not so imminent. Vertebrates abound, including over 200 mammals, 700 birds, nearly 300 reptiles and over 200 amphibians. There is an unknown number of freshwater fish, although 103 species have been identified in the Fly river alone. The estimates for invertebrates range from 80,000 to 100,000 species, but these are based on scant scientific knowledge and the true figure is probably much higher.

The threats facing the wildlife of New Guinea are many and varied. Agricultural land and settlements for the ever-increasing human populations continue to encroach upon wildlife habitats. Industry is also taking its toll. A recent scandal in Papua New Guinea over government corruption in the logging industry revealed that rates of forest destruction due to timber extraction are far higher than had previously been thought. Mining, with its destructive and polluting history, is becoming a major growth area. Trade in wildlife and traditional hunting play their roll in reducing populations, too. There is a flourishing trade (legal and illegal) in Irian Jaya, and hunting in Papua New Guinea has an effect on wildlife, especially when modern weapons are used and traditional practices ignored.

All these factors are putting pressure on New Guinea's largely endemic fauna. So far no vertebrate extinction can be attributed to the activities but it seems likely that many invertebrate and plant species were swept away with the rainforests that have been cleared to date. The next decade will be a critical period for the precious fauna of New Guinea and islands to the west. Currently, 23 mammals (excluding whales), 31 birds, 2 reptiles (excluding turtles), and 37 invertebrate species are listed as threatened. Again, these figures reflect our lack of knowledge about the region and probably grossly underestimate the extent of the problem.

——— The marsupials ———

New Guinea and Australia are the only two countries in the world that are home to both the marsupials (pouched mammals) and monotremes (egg-laying mammals). In Irian Jaya (and undoubtedly throughout New Guinea) approximately 50 per cent of the endemic marsupials are montane species, highlighting the importance of the rainforests covering the Central Dividing Range.

Little is known about some of the threatened marsupials, particularly the tree kangaroos. New Guinea has the largest number of these amazing animals, with seven species in all, including Scott's Tree-kangaroo. This is clearly extremely rare as no live specimen has yet been found! Tantalizing evidence of its existence has been collected by Australian scientists from the Torricelli Mountains of Papua New Guinea. The animal is the largest of the tree kangaroos yet known, possibly weighing as much as 20 kilograms (44 pounds), and is apparently jet black with a bright orange streak at the base of its tail. The other species of tree kangaroo over which there is concern include Doria's, Goodfellow's, the White-throated, the Grizzled and Matschie's Tree-kangaroo.

Among other threatened members of the kangaroo and wallaby family are two beautiful and vulnerable wallabies, Macleay's Dorcopsis and the Black

Below *The Ornate or Goodfellow's Tree Kangaroo* (Dendrolagus goodfellowi) *is under pressure from hunting in its forest home in the central highlands of Papua New Guinea. Although it is believed to have declined, little is known of its precise status.*

Dorcopsis. Macleay's Dorcopsis is an extremely rare animal, known only from a few specimens. It is found in mid-montane forests in the eastern part of New Guinea, and is considered vulnerable to any disturbance in its very restricted range. The Black Dorcopsis, another montane marsupial, is restricted to one, possibly two, islands off the northeast coast of New Guinea. Its very dense and luxuriant black fur, suiting its cold habitat, distinguishes this wallaby from its mainland relatives, most of which inhabit lowland forests.

The staggering variety among New Guinea's marsupials is exemplified by carnivorous marsupials like the Bronze Quoll, long-nosed bandicoots such as the Dimorphic or Clara Bandicoot, the beautiful Woodlark Island Cuscus and the Black-spotted Cuscus, and, the many gliders and possums, including the Torricelli or Northern Glider and D'Albertis Ringtail. Most of these are rare species with highly restricted distributions.

Amazing monotremes

Of even more concern is one of New Guinea's two monotremes. The Short-beaked Echidna also inhabits Australia and its status in New Guinea is unknown. The Long-beaked Echidna only occurs in New Guinea and is one of the most biologically important and threatened animals there. It is the largest of all monotremes, and also differs from its short-beaked relative in having a tongue uniquely adapted to feed on earthworms. It is found over most of New Guinea, but with increasing rarity, and it seems that wherever human populations are high, the species is unlikely to be found. It is extremely hard to locate in the field, and is becoming locally extinct in large areas of the central highlands. Hunting pressures appear to have seriously affected population levels.

Bats and birds

New Guinea's bat fauna has not escaped the depredations of a growing human society, for example the Lesser Naked-backed Fruit Bat and the Big-eared Flying Fox, both rainforest inhabitants. But New Guinea's longest list of threatened vertebrates is unfortunately provided by the birds. Four New Guinea birds of prey may be at risk, including the Black Honey Buzzard. A very rare endemic from New

Above *The Long-beaked Echidna* (Zaglossus bruijni) *is confined to humid montane forests at altitudes of up to 4,150 meters (13,600 feet) in New Guinea. These egg-laying mammals only occur where human populations are low, and have recently become extinct in large areas of the central highlands. They have also declined in other areas where traditional taboos against eating them have broken down under the influence of missionaries.*

Right *A female Blue Bird of Paradise* (Paradisaea rudolphi) *feeding on a pandanus fruit. One of the most spectacularly beautiful of all the birds of paradise, the male has long blue, purple and cinnamon plumes on the flanks and two very long black-tailed streamers.*

Far right *A male Lesser Bird of Paradise* (Paradisaea minor). *After being brought back to Spain by Magellan's crew in 1521, this bird was systematically hunted for its plumes until it finally received protection in the 1920s when the world-wide trade in bird plumes was stopped.*

Britain. it inhabits lowland forest that is continually being logged and destroyed for oil-palm plantations.

It is the region's birds of paradise that are simultaneously the most spectacular and the most sought after. These magnificent birds are highly prized for their extremely long and often iridescent plumes. both by indigenous peoples and overseas collectors. Fortunately. very few of the 43 species are actually threatened. and those that are suffer from habitat destruction rather than collection for feathers. Species of concern include the Blue and Goldie's Birds of Paradise.

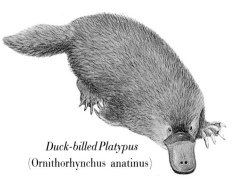

Duck-billed Platypus
(Ornithorhynchus anatinus)

—————— Reptiles ——————

The two reptile species officially recorded as threatened are the New Guinea Plateless Turtle and the New Guinea Crocodile. The Plateless Turtle (known as the Pitted-Shelled Turtle in Australia where it also occurs) is under pressure from local hunting. The New Guinea Crocodile was extensively exploited in the past and is now under

Short-beaked Echidna
(Tachyglossus aculeatus)

Left *A New Guinea Crocodile* (Crocodilus novaeguinea) *being reared on a crocodile farm in Papua New Guinea. This country has been at the forefront of efforts to breed and ranch crocodiles commercially, and so conserve wild stocks.*

CITES-approved ranching programs. Unfortunately. recent. severe budgetary cuts in Papua New Guinea are affecting the management programs. and the crocodile is still subject to heavy poaching in Irian Jaya.

—————— Australian megadiversity ——————

Australia is acknowledged by scientists as being one of a dozen "megadiversity" countries on Earth today. The criteria for achieving this lofty status include a nation's total number of species, and the proportion of species, genera. families and so on that are endemic. Australia has far more endemic families than any other country in the world. including seven endemic families of mammals. The (Short-beaked) Echidna and the Platypus occur together only in Australia. Of the marsupial species. 89 per cent are endemic, as are 73 per cent of the other mammals. At least 70 per cent of Australia's bird species are endemic, along with 88 per cent of the reptiles and 94 per cent of the amphibians.

In terms of sheer species numbers. Australia can claim the second largest reptile count in the world (700 species). the third highest number of amphibians in the Asia region (180 species), 850 bird species, and 260 species of mammal. With the inclusion of approximately 200 freshwater fish species, a "guesstimate" of around 100,000 insect species, and tens of thousands of molluscs, the island continent deserves its place on the global role of biological honor. Moreover, Australia has wilderness areas spread across a far wider range of habitats than in any other country.

Threats and losses

The bad news is that much of this staggering diversity has been severely affected by the activities of settlers from Europe. Since they first colonized Australia over 200 years ago, Australians have cleared about 75 per cent of the rainforests, 66 per cent of the country's original tree cover, and chronically degraded well over 50 per cent of the arid lands. As a result, Australia also holds some more unfortunate world records. It has the worst mammal extinction rate of any country in the world, 18 mammals having become extinct – approximately half of all the mammal species that have been lost globally in recent historical times. In addition, over 100 mammals, 100 birds, 100 reptiles, 40 frogs, 70 fish, and over 400 invertebrate species are now considered to be at some degree of risk.

Australia is home to only 17 million people and most of its vast lands are uninhabited, the southeastern and southwestern coastal areas supporting the bulk of urban and rural life. Yet it is in the central and arid zones with sparse human populations that species extinctions have been highest. A third of desert mammals have become extinct, and an alarming 90 per cent of all small to medium-sized mammals in the arid zones are now considered to be either extinct or endangered. What caused this biological catastrophe?

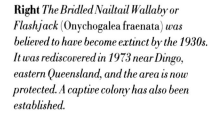

Right *The Bridled Nailtail Wallaby or Flashjack* (Onychogalea fraenata) *was believed to have become extinct by the 1930s. It was rediscovered in 1973 near Dingo, eastern Queensland, and the area is now protected. A captive colony has also been established.*

The affected mammals fall within the weight range 35–5500 grams (1¼–194 ounces), and have been described as "critical weight range species". It is believed that these species were susceptible to subtle changes in climatic conditions. Living in a harsh arid zone, survival was difficult enough at the best of times. When droughts came, their distribution contracted to smaller "refugia" with suitable vegetation, where they were prone to natural local extinctions. When the Europeans brought their stock animals to the central arid zones, the smaller mammals simply could not compete and the "refugia" became virtual prisons.

Scientists have also suggested that it was frequent burning of large areas of desert by Aboriginal communities over the past 40,000 years that had created suitable habitats for a large range of mammals. When the Aboriginals were forcibly moved from their lands by invading Europeans, many thousands of years of land management expertise were lost. Wildfires became the norm and conditions radically changed. Unable to disperse from their "refugia" when good rains fell, the remaining mammals were probably particularly vulnerable to predation by introduced foxes, animals that have caused tremendous damage to small and medium-sized mammal populations across Australia. Domestic cats gone feral, sheep, cattle, camels, pigs, goats, and an endless list of exotics all helped seal the mammals' fate.

The above are hypotheses and cannot now be proven, but, in deadly combination, they clearly played a role in the drastic decline of Australian wildlife. To the list of extinct Australian mammals can be added two species of rodents, Maclear's Rat and the Burrowing Rat, which once lived in the Australian Territory of Christmas Island in the Indian Ocean. This brings the total mammal extinction count to 20 species, and some scientists believe that the number may be as high as 22.

Marsupials and rodents at risk

Large numbers of other marsupials and rodents remain at risk, including some of Australia's most beautiful kangaroos and wallabies. The highly endangered Bridled Nailtail Wallaby has only one population remaining on Tauntan Scientific Reserve in Central Queensland. The Yellow-footed Rock-Wallaby in western New South Wales, the Black-footed Rock-Wallaby and Tammar Wallaby in Western Australia, and the Rufous Hare-Wallaby in the Northern Territory are all presenting wildlife managers

DISTRIBUTION

BRIDLED NAILTAIL WALLABY

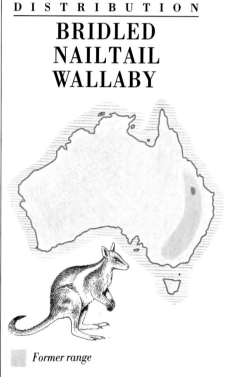

Former range

Current range

Range of the Bridled Nailtail Wallaby (Onychogalea fraenata). *Formerly abundant, it has been reduced to a small population in east Queensland.*

Right *The Southern Hairy-nosed Wombat* (Lasiorhinus latifrons) *is similar in appearance to the Common Wombat but has finer and softer fur and a hairy nose. It occurs in southern Australia where it is locally abundant but populations are fragmented and suffer from competition with rabbits.*

Below *The Numbat or Banded Anteater* (Myrmecobius fasciatus) *is, unusually for a marsupial, active by day. Its numbers have declined dramatically and it is now extinct in New South Wales, Victoria, Northern Territory and South Australia.*

with extremely tough problems. The Rufous Hare-Wallaby (or Mala), is the subject of a captive breeding and reintroduction program in the Northern Territory. It appears stable on two Western Australian islands, but there may be as few as 30 wild individuals remaining on the mainland. It is a classic example of the serious decline among desert mammal populations, for this species once inhabited more than 25 per cent of the continent.

The list of other famous marsupials in need of conservation help is extensive, but the following examples highlight the diversity in this marvelous animal group. The Northern Hairy-nosed Wombat remains in one isolated population (perhaps 65 animals) in Epping Forest National Park in central coastal Queensland. The Bilby, one of the most fragile and unusual looking of all the bandicoot family, is in much the same position as the Mala, with small threatened populations in three states. The Long-footed Potoroo, southeastern Australia's most endangered species, is being pushed to the brink by logging activities in Victoria and New South Wales. The Golden Bandicoot from north Western Australia and the Numbat from southwest Western Australia are two striking examples of species that have been lost from more than 90 per cent of their former ranges in recent times. There is a successful conservation program for the Numbat involving captive breeding, reintroductions and relocations to parts of its former range, and it has come to symbolize the conservation fight in Western Australia.

Among the possums, three of the most endangered are Leadbeater's Possum, the Mountain Pygmy-possum, and the Western Ringtail Possum. The first two are threatened by logging activities and ski resort development respectively. The ringtail possums in the east of Australia are often thought of as pests, living happily in urban gardens, and most Australians are surprised to learn of the difficulties facing the western cousin.

Also suffering heavily are the fascinating dasyurids, small insectivorous or carnivorous marsupials. The largest dasyurids left on the mainland are the native "cats" or quolls. Extremely beautiful, agile, and fierce, they remain secure only in

Left *The Rufous Bettong* (Aepyprymnus rufescens) *is a small nest-building kangaroo that lives in open forests. Although it is still reasonably widespread, development pressures, grazing and perhaps forestry practice are having their effect.*

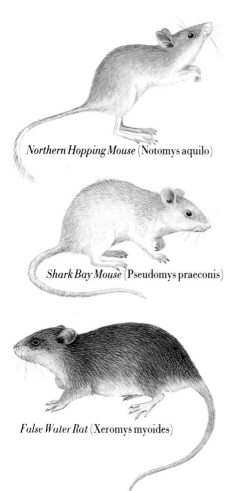

Northern Hopping Mouse (Notomys aquilo)

Shark Bay Mouse (Pseudomys praeconis)

False Water Rat (Xeromys myoides)

Tasmania. The Western Quoll or Chuditch is extremely endangered, surviving only in large jarrah forests in southwest Western Australia. Smaller dasyurids known to be at risk include the marsupial "mice," the Atherton Antechinus, the Kultarr, the Mulgara, the Dibbler, the Red-tailed Phascogale, and the Sandhill Dunnart.

The two endemic monotreme species, the Short-beaked Echidna, and the Platypus, are still common and maintain viable populations. But some scientists are concerned that the Platypus is a potentially vulnerable animal. It is extinct in South Australia, and is under increasing pressures from human use and pollution of its freshwater habitats in eastern Australia.

Although less appealing to many people than the marsupials, the rodents are a valuable component of the Australian fauna with a high degree of endemicity. A significant proportion of species, 8 out of 58, are extinct and at least 25 species are thought to be under some degree of threat, ranging from highly endangered to potentially vulnerable.

The Greater Sticknest Rat is probably the best known of the rodents in trouble. Once found across the entire southern half of Australia, the species has not been seen on the mainland since 1933. It is famed for building above ground large stick nests, which can reach 1 meter (3¼ feet) high and 1.5 meters (5 feet) across. Less than 1,000 individuals remain, only on the Franklin islands off the coast of South Australia. A new conservation program aims to reintroduce the rat to a part of its previous range in coastal and central Western Australia. One of this rat's close cousins, the Lesser Stick-nest Rat, has also not been seen since 1933, and is now listed as extinct. Reported sightings still occur in the desert regions of South Australia, leading to some hopes that it may one day be "rediscovered". The threatened rodent list also includes the False Water Rat, the Thornton Peak Melomys, and a significant number of indigenous mice. Among these are the Smoky Mouse, now extinct in New South Wales and occurring only in Victoria; the Shark Bay Mouse from the Shark Bay region of Western Australia; and the Northern Hopping Mouse found only on Groote Eylandt in the top end of Northern Territory.

Right *The Australian Sealion* (Neophoca cinerea) *is the only seal endemic to Australia. The total population is estimated at less than 5,000, breeding on offshore islands. Although they are no longer hunted, the populations do not appear to be increasing in number.*

DISTRIBUTION
SWAMP TURTLE

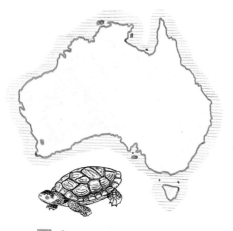

Current range

Western Swamp Turtle (Pseudomydura umbrina). *One of Australia's (and perhaps the world's) most endangered reptiles, there are probably fewer than 50 animals left in the wild. Although wildlife authorities have had some success with captive breeding, its future remains in peril.*

Endemic bats

Increasing numbers of endemic bats are worrying wildlife biologists. The Ghost Bat has recently been tagged as endangered by Australian bat specialists. It is the only carnivorous bat in Australia, and eats large insects, reptiles, frogs, birds, small mammals, and even other bat species. Occurring in the northern half of the continent, its habit of roosting in caves has contributed to its decline. In Queensland, for instance, a limestone mining company, with the full permission of the then Queensland government, blew up one of the species' main roosting caves at Mount Etna, near Rockhampton, causing international outrage. The spectacular, endemic Orange Horseshoe-Bat, also from northern Australia, has been badly affected by human interference, with entire colonies abandoning their roosts.

The Sealion and the Dugong

Two marine mammal species causing concern are the Australian Sealion and the Dugong. Hunted heavily in the last century, the sealion has still not recovered, and the estimated population in South Austalia and southeast Western Australia is no more than 3,500 to 5,000 animals. The Dugong, also heavily exploited in the past, is faring a little better with a population of around 50,000. Although this makes the Australian Dugong population one of the healthiest in the world, it still remains vulnerable in its northern tropical coastal home.

The birds

Australian birds have so far proved a little more resilient than mammals to the depredations of human society. Only two species, the Dwarf Emu and the Paradise Parrot, and one subspecies, the Western Rufous Bristle Bird, have become extinct. But many scientists believe that the forces that so drastically affected the mammals will soon start to adversely influence the birds.

Australia is renowned for its broad array of parrot species, and an alarmingly high proportion of these are threatened to some degree. Those of particular concern include the Glossy Black and Baudin's Black Cockatoos, and Alexandra's, the Night, the Golden-shouldered, the Hooded, the Orange-bellied, and the Scarlet-chested

Parrots. Habitat destruction has been mainly responsible for the decline of these species. Many are further threatened by the activities of wildlife smugglers, such as the Golden-shouldered Parrot and the potentially vulnerable Palm Cockatoo, both found in restricted habitats at the top end of the Cape York peninsula in Queensland.

Other well-known Australian birds continue to struggle against very stiff odds. The extremely beautiful Mallee Fowl builds a very large nesting mound – measuring 2–5 meters (6½–16½ feet) in diameter and one meter (3¼ feet) high – by filling an excavation with sand, dry leaves, twigs, and bark. The male carefully controls the temperature of the eggs inside this incubating mound by adding or removing sand as necessary. The Mallee Fowl is now vulnerable to extinction through loss of its essential mallee (dwarf eucalyptus), dry scrub habitat, and predation of eggs and chicks by introduced foxes.

Another attentive parent, the male Cassowary, has been observed sitting on its eggs for 48 days without getting up, feeding or drinking. This remarkable flightless bird, standing up to 1.8 meters (6 feet) tall, is also vulnerable to extinction, with possibly fewer than 4,000 birds left. Destruction of its rainforest home in north Queensland, illegal hunting, disease, and road kills have all taken their toll.

Far left *The cheeks of the Palm Cockatoo* (Probosciger aterrimus) *turn bright red when the bird is excited. In Australia, it occurs only at the extreme north of the Cape York peninsula, Queensland. It does also have an extensive range in New Guinea, but has been wiped out in most areas close to villages.*

Left *The Diamond Python* (Morelia spilota spilota) *is restricted to the eucalyptus and rainforests of New South Wales. It is a distinct subspecies of the more widespread Carpet Python and, because of its attractive markings, has been widely collected for the pet trade.*

The Gouldian Finch and the Rufous Scrub Bird are other examples of highly endangered mainland Australian birds. But it is among the birds of Australia's island territories that the bulk of avian extinctions have been experienced to date. The Lesser Noddy, the Norfolk Island Parrot, the Norfolk Island Boobook Owl, and Abbott's Booby are a few of the many species threatened in these island habitats.

Reptiles

The reptiles have lost only one of their number, the Adelaide Pygmy Blue-tongued Skink. Of the rest, the Western Swamp Turtle is easily the most endangered. There are fewer than 50 remaining in the wild, isolated in two small ephemeral swamps near Perth in Western Australia, and the turtle's future depends upon intensive captive breeding programs. Although there have been two successful batches of young to date, its long-term survival is still far from assured. Three snakes, the Diamond Python, the Broad-headed Snake, and the Western Black-striped Snake all suffer from the dual threats of habitat destruction and the wildlife trade.

The reptile with perhaps the worst public image in Australia is the Saltwater Crocodile. The subject of much controversy, it was hunted to near extinction in the years after the Second World War. The Western Australian population is now extremely small and isolated. In Queensland, the population is under increasing threat from habitat destruction, illegal trade and shooting, and removal from eastern coastal habitats by wildlife authorities for use in "farms." The Northern Territory's population is protected primarily so that it can be utilized in endorsed "ranching" operations, though skins have recently been exported to Japan in contravention of the spirit of an international convention designed to control such trade. The Saltwater Crocodile will never be "safe" in Australia, and therefore must be regarded as continually vulnerable.

On Australian islands, the reptile fauna has been as vulnerable as the mammals and birds, and includes three threatened skinks. The Pedra Branca Skink, while seemingly secure, is precariously linked to the well-being of Pedra Branca Island seabird colonies on which it feeds. Increasing commercial fishing near this Tasmanian island may have catastrophic results. The island home of the vulnerable Lord Howe Island Skink is located some 800 kilometers off the New South Wales coast. The endangered Lancelin Island Skink occurs off the southwest coast of Western Australia. Both skinks have been affected by introduced animals.

Amphibians and fish

The alarming declines among the amphibians of continental Australia have caused warning bells to ring around the country. In the last ten years or so, as many as a dozen frog species have disappeared from their rainforest haunts down the east coast of Australia. Nobody knows why, but one hypothesis is that the disappearances are linked to subtle effects of climatic change. Australia has the only frog that incubates its young in its stomach, the Platypus Frog, and one of the only two species in the world that uses sign language to communicate, the Eungella Torrent Frog. The former is highly endangered, having not been seen for a number of years, while the latter is described as being potentially vulnerable. The thirty or so other amphibians considered potentially vulnerable to extinction include the Baw Baw Frog from alpine habitats in Victoria, and the Mount Glorious Torrent Frog from the rainforests of southern Queensland.

Right *The Great White Shark* (Carcharodon carcharias) *is still widespread in most of the warmer waters of the world but has suffered in recent years from a bad press, particularly after the release of the film* Jaws, *and may be threatened in Australia. Very little is known of its life cycle or status.*

There is a relatively low number (about 200) of freshwater fish species in Australia, but this is made up for by their diversity and the high proportion of endemics. Australian biologists have lately realized that a greater number of freshwater fish species are under threat than was previously thought. Competition from introduced game fish, pollution, and the damming of rivers have all produced large declines in numbers and range. Many of Tasmania's well-known, minnow-like galaxids are causing concern, including the Swan Galaxias and the Lake Pedder Galaxias. On the mainland, the Blind Cave Eel, which lacks eyes, body pigmentation and fins, has been collected less than a dozen times and is found only in subterranean waters in Western Australia. The Spotted Barramundi from Queensland, and the Trout Cod from northeastern Victoria and southern New South Wales, both have very restricted distributions and need active conservation efforts.

So, too, do at least three species of marine sharks. Sport hunting, commercial fishing, beach netting and outright prejudice may finally be having an impact on the Great White Shark, the Gray Nurse Shark, and Herbst's Shark. Two other marine

Left *The Tuatara* (Sphenodon punctatus) *is a reptile virtually indistinguishable from its ancestors that lived 135 million years ago in the Jurassic. Once widespread in New Zealand, its range has contracted within historical times and it is now confined to offshore islands.*

species listed by Australian experts are the Black Cod and the Southern Bluefin Tuna. The Bluefin has been heavily over-exploited by national and international fishing fleets, and may be already commercially extinct.

New Zealand – land of the Old Night Bird

New Zealand evolved in isolation for some 80 million years after splitting from Gondwanaland. It is both the largest and most diverse of land forms to have developed in the absence of terrestrial mammals. The amazing results of this isolated gestation period were birds such as the flightless kiwis and the giant ostrich-like moas, the very ancient reptile, the Tuatara, and many other animals that have come to symbolize New Zealand's wildlife heritage – or what is left of it.

Evolution did not provide New Zealand with the sheer numbers of species found on islands such as New Guinea, but this is more than compensated for by the biological wonders among its endemic fauna. The endemic species comprised 3 mammals (excluding whales and dolphins), 173 birds, 40 reptiles, 3 amphibians, 25 fish, and 91 molluscs and arthropods. A further 195 birds and 3 freshwater fish were indigenous. Of these species, 21 vertebrates and 8 invertebrates are now extinct, while 59 vertebrates and 51 invertebrates are endangered or vulnerable.

New Zealand was a land of forests and superlative mountain ranges. It was only 1,000 years ago, with the arrival of the Polynesians, that New Zealand first felt the impact of human interference. By the time the Europeans had firmly established their colonies, almost 25 per cent of New Zealand's forests had disappeared, and with them a large percentage of the birds, including the giant moas. Due to vastly increased forest destruction by Europeans, approximately 75 per cent of the forests have now been lost, with the majority remaining as high-altitude remnants. The clearing of indigenous forests for the logging industry, agriculture, grazing, and other developments still represents one of the prime threats to New Zealand's wildlife.

Introduced species

Introduced and now feral species wrought terrible damage on native animals and plants. The list of destroyers is almost endless and includes rats, mice, ferrets, stoats, cats, dogs, possums, wallabies, cattle, sheep, goats, rabbits, and many introduced

Right *Until about 100 years ago Hooker's Sealions* (Neophoca hookeri) *bred on North Island, New Zealand, but they are now restricted to sub-Antarctic islands. During the nineteenth century they were exterminated on Macquarie island and the main population is now on Auckland island.*

plants. These exotic predators, browsers and colonizers killed and ate to extinction a large number of endemic vertebrates, and continue to seriously threaten many of the remaining species.

The only non-marine mammals indigenous to the country are three endemic bat species, called *pekapeka* by the Maori. The Greater Short-tailed Bat is already extinct, perhaps as recently as 1965. Some biologists hope that a few of these bats may still survive on one of the small rat-free islands near Big South Cape Island. The other two, the Short-tailed Bat and the Long-tailed Bat are threatened. What a catastrophe it would be if these remaining ambassadors of the mammals in New Zealand were also to be lost through the actions of humans.

Marine mammals

Among the marine mammals giving cause for concern are Hector's Dolphin, an animal found nowhere else in the world, and Hooker's Sealion, a species that inhabits Auckland and Campbell Islands just south of New Zealand. Hooker's Sealion is

Left *The Kea* (Nestor notabilis) *is found at high altitudes on South Island, New Zealand. In the past it was persecuted because it was thought to kill sheep, but it is now protected.*

Kakapo (Strigops habroptilus)

thought to be one of the world's rarest sealions, with an estimated population of between 6,000 and 7,000 animals. The species is threatened by the activities of Japanese, Korean, and Soviet trawlers hunting for squid. The sealion also hunts squid, and it is thought that hundreds of them become entangled in the trawling nets each trawling season.

The birds

The largest component of the vertebrate fauna, the birds, have borne the brunt of the unnatural extinction in New Zealand. Seventeen birds have already been lost, and it is estimated that one in every nine of the world's endangered birds now hails from New Zealand. The plight of the endemic parrots – some believe the most spectacular and fascinating of all the world's parrot species – epitomizes the dramatic effects of human invasion upon New Zealand's wildlife.

All the endemic parrots are subject to illegal capture for sale, normally in overseas markets, and other threats. The Kaka is suffering from the felling of indigenous forests and competition with exotic browsers, in existing habitat. The Kea is regionally threatened by illegal shooting and poisoning but it is the Kakapo that has become most prominent in the battle to conserve endangered species in New Zealand. Also known as the Old Night Bird or Owl Parrot, it is the most extraordinary parrot and the one nearest extinction, with only 43 remaining. This flightless creature of the night is the largest parrot in the world, weighing up to 3.5 kilograms (7¾ pounds). It may live to be 60 years old or more but even with such longevity, it may not see out the century unless drastic action is taken. The bird evolved in the absence of large predators, except for a now-extinct giant eagle. So it has no defences, other than its natural camouflage of mottled green and yellow feathers and the instinct to freeze when threatened, with which to stave off the onslaught of humans and their introduced species. The Kakapo exists now on only a few small islands, Little Barrier, Codfish, and Stewart. The two former are islands to which it was deliberately transferred from Stewart Island as part of a million dollar, long-term scheme.

The endemic Takahe, a beautiful and endangered flightless rail, was once widespread in the alpine grasslands and upper beech montane forests off Fiordland. Its decline in population has been caused by predation and competition for food with introduced species, in an already restricted range. The kiwis, familar throughout the world as symbols of New Zealand, are also in some trouble. Like all of New Zealand's flightless birds, they are finding difficulty in maintaining range and numbers under continuing human pressures. The North Island Brown Kiwi is threatened by land clearance and is apparently vulnerable to accidental killing during pig and possum hunting. The South Island Brown Kiwi is under threat in a number of areas due to logging, while the highly endangered Little Spotted Kiwi has only one viable and restricted colony, and requires urgent conservation action.

In contrast, the Black Robin provides a good-news story. About a decade ago, the species was on the brink of extinction with the last five Black Robins clinging on to survival on one of the Chatham Island group. Although the species was always restricted to the Chatham islands some 800 kilometers (500 miles) east of mainland New Zealand, it was once widespread throughout the island group. Gross habitat disruption, destruction and predation reduced the population to a mere handful of birds in a tiny remnant patch of forest. Thanks to the intervention of the New Zealand Wildlife Service, and the unusual longevity and breeding capacity of one of the two surviving females, the population of Black Robins today stands in excess of 116 birds – a spectacular and welcome recovery.

Reptiles, amphibians, and fish

While proving rather more resilient than the bird or mammal fauna, the endemic reptiles and amphibians of New Zealand have not been immune from the pressures of modern human society. That well-known reptilian curiosity, the Tuatara, has a very restricted distribution and is further threatened by the illegal reptile trade and predation by rats on a number of the islands it currently inhabits. New Zealand's only endangered reptile is the Great Barrier Skink, threatened by habitat destruction, and introduced predators. Five other reptile species thought to be vulnerable are Stephens

Below *The Takahe* (Notornis mantelli) *was confined to the Murchison mountains of South Island, New Zealand. There competition for food from introduced deer and predation by introduced mammals have caused a decline, and a population has been established on Maud Island.*

Below right *The Black Robin* (Petroica traversi) *was confined to Little Mangere Island in the Chatham islands of New Zealand, but in the 1970s the entire population was transferred to Mangere Island and there are now populations on Rangatira as well.*

Island Gecko, the Grand Skink, Whitaker's Skink, the Robust Skink, and Macgregor's Skink. The two losses to the forces of extinction have been the skink, *Leiolopisma gracilicorpus*, and the Giant Gecko.

New Zealand's three endemic amphibians are all frogs. Only one is listed as vulnerable to extinction in New Zealand – Hamilton's Frog, with only two main populations surviving. However, the other two species, Archey's Frog and Hochstetter's Frog, are regionally threatened by habitat destruction.

Many of New Zealand's galaxid fish have also found the pressures of human society too great. The Shortjawed Kokopu, the Canterbury Mudfish, and the Black Mudfish are listed as threatened. The only species known to have become extinct is the New Zealand Grayling.

Above *The New Zealand Hamilton's Frog,* (Leiopelma hamiltoni) *lives well away from standing water, in mists and clouds. It was discovered in 1915 on Stephens Island in the Cook Strait, but by 1942 was believed extinct. It has since been found again there and, although it is still very rare, another colony was discovered in 1958 on Maud Island, where this one was photographed. Because of the scientific interest in the species, it was given protection in 1921, together with all other New Zealand frogs.*

The future

This review has barely touched on the marine vertebrates and the land and marine invertebrates at risk. No one even really knows how many invertebrate species there are in the Australasian, region as a whole. Guesses range from half a million to one million, and are probably serious underestimates. This indicates the amount we have still to learn about the region's biological diversity. Yet we must learn quickly, for the scale of environmental, and consequent species, degradation, is already great.

There is, however, reason for optimism. The Indonesian, Papua New Guinean, Australian, and New Zealand governments have all embarked upon a new era in environmental management, both individually and, increasingly, in partnership. They are realizing that not only do we have an obligation to future generations to preserve the diversity and bounty of life for its own sake, but that well-managed natural resources will mean a better and longer life for us all.

SPECIES IN FOCUS

ANTARCTICA

Mark Carwardine is a zoologist, writer, photographer, and broadcaster. After graduating in zoology from London University, he worked for six years as the World Wide Fund for Nature's Scientific Officer. He later joined the Nairobi-based United Nations Environment Program, as resident Science writer, and then worked as a consultant for the International Union for Conservation of Nature and Natural Resources, in Switzerland. Since going freelance in 1986 Mark has become a regular contributor to radio and television programs. He has written more than 20 books on a variety of travel, wildlife and conservation subjects, and numerous articles for newspapers and magazines.

Right *The Antarctic peninsula near Argentine Island. The last nearly pristine wilderness in the world, Antarctica is now critically threatened by a wide range of developments, including mineral exploitation and other human activities.*

Below *Antarctica covers ten per cent of the world's land surface and doubles again in size when the seas freeze in the winter. A great sheet of ice containing 99 per cent of the world's ice covers 98 per cent of the continent.*

AUSTRALIA

ANTARCTICA

Antarctica is the only continent that has so far escaped most of the destructive human activities that are such a familiar problem in other parts of the world. Permanently concealed under a thick ice cap, cold and windy, isolated and inhospitable, it is the kind of place that many people assume will be safe forever. But there is growing concern about its future. As resources elsewhere in the world become even scarcer, certain governments and businesses are looking to Antarctica for new supplies of food and mineral wealth. This could cause irreversible damage very quickly. Yet many experts believe that the continent is of more long-term value to the world if left untouched and, for a growing number of people, it has come to symbolize the need for drastic measures to protect the world's last remaining wildernesses.

Antarctica is basically a huge island, separated from all other continents by a permanently frozen sea and the stormy waters of the Southern Ocean. About twice the size of Australia, it is roughly circular in shape with a spindly arm (called the Antarctic Peninsula) reaching northwards toward Tierra del Fuego. The continent is very important for a number of reasons. It is a critical component of the world's weather system, which is driven largely by the great temperature difference between the tropics and the poles. It provides a pristine open-air laboratory for monitoring global pollution. And it is the largest wildlife sanctuary on Earth.

Krill – a rich feeding ground

First impressions about the wildlife of Antarctica can be misleading. With a few exceptions, the land animals are predominantly microbes and small invertebrates, the largest of which is a wingless fly less than 13 millimeters (½ inch) long. Plant life is also rather limited, consisting of just two native vascular species (a pearlwort and a grass) and a few representatives of groups such as mosses, lichens, algae, and micro-organisms. But the surrounding sea, which covers more than twice the area of the land, is a thick soup of tiny shrimp-like creatures called krill, which are full of protein and live in dense swarms throughout the region. Directly or indirectly, the krill make the Southern Ocean a rich feeding ground for a significant number of the world's surviving great whales and millions of seals, penguins, and other animals.

Antarctica's wildlife has been exploited for a long time. Catch levels of krill are fairly modest, currently averaging less than half a million tons per year, but krill is widely considered to be one of the planet's largest remaining untapped sources of food and there are plans to increase the harvest. Yet competition for krill among the wildlife of the Southern Ocean is already intense, and there is concern that even a relatively small krill fishery could have a serious impact on the struggling populations of whales and other animals.

All other fishing was effectively unregulated for many years, the discovery of new stocks being followed characteristically by rapid overfishing. Since the late 1960s, several fish populations have declined by as much as 90 per cent and the overall annual catch has fallen dramatically. Nevertheless, all the world's major fishing fleets are still working the Antarctic waters.

Krill (Euphausia superba)

—————— Whaling ——————

Seals and whales were once killed in enormous numbers and even penguins have been harvested for their eggs, flesh, and skins. While most of the hunting has now stopped, or is adequately controlled, whaling remains a notable exception. Officially, all commercial whaling has been banned since October 1985. But the ban exists on paper only. More than 12,000 whales have been slaughtered since it came into effect.

The world's whalers first turned their attentions to Antarctic waters at the beginning of the century, when they had wiped out most whale populations everywhere else in the world. The most sought-after species was the largest animal

Below left *An American Sheathbill* (Chionis alba) *scavenging behind a Gentoo Penguin* (Pygoscelis papua) *among Chinstrap Penguins* (Pygoscelis antarctica). *Chinstraps may have increased since the slaughter of whales, with which they competed for Krill.*

Below *Numbers of Crabeater Seal* (Lobodon carcinophagus) *have increased dramatically since the 1930s and it is believed this is directly linked to the decline in whales. Like the great whales, these seals feed on Krill, sucking them in as they swim through a shoal open-mouthed, and then sieving them through their cheek teeth.*

ever to inhabit our planet, the Blue Whale. At the peak of the whaling operations, in the short 1930-31 season, an incredible 30,000 of these animals were killed in the region. There were about a quarter of a million Blue Whales there at the time; today, there are between 200 and 1,100 left. As the Blue Whale catch declined, the whalers concentrated on other species and, one by one, the Antarctic's great whales were hunted to commercial extinction. Yet the whaling continues to this day. The Japanese are still ploughing the southern seas for Minke Whales, stubbornly ignoring the official ban and in spite of strong world opinion against them.

———— Research and Tourism ————

Surprisingly, no human had set eyes on the Antarctic continent itself until the Russian explorer Thaddeus von Bellingshausen sighted it in January 1820. The first actual landing was many years later, in 1895, when a Norwegian whaling party stepped ashore beneath Cape Adare in Victoria Land. Human activities since have more than made up for lost time. There are more than 60 permanent scientific bases on the continent and surrounding islands, populated by some 800 people in the winter and as many as 3,000 during the brief southern summer. The largest is like a small town with a bank, a hotel, and even an airport built on the ice. They all compete with wildlife for the very limited ice-free space and cause local problems with waste (including human sewage) which is often dumped straight into the sea or on to the ice.

Antarctica is also becoming a popular tourist destination. Tourism in the region is already 25 years old and, although it is currently limited to a small number of cruise ships, there is concern that it may be approaching a rapid phase of expansion. There are proposals to build hotels, airstrips, and other land-based facilities to cope with the growing demand.

Below *The pollution on this beach on the British island of South Georgia is typical of an increasing problem throughout the Antarctic. Abandoned whaling and sealing stations, and modern scientific research facilities all contribute litter to what was until very recently a totally unspoiled region.*

Below right *The* Explorer *is one of an increasing number of tourist ships visiting the Antarctic. If properly controlled, tourism can be a relatively benign form of development.*

Mining

The greatest potential threat of all is mining, which could cause irreversible damage on a massive scale. Research by several nations suggests that Antarctica just might contain large quantities of oil and substantial deposits of other minerals, such as copper, platinum and coal. If these reserves were ever exploited, oil spills would be inevitable and the continent would be besieged with ever larger numbers of people, increased shipping operations, huge quantities of equipment, and a variety of new buildings and exploration facilities.

Restricting human activities – and environmental damage – in Antarctica is particularly difficult because it belongs to the world as a whole rather than to just one country. There were formal territorial claims to various sections of the continent as early as 1908 but, thanks largely to a remarkable international pact called the Antarctic Treaty, these have all been frozen. The treaty came into force in 1961 and provides a legal framework for all decision-making in the region. It has enabled the development of a wide selection of valuable agreements and guidelines on everything from expeditions and research bases to telecommunications and tourism.

The risks of mineral exploitation – even if it is carefully controlled – are simply too great to exchange for a few years' extra supply of raw materials. Many experts believe that there can be no half measures. If we do not give the continent *complete* protection it may be impossible to preserve it at all. With this in mind, several governments and many of the world's largest conservation organizations have proposed a very exciting idea: to establish Antarctica as a world park. This would ensure that environmental considerations came first in the planning and performance of all human activities. It would be the first park of its kind and would give the last virtually unspoiled continent on our planet the level of protection it deserves.

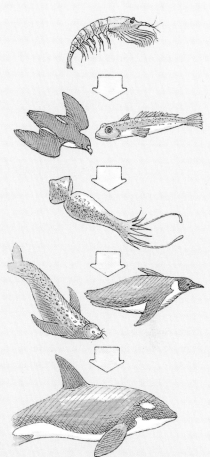

Above *Krill* (Euphausia superba), *a shrimp - like crustacean, occurs in such huge numbers that it dominates the Antarctic food chain. A wide range of animals feed directly on Krill, including fish, seabirds, penguins, Crabeater Seals, and the great whales, and many of these are, in turn, devoured by others. People's depletion of the great whales has irrevocably altered the balance of wildlife dependent on Krill.*

OCEANIA & MARINE

Oceania can be broadly defined as all those islands, scattered across the world, which rise directly from the seabed and have never been part of a continental land mass. Alternatively, it can be defined as the majority of the Pacific Ocean islands. Oceanic islands support a higher number of endemic animal and plant species than any other region.

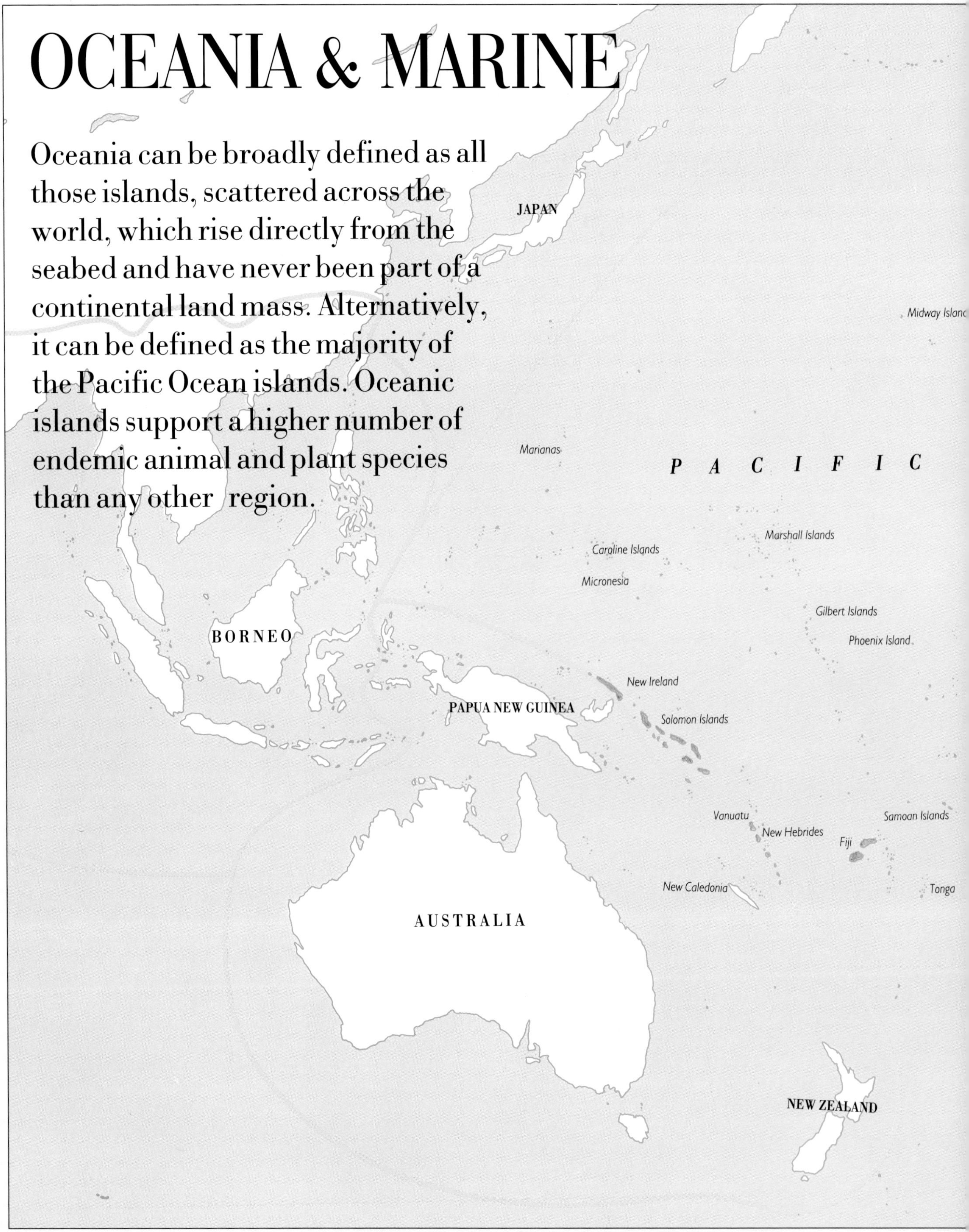

JAPAN

Midway Island

Marianas

PACIFIC

Caroline Islands

Marshall Islands

Micronesia

Gilbert Islands

Phoenix Island

BORNEO

New Ireland

PAPUA NEW GUINEA

Solomon Islands

Vanuatu

Samoan Islands

New Hebrides

Fiji

New Caledonia

Tonga

AUSTRALIA

NEW ZEALAND

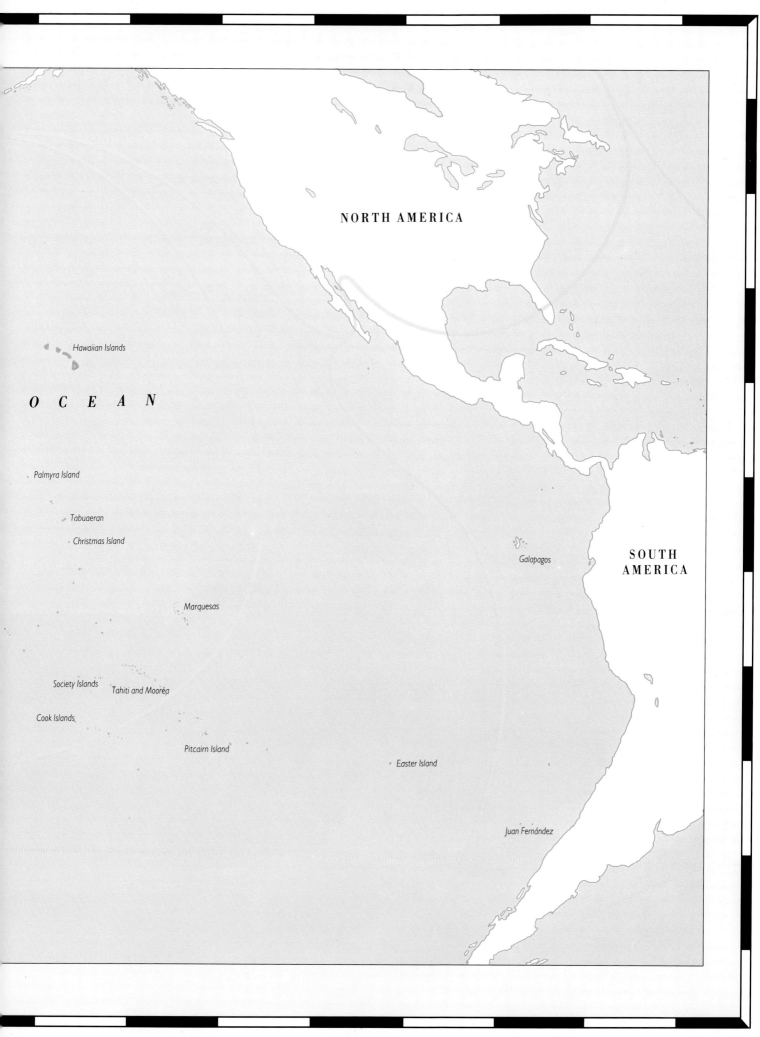

NORTH AMERICA

SOUTH AMERICA

O C E A N

Hawaiian Islands

Palmyra Island

Tabuaeran

Christmas Island

Galapagos

Marquesas

Society Islands

Tahiti and Mooréa

Cook Islands

Pitcairn Island

Easter Island

Juan Fernández

OCEANIA & MARINE

Teresa Farino is an ecologist, freelance writer, and environmental consultant with a special interest in the adaptations of animals and plants to the world's biogeographic zones. She is author of five books, and has contributed to many other publications. She has spent the last five years studying the flora, fauna, and traditional agricultural system of the Picos de Europa in northern Spain, where she now lives. She has a Masters degree in Conservation and is an honorary research associate of the University College of Wales, Aberystwyth.

Oceania can be broadly defined as all those islands, scattered across the world's oceans, which rise directly from the seabed and have never been part of a continental land mass. Oceanic islands are usually volcanic in origin, formed of lava pushed up through points of weakness in the Earth's crust. In tropical regions, coral reefs soon form around new volcanoes. Over the course of millennia, the cone gradually sinks under its own weight and vanishes beneath the waves, leaving a coral atoll as the only evidence of its past existence.

All volcanic islands rise pristine from the seabed and are totally devoid of life at their formation. Natural colonization by animals and plants is a slow process. Creatures which can swim or fly – seals, marine turtles, and seabirds – may arrive under their own steam, sometimes carrying the seeds of plants in their fur or feathers, or even in their stomachs. Microscopic seeds and small invertebrates may arrive at an island in the air streams of the upper atmosphere, while cyclones and hurricanes can cause rafts of fallen trees and other debris from the continents to be hurled far out to sea. Very occasionally such a raft may come ashore, depositing its living cargo.

Only a tiny fraction of the vast wealth of continental animals and plants will ever reach an oceanic island and, even then, survival is dependent upon finding a suitable habitat or a compatible mate. But those creatures that become successfully established on an oceanic island thrive in the absence of mainland predators and have a multitude of new niches to exploit. Such isolated island populations start to change, both physically and behaviourally. Thus, oceanic islands support a higher number of endemic animal and plant species than any other biogeographic region.

The Hawaiian archipelago, which lies almost 4,000 kilometers (2,500 miles) from the nearest major land mass and 1,600 kilometers (1,000 miles) from the closest

Right *The coast of Napali on the island of Kauai in the Hawaiian Islands. Although superficially unspoiled the impact of people can be discerned. Since their discovery by Captain Cook, the islands have been steadily depleted of their rich and varied fauna and flora through deforestation, hunting, and the introduction of exotic species.*

islands, is the most isolated island group in the world. Although most of the animals and plants that live there are related to families on other Pacific islands, over 90 per cent of the native flowering plants and almost all of the land birds and invertebrates – including some 8,000 insects – are found nowhere else in the world. But of the 69 endemic land birds known to be present on the Hawaiian Islands when Captain Cook arrived in 1798, 25 have since become extinct and most of the remainder are endangered, particularly forest species such as the honeycreepers. Similarly, Hawaii has already lost 600 of its 1,061 endemic snail species and it is estimated that between 200 and 400 of the remainder are endangered. Of the diverse endemic Hawaiian flora, about 300 species have disappeared forever and a further 800 are at risk.

Such horrifying statistics are unfortunately not confined to the Hawaiian archipelago. Generally speaking, oceanic islands have a greater number of endangered species than any other region of equivalent land area in the world. Only 20 per cent of all the bird species in the world are found on islands, but of the 94 species of bird known to have become extinct since 1,600, 85 were island endemics. Similarly, about one-third of the 25,000 flowering plants that are considered to be threatened with extinction in the world today are found only on islands. On the Juan Fernández archipelago off the Chilean coast, the majority of the 116 endemic plant species are endangered, as are two-thirds of the 229 endemic plants of the Galápagos archipelago. Over a quarter of the 600 plants which are endemic to the Canary islands are also at risk, while of the 280 plants native to Mauritius, 7 per cent are extinct and 79 per cent are in danger of vanishing forever.

Just why are so many island species threatened with extinction? One of the main reasons is that small islands are only able to support small populations of any species, no matter how successful that species may be. In addition, in the absence of large herbivores, many plants have stopped expending energy on the production of grazing deterrents such as thorns and toxic chemicals. Similarly, the paucity of predators means that island birds do not have to take to the air to escape, nor do they need to nest in high, inaccessible places. So, during the course of evolution, many birds have lost the power of flight.

Such isolated communities of animals and plants are relatively stable as long as they remain undisturbed, but there are now few islands that have not been visited by people. Humans and their introduced herbivores and predators have wreaked havoc on the unprotected flora and fauna. In addition, the world's oceanic islands are no more able to withstand large-scale forest clearance, burning, soil erosion, and other human disruptions than any other terrestrial ecosystems.

Exploiting island life

Hungry sailors rapidly annihilated the Dodo of Mauritius, which had previously never encountered large predators. The Hawaiian Goose, or Néné, a species with limited powers of flight, was hunted almost to extinction by the early twentieth century. Although reintroductions of captive-bred birds have saved this species from the grave, predation by mongooses, rats, and feral dogs and cats are preventing the population from expanding.

Top *The Silver Sword* (Argyroxphium sandvicense) *is one of the rarest flowering plants in the world, confined to the Haleakala Crater National Park, on the island of Maui, Hawaii. The spectacular flower grows 2 meters (6½ feet) high, takes 15 years to grow, and when it has bloomed the plant dies.*

Above *The Hawaiian Goose or Néné* (Branta sandvicensis) *was saved from extinction both by the introduction of strict protective measures in the Hawaiian Islands and also by a captive breeding program started by Sir Peter Scott in England, and the US Fish and Wildlife Service.*

Hunting has also depleted populations of Pacific-island pigeons, and those now endangered include the Tooth-billed Pigeon, reminiscent of the Dodo in appearance and endemic to the volcanic islands of Western Samoa; the Marquesas Pigeon found only on the island of Nuku Hiva in the Marquesas group; and the Society Islands Pigeon, which is restricted to Tahiti and nearby Makatea in the Tuamotu archipelago. In many areas hunting continues today, despite being illegal.

Birds are not the only island creatures to have suffered from over-exploitation. In the equatorial Pacific, the Galápagos Islands were originally home to 14 distinct subspecies of Giant Tortoise (*Geochelone elephantopus*), the largest measuring up to 122 centimeters (48 inches) in length and weighing some 270 kilograms (600 pounds). It is estimated that more than 200,000 Giant Tortoises were taken from the Galápagos Islands by passing ships between the seventeenth and nineteenth centuries, mostly for live storage in the hold, to provide sailors with a

Right *The Gálapagos Giant Tortoise* (Geochelone elephantopus) *once occurred on all the larger islands in the Gálapagos, but is now extinct on Floreana and Fernandina and much reduced on most other islands.*

continuous supply of fresh meat.

Of an original population of 250,000, only about 15,000 of these Giant Tortoises remain today. Two subspecies have vanished forever and many of the remainder may not survive for much longer. The Pinta Island Giant Tortoise, for example, is as good as extinct, with only a single male surviving – nicknamed "Lonesome George" – now in residence at the Charles Darwin Research Station.

Another species of Giant Tortoise (*Geochelone gigantea*) was once wide-spread on the islands of the Indian Ocean. Somewhat smaller than its Galápagos relative, measuring a maximum of 105 centimeters (41 inches), this tortoise has been systematically exterminated in much the same way. By the end of the nineteenth century, only the isolated coral atoll of Aldabra retained its Giant Tortoises, and today this island is home to about 150,000 of the huge reptiles.

Most of the 55 species of flying fox are restricted to single islands or small island groups in the Pacific and Indian Oceans. They are the largest bats in the world, with a wingspan of up to 1.7 metres (5½ feet). Flying foxes are long-lived creatures that have a very low reproductive rate compared with other mammals of similar size. They also have complex social structures, specific food requirements and a narrow

range of potential roost sites. As a consequence, flying foxes are vulnerable to a wide variety of threats associated with human interference, particularly forest destruction and hunting.

Archeological evidence suggests that the Chamorro people of the Marianas Islands have been eating flying foxes for over 1,000 years. Although traditional hunting practices are thought to have had little impact on the populations of flying foxes in the North Pacific, the introduction of firearms and a cash economy has proved disastrous for many species. Today, all trade in flying foxes serves a single consumer market – the island of Guam in the Marianas islands – where the bats' flesh is regarded as a delicacy. In the 1970s, having all but exterminated the Guam Flying Fox (now possibly extinct) and the Marianas Flying Fox, the hunters moved further afield. No fewer than 30,000 frozen flying fox carcasses were imported into Guam between 1981 and 1987, mainly from Micronesia and Samoa.

Another animal unfortunate enough to be considered a delicacy – and reputed to have aphrodisiac properties – is the Coconut or Robber Crab. Living almost exclusively on small islands in the western Pacific and eastern Indian Oceans, it is probably the largest terrestrial invertebrate in the world. A mature male Coconut Crab can measure a meter (3¼ feet) from leg tip to leg tip and weigh up to 3 kilograms (6½ pounds), females being somewhat smaller. Hunted intensively by island peoples, especially in the northern Marianas, it is also used as fishing bait, and whole crabs are dried and mounted for sale to tourists. As a result this species has declined in many areas and is now extinct on a number of islands.

Above *The Coconut or Robber Crab* (Birgus latro) *is widely distributed in the Indian and Pacific Oceans. Considered a delicacy, it is hunted extensively for food, and is declining throughout most of its range.*

Juan Fernandez archipelago

Sheep, cattle, horses, goats, and rabbits are threatening:

● Crusoe's mayu-monte *(Sophora fernandeziana)* – confined to Isla Robinson Crusoe.

● Selkirk's mayu-monte *(Sophora masafuerana)* – endemic to Isla Alejandro Selkirk.

● *Lactoris fernandeziana* – one of the archipelago's 98 endemic flowering plants.

● *Ranunculus capparum* – only known from a single locality on Isla Alejandro Selkirk and possibly extinct.

Over-exploitation is severely endangering:

● The Chonta Palm *(Juania australis)* – used for walking sticks, cabinet work, and its "edible heart" leaves.

Extinct in the wild since 1908:

● The semi-parasitic tree *Santalum fernandezianum* – felled for its sweet-scented reddish wood, used in the production of prayerbeads and boxes for saintly relics for export to Peru.

The dark red resin of the Macronesian Dragon Tree was once believed to be the blood of dragons and is reputed to have magical and medicinal properties. This small tree has thus been "harvested" from all but the most inaccessible sites and is now extinct on four of the Canary Islands and on Porto Santo in the Madeiran archipelago. Less than 200 specimens remain on Tenerife and La Palma, with a handful on Gran Canaria and Madeira and a small population in the Cape Verde.

Forest clearance

Although direct exploitation has been responsible for the near extinction of some island species, it is the wholesale destruction of the island habitat which has caused the most widespread damage.

When Mauritius, Réunion and Rodrigues (the Mascarenes), lying in the Indian Ocean due east of Madagascar, were colonized by people in the mid-1600s, they were almost entirely forested. Between 1638 and 1710, almost all the lowland ebony was removed for lumber, while in succeeding centuries widespread clearance of the lowland forests made way for valuable cash crops such as sugar, tea and pine plantations. Today, sugar cane covers more than 95 per cent of the lowlands of Mauritius and only a few square kilometres of dwarf upland forest remain.

The effect on the wildlife of these islands has been catastrophic. Among the endemic vertebrate species, Mauritius has lost 11 of its 21 birds, 2 of its 3 fruit bats, and 8 of its 12 reptiles, including *Leiolopisma mauritiana*, formerly the world's largest skink. Nearby Réunion has fared even worse, losing 16 of its 23 birds, both its fruit bats, and 4 of its 6 reptiles. On Rodrigues, all the native reptiles have been eliminated, including the world's largest gecko *Phelsuma gigas*, as well as one of the two fruit bats, and 10 of the 12 land birds endemic to the Mascarenes.

Similarly, people have wreaked havoc on natural ecosystems in the Seychelles, especially the once extensive forests of these granitic oceanic islands. Commercial logging and clearance for agriculture not only physically destroyed a large part of the native forests, but also led to the increased incidence of drought, accidental fires and soil erosion. Not surprisingly, almost all of the 72 endemic vascular plants of the Seychelles (not including Aldabra) are in danger of extinction.

The clearance of upland forests on the main island of Mahé, along with the increased incidence of fire on the denuded island, has reduced the population of the forest-dwelling Seychelles Scops Owl to only 80 pairs. The Seychelles Brush Warbler is found only on Cousin Island today, having disappeared from Marianne during the major forest clearances of the nineteenth century. A similar fate has befallen the Rarotonga Flycatcher, known only from the greatly reduced upland forests of the Cook Islands and not seen since 1976.

Introduced animals and plants

The native plants of oceanic islands are often unable to compete with the vigorous weeds which may become dominant following habitat degradation, while the indigenous animals are ill-adapted to feed on introduced vegetation. In the Mascarenes the invasion of exotic plant species is believed to have brought about the virtual extinction of the monotypic tree *Tetrataxis salicifolia*, now known only from seven individuals on the island of Mauritius, while only three individuals of the small tree *Badula crassa* survive today on the island of Réunion.

Perhaps the most insidious destruction has resulted from introduced domestic herbivores, especially the goat. Goats defoliate all vegetation within reach and can even climb trees to browse. They are also extremely prolific, the goat population on Pinta Island in the Galápagos increasing from just 3 individuals to around 20,000 in 12 years! In the sixteenth and seventeenth centuries, goats were automatically introduced to islands as soon as they were discovered to provide a ready supply of fresh meat for passing sailors.

One of the most tragic examples of environmental breakdown is that of St. Helena, a solitary island in the South Atlantic, perhaps best known as the site of Napoleon's final exile. St. Helena was discovered in 1502, at which time it was densely covered with forests. In 1513, a small herd of goats was introduced and by 1588, the original herd had proliferated into thousands. Their voracious appetites not only stripped the island of much of its herbaceous vegetation but also prevented forest regeneration. This goat-manufactured ruin was aided and abetted by human felling of mature trees to fuel the lime-kilns that were needed to supply mortar for fortifications during the Napoleonic wars.

By 1810, the original forest was confined to a few fragments on the central

Below left *The natural forest cover of the island of Mauritius has largely been destroyed and a significant proportion of the land is now under cultivation for sugar cane.*

Below *The Coco de Mer* (Lodoicea maldivica) *has the largest seeds in the plant kingdom. Their size together with their distinctive shape made the seeds much prized symbols of virility. The plant is confined to the Seychelles. Although extinct in many areas it has been protected in the Valle de Mai since 1966.*

ridges and precipices of the island, the remainder being overrun with some 260 species of European, American, and Australian weeds. Research carried out at that time suggests that, before human intervention, St. Helena had supported in the region of 100 endemic plant species. Today less than 40 endemics remain, about half of which are endangered. Among the more severely threatened are the St. Helenian Olive and the Bastard Gumwood, both of which have been reduced to only a single individual in the wild, while the False Gumwood is represented by only three trees.

The effect of introduced herbivores has been no less severe on a number of other oceanic islands. Only 24 kilometers (15 miles) from the northern tip of Mauritius, Round Island has the misfortune to lie on a major trade route. Following the introduction of goats and rabbits in 1850 to provide food for mariners, overgrazing has almost completely denuded the island. The hardwood forest that formerly clothed the volcanic crown of Round Island has been reduced to just a single tree, while its once luxuriant palm savanna today consists of a few mature trees which are unable to regenerate as the rabbits quickly dispose of any seedlings.

Ship-borne rats have probably had the most devastating impact on island

Right *The Flightless Cormorant*
(Nannopterum harrisi) *from the Gálapagos
Islands. Many species of birds occurring on
oceanic islands are flightless and it is thought
that this reduces their chances of being blown
away from their island home. Another theory is
that with few land predators and easily
available food, they had no need to fly.*

Round Island
Only 152 hectares (375 acres) in size,
Round Island is home to seven reptilian
species known only from the Mascarenes.
- Endangered:
  Gunther's Gecko *(Phelsuma guenther)*
  Round Island Skink *(Leiolopisma
  telfairii).*
- Approximately 75 individuals left: Keel-
  scaled Boa *(Casarea dussumieri).*
- Seen twice in last 20 years:
  Round Island Boa *(Bolyeria
  multocarinata).*

reptiles and birds of any unintentionally introduced animal. The Black Rat is
originally native to Asia but was spread by ship around the world during the great era
of trade and exploration in the fifteenth and sixteenth centuries. It climbs well,
raiding birds' nests for eggs and young, and takes a wide variety of terrestrial prey,
including lizards and large invertebrates.

In the Galápagos archipelago, predation by Black Rats has caused a severe
decline in the population of the endemic Galápagos Dark-rumped Petrel. Similarly,
rat predation on the nests of the Aldabra Brush Warbler is the main reason why this
bird is believed to be extinct. Apparently confined to a 10-hectare (25-acre) strip of
coastal vegetation on Aldabra, only five individuals have ever been seen. In 1977 only
two females were found, while a search in 1986 failed to locate any birds.

The stick insect *Dryococelus australis*, a 12-centimeter (4¾-inch) heavy-
bodied, wingless species, is endemic to Lord Howe Island off the east coast of
Australia. It was formerly abundant on the main island but was quickly exterminated
by rats when they were introduced in 1918. It is possible that a small colony still
survives on tiny Ball's Pyramid, a virtually unvegetated but presently rat-free
offshore islet. Some 40 per cent of Lord Howe Island's indigenous species of forest
bird had also become extinct within five years of the rats' arrival.

In a misguided attempt to control rats, the Indian Mongoose was introduced
to a number of Pacific islands. This voracious predator hunts primarily by day, and
so has relatively little effect on the nocturnal rats. After wreaking havoc on the native
avifauna of Hawaii, the mongoose was imported to Fiji in 1873. Eight species of
indigenous bird subsequently became extinct in the Fijian archipelago, while the
endemic Long-legged Warbler has virtually disappeared, with only a handful of
survivors confined to the montane forests of Viti Levu and Vanua Levu. The endemic
Barred-wing Rail was formerly known from the islands of Viti Levu and Ovalau, but
following mongoose predation it has been recorded only once this century.

In the late nineteenth century, cats were released on Mangere Island in the
Chatham group to control rabbits. This example of biological control did indeed
achieve its stated objective, but in the process no less than 12 indigenous bird species
were also eliminated, three of which were endemic and have therefore disappeared

from this world forever. In the Seychelles, predation by feral cats is thought to have been the main reason for the virtual extinction of the Seychelles Magpie-robin, known only from Frigate Island. The population of the Galápagos Hawk, a confiding species which was once abundant throughout the archipelago, has also been severely affected by cat predation. Only 130-150 pairs were recorded in a 1974 census, and these were found only in remote localities, far from human settlements.

In the 1970s, almost all of the 18 native birds on Guam in the Marianas Islands became extinct because of the Australian Brown Tree Snake, a venomous bird and egg predator introduced to the island after the Second World War. This snake, which locates its prey by smell and is capable of engulfing a chicken, has become so successful on Guam that its population is numbered in millions. One of its most spectacular victims was the endemic and flightless Guam Rail whose population on the island plummeted from over 80,000 individuals in 1968 to zero in 1988. Fortunately the bird is breeding prolifically in captivity, and an experimental population is to be introduced to the nearby, currently snake-free, island of Rota.

The world's largest terrestrial snail, *Achatina fulica*, native to Africa and Madagascar, was deliberately introduced to Réunion in the early nineteenth century.

Below left *The small Indian Mongoose* (Herpestes auropunctatus) *has been introduced into many islands including Mafia (Tanzania), Mauritius, Fiji, and several islands in the Caribbean and Hawaii. They have done considerable damage to populations of ground-nesting birds.*

Below *The Brown Tree Snake* (Boiga irregularis) *occurs in coastal northern and eastern Australia north to New Guinea and Indonesia. This very aggressive snake has been introduced from Australia into Guam, where it has wiped out many of the native birds.*

supposedly to make soup for the Governor's mistress. From there it has spread as far afield as the Society Islands and Hawaii, reaching plague proportions among crops on many Pacific islands. In 1977, in the Society Islands, the large carnivorous snail *Euglandina rosea*, of Florida was introduced in an attempt to control this pest. Rather than tackle the African giant, however, Euglandina rosea preferred a diet of viviparous tree snails, two genera of which (*Partula* and *Samoana*) are found only on the island of Moorea. By 1980, no viviparous tree snails were found in that part of Moorea occupied by the carnivore and it is feared that the majority of the 11 endemic species have become extinct in the wild.

Introduced animals also bring exotic diseases with them, such that native birds of Pacific islands have been seriously affected by bird pox, spread by mites and direct contact between birds, and avian malaria, spread by mosquitoes. The southern *Culex* mosquito, accidentally introduced to Hawaii in the mid-1800s, has carried avian malaria throughout the lowlands of the archipelago, killing off a great part of

Snails at risk
- Over half of the 41 *Achatinella* tree snails endemic to Oahu, Hawaii are extinct, the remainder are seriously endangered by the introduced *Euglandina rosea*, predation by rats and fire ants, shell-collectors, and forest clearance.
- More than 30 of 66 *Bulimulus* snails endemic to the Galapagos are seriously endangered by fire ants.
- All but two of the 13 endemic endodontid snails of Rarotonga in the Cook islands have been eliminated by the African ant.

the native bird life. At present the colder forests above 900 meters (2952 feet) have escaped, but it is only a matter of time before the more hardy northern *Culex* mosquito arrives.

Many of the endemic Hawaiian honeycreepers appear to have little immunity to avian diseases. Among the most severely affected have been the Nukupu'u, the Akialoa (now possibly extinct), the Akiapola'au, the 'Akepa, the Crested Honeycreeper, the 'O'u and the Maui Parrotbill. As usual, though, a single factor is not totally to blame for the honeycreepers' dramatic decline. Forest degradation, introduced mammalian predators such as rats and mongooses, and competition with exotic birds have also contributed to the rarity of this family today.

Marine

The oceans and seas cover more than 70 per cent of the face of the Earth and have an average depth of almost 4 kilometers (2½ miles). All are interconnected, forming one huge, continuous, three-dimensional habitat, which has been estimated to comprise about 99 per cent of all the life-supporting space available on this planet. And indeed, life exists at all levels – from the shallow waters of the continental shelves to the vast expanses of the open ocean, and from the sunlit waters at the surface to the abyssal trenches reaching depths over 11,000 metres (36,000 feet). Some marine organisms have a cosmopolitan distribution in the world's oceans, while others are limited to areas of particular temperature, depth, and salinity.

Over the centuries the oceans have been regarded as a limitless resource. People have vastly over-exploited most commercial fish species, hounded seals and Sea Otters unceasingly for their skins, driven the great whales to the brink of extinction and treated the oceans as a huge trashcan. Although the effects of such depredations are now becoming increasingly obvious, human ignorance is still perhaps the most severe threat to the world's seas and oceans.

Plastics are mong the amost dangerous of all human waste products as they break down very slowly. Over two million seabirds and 100,000 endangered marine mammals, and sea turtles are known to die each year from accidental entrapment in

Above *Discarded fishing nets are a major cause of mortality in seabirds; millions drown every year. This Manx Shearwater was found on a beach in west Wales, close to its breeding site. As a result, its young may have starved to death.*

Right *Huge quantities of garbage end up in the seas. In addition, several thousand tons of hazardous waste are dumped at sea each year.*

or ingestion of discarded plastics. Other forms of pollution also take a heavy toll. For example, in one of the worst single oil spills in history, the tanker *Exxon Valdez* ran aground on 24 March 1989 in Prince William Sound, Alaska. Millions of gallons of crude oil were spilt, contaminating almost 4,000 square kilometers (1,500 square miles) of sea and claiming the lives of 950 Sea Otters, 9 whales, millions of fish, and 300,000 birds.

Incidental catches have a detrimental effect on marine organisms, with one of the most wasteful examples of exploitation being that carried out by tuna-fishing fleets in the eastern tropical Pacific. Tuna in these waters are frequently associated with surface schools of dolphins and porpoises; a fact which enables fishermen to locate their prey with ease. The massive purse-seine nets used to trap the tuna also accidentally drown over 120,000 small cetaceans each year. Not surprisingly, the East Pacific Spinner Dolphin has been reduced by about 80 per cent.

In the Pacific Ocean, an estimated 48,000 kilometers (30,000 miles) of driftnets are set each night by the pelagic fisheries of Japan, Korea, and Taiwan. Each net is a plastic death trap which ensnares and drowns small cetaceans, seals, marine turtles, sharks and other non-target species. But the real threat is posed by the so-called ghost nets – nets which have come adrift and are swept along by the ocean currents, engulfing all creatures in their path. Japan, for example, is estimated to lose 16 kilometers (10 miles) of driftnets each night. When the weight of carcasses becomes too great, the ghost nets sink to the bottom, only to rise again to wreak yet more havoc when their cargo of corpses has rotted.

Shark barriers cause similar problems. These are weighted gill nets, set parallel to the shore to protect bathing beaches around the coasts of Australia and South Africa. Statistics from the Queensland nets alone make depressing reading, with 465 Dugongs, 317 porpoises, 2,654 marine turtles and 10,889 rays being trapped over a period of 16 years, as well as over 20,000 sharks, most of which belonged to species not remotely dangerous to people.

But it is probably over-exploitation that has had the greatest impact on marine life, as these examples from some animal groups show.

Whales and dolphins

One of the most tragic examples of over-exploitation of marine organisms is that of the great whales, hunted for over 1,000 years for their flesh and for the valuable fats and oils contained in the thick layer of blubber which insulates their bodies. In the early days of whaling the harvest was small, but when steel motor vessels appeared on the scene, armed with cannon and accompanied by factory ships able to process a large number of carcasses at sea, whaling began to have a serious impact on its target species. This century alone, over 1.25 million whales have been slaughtered.

The largest living animal, the Blue Whale, was originally found in all the world's oceans and seas, with an estimated total of around 200,000 individuals in the southern oceans alone. Recent surveys suggest that the oceans of the southern hemisphere today support a maximum of 2,000 Blue Whales, despite the species having been protected since 1965. Similar horror stories can be told for other great whales. The Fin Whale, or Common Rorqual, had an estimated pre-exploitation population of over 500,000 individuals, yet only 4,000 are thought to be present in the southern hemisphere today. While about 115,000 Humpback Whales formerly inhabited the oceans, a census in the 1980s revealed the presence of less than 7,000 individuals worldwide.

Above *An increasing amount of debris and waste litters beaches around the world. In many places, raw sewage is still pumped into the sea. Boatloads of household and industrial waste are dumped at sea, and most ocean-going vessels dump their garbage overboard. Plastics, in particular, can take many decades to decompose and may harm or kill birds and marine wildlife.*

Below *Sturgeon, like salmon, return to rivers in order to breed. The Atlantic Sturgeon* (Acipenser sturio) *was once extremely abundant but was fished to the point of extinction in most rivers and pollution has often prevented recolonization.*

Below right *The tail fluke of a diving Blue Whale* (Balaenoptera musculus) *in the Indian Ocean. The Indian Ocean has been created a whale sanctuary, but some scientists believe that Blue Whale populations have fallen so low they may never recover.*

The Bowhead, or Greenland Right Whale, which was once common in almost all arctic waters, has been virtually exterminated. Commercial whaling commenced in the sixteenth century, the prize being the Bowhead's enormously thick layer of blubber and long baleen plates. Bowheads swim close to the surface at low speeds while feeding, and conveniently float when dead, making them the "right" whales for people to exploit. By 1981 the North Pacific Bowhead population was estimated at about 2,200 individuals, with a few sporadic sightings in the North Atlantic. Its close relatives, the Northern Right Whale and the Southern Right Whale, once abundant along the coasts of major land masses, have also been brought almost to the point of extinction. Today these right whales are among the most threatened of all cetaceans, with an estimated world population of about 4,000 individuals.

Other baleen whales that have suffered huge losses through over-exploitation include the Sei Whale, Bryde's Whale, and the Gray Whale. Among the toothed whales, the Northern Bottle-nosed Whale is today believed to be heavily depleted, while only 2,000 to 4,000 Sperm Whales are thought to survive of an original southern hemisphere population of well over a million. Other toothed whales whose populations have declined dramatically include the Narwhal and the Beluga.

The slaughter of the great whales has now almost ended, but their smaller relatives – the dolphins and porpoises – continue to be threatened by hunting. Current estimates suggest that half a million small cetaceans are killed every year, particularly by Japan, Peru, and Sri Lanka. In Sri Lanka, dolphin meat represents a vital source of protein, and the kill is in the order of 40,000 small cetaceans each year. The Japanese claim that eating whale meat is an essential part of their culture and religion. In 1988, Japanese kills accounted for nearly 50,000 small cetaceans, including such endangered species as Dall's Porpoise, found only in the North Pacific.

———— Sharks ————

Another inoffensive beast hunted for centuries, especially in the North Atlantic, is the Basking Shark. It is the second-largest fish in the world, growing to lengths well in excess of 11 meters (36 feet). It feeds on plankton and occurs more or less all around the world, often frequenting shallow coastal waters. The surface-feeding habit and gregarious nature of this fish make it easy prey, while its huge liver yields up to 900 liters (240 gallons) of oil, used as lamp-fuel, lubricants, and in the preparation of cosmetics. In a classic case of over-exploitation, the Achill Island fishery managed to virtually eliminate the Basking Shark population along the western coast of Ireland, a kill of over 1,700 in 1950 dropping to an average of less than 50 sharks a year in the early 1970s. Although the Basking Shark is not considered to be endangered, numbers have declined dramatically in almost all fisheries, and it is feared that the remaining individuals may be too widely dispersed to reproduce efficiently.

In contrast, the Great White Shark is a fierce predator and it is this that has led to its relentless persecution around the world. Large predators always exist in far smaller numbers than the animals on which they feed, and the Great White is no exception: on average, only 27 have been caught for every 100,000 sharks of other species. Because Great Whites occasionally take a curious bite out of an unfortunate swimmer, the sensationalist press and the horror film industry have provoked an almost obsessive hatred of them. In addition, some sports fishermen regard the single-handed capture of a Great White as the ultimate "macho" status symbol, while its teeth fetch up to $200 on the open market and a full set of jaws around $5,000. Some researchers believe the Great White Shark is close to extinction, with only an estimated 35 to 40 remaining in southern Australian waters (once a stronghold of this species), most of which are virginal males.

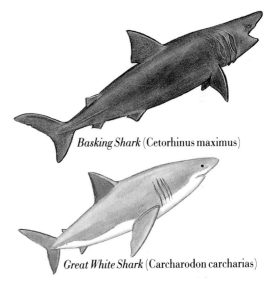

Basking Shark (Cetorhinus maximus)

Great White Shark (Carcharodon carcharias)

——————— **Seals and otters** ———————

Hunting for skins has severely affected many seal populations, especially those with a limited geographical distribution. The Juan Fernández Fur Seal, for example, is confined to five tiny islands off the Chilean coast, where it numbered over 3.5 million in pre-exploitation times. From the seventeenth century onwards, hunting was so intense that by the 1960s this seal was believed to be extinct. Fortunately a few small colonies of survivors were discovered in 1965, and following legal protection the Juan Fernández Fur Seal now numbers more than 2,500 individuals.

The Sea Otter, measuring up to 2 meters (6½ feet) from head to tail, possesses a thick pelt which is regarded as being among the most valuable of all mammal skins. Originally present all around the rim of the North Pacific, from Japan to the shores of central California, its population was estimated at over 200,000 at the beginning of the eighteenth century. By 1911, when hunting finally ceased, it was estimated that only 1,000 to 2,000 Sea Otters remained. Following legal protection the otters have repopulated much of their range, but are still apparently absent from the Pacific coast of North America south of Alaska, apart from an isolated Californian population.

Sea Otters are also severely affected by oil spills. They may ingest the toxic oil while swimming through oil-contaminated waters, eating contaminated food or preening. Alternatively they may die from hypothermia, as, unlike most marine mammals, Sea Otters possess no blubber beneath the skin, relying on their fur for insulation, and it has been suggested that in the cold waters of the Northern Pacific only 10 per cent contamination of the coat can kill.

Many seals are viewed as competitors for the fish harvest by fishermen, who respond by killing large numbers. In some cases a "cull" is associated with a barely concealed demand for seal products. For example, the massacre of Harp Seals and Hooded Seals in Canada in the 1980s took place ostensibly because these species were depleting local fisheries, but had the lucrative spin-off of valuable pelts.

Among the most victimized of the fisherman's supposed competitors are the monk seals, already greatly depleted by sealing expeditions in the eighteenth and

Right *The Sea Otter* (Enhydra lutris) *once widespread and abundant from the coast of Siberia to California, was hunted almost to extinction. Under strict protection, numbers are now rising and it has become a major tourist attraction in some areas, particularly southern California.*

Right *The Sea Otter* (Enhydra lutris) *once widespread and abundant from the coast of Siberia to California, was hunted almost to extinction. Under strict protection, numbers are now rising and it has become a major tourist attraction in some areas, particularly southern California.*

Below *The order of Sirenia contains four living species: the Dugong, the American (West Indian) Manatee, the Amazonian Manatee, and the African (West African) Manatee.*

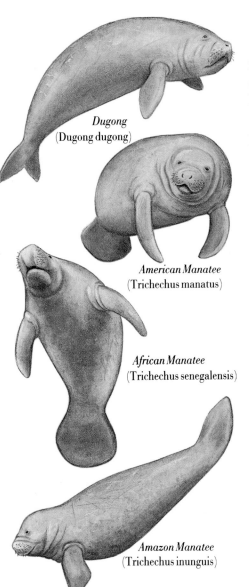

Dugong
(Dugong dugong)

American Manatee
(Trichechus manatus)

African Manatee
(Trichechus senegalensis)

Amazon Manatee
(Trichechus inunguis)

nineteenth centuries. The Caribbean Monk Seal is probably extinct, with no definite sighting since 1952, the last known colony of this species in Yucatan, Mexico, having been exterminated by fishermen in 1911. Although the Hawaiian Monk Seal was formerly widespread in the Hawaiian Islands, it is thought that the current population numbers no more than 1,500 individuals.

Similarly the Mediterranean Monk Seal occurs only sporadically in the eastern Mediterranean today, although its former range extended from Madeira and the Canaries throughout the Mediterranean to the Black Sea. Apart from persecution as a fish-eater, this seal is also suffering disturbance along its coastal habitats due to increased tourism, especially urbanization, pleasure boats and diving. Only about 500 Mediterranean Monk Seals remain, and there is a real possibility that this species will become extinct in the near future.

Sirenians

Possibly the only marine creature as yet annihilated by people is Steller's Sea Cow, a peaceable, slow-moving beast which measured 6–9 meters (20–30 feet) and weighed around 6,400 kilograms (14,100 pounds). This giant herbivore of the Pacific Arctic was discovered in 1741, but within 30 years it had been hunted to extinction for its oil, thick skin, and delicious meat.

Steller's Sea Cow was a member of the Sirenia, an order which contains four living species, all of which are gentle herbivores, totally independent of land and similarly threatened with oblivion by the activities of people. While the Amazonian Manatee is an inhabitant of the lakes, rivers, and channels of the Amazon Basin, the West Indian and West African Manatees both inhabit shallow coastal waters, estuaries and rivers, and the Dugong of the Indo-Pacific is entirely marine.

West Indian Manatees were formerly widespread and abundant around the coasts of the southern USA, the Caribbean and northern South America, but the main viable populations today are confined to Florida, Belize, Guyana, and Surinam. Of over 10,000 manatees in Floridian waters in the 1940s, less than 1,200 remain today. The West African Manatee has suffered less from human depredations and still occupies a large part of its former range from Senegal to Angola. The Dugong is now extinct in the Mediterranean and severely depleted in the northern Indian Ocean. The largest known populations today occur in northern Australia, with a world maximum of around 50,000 in the entire Indo-Pacific.

Sirenians are long-lived creatures with a low reproductive rate. Female Dugongs live for about 50 years but have their first calf betwen the ages of nine and fifteen years, and subsequent offspring at intervals of three to seven years. A stable population of Dugongs can thus increase at a maximum of about 5 per cent per year; similar rates of increase apply to manatees. But many populations of sirenians regularly sustain losses far in excess of this meager figure.

Despite legal protection in many countries, all living sirenians are still hunted for their meat, oil, and hides. In addition, they become entangled and drown in the nets of commercial fishermen, while Dugongs are frequently counted among the unintentional victims of shark nets in Australian waters. Of the total population of around 1,200 Florida manatees, no less than 160 died in 1989, about a third as a result of collisions with an ever increasing number of powered pleasure boats.

Undersea meadows provide the main source of food for manatees and Dugongs, each animal needing to eat at least 5 per cent of its body weight in sea-

grasses per day to sustain its bulk. But onshore forest destruction and soil erosion are increasing the turbidity of the water, thus killing off these meadows and starving the resident sirenians to death. In Florida's Boca Ciega Bay, about a fifth of the sea-grass beds have been destroyed by trawling and dredging activities, while herds of Dugong which feed on the sea-grass beds of the Arabian Gulf are threatened by reclamation schemes off Bahrain.

Left *A West Indian Manatee* (Trichechus manatus) *in the Crystal River, southern Florida. Elsewhere in the world they are hunted for their flesh. In Florida, they are strictly protected against hunters but face the new threat of damage from the propellers of speedboats.*

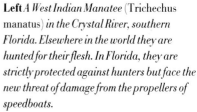

Green Turtle (Chelonia myas)

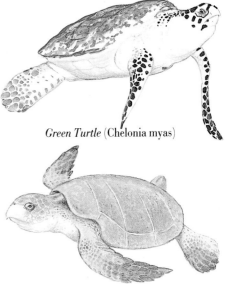

Kemp's Ridley (Lepidochelys kempii)

—— **Sea turtles** ——

Perhaps the most endangered group in the world's oceans today is the marine turtles, six of the seven living species having been severely depleted by over-exploitation and incidental capture, pollution and coastal development.

The Green Turtle is a 1-meter (3¼-foot) long, herbivorous, circumtropical

Triton's Trumpet (Charonia gigas)

Queen Conch (Strombus gigas)

Right *The Hawksbill Turtle* (Eretmochelys imbricata) *is widespread in warmer waters and is the species most valued for "tortoiseshell." It is now protected in most parts of the world and the trade in its shell is controlled.*

species. The females do not mature until 15-50 years of age, when they return to their ancestral beaches to lay their eggs. Many traditional nest sites support depleted numbers of females today, while others have been lost altogether. For example the largest Green Turtle rookery the world has ever known, on the Cayman islands, had been completely exterminated by 1900. The Hawksbill Turtle is another circum-tropical species which feeds mainly on invertebrates of the seabed associated with coral reefs. Unlike the Green Turtle, Hawksbill females emerge to lay their eggs singly or in small numbers. Although many nesting localities survive, their breeding populations are severely depleted.

The Loggerhead Sea Turtle is a circumglobal, carnivorous species about the same length as the Green Turtle. Breeding densities have declined dramatically, the main nesting sites today being found on Masirah Island off Oman and in Florida. The largest sea turtle, the Leatherback, reaches some 1.8 meters (6 feet) in length and lacks a well-developed bony carapace. It is another circumglobal species, but today nesting occurs mainly in Pacific Mexico, French Guiana and western Malaysia.

Kemp's Ridley is a critically endangered turtle whose females choose to lay their eggs only on a 20 kilometer (12 mile) stretch of beach near Rancho Nuevo, Tamaulipas in Mexico. This species is noted for its *arribadas,* in which thousands of female turtles emerge on to the beach simultaneously. In 1947 some 40,000 females emerged at Rancho Nuevo in a single day, but by the late 1970s average figures of only about 500 per season were recorded. The related Olive Ridley is a more widespread species, known from the tropical Atlantic, Indian, and Pacific Oceans. While *arribadas* of more than 150,000 females were once common throughout the breeding range, today such numbers are encountered in only two localities.

The most severe threat to marine turtles is the collection of eggs for food, since whole generations of turtles are liable to be eliminated in one fell swoop. Loggerhead eggs are exploited on a large scale in Mexico, Cuba, Mozambique, and the Macronesian islands, while almost all the Green Turtle eggs laid in Sarawak over the past few decades have been collected by local people, mainly because they are regarded as an aphrodisiac.

All marine turtles are also hunted for food, mainly for local consumption,

although the flesh of the Green Turtle is considered a great delicacy in the Western world. Green Turtles have also been exploited commercially as a source of oil and leather, while leatherback oil was formerly used for caulking boats, as lamp fuel and in local medicine. Commercial harvesting of Olive Ridleys for the leather industry is still widespread, with more than two million adults being taken in Mexico between 1964 and 1969. Only the skin from the neck, shoulders and limbs is removed, the rest of the carcass being discarded. Stuffed juveniles of several species are sold to tourists as curios, particularly Hawksbills. In addition, the strikingly patterned shell obtained from this species has been highly valued since the time of the Pharoahs.

Since most adult marine turtles are bottom-feeding creatures, accidental capture in shrimp trawls causes high mortality. Some 4,000 Loggerheads a year, for example, are drowned or battered to death in this manner in the south-eastern USA alone. Large numbers of Kemp's Ridleys are trapped in shark nets in Australian waters, while drift nets, long lines and ships' propellers cause problems for surface-feeding species such as the Leatherback.

Marine pollution is accounting for large numbers of juvenile turtles, especially Greens and Loggerheads, which are indiscriminate feeders and have been found choked to death on tar balls, styrofoam plastics, and plastic bags. Riverborne pollution in the Mississippi Delta is adversely affecting adult Kemp's Ridley Turtles.

In addition, uncontrolled coastal development is devastating marine turtle populations in many parts of the world. Even where such activities do not completely destroy breeding habitat, sand compaction by vehicles prevents the emergence of the hatchlings and deters further nesting, while speedboats kill and mutilate females waiting to come ashore. Also, the bright lights of coastal resorts cause disorientation both of nesting females and emergent hatchlings. Instead of making their way down to the sea, the turtles head inland.

—— Invertebrates ——

Neither have invertebrates escaped over-exploitation, and endangered species include a number of large marine molluscs. Large-scale exploitation for food and ornament is chiefly responsible for their decline.

Left A Giant Clam (Tridacna gigas) *among branching corals in the Galápagos Islands. Many of the larger and more spectacular molluscs have suffered from overcollection both for food and as souvenirs.*

CONSERVATION
— IN —
ACTION

NATIONAL PARKS

John Burton began his career in the British Museum in the Natural History Department. He moved into freelance writing and journalism and, from 1970 onward, became increasingly involved with wildlife conservation. John has written 15 books and contributed to many others. He was the Executive Secretary of the Fauna and Flora Preservation Society for many years, has been involved with numerous other conservation projects and is currently the UK Representative for the Programme for Belize.

Peter Earland-Bennett is a freelance natural history researcher with an honors degree in Geology and a special interest in lichens and fungi.

The scale of destruction of the world's wild places is escalating rapidly. In the developing world, the demand for natural resources is often one of the prime reasons for this. In the developed world, other factors such as the increase in leisure pursuits can add to the degradation and destruction of habitats. Whatever the reasons, the need for the protection of natural habitats becomes ever more urgent.

Although parks and areas of forest and other habitats were set aside for hunting by monarchs in medieval times and even earlier, the establishment of nature reserves, national parks, and similar protected areas is much more recent. By the end of the eighteenth century the vast expansions in human populations associated with the Agricultural Revolution and then the Industrial Revolution, were taking an increasing toll on nature. Among the earliest naturalists to realize this was the Englishman Squire Charles Waterton, who in 1824 expressed his horror at the way Americans were commercializing Niagara. By 1826 he had enclosed his estate with a high brick wall, protecting all the wildlife within it and creating a sanctuary very much in the modern style. However, the origin of protected areas is not normally traced to the eccentric behavior of an English squire, but to an American cemetery.

In 1831 a rural cemetery known as Mount Auburn was created in the outskirts of Boston. As well as providing a place for burying the dead, within a few years of its

creation, its attractively planted landscape had made it a popular place of recreation for Bostonians. Today it is a mature arboretum and, during the migration season, an important locale for viewing myriad warblers and other songbirds on passage.

A year after the creation of Mount Auburn, the famed artist of native Americans George Catlin proposed that a "nation's park" be created in the west of the emerging USA. Another American, Frederick Law Olmsted, inspired by London's Victoria Park, was one of the designers of New York's Central Park in the 1850s. Although such city parks are far removed from modern concepts of a nature reserve, the seeds of the idea had been sown. They soon germinated and between 1879 and 1885, Frederick Law Olmsted got the state of New York to restore the cataracts of Niagara and its environs to their natural state. Ontario followed suit and made the Canadian side a provincial park in 1888.

It was in 1864, when Yosemite valley was set aside by Congress for protection as a state park, that the modern national park movement can be said to have been truly born. A national park surrounding the Yosemite valley was established by Congress in 1890, but by then Yellowstone had been a national park for nearly two decades. Like the majority of the early parks in America, both Yosemite and Yellowstone were preserved for their monumental scenery rather than their wildlife. It was not until the Everglades of Florida became a national park in 1947 that an area can be said to have been put aside in the USA purely for the wildlife it contained.

While the Americans undoubtedly created the concept of national parks, there were significant developments in other parts of the world. The Gran Paradiso National Park in Italy has a strong claim to be one of the oldest parks, and colonial powers subsequently set aside for protection large areas in Africa and Asia.

As the twentieth century nears its end, the heightened awareness of the plight of wildlife is leading to the establishment of a rapidly growing network of national

Above *China's nature reserves. The ones shown on this map were all established to protect endangered species of animals. In addition, there are reserves established to protect important ecosystems, and others to protect endangered vegetation types. (Based on* China's Nature Reserves *by Li Wenhua and Zhao Xianying.)*

Far left *Yosemite National Park, California, like most other parks in North America, was created primarily for its scenic value rather than as a wildlife refuge. However it does contain a wide range of animals and plants, including many rarities.*

Left *The alpine meadows of Gran Paradiso National Park provide a refuge for some of Europe's rarest fauna and flora. It was there that the Ibex (*Capra ibex*) was saved from extinction. Situated close to the border with France, it adjoins the Vanoise National Park.*

parks and other protected areas. The following examples illustrate some of the better known, more accessible and larger ones, arranged on a geographical basis. Those selected are intended to give an idea of the diversity of wild life to be found within a region's parks.

Africa

Ethiopia has created spectacular parks, including the Awash National Park (72,000 hectares/180,000 acres). This contains mainly a grassy plain in the Ethiopian highlands, crossed by the Awash river. Here the rare Swayne's Hartebeest can still be seen, together with Beisa Oryx, Anubis Baboon, Ostrich, and other wildlife.

The national parks of Kenya are among the best known in the world. Despite its small size and proximity to the city, Nairobi National Park with its backdrop of downtown skyscrapers is still a haven for big game. Nakuru National Park (20,000 hectares/50,000 acres) was established in 1967 around the large shallow Lake Nakuru and swamps. Greater and Lesser Flamingo congregate there in flocks reaching over a million strong at times, as well as Spoonbill, pelican, cormorant and Night Heron. Tsavo, Amboseli, Samburu, the Aberdares, and Malindi Watamu Marine national parks are just a few of the other areas that make Kenya justly popular with tourists.

Right *Tsavo West National Park in Kenya was the center of a controversy over elephant culling in the 1970s. Some people thought that the numbers of African Elephant (Loxcodonta africana) were so high they would totally destroy the natural habitat. Culling did not occur and now the populations are threatened by poaching.*

Tanzania's protected areas included the Ngorongoro Conservation Area (528,000 hectares/1.3 million acres). This provides an extraordinary variety of important habitats for wildlife in a huge volcanic bowl, and also encompasses the Olduvai gorge, rich in fossils of early humans. There are large populations of ungulates, such as wildebeest, Zebra, Eland, and both Thomson's and Grant's Gazelles, alongside Elephant, Lion, rhinoceros, Leopard, African Buffalo, and flamingo, stork and Ostrich. Close by, the Serengeti National Park (1.47 million hectares/3.65 million acres) is perhaps the most spectacular of all the African parks. The undulating plains are filled with the greatest concentration of plains game in Africa, particularly during the annual migration in May to June when huge herds trek in search of water. Wildebeest, zebra, Thomson's Gazelle, Lion, Leopard, Cheetah, African Hunting Dog, Spotted Hyena, Elephant, Black Rhinoceros, Hippopotamus,

Giraffe, oryx, and African Buffalo are among the many animals still abundant there.

In Uganda, Kabalega Falls National Park (384,000 hectares/950,000 acres) contains these magnificent falls on the River Nile. Most of the park is rolling grassland and savanna, with isolated forest patches, swamp and river. It once held some of Africa's largest concentrations of crocodiles, Buffalo, Giraffe, Lion, and Black and White Rhinoceros, as well as Elephant and Hippopotamus. Unfortunately the White Rhino is extinct there and the security of several other species is in doubt.

In West Africa, Senegal's Niokolo-Koba National Park (913,000 hectares/ 2.26 million acres) was established in 1954. It has impressive savannas, flooded grassland, marsh, and dry forest. The mammals include Lion, Leopard, Elephant, and Giant Eland. All three African crocodiles, the Abyssinian Ground Hornbill, and Martial Eagle are also found there.

The 'W' National Park (1 million hectares/2.5 million acres), also established in 1954, straddles the borders of Benin, Niger, and Burkino Faso in West Africa. The habitats protected include forest, savanna, and semi-desert, with populations of Elephant, Lion, Cheetah, Leopard, Hippopotamus, Buffalo, reedbuck, hyena, crocodile and African Fish Eagle.

In the Cameroon the Bouba Ndjida National Park (220,000 hectares/ 540,000 acres) encompasses closed-canopy woodland and light forest with

Below *Mount Kilimanjaro in Tanzania seen from Amboseli National Park, Kenya, with a Giraffe* (Giraffa camelopardalis) *in the foreground.*

Right *Robin's Camp, Hwange National Park, Zimbabwe. Essential components of most national parks are facilities for visitors, since tourists provide vital revenue. The facilities should be as unobtrusive as possible, as in this example.*

White Rhinoceros

The story of the survival of the White Rhino is one of markedly fluctuating fortunes. By the early part of the present century it had been wiped out from most of the southern part of its range, surviving only in the Umfolozi and Hluhluwe Game Reserves in South Africa. However, it was still widespread in the northern parts of its range, with as many as 1,000 in Zaire in the 1960s, and substantial populations in the Sudan, Uganda and elsewhere. By the late 1980s less than 20 of the northern population survived, in the Garamba National Park in Zaire. But the southern population had increased to such an extent that they were being reintroduced elsewhere, sent to zoos, and even culled.

populations of Black Rhinoceros, Giant (Derby) Eland, Elephant, Cheetah, Lion, Hippopotamus, Giraffe, kob (waterbuck), and Buffalo. More recently, with help from the World Wide Fund for Nature (World Wildlife Fund), a large area of forest has been protected in Korup.

Zaire contains some of the largest tropical forests in the world, and the Virunga National Park (780,000 hectares/1.9 million acres) was among the first areas there to be protected as a national park in 1925. The park, contiguous with Ruwenzori National Park in Uganda and Volcanoes National Park in Rwanda contains lakes, marshy deltas, peat bogs, savanna, lava plains, equatorial forest, high altitude glaciers and snow fields. The animals found there include Elephant, Lion, Hippopotamus, Buffalo, kob, Topi, Defassa Waterbuck, Okapi, the endangered Mountain Gorilla and the Chimpanzee. Zambia's Kafue National Park (2.24 million hectares/5.53 million acres) includes open grassy floodplains, forest and swampland. The animals found there include Giant Eland, Kudu, Little Duiker, the rare Red Lechwe, Elephant, Black Rhinoceros, Buffalo, Lion, and the Yellow and Chacma Baboons.

Zimbabwe's network of parks includes the famous Hwange National Park (1.46 million hectares/3.62 million acres) which was established in 1928. It has great teak forests, moist woodland, savanna and grassy plains with substantial populations of Elephant, Buffalo, Giraffe, zebra, wildebeest, Impala, eland, Lion, Leopard, Cheetah, Bateleur Eagle, and vultures.

South Africa has lost much of its wildlife, but does have some impressive protected areas. The Kalahari Gemsbok National Park (959,103 hectares/2.36 million acres) established in 1931, crosses the border of South Africa and Botswana, and joins an area of over 1 million hectares (2.5 million acres) in Botswana. A huge, open expanse of sand dunes with scattered grass and trees, it is home to substantial populations of Gemsbok, Springbok, wildebeest, eland, Cape Pangolin, Cheetah, Lion, jackal, Bat-eared Fox, Secretary Bird, Giant Eagle Owl, and Ostrich.

The Kruger National Park (2 million hectares/5 million acres), established in 1926, was one of the first parks and is among the best-known wildlife reserves in the world. Despite limited rainfall, it supports about 1 million large mammals, including Elephant, Buffalo, Impala, zebra, introduced Black and White Rhinoceros, Hippopotamus, Giraffe, Lion, Cheetah, and Vervet Monkey.

In Namibia's Etosha National Park (2.2 million hectares/5.5 million acres) the arid savannas are scattered with some trees and shrub acacia, but it is largely open arid country. The animals present include Elephant, Lion, Leopard, Cheetah, zebra, Black Rhinoceros, Giraffe, eland, Black-faced Impala, Ostrich, and Red-crested Korhaan.

Asia

Although not as widely known as many of the African and North American parks, there are many impressive reserves throughout Asia. Since these lack the extensive savannas and open grasslands that dominate many of the African parks, the wildlife is generally less obvious, but nonetheless exciting.

India's Gir National Park (130,000 hectares/320,000 acres) is the last home of the Asian population of Lion, which earlier this century ranged from Arabia across the Middle East to India. It comprises mostly arid, overgrazed scrub forest of stunted acacia and teak trees. In addition to Lions there are Leopard, Sloth Bear, Nilgais, Spotted (Chital) Deer, Sambar Deer and Wild Boar.

The habitats of Kanha National Park (46,000 hectares/114,000 acres) include grassland, forests and dense bamboo thickets. It is home to some of the largest populations of several endangered mammals, including Tiger, Barasingha (Swamp Deer), Leopard, Sloth Bear, Dhole (a wild dog), Striped Hyena, and Asiatic Jackal.

Kaziranga Wildlife Sanctuary (43,000 hectares/106,240 acres) is an amply watered area, with swampy plains, open grassland and reedbeds. It is one of the remaining strongholds of the Great Indian (One-horned) Rhinoceros (the largest

Below *Giraffe* (Giraffa camelopardalis), *Thomson's Gazelle* (Gazella thomsoni), *Ostrich* (Struthio camelus) *and Gemsbok* (Oryx gazella) *at a waterhole in the Etosha pan, Namibia.*

Below left *The Gemsbok Kalahari National Park on the borders of Namibia and Botswana is one of the largest areas of wilderness in the world. It has spectacular sand deserts as well as large herds of Gemsbok* (Oryx gazella) *and other antelopes.*

rhino species) and its other inhabitants include wild Water Buffalo, Asian Elephant, Tiger, Leopard, and Himalayan (Asiatic) Black Bear.

Keoladeo Ghana Wildlife Sanctuary covers a relatively small area (2,850 hectares/7,000 acres) consisting of a sparsely wooded, shallow basin. After monsoon rains this becomes a vast expanse of lake and marsh, and attracts huge flocks of water-loving birds, such as cranes, storks, ducks, geese and waders, and birds of prey including Steppe Eagle, Pallas's Fishing Eagle and Marsh Harrier.

Nepal's Royal Chitwan National Park (55,000 hectares/13,600 acres) ranges from low grassy plains to the icy heights of Mount Everest, and is home to Tiger, Leopard, Himalayan Black Bear, Sloth Bear, the endangered Gaur (a wild ox), sightless Ganges Dolphin, and crocodile.

Sri Lanka's Wilpattu National Park (Yala Park) (131,000 hectares/324,500 acres) covers a wide coastal strip and shorelines along Portugal and Dutch Bays. It is noteworthy for its great concentrations of Leopard, which on this island are normally diurnal, and for being the last refuge in the area of the nearly extinct Dugong. Other inhabitants include Sambar and Spotted Deers, Muntjac, Buffalo, Leopards, a small

Above right *A grassy plain in the Royal Chitwan National Park, Nepal, with the permanent snows of the Himalayas in the background.*

Right *A solitary Asiatic Elephant (Elephas maximus) in the Yala National Park in Sri Lanka. The park is also renowned for its spectacular rock formations.*

population of Asian Elephant, herons, egrets, Spoonbill, and White Ibis.

The hundreds of islands that comprise Indonesia are home to a wide diversity of wildlife. They are also home to some of the most rapidly expanding human populations in the world, and a network of protected areas is essential if the wildlife is to survive. The Ujung Kulon Nature Reserve in the lowlands with many streams and swamps is mostly covered by dense tropical vegetation. It was established primarily to provide a refuge for the last survivors of the nearly extinct Javan Rhinoceros, and also harbors Banteng, Muntjac, giant squirrel, Javan Macaque, and monitor lizard.

Borneo's Kinabalu National Park contains forested mountains and tropical lowlands. Among the species found there are the rare Sumatran (Asiatic Two-horned) Rhinoceros, Orang Utan, gibbon, tarsier, Flying Lemur, Giant Ground Squirrel and pangolin.

Thailand's Khao Yai National Park (over 200,000 hectares/512,000 acres) is mostly lush tropical rainforest, with palms, bamboos, evergreens, and deciduous trees. There are healthy populations of Asian Elephant, Sun Bear, Tiger, Leopard, gibbons, and great numbers of hornbills.

Japan has many parks, the majority chosen for their scenic beauty, but an increasing awareness of wildlife has led to more areas being given protection to preserve threatened species. The Akan National Park comprises mountains, forests and lakes, including Kutcharo, the largest crater lake in the world, and Mashu. The scenery is spectacular, especially in autumn when maple and birch turn crimson and yellow, and spring with rhododendrons and azaleas. It also provides a refuge for Eurasian Brown Bear, Raccoon Dog, Sika Deer, and other wildlife.

Turkey's Lake Manyas National Park (50 hectares/125 acres) contains a shallow lake fringed with willows and reedbeds, and nearby woods and low-lying, often flooded areas. Although tiny it is a veritable bird paradise, harboring White Stork, Glossy Ibis, Squacco Heron, White-winged Black Tern, huge flocks of migratory pelicans, and many other birds.

The USSR has an impressive network of protected areas covering habitats that range from arctic tundra to tropical forest. The Barguzin State Nature Reserve (260,000 hectares/650,000 acres), established in 1916, is a refuge for the varied and fascinating fauna and flora of the Lake Baikal taiga. Over 600 species of flowering plant have been recorded there, while the freshwater lake, the deepest in the world, is home to the endemic Baikal Seal and many other unique animals.

The Kavkaz (Caucasus) Biosphere Nature Reserve (260,000 hectares/ 650,000 acres) was created in 1924. A mountain reserve, it has over 1,500 plant species, including many endemic forms, plus 157 birds and 59 mammal species.

"Kedrovaya Pad" Nature Reserve (17,900 hectares/44,000 acres) protects 17 species of plant listed by the USSR as endangered, including Ginseng (*Panax ginseng*) and *Rhododendron schlippenbachii*. It also harbors Leopard and endemics such as Maack's Swallowtail Butterfly.

The USSR's Repetek Biosphere Nature Reserve (34,700 hectares/85,800 acres) is a remarkable area in the Kara-Kum sandy desert, close to the Iranian border. Around 200 species of bird, including Rufous Bush Chat and Pander's Ground Jay, have been recorded, as well as a wide range of reptiles.

Wrangel Island Reserve (796,000 hectares/1.96 million acres) in the Chukchi sea off northeast Siberia is a sanctuary for breeding Snow Goose, sandpiper and other shorebirds, and Polar Bear and Walrus.

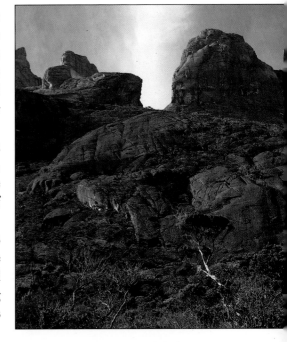

Above *The peaks of Mount Kinabalu from Panar Laban, Sabah Malaysia. Mount Kinabalu which towers to a height of 4,090 meters (13,455 feet) is the highest peak between the Himalayas and New Guinea. The park embraces all the ground over 610 meters (2,000 feet) and pitcher plants are especially abundant.*

Australia and New Zealand

Australia includes some huge areas of largely unexplored natural habitats ranging from arid deserts to the 2,000 kilometer (1,250 mile) long Great Barrier Reef. Green Island, off Queensland (7 hectares/17 acres plus 3,000 hectares/7,500 acres of surrounding waters) is a small coral cay giving access to the Great Barrier Reef. There much of the undersea wildlife typical of the reef can be seen including staghorn, golden leaf, brain and many other living corals together with a wide variety of brilliantly colored fish.

Lamington National Park, Queensland (18,100 hectares/44,800 acres) is a rugged volcanic plateau, deeply cut by winding river gorges providing hundreds of waterfalls. The plentiful rainfall supports varied plant life including rainforest. More than 20 species of orchid, King Parrot, Crimson Rosella, Red-necked Wallaby, bandicoot, Brush-tailed Possum, Sugar Glider, and many others have been recorded.

The fantastic sandstone formations of Ayres Rock – Mount Olga National Park, Northern Territory, are among the better-known natural features of Australia. In contrast, Phillip Island in Victoria (530 hectares/1,300 acres), once a farming community, is now several small reserves, providing refuge for such typically Australian animals as Fairy Penguin and Koala. There are also large breeding colonies of Short-tailed Shearwaters.

Sherbrooke Forest Park in Victoria (800 hectares/2,000 acres) is richly vegetated with luxuriant tree ferns and towering Mountain Ash (Giant Gum Tree). Among the special attractions is the lyrebird.

Tidbinbilla Nature Reserve in New South Wales is a treasury of plant and animal life, and striking geological formations. Grey and Red Kangaroo, reintroduced Emu, Red-necked and Swamp Wallaby, Wombat, Kookaburra, honeyeaters, and Peregrine Falcon are among the animals that can be seen.

The Stirling Ranges National Park, Western Australia, is an area of rugged peaks with cloud forest remnants, dry eucalyptus forest and mallee heath. It contains many rare wildflowers, as well as Grey Kangaroo, wallaby, wombat, Emu, Purplecrowned Lorikeet, and several species of honeyeater.

Mount Field National Park, Tasmania, encompasses forested mountains,

Left *The horses of the Camargue, though not wild, typify the region. Much of the Camargue has been heavily modified by people but it remains important for breeding birds such as flamingoes and herons and rare mammals such as Wild Boar* (Sus scrofa) *and beaver* (Castor fiber).

waterfalls and high bogs. Its wildlife inhabitants include Platypus, Tasmanian Devil, Tasmanian Echidna, bandicoot, wombat, wallaby, Tasmanian Native-hen, Yellow Wattlebird, and Green Rosella.

New Zealand's Egmont National Park, North Island, is in forested mountains. Several of the birds unique to New Zealand still occur there, including Brown Kiwi, Kaka, Shining Cuckoo, North Island Tomtit, and North Island Wattled Crow. Urewera National Park, North Island, covers an area of densely forested mountains, waterfalls, and lakes. Many of New Zealand's rare endemic birds are found there including kiwi, Weka, Paradise and Blue Duck, Kaka, Shining Cuckoo, New Zealand Pigeon, and Morepork.

Fiordland National Park, South Island (1.2 million hectares/3 million acres) is one of the world's largest national parks and also one of the most unspoiled. Among the birds found there are two species of kiwi, and Takahe, Kakapo (Old Night Bird), and South Island Wattled Crow. In addition there are fur seal and sealion.

Europe

Almost everywhere in Europe shows signs of human activities, but there are still some remarkable parks and reserves. Although these may be modified or even managed, they are often spectacularly beautiful, particularly in spring, and home to the remnants of the large mammal fauna that was once widespread over the continent.

Austria's Marchauen-Marchegg Nature Reserve (1,120 hectares/2,760 acres) contains some of the most luxuriant of Europe's remaining riverine forests. Inhabitants include Red Deer, Roe Deer, Wild Boar, marten, European Lynx, seven species of woodpecker, Black Kite, White-tailed Eagle, Honey Buzzard, and heron. Neusiedlersee and Seewinkel Reserves (34,000 hectares/85,000 acres) on the Austro-Hungarian border encompasses a remarkable steppe lake and shallow marsh. These form a vast breeding ground that attracts more than 300 species of bird including Great White Egret, European Spoonbill, Baillon's Crake, and Red-necked Phalarope.

The Hautes Fagnes Nature Reserve is in Belgium, one of Europe's smallest and most densely populated countries. It protects a high plateau of peat moor ringed by woodland and is inhabited by Red Deer, Roe Deer, Wild Boar, and the rare

Otter Trust

Over the majority of its European range, the otter is critically endangered, if not already extinct. The causes for its decline include pesticide poisoning, hunting, and probably road deaths. In areas where adequate protection can be given reintroductions have taken place, and in England the Otter Trust has been breeding them very successfully in captivity. In cooperation with the Nature Conservancy Council, the Otter Trust has successfully reintroduced into the wild captive-bred otters. Subsequent monitoring of these animals has shown that they have bred in the wild and reared cubs.

European Wild Cat. The flora includes many rare species such as Marsh Gentian, Bog Asphodel, Bog Pimpernel, White Beak-sedge, and Common Sundew.

One of France's most spectacular protected areas is the Camargue Zoological and Botanical Reserve (10,500 hectares/26,000 acres) around the Rhône Delta on the Mediterranean coast. It is one of Europe's most important bird reserves and over 320 species of bird have been recorded. Flamingo, four species of tern, Bee-eater, Roller, and Great Spotted Cuckoo are among the birds breeding there.

La Vanoise National Park adjoins the Gran Paradiso of Italy on the French side. It has magnificent alpine scenery containing coniferous forest, interspersed with heath, alpine meadowland, glaciers, and permanent snow. The mammals include Ibex, Chamois, and Alpine Marmot. Among the 115 species of bird found there are Water Pipit, Alpine Accentor, and Black Grouse.

In Eire's Killarney National Park, the oceanic climate encourages luxuriant growth of mosses and ferns within the fine natural oak and yew woodland. Unusual species include strawberry tree, Irish Spurge, the large-flowered butterwort and kidney saxifrage, and Red Deer and the introduced Sika Deer.

Much of Germany is forested, though mostly with second-growth forests or plantations. The Bavarian Forest National Park (13,000 hectares/32,000 acres) is

Right The Farne Islands off the coast of Northumberland, England are a breeding ground for large colonies of seabirds such as these puffins, kittiwakes, and guillemots.

inhabited by three species of grouse – the Capercaillie, Black Grouse and Hazel Hen – Tengmalm's Owl, Goshawk, Three-toed Woodpecker, and Ring Ouzel as well as Roe and Red Deer, and Pine Marten. The Berchtesgaden National Park is a stunningly beautiful enclave of alpine scenery. It offers a wide range of habitats including deciduous woodland, spruce-beech-fir woodland, subalpine coniferous forest, mountain-pine scrub, and alpine grassland. Among the rarer inhabitants are juniper, Arolla Pine, Dragonmouth, Apollo butterfly, Marmot, and Golden Eagle.

Great Britain's wildlife is among the most impoverished in Europe but the Cairngorm National Nature Reserve, Scotland (26,000 hectares/64,000 acres) is a magnificent wilderness area containing vertical rocky cliffs, cauldron-like corries, steep-sided glens, and vast areas of high moorland. Among the birds to be encountered are Golden Eagle, Osprey, Peregrine Falcon, Merlin, Snow Bunting and Ptarmigan, while the flora includes Bell Heather, Mountain Crowberry, Creeping

Azalea, Dwarf Cornel, and Alpine Lady's Mantle.

Lindisfarne National Nature Reserve and the Farne islands, England, comprise 28 small islands renowned for their wildfowl, seabird, and Gray Seal populations. In contrast, the New Forest, was formerly a royal forest, created by the Norman kings in the eleventh century. Although without formal status overall, it includes extremely important conservation sites, being among the richest areas in the British Isles for both plants and animals. Uncommon species include Honey Buzzard, Hobby, Goshawk, Nightjar, Sand Lizard, Smooth Snake, Mole Cricket, and several of Britain's rarest butterflies.

Minsmere Bird Reserve, England (600 hectares/1,500 acres) is one of the most outstanding in Britain. Its reedy marshes and pools, woodland, heathland, and hedge are mainly human-made habitats, but they attract some 250 species of bird, mostly waterfowl and shorebirds. These include Avocet, Bittern, Nightjar, Marsh and Hen Harrier, Garganey, Snow Bunting, and Black Tern.

Dartmoor National Park, England, is a high plateau of ancient granitic rocks comprising moors and bogs, rocky outcrops and steep-sided, wooded valleys with fast-flowing streams. The rich and distinctive flora includes the rare Heath Lobelia, Sanicle, Royal Fern, and Opposite-leaved Golden Saxifrage.

Left *Dartmoor, Devon, England seen from Pew Tor. Like most of Britain's national parks, there is much evidence of human activity with the landscape heavily modified by grazing and farming. The Dartmoor National Park contains many important archeological sites and herds of semi-wild primitive ponies.*

Greece's Lake Mikri Prespa National Park, established in 1971, is one of the least known but certainly one of the most important of Europe's protected areas. The lake and its shores harbor an extraordinary variety of birds. They include nesting colonies of Dalmatian and White Pelicans, both of which are declining rapidly, Spoonbill, Pygmy Cormorant, Gray and Purple Herons, Squacco Heron, Night Heron, Little Bittern, Glossy Ibis, Great White and Little Egret.

Italy's Gran Paradiso National Park (63,500 hectares/157,000 acres), one of the world's oldest protected areas, is in a beautiful part of the Italian Alps. Created in the last century as a reserve for Ibex, it also harbors 1,500 species of alpine plants, Chamois, and Golden Eagle, Alpine Swift, Crag Martin, Alpine Chough, Snowfinch, Black Grouse and Ptarmigan.

The Texel and Terschelling Reserves (280,000 hectares/700,000 acres) of the Netherlands are very valuable bird reserves in the Waddensee, a huge expanse of

Above *Sandhill Cranes* (Grus canadensis) *against a backdrop of scorched trees in the Yellowstone National Park, Wyoming, USA. In the past, fires were normally controlled even within parks but in recent years the National Park Service has occasionally allowed them to take their natural course.*

tidal flats and shallows. They are home to breeding colonies of Spoonbill, Avocet, Eider, Curlew, Black-tailed Godwit, Ruff, Redshank, Shelduck, and tern.

Norway has a small human population spread over a huge area and in its Rondane National Park, an area of largely unspoiled high mountain ranges, some of Europe's rarest mammals can be found, including wild Reindeer and Wolverine.

Poland's Bialowieza National Park was formally established only in 1947 but has a much longer history. Together with its neighboring Russian area, it preserves remnants of the primeval forest which once spread over the central European plain. For four centuries it has been the principal home of the once greatly endangered European Bison. It also contains Elk (Moose), European Lynx, Grey Wolf, Beaver, Bechstein's Bat, and most other species associated with the great forests.

The Danube Delta Reserve (440,000 hectares/1.1 million acres) in Romania is a maze of shifting channels, reedy swamps, sandbars, low islands, and floodplains rising barely above sea level. Although a large part has been destroyed or drastically modified in the past few decades it is still among the most important wetlands in Europe. There are herds of Wild Boar, as well as small populations of Gray Wolf, and European Wild Cat, Mink, and Otter. The birds include White and Dalmatian Pelicans, nesting Pygmy Cormorant, Glossy Ibis, and Night Heron.

Spain's Coto Doñana National Park (33,700 hectares/83,200 acres) is one of the most valuable wildlife areas of western Europe and, sadly, one of the most threatened. Amid the sand dunes and marshes of the Guadalquivir river delta lives one of the last of the Iberian populations of the European Lynx. Also present are Wild Boar, Red and Fallow Deer, Avocet, Black-winged Stilt, Slender-billed Gull, Crested Coot, Black-necked Grebe, and Griffon, and Black Vultures.

Just south of the high peaks of the Pyrenees lie the spectacular crags and escarpments of the Valle de Ordesa National Park (2,000 hectares/5,000 acres).

There are a number of rare species including Spanish Ibex, Chamois, Wild Boar, Wild Cat, European Brown Bear, Lynx, and, among the birds, Lammergeier, Alpine Swift, Alpine Chough, Rock Thrush, and Ptarmigan.

Sweden's Stora Sjöfallet National Park (540,000 hectares/1.3 million acres) is by far the largest reserve in Europe. It is mostly primeval coniferous forest mixed with birch woods, dwarf birch and willow scrub, alpine heath and tundra, and also includes extensive areas of marsh and bog. It shelters some of the last populations of Europe's larger mammals including European Brown Bear and Lynx, Gray Wolf, Wolverine, Pine Marten, and Elk (Moose). Birds found there include Golden Eagle, Gyrfalcon, Merlin, and Rough-legged Buzzard.

The Swiss National Park (2,000 hectares/5,000 acres) was an early reserve, established in 1914. It contains long stretches of magnificent pine forest, remote untouched valleys and impressive peaks of dolomitic limestone. The mammals found there include Ibex, Chamois, Marmot, while among the birds are Alpine Swift, Snow Finch, Ptarmigan, Black Grouse, Alpine Chough, Capercaillie, Raven, and Nutcracker.

North America

The vast, largely unexplored, northern tundras of Canada and Alaska include some of the world's largest protected areas. Wood Buffalo National Park, Alberta (4.5 million hectares/11 million acres) was established in 1922 to protect the last remaining herd of Wood Bison. Today's descendants, numbering 12,000, are mostly hybrids of Wood and Plains Bison, but a pure isolated herd of about 200 Wood Bison was found in 1957 in the Nyarling river–Big Buffalo lake area of the park. The park also contains Moose (Elk), Woodland Caribou, Black Bear, and Timber (Gray) Wolf.

The United States park system got underway with the protection by Congress of the spectacular Yosemite valley and surrounding countryside, but this still did not save California's symbol, the Grizzly Bear, from extinction in the state. Yellowstone National Park, Wyoming (880,000 hectares/2.2 million acres) is the oldest and, together with the Grand Teton National Park and other contiguous protected areas, forms one of the largest wilderness areas in the United States. It is a high rolling

Bald Eagle
The Bald Eagle was chosen by the United States of America as the nation's Geat Seal, soon after Independence. It was a controversial decision, since not everyone liked the idea of a scavenger being used. However, there is no doubt that it is a majestic and impressive bird. Despite its status as the national bird, Bald Eagles were persecuted widely, and then in the 1950s and 1960s their populations declined catastrophically, almost entirely due to pesticide poisoning. The bird disappeared from many states, and became rare almost everywhere except Alaska. Fortunately, with the introduction of some controls on the use of pesticides, strict protection and imaginative reintroduction programs, the species is now re-established over most of its former range.

Left *Great Egrets* (Egretta alba) *in the Everglades National Park, Florida, USA. Public outrage at the hunting of breeding egrets for their plumes eventually led to the protection of the Everglades, making it one of the few parks in the USA established primarily to preserve wildlife.*

volcanic plateau bounded by rugged mountains and containing the spectacular geothermal features, most famous of which is the geyser, Old Faithful. There are huge numbers of Elk (Wapiti), as well as Black Bear, Grizzly Bear, Bison, Moose (Elk), Mule Deer, Pronghorn Antelope, Golden Eagle, and Trumpeter Swan.

The Badlands National Park, South Dakota, contains remnants of one of the world's great grasslands, on the edge of the prairies. Bison, Pronghorn Antelope, prairiedog, Bighorn Sheep, and Mule Deer roam there and it was among the last natural habitat for the Black-footed Ferret.

Big Bend National Park, Texas, encompasses wide expanses of arid flatland, sheer canyons, forested slopes and mountain meadows. Although in the USA, much of its flora and fauna is more typical of Mexico and Central America. In the desert areas there are cacti, yucca, and agave as well as many species of desert rodent, Kit Fox, and peccary. The wooded areas are home to Mountain Lion and Gray Fox while 385 species of bird have been recorded there.

The Great Smoky Mountains National Park in Tennessee and North Carolina is connected to Shenandoah National Park in Virginia by a 755-kilometer (469-mile) scenic road known as the Blue Ridge Parkway. It was established to preserve

Right *A herd of Marine Iguanas* (Amblyrynchus cristatus) *sunning themselves on the dark volcanic rocks of the Galapagos islands. They swim out to sea to graze on marine algae.*

remnants of the eastern hardwood forest.

The Everglades National Park, Florida comprises over 540,000 hectares (1.3 million acres) of subtropical swamps. It is home for a large number of North America's endangered animals; Florida Cougar, North American Manatee, sea turtles, American Crocodile and Alligator, Everglades Kite, and huge nesting colonies of herons and egrets.

South America

Tikal National Park, Guatemala covers an area of 57,500 hectares (142,000 acres) around a restored Mayan temple city in dense tropical forest. Although the main attraction is the archeological site, the park is rich in mammals, such as Brocket Deer, peccary, agouti, Jaguar, Puma (Mountain Lion), Ocelot, and Coatimundi, and birds including trogons, tanagers, motmots, and hummingbirds.

The Rio Bravo Conservation and Management Area in Belize is owned by private groups which bought it with the intention of developing tourism as a long-term sustainable resource. The wildlife includes Jaguar, Ocelot, Margay, Tapir, Howler and Spider Monkeys, Morelet's Crocodile, and Ocellated Turkey.

Trinidad is important for migrant birds and has significant breeding

populations. The Caroni Swamp Wildlife Sanctuary and Asa Wright Nature Center contain brackish shallow waters, mud flats and rainforest. Some 10,000 Scarlet Ibis breed there as well as Cattle Egret, Roseate Spoonbill, Limpkin, White, Little Blue and Louisiana Herons, Blue-gray, palm, Silver-beaked, White-lined and Bay-headed Tanagers; and hummingbirds.

Galápagos National Park, Ecuador, in the Pacific contains the 16 major islands, and many more smaller ones, spread over 520,000 hectares (1.28 million acres) of ocean. On the islands are some damp forests, but much of the habitat is arid with the remains of volcanic cinder cones and craters. The many endemic animals, several of which are endangered, include sea lion, Galápagos marine and land iguana, Giant Tortoise, Galápagos Hawk, Flightless Cormorant, Galápagos Penguin, and 13 species of Darwin's finch. There are also huge colonies of Magnificent Frigate Bird, Waved Albatross, and Masked, Red-footed, and Blue-footed Booby.

The mighty falls of Iguazú, one of the world's most spectacular sights, are now protected in Iguazú National Park, Argentina and Iguaçu National Park, Brazil. Luxuriant tree ferns, bamboos, and palms border the falls, and bromeliads, orchids and vines festoon the trees, where macaws and other parrots are still common.

Nahuel Huapi National Park, Argentina, contains over 770,000 hectares (1.9 million acres) of dense forest with Antarctic Beech, myrtle and larch. Above the treeline are perpetual snowfields and glaciers. The mammals include Pudu, Guemal, Vicuña, and Guanaco and among the birds there are Black-necked Swan, Ashy-headed Goose, Steamer Duck, Blue-eyed Cormorant, Chilean Flamingo, Austral Parakeet, and Austral Pygmy Owl.

High in the Andes of Peru is the Pampa Galeras National Reserve, containing rolling, treeless grasslands, with broad valleys separated by flat-topped ridges. The reserve was established to preserve the Vicuña, which has steadily increased in numbers under strict protection.

Itatiaia National Park in Brazil was one of the earliest to be established in South America, dating back to 1937. It includes mountainous tropical rain and cloud forest, and among their large inhabitants are Maned Wolf, Jaguar, Ocelot, Tapir, Giant Anteater, Woolly Spider Monkey, sloth, harpy eagle, guan, and toucan.

Above *These parks have been identified by The Nature Conservancy (TNC) of the USA as being threatened.*

PROTECTED AREAS

Protected regions

With the rapid expansion of the world's human population, natural areas are increasingly confined to national parks and reserves. Those shown here are a selection, chosen from those listed by World Heritage. It is notable that some of the largest protected areas occur in the poorer countries of the world, while the wealthier nations of the developed world often protect only a tiny fraction of their land, usually in areas too small to be of major significance. Antarctica is still the subject of dispute between those nations which recommend a World Park and those which refuse to give up mineral exploitation rights.

Percentage of country area classified as protected in 1989

- 20% and over
- 10-19.9%
- 5-9.9%
- 1.0-4.9%
- Under 1.0%
- Insufficient data

World Heritage Sites

- Natural sites
- Combined natural and cultural sites

GREENLAND

ICELAND

CANADA

UNITED STATES OF AMERICA

MEXICO

BAHAMAS

CUBA
BELIZE
GUATEMALA
HONDURAS
EL SALVADOR
NICARAGUA
PANAMA
COSTA RICA

JAMAICA HAITI
DOMINICAN REPUBLIC
ANTIGUA AND BARBUDA
DOMINICA
ST LUCIA
ST VINCENT BARBADOS
GRENADA
TRINIDAD AND TOBAGO

VENEZUELA
COLOMBIA
GUYANA
SURINAM
FRENCH GUIANA

ECUADOR

PERU

BRAZIL

BOLIVIA

PARAGUAY

CHILE

ARGENTINA

URUGUAY

GREAT BRITAIN
IRELAND
DEN
NETHERLAN
BELG
FRAN

PORTUGAL
SPAIN

MOROCCO
ALGER

MAURITANIA

MALI

CAPE VERDE

SENEGAL
GAMBIA
GUINEA-BISSAU
GUINEA
SIERRA LEONE
LIBERIA
IVORY
COAST
BURKINA
GHANA

EQUITORIAL GUI
SAO TOME & PRIN

INTERNATIONAL CONVENTIONS

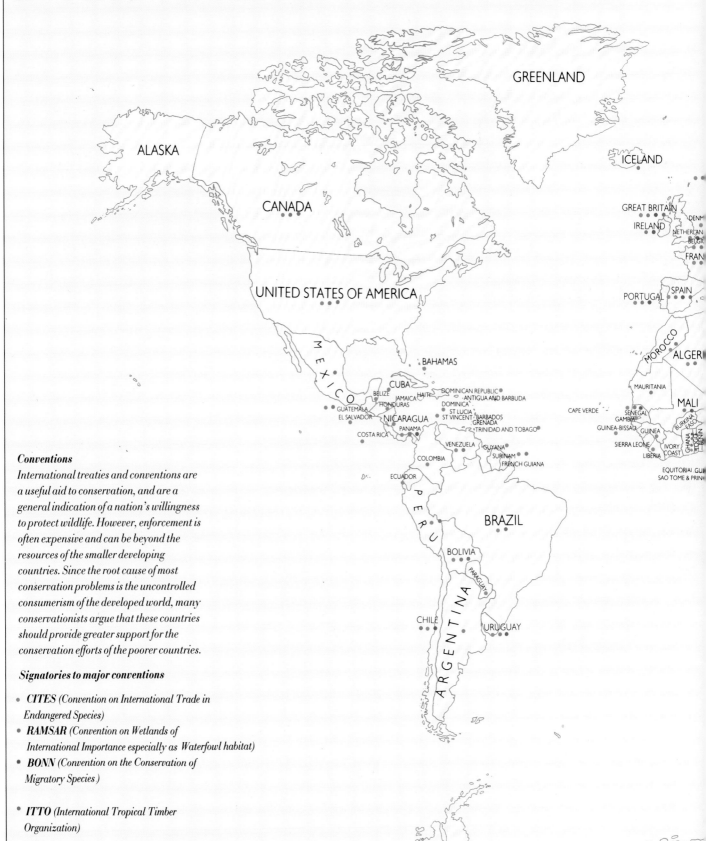

GREENLAND

ICELAND

ALASKA

GREAT BRITAIN

DENM

IRELAND

NETHERLAN

BELGI

CANADA

FRAN

SPAIN

UNITED STATES OF AMERICA

PORTUGAL

MOROCCO

ALGER

BAHAMAS

MAURITANIA

MALI

CUBA

DOMINICAN REPUBLIC

BELIZE

ANTIGUA AND BARBUDA

JAMAICA HAITI

DOMINICA

HONDURAS

ST LUCIA

CAPE VERDE

SENEGAL

GUATEMALA

ST VINCENT BARBADOS

GAMBIA

EL SALVADOR

NICARAGUA

GRENADA

GUINEA-BISSAU

GUINEA

COSTA RICA

PANAMA

TRINIDAD AND TOBAGO

SIERRA LEONE

IVORY

LIBERIA

COAST

VENEZUELA

GUYANA

EQUITORIAL GU

COLOMBIA

SURINAM

SAO TOME & PRIN

FRENCH GUIANA

ECUADOR

P
E
R
U

BRAZIL

BOLIVIA

PARAGUAY

A
R
G
E
N
T
I
N
A

CHILE

URUGUAY

M
E
X
I
C
O

Conventions

International treaties and conventions are a useful aid to conservation, and are a general indication of a nation's willingness to protect wildlife. However, enforcement is often expensive and can be beyond the resources of the smaller developing countries. Since the root cause of most conservation problems is the uncontrolled consumerism of the developed world, many conservationists argue that these countries should provide greater support for the conservation efforts of the poorer countries.

Signatories to major conventions

- **CITES** *(Convention on International Trade in Endangered Species)*
- **RAMSAR** *(Convention on Wetlands of International Importance especially as Waterfowl habitat)*
- **BONN** *(Convention on the Conservation of Migratory Species)*

- **ITTO** *(International Tropical Timber Organization)*

SWEDEN
FINLAND
POLAND
GERMANY
CZECH
AUS
HUN
ROMANIA
YUGOSLAVIA
BULG
ALB
GREECE
TURKEY
TUNISIA
LEBANON
SYRIA
ISRAEL
IRAQ
JORDAN
IRAN
AFGHANISTAN
PAKISTAN
LIBYA
EGYPT
SAUDI
ARABIA
OMAN
PDR YEMEN
NEPAL
BHUTAN
BANGLADESH
INDIA
BURMA
SRI LANKA

SOVIET UNION

MONGOLIA

NORTH KOREA
SOUTH KOREA
JAPAN

CHINA

TAIWAN

LAOS
THAILAND
VIETNAM
KAMPUCHEA
PHILIPPINES

MALAYSIA

INDONESIA

GER
CHAD
SUDAN
CENTRAL
AFRICAN
REPUBLIC
ETHIOPIA
SOMALIA
CONGO
CAMEROON
RWANDA
UGANDA
KENYA
BURUNDI
ZAIRE
TANZANIA
SEYCHELLES
ANGOLA
MALAWI
COMOROS
ZAMBIA
MOZAMBIQUE
NAMIBIA
ZIMBABWE
MADAGASCAR
BOTSWANA
SOUTH
AFRICA

PAPUA
NEW GUINEA
SOLOMON ISLANDS

AUSTRALIA

NEW ZEALAND

CONCLUSION

I
t is difficult not to be pessimistic about the future of the world's wildlife. Everywhere we look, species are threatened with extinction and habitats are being lost at an alarming rate. As this book was being written, plans were being approved to destroy one of the most important habitats for Britain's rarest reptiles. If a wealthy country such as Britain considers endangered species to be so low on its list of priorities, what hope is there in the poorer tropical countries?

Fortunately, some of the poorest countries have led the way in conservation. The central African country of Rwanda's efforts to conserve the Mountain Gorilla and much of its other wildlife have not only benefited the wildlife itself, but also brought much needed revenue to the people. It is a country one-tenth of the size of Britain, with a largely rural population, which grew from 2.7 million in 1960 to 7.7 million in 1990, and is predicted to reach over 18 million by 2025. Despire enormous political problems within the country, one tenth of the land has been protected as national parks and, until recent upheavals, tourism centered around the gorillas and other wildlife was a major source of foreign exchange.

Belize in Central America is only slightly smaller than Rwanda and, in contrast, has a population of well under a quarter of a million. After a long history of logging it is attempting to save much of its tropical forests through cooperation between government and private organizations. This far-sighted program aims to develop sustainable use of the land, preserving as much as possible of the forest cover, wetlands, barrier reef, cays, and other remaining natural habitats, while at the same time providing employment and revenue.

Costa Rica also has an impressive network of parks and reserves and the Guanacaste reserve has started to regrow a climax tropical forest. Almost all parts of the world have some parks and reserves of which to be proud (see pages 224–243). Yet reserves alone cannot provide the answer. To be effective, almost any mainland reserve or park, however large, needs to be connected by natural lands with other areas. Otherwise, it is an isolated island doomed in the long term.

A lot of publicity is given to the captive breeding of animals. Important and invaluable work is being done by places specializing in breeding for conservation purposes, such as the Jersey Wildlife Preservation Trust and the

Otter Trust. But there are only a tiny number of such places compared with the scores of zoos, mostly little better than nineteenth century menageries, that are jumping on the bandwagon of conservation. Very few of the world's zoos are able to save more than a handful of species and many of the species that zoos use to justify their involvement in conservation, such as African Elephants and tigers, are not in need of captive breeding programs. Before supporting the programs publicized by most zoos, the public would do well to ask searching questions about the overall benefits of captive breeding, and how it fits in with the long-term needs of the animals concerned in their natural habitats.

The arguments concerning economic development and conservation are complex, interwoven, and often apparently in conflict. For example, tourism can provide an incentive for conservation and bring much needed foreign currency to a country hard-pressed to save its wildlife. Yet tourism can also wreak havoc in habitats, and tourists consume huge quantities of energy traveling. Ultimately the only long-term solution is smaller human populations. Few of us are going to be prepared to give up our opportunities to travel, to own cars, computers and all the other energy-consuming paraphernalia of life in the twentieth century. If there were incentives for smaller families, there would be more of the cake for everyone.

On a more practical level there are many things the individual can do. By joining one or more of the environmental groups (see p250), individuals can increase their awareness of the problems. They can also make contributions, from digging ponds at weekends to protesting against ships dumping nuclear waste, from fund-raising for orphan elephants to buying thousands of acres of wilderness. Perhaps most importantly, individuals can influence governments. As was demonstrated in the latter part of the 1980s, politicians start to take note when any group numbers hundreds of thousands. Many of the changes needed are of such magnitude that they can be made only by governments. In those countries where governments are elected, it is the responsibility of each individual to ensure that by the year 2000 only politicians sensitive to the environment are elected.

ENDANGERED WILDLIFE

The IUCN definition of endangered refers to species in danger of extinction if there is no change in their current circumstances. This includes species whose numbers have been reduced to a critical level, species whose habitats have been so drastically reduced that they are considered to be in imminent danger of extinction and species that may be extinct but have been seen in the wild in the past 50 years. The following is a listing of endangered mammals, birds, reptiles and amphibians. Only full species are listed. However, many subspecies are also endangered.

Key:
1 Palearctic	5 Indian and Oriental
2 Nearctic	6 Australasian
3 Neotropic	7 Oceania
4 Ethiopian	8 Marine

——— CLASS MAMMALIA ———

Family Macropodidae
Bettongia penicillata Brush-tailed Bettong	6
Onychogalea fraenata Bridled Nailtail Wallaby	6

Family Phalangeridae
Phalanger lullulae Woodlark Island Cuscus	6

Family Vombatidae
Lasiorhinus krefftii Northern Hairy-nosed Wombat	6

Family Thylacomyidae
Macrotis lagotis Greater Bilby	6

Family Myrmecobiidae
Myrmecobius fasciatus Numbat	6

Family Solenodontidae
Solenodon cubanus Cuban Solenodon	3
Solenodon paradoxus Haitian Solenodon	3

Family Potamogalidae
Micropotamogale lamottei Nimba Otter-shrew	4

Family Pteropodidae
Nyctimene rabori Philippines Tube-nosed Fruit Bat	5
Pteropus insularis Truk Flying Fox	7
Pteropus livingstonei Comoro Black Flying Fox	7
Pteropus mariannus Marianna Flying Fox	7
Pteropus molossinus Pohnpei Flying Fox	7
Pteropus phaeocephalus Mortlock Flying Fox	7
Pteropus rodricensis Rodrigues Flying Fox	7
Pteropus samoensis Samoan Flying Fox	7
Pteropus voeltzkowi Pemba Flying Fox	4

Family Emballonuridae
Coleura seychellensis Seychelles Sheath-tailed Bat	7

Family Mystacinidae
Myotis grisescens Grey Bat	2

Family Cheirogaleidae
Allocebus trichotis Hairy-eared Dwarf Lemur	4

Family Lemuridae
Hapalemur aureus Golden Bamboo Lemur	4
Hapalemur simus Greater Bamboo Gentle Lemur	4
Lemur coronatus Crowned Lemur	4
Lemur macaco flavifrons Sclater's Lemur	4
Lemur mongoz Mongoose Lemur	4
Varecia variegata Ruffed Lemur	4

Family Indriidae
Indri indri Indri	4
Propithecus diadema Diademed Sifaka	4
Propithecus tattersalli Golden Crowned Sifaka	4

Family Daubentoniidae
Daubentonia madagascariensis Aye-aye	4

Family Tarsiidae
Tarsius syrichta Philippine Tarsier	5

Family Cebidae
Brachyteles arachnoides Woolly Spider Monkey	3
Callicebus personatus Masked Titi	3
Chiropotes satanas satanas Southern Bearded Saki	3
Lagothrix flavicauda Yellow-tailed Woolly Monkey	3
Saimiri oerstedi Central American Squirrel Monkey	3

Family Callitrichidae
Callithrix aurita Buffy-tufted-ear Marmoset	3
Callithrix flaviceps Buffy-headed Marmoset	3
Leontopithecus caissara Black-faced Lion Tamarin	3
Leontopithecus chrysomelas Golden-headed Lion Tamarin	3
Leontopithecus chrysopygus Black Lion Tamarin	3
Leontopithecus rosalia Golden Lion Tamarin	3
Saguinus bicolor Pied Tamarin	3
Saguinus leucopus White-footed Tamarin	3
Saguinus oedipus oedipus Cottontop Tamarin	3

Family Cercopithecidae
Cercocebus galeritus galeritus Tana River Mangabey	4
Cercocebus galeritus sanje Sanje Crested Mangabey	4
Cercopithecus erythrogaster White-throated Guenon	4
Cercopithecus erythrotis sclateri White-throated Guenon	4
Cercopithecus preussi Preuss's Guenon	4
Colobus satanas Black Colobus	4
Mandrillus leucophaeus Drill	4
Procolobus (b.) badius waldroni Miss Waldron's Bay Colobus	4
Procolobus (b.) gordonorum Uhehe Red Colobus	4
Procolobus (b.) kirkii Zanzibar Red Colobus	4
Procolobus (b.) pennanti Pennant's Red Colobus	4
Procolobus (b.) pennanti bouvieri Bouvier's Red Colobus	4
Procolobus (b.) pennanti pennanti Pennant's Red Colobus	4
Procolobus (b.) pennanti preussi Preuss's Red Colobus	4
Procolobus (b.) rufomitratus rufomitratus Tana River Red Colobus	4
Macaca fuscata yakui Yakushima Macaque	1
Macaca pagensis Mentawai Macaque	5
Macaca silenus Lion-tailed Macaque	5
Presbytis comata Javan Leaf Monkey	5
Presbytis potenziani Mentawai Leaf Monkey	5
Pygathrix nemaeus Red-shanked Douc Langur	5
Pygathrix nigripes Black-shanked Douc Monkey	5
Rhinopithecus avunculus Tonkin Snub-nosed Monkey	5
Rhinopithecus bieti Yunnan Snub-nosed Monkey	1
Rhinopithecus brelichi Guizhou Snub-nosed Monkey	1
Simias concolor Pig-tailed Langur	5
Trachypithecus francoisi Tonkin Leaf Monkey	5
Trachypithecus johnii Nilgiri Leaf Monkey	5
Trachypithecus leucocephalus White-headed Black Leaf Monkey	1

Family Hylobatidae
Hylobates klossi Kloss's Gibbon	5
Hylobates moloch Javan Gibbon	5
Hylobates pileatus Pileated Gibbon	5
Pongo pygmaeus Orang Utan	5

Family Pongidae
Gorilla gorilla berengei Mountain Gorilla	4
Gorilla gorilla graueri Eastern Lowland Gorilla	4
Pan troglodytes verus West African Chimpanzee	4

Family Bradypodidae
Bradypus torquatus Maned Sloth	3

Family Leporidae
Bunolagus monticularis Riverine Rabbit — 4
Caprolagus hispidus Hispid Hare — 5
Lepus flavigularis Tehuantepec Hare — 2, 3
Pentalagus furnessi Amami Rabbit — 1
Romerolagus diazi Volcano Rabbit — 2, 3
Sylvilagus graysoni Tres Marias Cottontail — 3

Family Sciuridae
Cynomys mexicanus Mexican Prairie Dog — 2, 3
Marmota vancouverensis Vancouver Island Marmot — 2

Family Heteromyidae
Dipodomys gravipes San Quintin Kangaroo Rat — 2, 3
Dipodomys stephensi Stephens Kangaroo Rat — 2

Family Cricetidae
Neotoma anthonyi Anthony's Wood Rat — 2, 3
Neotoma bunkeri Bunker's Wood Rat — 2, 3
Neotoma martinensis San Martin Island Wood Rat — 2, 3
Reithrodontomys raviventris Salt-marsh Harvest Mouse — 2
Sigmodon arizonae plenus Colorado River Cotton Rat — 2

Family Muridae
Solomys ponceleti Poncelet's Giant Rat — 6
Zyzomys pedunculatus Central Rock-rat — 6

Family Dinomyidae
Dinomys branickii — 3

Family Capromyidae
Capromys angelcabrerai Cabrera's Hutia — 3
Capromys auritus Large-eared Hutia — 3
Capromys garridoi Garrido's Hutia — 3
Capromys nanus Dwarf Hutia — 3
Capromys sanfelipensis Little Earth Hutia — 3

Family Platanistidae
Lipotes vexillifer Baiji, Yangtze River Dolphin — 1
Platanista minor Indus River Dolphin — 1, 5

Family Delphinidae
Phocoena sinus Vaquita — 2, 3

Family Balaenopteridae
Balaenoptera musculus Blue Whale — 8

Family Balaenidae
Eubalaena glacialis Northern Right Whale — 8

Family Canidae
Canis rufus Red Wolf — 2

Canis simensis Simēn Jackal — 4
Lycaon pictus African Wild Dog — 4

Family Ursidae
Ailuropoda melanoleuca Giant Panda — 1

Family Mustelidae
Mustela nigripes Black-footed Ferret — 2

Family Viverridae
Bdeogale crassicauda omnivora Sokoke Bushy-tailed Mongoose — 4
Liberiictis kuhni Liberian Mongoose — 4
Paradoxurus lignicolor Mentawai Palm Civet — 5
Viverra civettina Malabar Civet — 5

Family Felidae
Felis iriomotensis Iriomote Cat — 1
Felis pardina Pardel Lynx — 1
Panthera tigris Tiger — 5
Panthera uncia Snow Leopard — 1, 5

Family Phocidae
Monachus monachus Mediterranean Monk Seal — 8
Monachus schauinslandi Hawaiian Monk Seal — 7
Phoca hispida saimensis Saimaa Seal — 1

Family Elephantidae
Elephas maximus Indian Elephant — 5

Family Equidae
Equus africanus African Wild Ass — 4
Equus grevyi Grevy's Zebra — 4

Family Tapiridae
Tapirus indicus Malayan Tapir — 5

Family Rhinocerotidae
Diceros bicornis Black Rhinoceros — 4
Didermocerus sumatrensis Sumatran Rhinoceros — 5
Rhinoceros sondaicus Javan Rhinoceros — 5
Rhinoceros unicornis Great Indian Rhinoceros — 1, 5

Family Suidae
Sus salvanius Pygmy Hog — 1, 5
Cervus alfredi Visayan Spotted Deer — 5
Cervus duvauceli Swamp Deer — 1, 5
Cervus eldi Brow-antlered Deer — 5
Dama mesopotamica Persian Fallow Deer — 1
Hippocamelus bisulcus South Andean Huemul — 3
Muntiacus feaei Fea's Muntjac — 5
Ozotoceros bezoarticus celer Argentinian Pampas Deer — 3

Family Bovidae
Bos grunniens Wild Yak — 1

Bos sauveli Kouprey — 1
Bubalus bubalis Wild Asiatic Water Buffalo — 1, 5
Bubalus depressicornis Lowland Anoa — 5
Bubalus quarlesi Mountain Anoa — 5
Bubalus mindorensis Tamaraw — 5
Addax nasomaculatus Addax — 1
Cephalophus jentinki Jentink's Duiker — 4
Gazella cuvieri Cuvier's Gazelle — 1
Gazella dama Dama Gazelle — 1
Gazella leptoceros Slender-horned Gazelle — 1
Hippotragus niger variani Giant Sable Antelope — 4
Oryx dammah Scimitar-horned Oryx — 1
Oryx leucoryx Arabian Oryx — 1
Tragelaphus buxtoni Mountain Nyala — 4
Hemitragus jayakari Arabian Tahr — 1
Capra walie Walia Ibex — 4

─────────── **CLASS AVES** ───────────

Family Podicipedidae
Tachybaptus rufolavatus Alaotra Grebe — 4
Podiceps taczanowskii Junin Grebe — 3

Family Diomedeidae
Diomedea amsterdamensis Amsterdam Island Albatross — 1

Family Procellariidae
Pterodroma cahow Cahow — 3
Pterodroma madeira Freira — 1
Puffinus auricularis Townsend's Shearwater — 2, 3

Family Pelecanidae
Pelecanus crispus Dalmatian Pelican — 1

Family Sulidae
Sula abbotti Abbott's Booby — 6

Family Fregatidae
Fregata andrewsi Christmas Frigatebird — 6

Family Ardeidae
Gorsachius magnificus White-eared Night-heron — 1
Egretta eulophotes Chinese Egret — 1
Ardea imperialis White-bellied Heron — 5

Family Ciconiidae
Leptoptilos dubius Greater Adjutant — 5

Family Threskiornithidae
Pseudibis gigantea Giant Ibis — 5
Geronticus eremita Northern Bald Ibis — 1
Nipponia nippon Crested Ibis — 1
Platalea minor Black-faced Spoonbill — 1

Family Anatidae
Tadorna cristata   Crested Shelduck   1
Aythya innotata   Madagascar Pochard   1

Family Cathartidae
Gymnogyps californianus   California Condor   2

Family Accipitridae
Haliaeetus vociferoides   Madagascar Fish-eagle   4
Eutriorchis astur   Madagascar Serpent-eagle   4
Pithecophaga jefferyi   Philippine Eagle   5
Aquila adalbertii   Spanish Imperial Eagle   1

Family Falconidae
Falco punctatus   Mauritius Kestrel   4

Family Cracidae
Penelope albipennis   White-winged Guan   3
Penelope perspicax   Cauca Guan   3
Pipile jacutinga   Black-fronted Piping Guan   3
Oreophasis derbianus   Horned Guan   2,3
Mitu mitu   Alagoas Curassow   3
Crax blumenbachii   Red-billed Curassow   3

Family Phasianidae
Odontophorus strophium   Gorgeted Wood-quail   3
Francolinus ochropectus   Djibouti Francolin   4
Arborophila rufipectus   Sichuan Partridge   1
Arborophila ardens   White-eared Partridge   1
Agelastes meleagrides   White-breasted Guineafowl   4

Family Gruidae
Grus americana   Whooping Crane   2

Family Rallidae
Nesoclopeus poecilopterus   Bar-winged Rail   7
Gallirallus owstoni   Guam Rail   7
Gallirallus sylvestris   Lord Howe Rail   6
Notornis mantelli   Takahe   6

Family Rhynochetidae
Rhynochetos jubatus   Kagu   7

Family Otididae
Houbaropsis bengalensis   Bengal Florican   5
Sypheotides indica   Lesser Florican   5

Family Haematopodidae
Haematopus chathamensis   Chatham Island Oystercatcher   6

Family Recurvirostridae
Himantopus novaezelandiae   Black Stilt   6

Family Charadriidae
Thinornis novaeseelandiae   Shore Plover   6

Family Scolopacidae
Numenius borealis   Eskimo Curlew   2

Family Columbidae
Nesoenas mayeri   Pink Pigeon   4
Zenaida graysoni   Socorro Dove   2,3
Leptotila wellsi   Grenada Dove   3
Geotrygon caniceps   Grey-headed Quail-dove   3
Gallicolumba erythroptera   Polynesian Ground Dove   7

Family Loriidae
Cacatua moluccensis   Salmon-crested Cockatoo   5
Cacatua alba   White Cockatoo   5
Cacatua haematuropygia   Red-vented Cockatoo   5
Cacatua goffini   Tanimbar Corella   5

Family Psittacidae
Psephotus pulcherrimus   Paradise Parrot   6
Pezoporus wallicus   Ground Parrot   6
Psittacula eques   Mauritius Parakeet   4
Anodorhynchus leari   Lear's Macaw   3
Cyanopsitta spixii   Little Blue Macaw   3
Rhynchopsitta terrisi   Maroon-fronted Parrot   2,3
Amazona vittata   Puerto Rican Parrot   3
Amazona brasiliensis   Red-tailed Parrot   3
Amazona arausiaca   Red-necked Parrot   3
Amazona imperialis   Imperial Parrot   3
Strigops habroptilus   Kakapo   6

Family Musophagidae
Tauraco bannermani   Bannerman's Turaco   4

Family Cuculidae
Centropus chlororhynchus   Green-billed Coucal   5

Family Strigidae
Otus ireneae   Sokoke Scops-owl   4

Family Trochilidae
Glaucis dohrnii   Hook-billed Hermit   3

Family Picidae
Dryocopus galeatus   Helmeted Woodpecker   3
Campephilus principalis   Ivory-billed Woodpecker   2,3
Campephilus imperialis   Imperial Woodpecker   2,3
Sapheopipo noguchii   Okinawa Woodpecker   1

Family Formicariidae
Formicivora erythronotos   Black-hooded Antwren   3
Pyriglena atra   Fringe-backed Fire-eye   3

Family Pittidae
Pitta schneideri   Schneider's Pitta   5
Pitta gurneyi   Gurney's Pitta   5

Family Atrichornithidae
Atrichornis clamosus   Noisy Scrub-bird   6

Family Mimidae
Mimodes graysoni   Socorro Mockingbird   3
Ramphocinclus brachyurus   White-breasted Thrasher   3
Alethe choloensis   Thyolo Alethe   4
Copsychus cebuensis   Black Shama   7
Copsychus sechellarum   Seychelles Magpie Robin   7
Myadestes myadestinus   Kamao   7
Myadestes lanaiensis   Olomao   7
Myadestes palmeri   Puaiohi   7
Turdus helleri   Taita Thrush   4
Acrocephalus rehsei   Nauru Reed-warbler   7
Acrocephalus rodericanus   Rodrigues Brush Warbler   7
Nesillas aldabranus   Aldabra Warbler   7
Petroica traversi   Chatham Island Robin   6
Platysteira laticincta   Banded Wattle-eye   4
Pomarea dimidiata   Rarotonga Monarch   6
Pomarea nigra   Tahiti Monarch   7
Myiagra freycineti   Guam Flycatcher   7

Family Nectariniidae
Nectarinia prigoginei   Marunga Sunbird   4

Family Zosteropidae
Zosterops albogularis   White-chested White-eye   6
Zosterops modestus   Seychelles White-eye   7

Family Meliphagidae
Moho braccatus   Kauai Oo   7
Moho bishopi   Bishop's Oo   7

Family Emberizidae
Nemosia rourei   Cherry-throated Tanager   3

Family Parulidae
Vermivora bachmanii   Bachman's Warbler   2,3
Dendroica kirtlandii   Kirtland's Warbler   2,3
Leucopeza semperi   Semper's Warbler   3

Family Drepanididae
Hemignathus obscurus   Akialoa   7
Hemignathus lucidus   Nukupuu   7
Paroreomyza maculata   Oahu Creeper   7
Psittirostra psittacea   Ou   7

Family Fringillidae
Carduelis cucullata   Red Siskin   3

Family Ploceidae
Ploceus golandi   Clarke's Weaver   4
Malimbus ibadanensis   Ibadan Malimbe   4
Foudia rubra   Mauritius Fody   7
Foudia flavicans   Rodrigues Fody   7

Family Sturnidae
Aplonis cinerascens   Rarotonga Starling   7
Leucopsar rothschildi   Bali Starling   5

Family Corvidae
Corvus hawaiiensis   Hawaiian Crow   7

CLASS REPTILIA

Family Chelidae

Pseudemydura umbrina   Western Swamp Turtle   6

Family Cheloniidae

Chelonia mydas   Green Turtle   8
Eretmochelys imbricata   Hawksbill Turtle   8
Lepidochelys kempii   Kemp's or Atlantic Ridley   8
Lepidochelys olivacea   Olive or Pacific Ridley   8

Family Dermochelyidae

Dermochelys coriacea   Leatherback   8

Family Emydidae

Batagur baska   River Terrapin   5
Callagur borneoensis   Painted Terrapin   5

Family Pelomedusidae

Podocnemis expansa   South American River Turtle   3

Family Testudinidae

Geochelone yniphora   Angonoka   **4**
Gopherus flavomarginatus   Bolson Tortoise   **2, 3**
Testudo hermanni hermanni   Hermann's Tortoise   8

Family Gekkonidae

Phelsuma edwardnewtonii   Rodrigues Day Gecko   7
Phelsuma guentheri   Gunther's Gecko   7

Family Iguanidae

Anolis roosevelti   Culebra Island Giant Anole   3
Cyclura collei   Jamaican Ground Iguana   3
Cyclura pinguis   Anegada Ground Iguana   3
Gambelia silus   San Joaquin Leopard Lizard   2

Family Lacertidae

Gallotia simonyi   Hierro Giant Lizard   **1**

Family Teiidae

Ameiva polops   St Croix Ground Lizard   3

Family Boidae

Bolyeria multicarinata   Round Island Boa   7
Casarea dussumieri   Round Island Keel-scaled Boa   3
Epicrates inornatus   Puerto Rican Boa   3

Family Colubridae

Thamnophis sirtalis tetrataenia   San Francisco
   Garter Snake   2

Family Elapidae

Naja oxiana   Central Asian Cobra   5

Family Viperidae

Vipera latifii   Latifi's Viper   **1**
Vipera schweizeri   Milos Viper   **1**
Vipera ursinii rakosiensis   Orsini's Viper   **1**

Family Alligatoridae

Alligator sinensis   Chinese Alligator   **1**

Caiman latirostris   Broad-nosed Caiman   3
Melanosuchus niger   Black Caiman   3

Family Crocodylidae

Crocodylus acutus   American Crocodile   **2, 3**
Crocodylus intermedius   Orinoco Crocodile   3
Crocodylus mindorensis   Philippines Crocodile   5
Crocodylus moreletii   Morelet's Crocodile   **2, 3**
Crocodylus rhombifer   Cuban Crocodile   3
Crocodylus siamensis   Siamese Crocodile   5
Tomistoma schlegelii   False Gharial   5

Family Gavialidae

Gavialis gangeticus   Gharial   **5**

CLASS AMPHIBIA

Family Ambystomatidae

Ambystoma macrodactylum croceum   Santa Cruz
   Long-toed
   Salamander   2

Family Plethondontidae

Batrachoseps aridus   Desert Slender Salamander   2
Typhlomolge rathbuni   Texas Blind Salamander   2

Family Bufonidae

Bufo houstonensis   Houston Toad   2
Bufo periglenes   Golden Toad   3

Family Discoglossidae

Alytes muletensis   Mallorcan Midwife Toad   **1**

Family Myobatrachidae

Rheobatrachus silus   Conondale Gastric-brooding
   Frog   **6**

CONSERVATION ORGANISATIONS

The following list gives a selection of international organisations, (i.e. those with offices in more than one country) and organisations which are particularly influential. The list has been chosen to give wide coverage, and those included are known to welcome enquiries. They are all membership organisations and most publish regular bulletins or newsletters. Government and state conservation agencies have not been listed; details of these can usually be obtained from public information services or public libraries.

Greenpeace

A direct action group mostly involved with marine issues; many local groups and chapters. Head Office UK:
> 3031 Islington Green,
> London N1 8XE

National Audubon Society

Has chapters in many states of the USA, but some State Audubon Societies are independent.
> 950 Third Avenue,
> New York,
> NY 10022, USA

World Wildlife Fund/Worldwide Fund for Nature

Headquarters in Switzerland and offices in many countries including:
> UK: Panda House,   USA: 1250 24th Street,
> Weyside Park,   Washington DC,
> Godalming,   20003, USA
> Surrey, GU17 1XR

International Council for Bird Preservation

Coordinates bird protection, with national sections in most countries with any conservation activity.
> ICBP International HQ,
> Cambridge Road, Girton,
> Cambridge.

Friends of the Earth

An international lobbying group, with many national offices and numerous local groups (chapters).
> UK: 2628 Underwood St,   USA: 218D Street S.E.,
> London N1 7JQ   Washington DC,
>   20003, USA

The Nature Conservancy

One of the largest conservation organisations in the world, owning or managing large amounts of land, mostly wilderness, in North and South America.
> 1815 North Lynn Street,
> Arlington,
> VA 22209, USA

Royal Society for the Protection of Birds

Has one of largest memberships of any conservation body, with a rapidly growing international section.
> The Lodge,
> Sandy, Beds,
> SG19 2DL

BIBLIOGRAPHY

The sources of information used in compiling the present work are very extensive. The works listed in the bibliography have been selected to enable the reader who wants to research further to obtain access to the widest possible selection of literature. The bibliographies of all the works listed will in turn lead on to more extensive references.

Anon., 1990, *1990 IUCN Red List of Threatened Animals*, IUCN, Cambridge, 1990.
Lists all species believed to be threatened throughout their range. IUCN also publish a wide range of "Red Data Books" dealing with threatened species.

Anon., *UNEP Environmental Data Report*, 2nd Edition, Blackwell, Oxford, 1989.

Burton, John A., "A Bibliography of Red Data Books (Part 1: Animal Species)", *Oryx*, 18:61-64, 1984.
Lists all known publications considered as "Red Data Books", both regional and taxonomic.

Collar, N.J. and Andre, P, *Birds to Watch*, ICBP, Cambridge, 1988. ICBP publishes a range of reports on threatened birds.

Jarvis, C., Leon, C. & Oldfield, S., "Bibliography of Red Data Books and Threatened Plants Lists. in Synge, H. Ed. Biological Aspects of Rare Plant Conservation, pp513-29, Wiley, Chichester, 1981.

Page numbers in *italic* indicate
illustrations

Abbott's Booby 167
Aberdares National Park, Kenya 226
Abies densa 155
Abyssinian Ground Hornbill 227
acacias 180
Acajou 145
Addax *128*, 128, *129*
Adelaide Pygmy Blue-tongued Skink
193
afforestation 33, 37, 40, 41, 154
African Dwarf Crocodile *137*, 137
African Hunting Dog 140, *141*, 226
African Violet 123, 125
African wilderness, destruction of 120
Afrormosia 145–6
agaves, night-blooming 75
agouti 238
Ailnathus fordii 152
air plants *see* bromeliads
Akan National Park, Japan 231
Akialoa 214
Akiapola'au 214
Alagoas Curassow 98
Alcon Large Blue Butterfly 37
Aldabra Brush Warbler 212
Aldabra Giant Tortoise *142*, 143, 208
Alexandra's Parrot 192
algae 170
alligators 62, *63*, 111, 165, 238
Alpacas 107, *109*
Alpine Accentor 234
Alpine Chough 235, 237
alpine daisies 183
Alpine Marmot 234
alpine meadows *29*
Alpine Swift 235, 237
Altai Snowcock 41
Altamira Yellowthroat 111
Amani Sunbird 137
Amazon Parrot 96, 113
Amazonia, wildlife 98–101
Amboseli National Park, Kenya 226
American Alligator 62, *63*, 238
American (Canadian) Beaver *60*, 60
American Sheathbill *201*
Amur (Siberian) Tiger *36*
anaoas 169
Ancistrocactus tubuschii 58
Andean Flamingo *109*, 109
Andean floristic region 91–3
Andes, wildlife 106–10
Angonoka Tortoise 140, 143
animal skin trade 111
animals, breeding for conservation
244–5
Anisoptera thurifera 177
Antarctic Beech 239
Antarctic Peninsula *200*
Antarctic Treaty 203
Antarctica *200*, 200–3
antbirds 103
anteaters *106*, 106, *190*, 190, 239
antelope 36, 132, 133, 138, 159, 228
desert *128*, 128

forest 133
see also eland; gazelle
Antioch dunes, California, protected
habitat 57
Antioch Dunes Evening Primrose 57
Anubis Baboon 226
Aoudad *see* Barbary Sheep
Apache Trout 77
Apalachicola National Forest 56
Apollo Butterfly *37*, 234
Apple Snails 65
aquaculture 116
Aquatic Box-turtle 70
Arabian Bustard 35
Arabian Oryx 33, 36
Arabian Tahr 36
Archduke Butterfly *51*
Archey's Frog 199
Arctic Tern 45, *82*, 83
Areca concinna 152
arid zones, threats of changes to 36–7
armadillos 106
Arolla Pine 234, *234*
Arrow Poison Frog *101*
arum lily *178*, 178–9
Asa Wright Nature Center, Trinidad 239
Ashy-headed Goose 239
Asian Cobra 162
Asian Tapir 166
Atherton Antechinus 191
Atitlan Grebe 109
atolls 170, 206
Attwater's Prairie Chicken 68, *69*
Audouin's Gull *46*, 46
aurochs 9
Austral Parakeet 239
Austral Pygmy Owl 239
Australia, habitat and plants 179–81
Australian laurel 182
Australian Sealion *192*, 192
avian malaria 213–14
Avocet 235, 236
Awash National Park, Ethiopia 226
Aye-aye 141
Ayres Rock–Mount Olga National Park,
Australia 232
Ayuque 58
Azores 45

Barbary Macaque (Barbary Ape) 47
Babirusa 169
Bactrian Camel *36*, 36
Badlands National Park, USA 238
Badula crassa 210
Baiji 165
Baikal, Lake 30
Baikal Seal 44, 231
Baillon's Crake 233
Baja California Pronghorn 72
Black Cod 195
Bald Cypress 54–5, *55*
Bald Eagle *62*, *83*, 237
Bald Ibis 33, 37, 129–30, *130*
Bali Starling 167, 169
bamboo 79
bamboo forest 151
China 34

Banded Wattle-eye 135
bandicoots 186, 190, 232, 233
Banksia goodii 181
banksias 181
Bannerman's Turaco 135
Banteng 231
Barasingha *see* Swamp Deer
Barbary Falcon 45
Barbary Sheep 128–9, *129*
Barguzin State Nature Reserve, USSR
231
Barn Swallow *84*, *85*, 165
Barred-wing Rail 212
barrier reefs 170
Basking Shark 216–17, *217*
Bastard Gumwood 211
Bat-eared Fox 229
Bateleur Eagle 228
bats 41–2, 45, 68, 69, 168, 186, 196,
208–9, 236
Australian 192
flying foxes 143, 186, 208–9, *209*
long-tongued 75
New Guinea 186–7
Baudin's Black Cockatoo 192
Bavarian Forest National Park,
Germany 234
Bavarian Pine Vole 34
Baw Baw Frog 194
Bay Checkerspot Butterfly 75
beach pollution *215*
Bearded (Red-backed) Saki 98–9
Bearded Vulture *see* Lammergeier
bears 9, 72, *80*, 81, 104, 231, 237, 238
beavers 9, 39, *60*, 60, *233*, 236
Bechstein's Bat 42, 236
Bedford-Russell's Idea Butterfly 51
Bee-eater 234
beech, southern 176, 177, 180
Beira 132–3
Beisa Oryx 226
Belize, attempts to save tropical forest
244
Beluga Whale 43, 216
Bengal Florican 158, 169
Bengal Tiger 115
Bermuda Petrel 62
Bialowieza National Park, Poland 236
Big Bend Gambusia 69
Big Bend National Park, USA 75
Big-eared Flying Fox 186
Bilby 190
biogeographical regions 8
biological resources, disappearance of
155
birds of paradise *186*, 187
birds of prey 36, 41, *73*, 73–4, 101,
168, 186–7, 213, 230, 233, 234, 235,
237
bison 77, 79, 236, 237
American 66, 67, *68*, 68
European *see* Wisent
Plains Bison 68, 77
Bittern 235
Black Bear *80*, 237, 238
Himalayan (Asiatic) 163, 230
Black Caiman 111
Black Colobus 135

Black Dorcopsis 185–6
Black Grouse 234, 235, 237
Black Honey Buzzard 186–7
Black Kite 233
Black Mudfish 199
Black Oystercatcher 45
Black Rat 212
Black Robin *198*, 198
Black Spider Monkey 99
Black Tern 235
Black Vulture *41*, 41, 236
Black-bordered Charaxes *50*
Black-capped Vireo 68
Black-faced Impala 229
Black-faced Lion Tamarin 97
Black-handed Spider Monkey 96
Black-necked Grebe 236
Black-necked Swan 239
Black-spotted Cuscus 186
Black-tailed Deer 78
Black-tailed Godwit 236
Black-winged Stilt 236
Blackbuck 159
Blackfin Cisco 66
bladderworts 55
Blaubok 138
Blind Cave Eel 195
Blue Bear *see* Black Bear
Blue Bird of Paradise *186*, 187
Blue (Canary Island) Chaffinch 45
Blue Duck 233
Blue Pike 67
Blue Vanda 152
Blue Whale 80, 202, 215, *216*
Blue-eared Pheasant 41
Blue-eyed Cormorant 239
Bluebearded Iris 126
Bluefin Tuna, Southern 195
Bog Asphodel 234
Bog Orchid 31
Bog Pimpernel 234
bogs, "improved" 56
Bolson Tortoise 70–1, 113
Bonobo 136
Bonthain Tiger Butterfly 51
Bory's Gentian 29
Bottle-nosed Whale, Northern 216
Bouba Ndjida National Park,
Cameroon 227–8
Bowhead Whale 80, 216
Bridled Nailtail Wallaby *188*, *189*, 189
Broad-headed Snake 193
Broad-nosed Caiman 111
Brocket Deer 238
Bromelia serra 91
bromeliads *91*, 91
Bronze Quoll 186
brooms 29
Brown Bear 32, *33*, 33–4, 34
Eurasian 231
European 237
Brown Hyena *138*, 138
Brown Kiwi *198*, 233
Brown Lemur 141
Brown Tree Snake *213*, 213
Brown-eared Pheasant 41
Brown-headed Cowbird 67, 74
Brush-tailed Possum 232

Buffalo, African 226, 227, 228, 229,
230
Buffalo Runner *see* Great Plains Wolf
Buffy Tufted-eared Marmoset 98
Buffy-headed Marmoset 98
Bung Boraphet marsh, Thailand 165,
167
Burma, forests of 153
Burrowing Rat 189
Bush Dogs 100
bush-brown butterflies *51*
bustards 34, *35*, 35, 36, 158, 159
butterflies 48–51, 65, *70*, 72, 75, 137,
159, 168, 235
European 37
island 50–1
Palearctic 34
butterfly reserves 49, 51

Cabot's Tragopan 41
cacti *57*, *58*, 75, 92
button 58
cactus rustling 57–8
Cahow 62
caimans 111
Cairngorm National Nature Reserve
234–5
Calamian Deer 168
California Clapper Rail 75
California Condor *73*, 73–4
California Least Tern 72–3
Calliope Silverspot Butterfly 75
Camellia crapnelliana 152
camels 36, *107*, 107–8, *108*, *109*
Canaries White-toothed Shrew 45
Canary Islands 45, 207
canopies 90, 90–1
Canterbury Mudfish 199
Caoba 90
Cape Pangolin 229
Cape Platana Frog 139
Cape, South Africa 125–6
Capercaillie 32, *34*, 34, 234, 237
Caracal 36
Caranthus coriaceus 127
Caribbean Monk Seal 218
Carmargue 30, *84*, *233*
Carmargue Zoological and Botanical
Reserve 234
Caroni Swamp Wildlife Sanctuary,
Trinidad 115, 239
Cascade Wolf 79
Cassowary 193
catastrophes, natural 8
cats 68–9, 140, 157–8, 159, 163, 166,
227, 228, 229, 234
feral 212–13
forest 96–7, 104
large 36, 60–1, 115, 230, 231, 238
spotted 96–7, 97, 111
Cattle Egret
cattle ranching 93, 104, 124
Cattleya skinneri 9
Caucasian Black Grouse 41
caves, Palearctic 41–2
Celmisia adamsii 183, 183
chacalacas 98

Chacma Baboon 228
Chamois 40–1, 182, 234, 235, 237
Chapman's Rhododendron 56
Charaxes butterflies 48, *50*
Chatham Island 182–3
Chatham Island (Giant) Forget-me-not 182–3
Checkered Killifish 70
Cheer Pheasant 159
Cheetah 36, 140, *141*, 226, 227, 228, 229
Chilean Flamingo 239
Chimpanzee *136*, 136–7, 228
China, nature reserves *225*
Chinchillas 108–9
Chinese Alligator 165
Chinese Giant Salamander 165
Chinese Monal 41
Chinese Pangolin *163*, 163
Chinstrap Penguin *201*
Chipko Andolan movement 157
Chonta Palm 210
Christmas Frigatebird 167
Christmas Island 167
ciscos 66
city parks 225
Clarke's Gazelle 133
Clarke's Weaver 137
clearfelling 147, 179
Clianthus puniceaus 183
cloud forest 239
Clouded Leopard 166
coastal development 221
Coastal Redwood 59
cockatoos 168, 169, 192, *193*, 193
Coco de Mer *211*
Coconut (Robber) Crab *209*, 209
Colombian Grebe 109, 110
colonization, natural 206
Colorado River Squawfish 78
Comanche Springs Pupfish 69
commercial fisheries *114*, 171
Common Goral 163
Common (Harbor) Seals 44, 45
Common Rorqual Whale 215
Common Sundew 234
condors 73, 73–4
Congo Peacock *136*, 137
coniferous forests 78
  primeval 237
conifers 27, 28, 58, 177
  deciduous 54–5
conservation 7, 183
  and butterflies 50–1
  the case for 11
  of mangroves 117
  and marsupials 189–90
  of reefs 173
Contra Costa Wallflower 57
Convention on Environmental Modification 8–9
Copper Band Butterfly Fish *171*
coral reefs 170–3, 206
corals, over-exploited 44
Cork Oak 30
corncrakes 35, 84
Corsican Nuthatch 45
Corsican Swallowtail Butterfly 48

Corybas fornicatus 155
Coryphantha minima Baird (Nellie Cory Cactus) *58*
Coto Doñana 84
Coto Doñana National Park, Spain *31*, 236
Cotton Mouse 65
Cotton-top Tamarin *96*, 96
Cougar *see* Lion, Mountain
Coyotes 63, 68
Crab-eating Macaque 115
Crabeater Seal *201*
Crag Martin 235
cranes 34, 37, *38*, 68, 79–80, *82*, 140
  declines noted 37
creepers 90
Crested Coot 236
Crested Eagle 101
Crested Honeycreeper 214
Crested (Japanese) Murrelet 46
Crimson Rosella 232
critical weight range species 189
crocodile farms *187*, 194
crocodiles *110*, 111, 114–15, *137*, 161, *187*, 194, 227, 230, 238
  American 65, 238
  freshwater 167
crop plants, native to SE Asia 153
crops, modern, ancestors of 31
Crown of Thorns Starfish 171, *172*, 172, 173
Crusoe's Mayu-monte 93, 210
culture and religion, influence of 156–7
curassows 98
curlews 83–4, 236

Daintree River 180
D'Albertis Ringtail 186
Dalmatian Pelican *84*, 84, 235, 236
Dama Gazelle 128, *129*
dams 78
Danube delta 84
Danube Delta Reserve 236
Danube, River 38–9
darters 64
Dartmoor National Park, England *235*, 235
Darwin's Finch 239
dasyurids 190–1
DDT 62, 81
deciduous forest 154
  mixed 153
  neotropic, wildlife 101–4
  temperate, clearance of 27–8
  tropical 88
  tropical dry 150
  tropical moist 150, 153
Deepwater Cisco 66
deer 35, *64*, 65, 78, 79, *104*, 105–6, 110, *111*, 163, 168, 169, 230, 231, 233, 236, 238
  see also elk; wapiti
Defassa Waterbuck 228
defoliants 9
deforestation 33–4, 41, 96, 146, 147, *151*, 151, 159, 163–4
  and coral reefs 172–3
Demoiselle Crane 37
Dendrobium pauciflorum 151, 152
Desert Pupfish 112
Desert Tortoise 75
desertification *122*, 123
deserts 89, 91–2
  Africa 123–4
  Australia 176, 184

India 159
  Neotropic, wildlife 112–13
  springs in 70
  USA 75–7, *76*
Desman, Pyrenean 39–40
developing countries, exploitation to pay foreign debt 10–11
Devil's Hole Pupfish 78
Dhole 229
Diademed Sifaka 142
Diamond Python *193*, 193
Diana Monkey 134
Dibatag 133
Dibbler 191
Dicliptera dodsonii 91
Dimorphic (Clara's) Bandicoot 186
Diospyros species 144
dipterocarp forest 153, 155
dipterocarps *146*, 146–7, 154
disease 44, 110, 213–14
Diuris purdiei 181
Djibouti Francolin 133
Dodo 143, 207
dogs 99–100, 130, *131*, 131, 140, *141*, 226, 229
dolphins 43, 100, 115–16, 161, 196, 216, 230
  river 165
Doria's Tree-kangaroo 185
Dove Tree 155
dragonflies 38, 159
Dragonmouth 234
Drakaea jeanensis 181
Drill 134, 137
Dromedary Camel 36
droughts, result of 85
Dryococelus australis 212
drystone walls 29
Duck-billed Platypus *187*, 187, 191, 233
ducks 39, 65, 166, 233, 236, 239
Dudhwa National Park, India 158
Dugong 192, *218*, 219, 230
Dusky Canada Goose 80
Dusky Seaside Sparrow 65–6
Dwarf Emu 192
Dwarf (Robbin's) Cinquefoil 54

eagles 41, 47, *62*, *100*, 101, 168, 228, 234, 235, 237, 238, 239
  fish eagles 142, 161, 227, 230
Eastern Brown Pelican 62
Eastern Tailed Blue Butterfly 48
Eastern Wapiti (Elk) 65
ebony 144, 152
Echidnas
  Short- and Long-beaked *186*, 186, *187*, 187, 191
  Tasmanian 233
economic plants, originating in Malaysian zone 155
Egadi Cabbage 31
Egmont National Park, New Zealand 233
egrets 231, 233, 235, *237*, 238, 239
Eider Duck 236
El Segundo Blue Butterfly 72
eland 226, 227, 228, 229
Elephant
  African 32, *138*, 139, 226, 227, 228, 229, 245
  Asiatic (Indian) *162*, 162–3, *163*, 230, 231
Elephant Seals, Northern 74

Elk 236, 237, 238
  see also wapiti
endemism 8, 50–1, 169
  Australia 180, 187–8
  Channel Islands, California 58–9
  Chatham Island 182–3
  Ethiopian highlands 131
  and extinction 207
  island 206, 212–13
  Juan Fernandez 93
  New Guinea 178, 185
  New Zealand 182, 183, 195–8
  Sri Lanka 152, 160
  Sulawesi 168, 168–9
Endrin, effects of 62
environmental problems, blame for 7
Epiophlebia laidlawi 159
epiphytes 90, *91*
  and collectors 91
Epithelantha bokei 58, 58
Erica verticillata 126, 126
erosion, from mouatin logging 150, 219
Eskimo Curlew 80–1, *81*, 83
Eskimos, subsistence hunting 43
Estuarine Crocodile 114–15
Ethiopian Bush Crow 131
Ethiopian Highlands 130–2
Etosha National Park, Namibia 229
Etosha Pan 229
eucalypts 180
Eungella Torrent Frog 194
European Community (EC), and bird protection 35
European Spoonbill 233
Everglades 56
  shrinkage of 65–6
Everglades Kite 238
Everglades National Park, USA 56, 117, 225, *237*, 238
Evros Delta 84
extinctions
  Australia 188–9, 193
  causes of 9–11
  famous Nearctic 65
  Indian Ocean Islands 143
  New Zealand 197

Fairy Armadillo 106
Fairy Penguin 232
falcons 24, 45, *61*, 61–2, 81, 234, 237
Fallow Deer 236
False Larch *92*, 92–3
False Water Rat *191*, 191
Farne Islands *234*, 235
Felton's Flower 93
fiddler crab *8*
Filfola Lizard 45
Fin Whale 215
Finn's Baya Weaver 158
Fiordland National Park, New Zealand 233
firs 155
fish
  annual 112
  forest 101
  freshwater 38, 195
  W Texas 69
Fish Eagle
  African 227
  Madagascan 142
  Pallas's Fish Eagle 161, 230
fishing, commercial 80
fishing nets 215
flamingoes *109*, 109, 226, *233*, 234, 239

Flashjack *see* Bridled Nailtail Wallaby
Flightless Cormorant *212*, 239
Florida Cougar 238
Florida Everglade (Snail) Kite 65
Florida Panther 65
Florida Torreya 56
Florida Yew 56
Flying Lemur 231
flyways 82, 83–4
food plants, New Guinea 178
forest clearance/destruction 28, 90, 95, 110, 210, 219
forest degradation 151, 214
forest loss 35, 155, 179
forestry plantations 29
forestry practice, destructive 27
forests 58
  boreal 79
  broadleaved subtropical 150
  closed, threatened 180
  dry 91
  evergreen Mediterranean oak 27–8
  Indian zone 150–1
  Mediterranean 34
  monsoon 154
  Nearctic 54
  Neotropic 99, 101–4
  Palearctic 27–8, 33–4
  primary evergreen 166
  second growth 27
  semi-evergreen 150
  subtropical evergreen 154
  temperate 159
  tropical 88, 89, 150, 228, 231
  see also bamboo forest; deciduous forest;
  dipterocarp forest; montane forest; rainforest; tropical rainforest; woodlands
Fossa 142
Fringe-eared Oryx 229
fringing reefs 170
frogs *101*, 135, 139, 162, 194, 199
Fruit Bats, Egyptian 42
Fuerteventura Stonechat 45
fur trade 96-7
Furbish Lousewort 54
Fynbos *126*

Galápagos archipelago 207, 208
Galápagos Dark-rumped Petrel 212
Galápagos Giant Tortoise *208*, 208, 239
Galápagos Penguin 239
galaxids 195, 199
gambusias 69
Ganges River Dolphin 116, 230
Ganges Susu 161
garden plants, originating in Sino-Japanese zone *153*, 153
Garganey 235
garigue 31
Gaur *164*, 164, *230*, 230
gazelle 36, 128, *129*, 133, 226, *229*
geckos 199, 210, 212
Gelada Baboon *131*, 131
Gemsbok 229
gene banks 183
Gentian, Indian 155
Gentoo Penguin *201*
Geometric Tortoise 138-9
Gharial 114, *161*, 161
Ghost Bat 192
ghost fishing nets 10, 215
Ghuditch *see* Western Quoll
Giant Anteater *106*, 106, 239

Giant Armadillo 106
Giant Carrion Beetles 62
Giant Catfish 165
Giant Clam 173, *221*
Giant (Derby) Eland 227, 228
Giant Eagle Owl 229
Giant Gecko 199
Giant Golden Mole 138
Giant Ground Squirrel 231
Giant Gum Tree (Mountain Ash) 180
Giant Nuthatch 164
Giant Otter 100
Giant Panda 32, 34-5, *35*
Giant Protea *126*, 126
Giant Sequoia *59*, 59
giant squirrels 166, 231
Giant Swallowtail Butterfly, African 137
Giant Tortoise *208*, 208
gibbons 165, 231
Gibraltar 47
Gila Monster *75*, 75
Gila Trout 77
Ginseng 231
Gir National Park, India 229
Giraffe *227*, 227, 228, *229*, 229
    see also okapi
Glacier Bear *see* Black Bear
Glacier National Park, USA 77
Glaucous Macaw 102
global ecosystem, and human survival
    11
Glomeropitcairnia erectiflora 91
Glossy Black Parrot 192
Glossy Ibis 231, 235, 236
goats 58-9, 182, 210-11
goby 171
Golden Bamboo Lemur 141-2
Golden Bandicoot 190
Golden Eagle 234, 235, 237, 238
Golden Langur *157*, 158
Golden Lion Tamarin 97
Golden-cheeked Warbler 68
Golden-headed Lion Tamarin 97
Golden-rumped Lion Tamarin 97
Golden-shouldered Parrot 192, 193
Goldie's Bird of Paradise 187
Goliath Frog 135
Gon-Gon Petrel 45
Gondwanaland forest 180
Goodfellow's (Ornate) Tree-kanagaroo
    185, 185
Gopher Tortoise 64
Goral 40
Gorillas *134*, 136
    Mountain Gorilla 136, 228, 244
gorses 29
Goshawk 234, 235
Gouldian Finch 193
Gran Paradiso National Park, Italy *225*,
    225, 235
Grand Skink 199
Grand Teton National Park, USA 237
Grant's Gazelle 226
grasses, drought-tolerant 28
grasslands 76, 85, 126-7, 178
    African 120
    conversion to agriculture 35-6
    and heathlands, Palearctic 28-9
    neotropic, wildlife 104-6
    prairies *57*, 57
    temperate (pampas) 88, *89*, 93, 104
    tropical 88
Gray Fox 238
Gray Heron 235
Gray Kangaroo 232
Gray Nurse Shark 195

Gray Seal 44, 235
Gray Whale *72*, 80, 216
Gray Wolf 32, *33*, 33-4, 34, *67*, 67-8,
    236, 237
    Mexican 72
Gray-cheeked Parakeets 103
Gray-necked Rock-fowl (Pithacartes)
    135
Gray's Monitor 168
Great Auk 65
Great Barrier Reef 172, 173
    tourism and recreation 171
Great Barrier Skink 198
Great Bustard *35*, 35
Great Egret 237
Great Indian Bustard 159
Great Lakes Fishery, demise of 66
Great Plains 57
Great Plains Wolf 68
Great Smoky Mountains National Park,
    USA 238
Great Spotted Cuckoo 234
Great White Egret 233, 235
Great White Shark *194*, 195, *217*, 217
Greater Adjutant 161
Greater Bamboo Lemur 141-2
Greater Short-tailed Bat 196
Greater Sticknest Rat 191
grebes 109-10
Green Peafowl *167*
Green Pitcher Plant 55
Green Turtle 47, *65*, 171, *219*, 219-20,
    220-1
Greenland White-fronted Goose 37-8
Grevy's Zebra *132*, 132-3
Griffon Vulture 41, 236
Grizzled Tree-kangaroo 185
Grizzly Bear 81, 237, 238
    Mexican 72
Ground Roller 142
grouse 34, 41, 234, 235, 237
Guadalquivir delta, a threatened
    wetland 30-1
Guam Flying Fox 209
Guam Rail 213
Guanacaste Reserve, Costa Rica 244
Guanacos 107, *109*, 239
guans 98, 239
Guasupucu *see* Swamp Deer
Guatemalan Fir 58
Guemal 239
Gulf (of California) Porpoise *72*, 72
gulls 45, *46*, 46, *81*, 236
    inland 39
Gunther's Gecko 212
Gurney's Pitta 166, *167*
Gypsum Wild Buckwheat 58
Gyrfalcon 237

habitat destruction 10-11, 193, 194
    and migrating birds 85
habitat "islands" 8
habitat loss 77, 98, 130
    African woodlands and grasslands
    122-3
habitat and plants
    Australasian region 176-83
    Ethiopian region 120-7
    Indian and Oriental region 150-5
    Nearctic region 54-9
    Neotropic region 88-93
    Palearctic region 26-31
Hairy-eared Dwarf Lemur 141
Hamilton's Frog *199*, 199
Harp Seal 217

Harpers Beauty 56
Harpy Eagle *100*, 101, 239
Haute Fagnes Nature Reserve, Belgium
    233-4
Hawaiian Goose (Néné) *207*, 207
Hawaiian islands *206*, 206-7
Hawaiian Monk Seal 218
hawks 98, 101, 213, 234, 235, 239
Hawksbill Turtle 171, *220*, 220, 221
hay meadows, traditional 29
Hazel Hen 234
Heath Hen 61
Heath Lobelia 235
heathland 29, 61, 180-1, *181*
Hebe salicifolia 183
Hebe speciosa 182, 182
Hector's Dolphin 196
Helmeted Woodpecker 103
Hen Harrier 235
HEP developments 112
herbaceous plants, rainforest 91
herbs 31
Herbst's Shark 195
Hermann's Tortoise 37
herons 37, 231, *233*, 233, 235, 236,
    238, 239
Herring Gulls *46*, 46
Hierro Giant Lizard 45
Hippopotamus 226, 227, 228, 229
Hobby 235
Hochstetter's Frog 199
holiday activities, damaging to rivers 39
Honey Buzzard 186-7, 233, 235
honeycreepers 207, 214
honeyeaters 169
Hooded Parrot 192
Hooded Seal 217
Hook-billed Hummingbird 98
Hooker's Sealion *196*, 196-7
Hoop Pine 177
hornbills 231
Horned Coot 109
Horseshoe Bats *42*, 42
housing, on drained land 66
Houston Toad 69
Howler Monkey 238
Huemul *104*
    North and South Andean 105
hummingbirds 103, 238, 239
Humpback Chub 78
Humpback Whale 60, *80*, 215
hunters, and migratory flyways 83
Hunter's Antelope (Hartebeest) 132-3,
    133
hunting 9-10, 168, 208
    commercial 10
hunting pressures, Indochina 162
hurricanes 171
Hwange National Park, Zimbabwe 228
Hyacinth Macaw *102*, 102
hyena 227, 229

Ibex *40*, 40, 130-1, *131*, 234, 235, 237
ibis 33, 37, 115, 129-30, *130*, 231,
    235, 236, 239
Ice Ages, influence of 26
Idiospermum australiense 179
igapo 101
Iguaçu National Park, Brazil 239
iguanas *238*, 239
Iguazu National Park, Argentina *239*,
    239
Impala 228, 229
Imperial Eagle 41
Imperial Woodpecker 103

India, protected areas 157-8
Indian Mongoose 212, *213*
Indian Pangolin *163*, 163
Indian Python 162
Indiana Bat 68
Indri 141
insect zoos 49
International Council for Bird
    Preservation (ICBP) 85, 156
introduced animals and plants,
    effects of 210-11
invertebrates, over-exploitation of 221
Irish Spurge 234
islands, single and group 8
islands and coastlines, Palearctic 45-7
Islay (island) 37-8
Isle Royale National Park (Canada) 67
Itatiaia National Park, Brazil 239
Ivory-billed Woodpecker 62-3

jackal 229
    Asiatic 229
Jaguar *97*, 97, 238, 239
    Arizona 76
Jaguarundi *69*, 69
Japanese Cranes *38*
Japanese Crested Ibis 37
Javan Macaque 231
Jentink's Duiker 133
Jerdon's Courser 160
Jersey Wildlife Preservation Trust 245
Juan Fernandez 93, 210
Juan Fernandez Fur Seal 217
Junin Grebe 109

Kabalega Falls National Park, Uganda
    227
Kafue National Park, Zambia 228
Kaiser-I-Hind butterfly 159
Kaka 197, 233
Kakapo *197*, 197-8, 233
Kalahari Gemsbok National Park,
    Southern Africa 228-9, *229*
kangaroos 189-90, 232
Kanha National Park, India 159-60,
    229
Kapur 146
Kauri trees 181, *182*
Kavkaz (Caucasus) Biosphere Nature
    Reserve, USSR 231
Kaziranga Wildlife Sanctuary, India
    229-30
Kea *197*, 197
Kedrovaya Pad Nature Reserve, USSR
    231
Keel-scaled Boa 212
Kemp's Ridley Sea-turtle 70, *113*, 113,
    219, 220, 221
Keoladeo Ghana National Park (Wildlife
    Sanctuary), India 160-1, 230
Kern Rainbow Trout 75
Keruing 146
Key Largo (Eastern) Woodrat 65
Khao Yai National Park, Thailand 231
Killarney National Park, Eire 234
Kinabalu National Park, Borneo 231
King Parrot 232
Kirtland's Warbler 67, 82
Kit Fox 72
kiwis 198, 233
Koala 232
kob (waterbuck) 228
Komodo Monitor (Dragon) *169*, 169
Korup National Park, Cameroon 134

Korup protected forest, Cameroon 228
Kouprey 164
Krill 200-1, *201*, 203
Kruger National Park, S Africa 229
Kuekenthal's Tiger Butterfly 51
Kultarr 191
Kunai Grass 179
Kuth 151-2, 155

La Vanoise National Park, France 234
Labrador Duck 65
Lactoris fernadeziana 210
Ladies-slipper Orchid *28*
Lady Amherst's Pheasant 41
Lake Lerma Salamander 71
Lake Manyas National Park, Turkey
    231
Lake Mikri Prepa National Park,
    Greece 235
Lake Patzcuaro Salamander 71
Lake Pedder Galaxias 195
Lake Sturgeon *66*, 66-7
lakes and rivers, Palearctic 38-40
Lamington National Park, Australia
    179, 232
Lammergeier 41, 237
Lancelin Island Skink 194
land management, and butterflies 49-
    50
landscapes
    managed 28-9
    mixed, woodland and agriculture 27
Langtang National Park, Nepal 159
Large Blue Butterfly *37*, 37
Large Copper Butterfly (English) 49
Latin America, pressure on timber 147
laurel pigeons 45
Leadbeater's Possum 190
Least Bell's Vireo 74
Leech, Medicinal 40
Leiolopisma gracilicorpus 199
Leiolopisma mauritania 210
lemurs 10, 140, 140-2, *141*, 141,
    141-2, 231
Leon Springs Pupfish 69
Leopard 36, 163, 226, 227, 228, 229,
    230, 231
Lesser Adjutant Stork 115
Lesser Bird of Paradise 186
Lesser Naked-backed Fruit Bat 186
Lesser (Red) Panda *159*, 159
Lesser Stick-nest Rat 191
lianas 91, 177
Liberian Mongoose 133-4
Light-footed Clapper Rail 73
lilies 56
Limpkin 239
Lindisfarne National Nature Reserve
    235
Lion-tailed Macaque *160*, 160
Lions 9, 32, 226, 227, 228, 229, 238
    Asian 229
    Mountain 60-1, *65*, 67, 238
Little Bittern 235
Little Duiker 228
Little Egret 235
Little Spotted Kiwi 198

253

lizards 36, 45, 168, *169*, 169, 235
  monitor lizards 168, *169*, 169, 231
Llamas 107, *109*
lobsters 44
Loggerhead Sea Turtle 45, *47*, 47, 220
logging 78, 133, 146, 168, 190, 210
  Australia 179
  banned in Thailand 147
  Latin America 147
  New Guinea 185
  pressure from 70, 153
Long-footed Potoroo 190
Long-haired Spider Monkey 99
Long-legged Warbler 212
Long-tailed Bat 196
Long-tailed Chinchilla *108*, 108
Longjaw Cisco 66
Lord Howe Island Skink 194
Lost Franklinia 56
Luzon Peacock Swallowtail Butterfly 168
Lynx 237
  European 30, 33-4, 233, 236

Maak's Swallowtail Butterfly 231
macaws 98, *102*, 102
Maclear's Rat 189
Macleay's Dorcopsis 185-6
Macronesian Dragon Tree 210
Madagascan Boa *142*
Madagascar 126-7
  forest 140
  wildlife 140-3
Madeira 45
Madeiran Petrel 45
mahoganies *146*
  African 144, 145
  Philippine 146
  true, Latin America 147
mahogany 6, *90*, 90
Mala *see* Rufous Hare-Wallaby
Malay Archipelago, butterfly species *48*, 50-1
Malayan Pangolin *163*, 163
Malco 169
Maleo *168*
Malindi Watamu Marine National Park, Kenya 173, 226
Mallee Fowl 193
Mallorcan Midwife Toad 45-6
Mammillaria pectinifera 57
Manatee 100-1, *111*, 218-19
  African 129, 218-19, *218*
  American 64-5, 218-19, *218*, *219*, 238
  Amazonian 100-1, 218
  West African (see African)
  West Indian (see American)
Mandrill 134, *135*
Maned Wolf *106*, 106, 239
Mangrove Hummingbird 115
mangroves 114-19, *152*, 153-4
  black and red 114
  coastal 177
  destruction of 167
  exploitation of 116-17
maquis 31, 84

Marbled Murrelet 78
Marbled Teal 85
Marchauen-Marchegg Nature Reserve, Austria 233
Margay 97, *97*, 238
Marianas Flying Fox 209
Marine Otters 113
marine reserves 44-5
Markhor 40, 41
marmosets 98
Marmot 234, 237
Marojejya darienii 127
Maroon-fronted Parrots 70
Marquesas Pigeon 208
Marsh Deer *see* Swamp Deer
Marsh Gentian 234
Marsh Harrier 230, 235
marsupial "mice" 191
marsupials 185-6
  at risk 189-90
marten 233
Martial Eagle 227
Mascarene fauna, fate of 143
Mascarene Islands 143, 210
Masked Bobwhite quail 76
Masked Finfoot 115
Masked Titi 98
Matschie's Tree-Kangaroo 185
Maui Parrotbill 214
Mauritius 207, 210, *211*
Mauritius Kestrel *143*, 143
Maxburretia rupicola, 155
Meadow Viper 37
medicinal compounds, from reefs 171-2
medicinal plants 151, 155, 178, 178-9
Mediterranean area 31, 34, 83
Mediterranean Monk Seal 218
Megaladapis edwardsi 141
Mekong delta 84
Menzbier's Marmot 37
Meranti 146
Merganser, Brazilian 112
Merlin 234, 237
Merrillia calaoxylon 152
Mexican Axolotl 70, 71
Mexican Blindcat 70
mice 75, 191
migrating birds 82-5
  habitat destruction 85
  stop-over and wintering sites 84-5
milkweed butterflies 51
mineral extraction, a threat 29-30
mining 106-7, 133, 185
  Antarctica 203
  raised mercury levels 110
Mink 236
  European and American 40
Minke Whale 202
Minsmere Bird Reserve, England 235
miombo woodland 122
Mission Blue Butterfly 75
Mole Cricket 235
Monarch Butterfly 70, *71*, 71
Mongoose Lemur 140, *141*
mongooses 133-4
Monk Seals *43*, 45
Monkey Puzzle Tree *92*, 92, 93
monkeys 47, 115, 134, 134-5, 135, *157*, 158, 238
  large *131*, 131, 226, 228
  spider monkeys 96, 99, 216, 239
  woolly monkeys 96, 98, 99, 99
monotremes 185, 186, 191
Montague's Harrier 35
montane forest 155, 164, 181
moorland 29

Moose *see* Elk
mopane woodland 122
Morepork 233
Moreton Bay Chestnut 178
Morlet's Crocodile 238
Morpho butterflies 48
Mosquito Fish 38
mossy forest 177-8
Mouflon *40*, 40
  Sardinian and Cyprus 46
Mount Auburn, USA 224-5
Mount Field National Park, Tasmania 232-3
Mount Glorious Torrent Frog 194
Mount Iti Speedwell 30
Mount Kupe Bush-shrike 135
Mountain Cat 97
Mountain Golden Heather 56
Mountain Nyala 130
Mountain Pygmy Possum 190
Mountain Tapir 109
Mountain Zebra 138
mountains
  Andes, wildlife 106-10
  Ethiopian region 124-5
  Himalayas 158-9
  Nearctic region 77-9
  Palearctic 29-30
  threats to 30
mudskippers *114*
Mugger Crocodile 114, *160*, 161
Mulanje Cedar *125*
Mule Deer 238
Mulgara 191
Muntjac 230, 231
Musk Deer 163, 169
Musk Ox 81
mussels, freshwater 64

Nahuel Huapi National Park, Argentina 239
Nairobi National Park, Kenya 226
Nakuru National Park, Kenya 226
Narwhal Whale 43, 216
National Elk Refuge, USA 79
national parks 59, 158, 159, 224-39
Natterer's Longwing 98
natural causes, as threat 151
natural events, devastating effects 113
nature reserves 183
Nellie Cory Cactus 58, *58*
Neusiedlersee and Seewinkel Reserves, Austro-Hungary 233
New Forest, England 235
New Guinea
  habitat and plants 176-9
  wildlife 184-7
New Guinea Crocodile *187*, 187
New Zealand
  habitat and plants 181-3
  wildlife 195-9
New Zealand Grayling 199
New Zealand Pigeon 233
Newfoundland White Wolf 60
Ngorongoro National Park, Tanzania 226
Niangua Darter 64
Nicobar Pigeon *168*
Night Heron 226, 235, 236
Night Parrot 192
nightjars 106, 169, 235
Nilgiri Tahr 160
Niokolo-Koba National Park, Senegal 227
North Island Tomtit 233

Northern Hairy-nosed Wombat 190
Northern Hopping Mouse *191*, 191
Northern Pronghorn 77
Northern Pudu 109
Northern Spotted Owl 79
Nubian Dragon Tree 123
Nukupu'u 214
Numbat (Banded Anteater) *190*, 190

Oceania 206-14
Ocellated Turkey 238
Ocelot 104, 238, 239
oil pollution 10, *44*, 44, 215
Okapi 136, 137, 228
Okavango delta 140
Old Night Parrot (Owl Parrot) *see* Kakapo
Olduvai Gorge 226
Olive Colobus 134
Olive Ridley Turtle 221
Onager 36
Opposite-leaved Golden Saxifrage 235
Orang Utan *165*, 165, 231
Orange Horshoe Bat 192
Orange-banded Thrush 169
Orange-bellied Parrot 192
orchids 91, 151, 152, 155, 177, 181, 232
Oregon Giant Earthworms 79
Oriental Rat Snake 162
Orinoco Crocodile *110*, 111
Orm 42
Ormer 44-5
Orthophytum burle-marxi 91
oryx 33, 36, 128, *129*, 226, *229*
Osprey 234
Ostrich *229*, 229
otingas 103
Otter Trust 245
otters 38, 39, 74, 100, 113, 214, 217, *218*, 236
'O'u 214
ovenbirds 103
over-collection, for horticulture 152
over-exploitation 43, 44, 67, 72, 210
  coral reefs 173
  of fish stocks 214
  of marine life 151-21
over-logging 145
overfishing 66
  Antarctica 201
overgrazing 70-1, 77, 78, 85, *93*, 93, 124
Pahrangat Spinedace 78
Painted Whitestart 76
Paiute Cut-throat Trout 75
Pallas's Fish Eagle 161, 230
Palm Cockatoo *193*, 193
palms 155, 177
Pampa Galeras National Reserve, Peru 239
pampas 88, *89*, 93, 104
Pampas Deer *105*, 105-6
Pancake Tortoise *137*, 137
Pander's Ground Jay 231
pangolins *163*, 163, 229, 231
Pantanal wetlands 110-11
Paphiopedilum druryi 151, 152, *153*
Paphiopedilum micranthum 153
Paradise Duck 233
Paradise Parrot 192
parakeets 102-3, *103*, 239
parasites 154, 155
Paris Peacock Butterfly *49*
Parras Pupfish 70

parrots 70, 76-7, 96, 98, *102*, 102-3, *103*, 113, 169, 192-3, 197, 232
partridges 36, 41
Passenger Pigeon 10, 67
Patagonia 93
Peacock Butterfly 48, *51*
Pearl Fish *112*
Pearly Parakeets 102
peat 28
peat bogs, after cutting, Ireland *31*
peat digging 37
peccary 238
Pecos Gambusia 69
Pedra Branca Skink 194
pelicans 37, 38, 39, 62, *84*, 84, 161, 226, 231, 235, 236
Père David's Deer 33
Peregrine Falcon 61, 61-2, 81, 234
Periphyton 56
Peruvian Penguin 113
pesticide poisoning 61, 68
pesticide pollution *112*
pesticides 10, 62, 81, *85*
pet trade 103, 112-13, 137
petrels, conservation measures 45
pheasants 32, 41, 136, 159
  see also tragopans
Phelsuma gigas 210
Philip Island Hibiscus *181*
Philip Island Reserve, Australia 232
Philippine Cockatoo 168
Philippine Eagle 168
Philippines 51
  crisis in 146-7
  endemism 168
Pie-billed Grebe 110
pigeons 10, 45, 67, 143, *168*, 208, 233
pigs 182
Pilot Whales 43
Pinabete 58
Pine Marten 237
pines, long- and short-needled 58
Pink Pigeon 143
Pinta Island Giant Tortoise 208
Piping Plover 61, 61, 82, 83
pitcher plants *55*, 55, 155, 178
pittas 166, 168
Pitted-shell Turtle *see* Plateless Turtle
Plains Bison 68, 77
plant collectors 183
plant gene reservoirs 31
plant species, loss of 26-7
plantations 98
plants, Nearctic 54-9
plastics, dangerous waste 214-15, *215*
Plateless Turtle 187
Platypus Frog 194
podocarp-hardwood forest 181
Podophyllum, Indian 151, 152
poisoning, of birds 39
Polar Bear 44, 81, 231
polderlands, Netherlands 38
pollution 10, 40, 160, 191, *215*
  agricultural 78
  Antarctica *202*
  atmospheric 10
  and epidemics 44
  Great Lakes 66
  hazardous waste at sea *214*
  mangroves vulnerable 116
  marine 43, *44*, 44, 221
  oil 10, *44*, 44, 215
  pesticide *112*
  of rivers 38-9
  water 165
  of wetlands 30

polyps 170
Pond Bat 42
population pressure 151
  and wildlife destruction 6
porpoises 43, 72, 216
possums 182, 186, 190, 232
  ringtail possums 190
potoos 103
prairie dogs 77
prairies, shortgrass and tallgrass 57, 57
primeval forest, lowland 28
Prince Ruspoli's Turaco 130, 132
Project Tiger, India 157-8
pronghorns 72, 76, 77, 78, 238
Prunus africana 121, 121-2
Przewalski's Horse 35-6
Ptarmigan 234, 235, 237
Pudu 109, 239
Puffin *43*
Puma *see* Mountain Lion
Puna Flamingo 109
Purple Heron 235
Purple-naped Lory 169
Purple-winged Ground Dove 79, *102*
purse-seine nets 215
Pygmy Cormorant 39, 235, 236
Pygmy Hippopotamus 133, *134*

Quagga 138
quails 84
Queen Alexandra's Birdwing Butterfly
  49, 51
Queen Conch *220*
Quetzal *see* Resplendent Trogon
quolls 190-1

Raccoon Dog 231
Rafflesia arnoldii 154, 155
Rahjah Pitcher Plant 155
rails 73, 75, 111, 198, 212, 213
rainfall patterns, New Guinea 177
rainforest *179*
  Amazonian 90
  central African 134-7
  cool temperate 179-80
  east African 137
  montane 155
  New Guinea *176*
  semi-evergreen 155, 176
  subtropical 179
  west African 133-4
  see also tropical rainforest
Rajah Brooke's Birdwing Butterfly *49*
Rallus antarcticus 111
Rallus semiplumbeus 111
Ramsar Convention 117
Ranunculus capparum 210
raptors 84
Raratonga Flycatcher 210
rats, ship-borne, effects of 211-12
rattans 155
Rauwolfia 151, 152
reafforestation 33, 117
recreation, danger to wetlands 30
Red Admiral Butterfly *48*, 48
Red Deer 233, 234, 236
  Corsican and Sardinian 46
Red Kangaroo 232
Red Kite *84*, 85
Red Lechwe 228
Red Siskin *102*
Red Wolf 63-4
Red-bellied Lemur 142
Red-billed Curassow *98*

Red-cockaded Woodpecker 68
Red-crested Korhaan 229
Red-necked Phalarope 233
Red-necked Wallaby 232
Red-tailed Phascogale 191
Redshank 236
redwoods 59
Redwoods National Park 59
reedbuck 227
reef damage, reduction of 173
reef inhabitants 171
reef loss, costs of 171
reefs, exploitation of 172
Reeves Pheasant 41
refugia 189
Reindeer 34, 236
Repetek Biosphere Nature Reserve,
  USSR 231
Resplendent Trogon *95*
reptiles 111, 187, 193-4
  desert 75, 184
  European 37
research, Antarctica 202
reservoirs, as wildlife areas 38
Rhine, River 38-9
Rhinoceros
  Black *138, 139*, 139, 226, 227, 228
  Great Indian (One-horned) *158*, 158,
    229-30
  Javan 166, 231
  Sumatran (Asiatic Two-horned) *166*,
    166, 231 White 138, 227, 228
Rhizanthella gardneri 181, 181
Rhododendron schlippenbachii 231
Ridge-nosed Rattlesnake 77, *77*
Right Whales
  Greeland, Northern and Southern
    216
  North Atlantic 60
Ring Ouzel 234
Ringed Seal 44
Rio Bravo Conservation and
  Managment Area, Belize 238
River Otter 38, 39
River Terrapin 115
River Turtle, South American 111
Robust Skink 199
Rock Thrush 237
rockroses 56
Rocky Mountain Wolf, Northern and
  Southern 77
rodents 37, 108-9, 168, 189, 191, 238
Rodrigues Flying Fox 143
Roe Deer 233, 234
Roller 234
Rondane National Park, Norway 236
Roosevelt Wapiti (Elk) 78
Roseate Spoonbill 239
Roseate Tern 45
Ross's Gull *81*
Rosy Periwinkle (Madagascan) 6, 123,
  127
Rough-necked Buzzard 237
Round Island 211, 212
Round Island Boa 212
Roiund Island Skink 212
Royal Bardia National Park, Nepal 158
Royal Chitwan National Park, Nepal
  158, *230*, 230
Royal Fern 235
rubber trees 90
Ruff 236
Ruffled Lemur *10*, 142
Rufous Bettong *191*
Rufous Bush Chat 231
Rufous Hare-Wallaby 189-90

Rufous Scrub Bird 193
Rufous-necked Hornbill 164
Ruwenzori National Park, Uganda 228
Rwanda, conservation of Mountain
  Gorilla 244

Sable 34
Sacred Mud Turtle 161-2
Saguaro Cactus *58*, 75
Sailfin Lizard 168
St. Helena, environmental breakdown
  211
St. Helena Ebony 144
St. Helena Redwood 144
St. Helenian Olive 211
Sal 150-1
salamanders 69, *70*, 71, 74, 78, 165
  aquatic 71
  cave
Salmon 39
Salmon-crested Cockatoo 169
Salt Marsh Harvest Mouse 75
saltmarsh 61, 65-6, *73*, 75
Saltwater Crocodile 194
Sambar Deer 230
Samburu National Park, Kenya 226
San Clemente Broom 58
San Clemente Bushmallow 58
San Clemente Larkspur 58
San Clemente Paintbrush 58
San Francisco Garter Snake 75
San Joaquin Kit Fox *74*
Sanborn's Long-nosed Bat 75
Sand Lizard 235
Sandalwood, East Indian 155
Sandhill Crane 80, *236*
Sandhill Dunnart 191
Sanicle 235
Santa Cruz Long-toed Salamander 74
Santalum fernadezianum 210
Sapele 145
Sapo National Park, Liberia 134
Satanic Nightjar 169
savanna 85, *104*, 104, 120, 227
sawgrass *56*
Scarlet Ibis 115, 239
Scarlet Tanager *11*
Scarlet-chested Parrot 192-3
Schaus' Swallowtail Butterfly 65
Scimitar-horned Oryx 128, *129*
Scops Owl 137
  Seychelles Scops Owl 210
Scott's Tree-kangaroo 185
Sea Lamprey *66*, 66
Sea Mink 65
Sea Otter 214, 217, *218*
  Southern 74
sea turtles 45, *47*, 47, 65, 214-15,
  219-20, 220, 238
sea-lions *192*, 192, 239
sea-urchins 44
seabirds, mortality in *214*
sea cull 217
seals *43*, 44, 45, 74, 80, *192*, *196*,
  196-7, *201*, 214, 233, 235, 239
  monk seals 217-18
seas and oceans, Palearctic 43-5
Secretary Bird 229
Sei Whale 216
Selkirk's Mayu-monte *93*, 210
Senecio dendrosenecio 124, 124-5
sequoias *59*, 59
Serbian Spruce 28
Serengeti National Park, Tanzania 226
Serpent Eagle, Madagascan 142

Seven-colored Tanager *98*
sewage pollution 215
Seychelles 143, 210
Seychelles Brush Warbler 210
Seychelles Magpie-robin 213
shark barriers 215
Shark Bay Mouse *191*, 191
sharks 195
  over-exploited 216-17
Sharphead Darter 64
Sharptooth Minnow 70
shearwaters 62
Shenandoah National Park, USA 238
shifting cultivation 151
Shining Cuckoo 233
Shoebill Stork 140
Short-tailed Bat 196
Short-tailed Chinchilla 108
Short-tailed Shearwaters 232
Shortjawed Kokopu 199
Siamang 165
Siamese Freshwater Crocodile 167
Siberian Crane 84, 160-1, *161*
Siberian White Crane 37
Sicilian Fir 28
Sika Deer 231
silt 78, *150*, 172, 173
silting of rivers 77
Silver Sword *207*
Simên Jackal 130, 131
Sipo 145
Sirenians 192, *218*, 219, 230
  over-exploited 218-19
Six-Fingered Frog 162
skinks 194, 198-9
slash-and-burn cultivation 126-7, 140
Slater's Monal 41
Slender-billed Curlew 37, 83, *83*-4
Slender-billed Gull 236
Slender-horned Gazelle 128, *129*
Sloth Bear 229, *230*, 230
Slow Loris 165, *166*
Small-eared Dog 99-100
Smoky Mouse 191
Smooth Snake 235
Snail Darter 64
Snail-eating Coua 142
snails
  at risk 213
  viviparous tree snails 213
snakes 36, 75, *142*, 162, *193*, 193-4,
  212, 235
Snow Bunting 234, 235
Snow Finch 235, 237
Snow Goose *83*, 231
Snow Leopard *36*, 159
snowcock 41
Society Islands Pigeon 208
Socotra 124
Socotran Fig *120*
Socotran Pomegranate 123
soil fertility, rainforest 95
soils, tropical *94*
solitaires 143
Somali-Masai 132-3
Song Sparrows 75
Sonoran Pronghorn 76
Southern Africa wildlife 138-9
Southern Andean Deer *see* Huemul
Southern Hairy-nosed Wombat 190
Spanish Ibex 237
speciation 156
species diversity
  Amazonia 100
  Cape, South Africa 126
  Neotropic 89-90

species range, reduction in 32-3
Spectacled Bear 104
Spectacled Caiman 111
Speke's Gazelle 133
Sperm Whales 216
Spiral Aloe 125
Spix Little Blue Macaw 98
Splendid Parakeet *103*
Spoonbills 231, 233, 235, 236, 239
Spot-billed Pelican 161
Spotted Barramundi 195
Spotted Deer 230
Spotted Hyena 226
Springbok 229
Squacco Heron 231, 235
Squirrel Monkey 95
Steamer Duck 239
Steller's (Northern) Sea Lion 80
Steller's Sea Cow 43-4, 218
Steller's (Short-tailed) Albatross 46
Stephen's Island Gecko 199
Steppe Eagle 230
steppes 28
  Patagonia *93*
Stirling Range National Park, Australia
  232, 232
Stone Curlew 35
Stora Sjöfallet National Park, Sweden
  237
storks 37, 84, 115, 140, 161, 230, 231
Strawberry Tree 234
Striped Hyena 229
Strophanthus thollonii 122, 122
Sturgeon *216*
Sudd 140
Sugar Glider 232
Sulawesi 51, 168
  butterflies *50*
Sulawesi Palm Civet 169
Sun Bear 231
sundews 55
swallowtail butterflies 37, 48, 65, 137,
  168, 231
swamp 55, 111, 177, 231, 238, 239
  coastal 84
  tropical 178
Swamp Deer 110, *111*, *159*, 160, 229
swamp forest, clearance of 167
Swamp Turtle 192, 193
Swamp Wallaby 232
Swan Galaxias 195
swans 39
Swayne's Hartebeest 226
Swift Fox 68
Swiss National Park 237
Syrian Wild Ass 36

tahrs 36, 160
Tai National Park, Ivory Coast 134
taiga 28
  erosion of 34
Takahe *198*, 198, *232*, 233
Tamaraw 168
tamarins 96
  lion tamarins 97, 98
Tamarugo Conebill 109

256

Tammar Wallaby 189
tanagers 11, 98, 238, 239
tapirs 96, 96, 109, 166, 238, 239
Tarpan 36
tarsier 231
Tasmanian Devil 233
Tasmanian Echidna 233
Tassel-eared Marmoset 98
Teak 150, 153
teak forests 154
Tecomanthe speciosa 182, 182
Tengmalm's Owl 234
Terai 150-1
terns 45, 72-3, 82, 83, 231, 234, 235, 236
terrapins 115
Tetrataxis salicifolia 210
Texas Blind Salamander 69
Texas Ocelot 69
Texas Poppy Mallow 57
Texel and Terschelling Reserves, Netherlands 235-6
Thames, River 39
Thick-billed Parrot 76-7, 77
Thicktail Chub 75
Thin-spined Porcupine 98
Thomson's Gazelle 226, 229
Thonningia sanguinea 121, 122
Thornton Peak Melomys 191
Three-banded Armadillo 106
Three-toed Sloth 98
Three-toed Woodpecker 234
Tiama 145
Tidbinbilla Nature Reserve, Australia 232
Tiger Cat 97, 97
tigers 36, 115, 157-8, 229, 230, 231, 245
Tikal National Park, Guatemala 238
Tillandsia 91, 91
timber 95, 144
Timber Wolf see Gray Wolf
tinamous 106
toads 45-6, 69

Todsen's Pennyroyal 58
Tooth-billed Pigeon 208
Topi 228
topminnows 112
Torricelli (Northern) Glider 186
tortoises 34, 36, 37, 64, 70, 113, 137, 137, 138-9, 140, 142, 143, 208, 208
Totoaba 72
tourism 45, 71, 171, 183, 202, 202
  and habitat loss 85
  two sides of 245
  uncontrolled development 46, 47
tragopans 41, 159
tree ferns 177, 177, 178
Trispot Darter 64
tritons 76, 95, 238
Tritons Trumpet 220
trogons 76, 95, 238
tropical rainforest 6, 89, 89-91, 94-8, 120-1, 179, 184, 231, 239
  evergreen 150, 153, 154, 155, 176
  semi-evergreen 153
  wildlife 94-8
tropical timbers 144-7
  import bans 6
trout 75, 77
Trout Cod 195
Trumpeter Swan 79, 238
Tsavo National Park, Kenya 226, 226
Tuatara 195
Tule Lake National Wildlife Refuge 83
Tule Wapiti (Elk) 74, 75
tundra 29, 34, 79, 80-1
Tundra Peregrine Falcon 81
turtles 47, 65, 70, 111, 113, 115, 161-2, 171, 187
turtle's eggs 220
tyrant flycatchers 103

Uakari 101, 101
Ujung Kulon Nature Reserve, Indonesia 231
Umbrella Pine 30
Urewera National Park, New Zealand 233
Utah Prairie Dog 77

Valencia Toothcarp 38
Valle de Ordesa National Park, Spain 236-7
Vampire Bat 75

varzea 101, 101
Vegas Valley Leopard Frog 78
vegetation
  alteration of 75
  Mediterranean 31
Venus Flytraps 55, 55
Vervet Monkey 229
Vicuña 107, 107-8, 108, 239
Vinaceous-breasted Parrot 95, 103
vines 91
Virginia Roundleaf Birch 56
Virunga National Park, Zaire 228
volcanic eruptions 8
Volanuoes National Park, Ruanda 228
Volga delta 30
Vriesea hieroglyphica 91
vultures 41, 41, 228, 236, 237

'W' National Park, W Africa 227
waders 84
Waldrapp see Bald Ibis
Walia Ibex 130-1, 131
wallabies 185-6, 188, 189, 189-90, 232, 233
Walrus 44, 231
Wanderoo 160
wapiti (elk) 65, 67, 74, 75, 78, 238
warblers 67, 68, 82, 85, 109, 111, 210, 212
  migratory 82, 83
Warbling Antbird 111
Water Buffalo 230
water extraction, danger to wetlands 30, 31
Water Pipit 234
water-tables, lowering of 30, 69
Wattled Crane 140
Wattled Crow, North and South Island 233
wealth, disparities in 6
Weka 233
Welwitschia bainesii 123, 124
Western Blue-striped Snake 193
Western Quoll 191
Western Ringtail Possum 190
Western Rufous Bristle Bird 192
Western Tragopan 159
wetlands 85, 167, 236
  African 140
  coastal 38
  danger to 30-1

Indochina 164-5
international convention for preservation of 37
  Mediterranean 84
  migration refueling sites 82
  Neotropic 110-12
  threatened habitat 37-8
  value of to birds 37
wetlands drainage 85, 160
  and butterflies 49
whale sanctuaries 72
whales 43, 72, 80, 80, 201-2, 202, 214, 215, 216, 216
  over-exploited 215-16
  right whales 60, 216
  toothed 216
whaling 43
  Antarctica 201-2
Whiskered Pitta 168
Whitaker's Skink 199
White Beak-sedge 234
White Ibis 231
White Pelican 235, 236
White (Silvery) Marmoset 98
White Stork 84, 231
White-breasted Guinea Fowl 134
White-eyed River Martin 165
White-footed Tamarin 96
White-headed Duck 39
White-necked Hawk 98
White-necked Pithacartes 135
White-tailed Deer 61, 64, 65, 79
  Florida Keys 64, 65
White-tailed Eagle 233
White-throated Tree-kangaroo 185
White-winged Black Tern 231
White-winged Wood Duck 166
Whooping Crane 68, 79-80, 82, 85
Wiest's Sphinx Moth 68
Wild Ass, African 133
wild asses 36
Wild Boar 233, 233, 236, 237
Wild Cat, European 234, 236, 237
wild horses 35-6
Wild Service Tree 28
wildebeest 226, 227, 228, 229
wilderness nature reserves 50
wildlife
  Australasian region 184-99
  Ethiopian region 128-43
  Indian and Oriental region 156-69
  Nearctic region 60-81

Neotropic region 94-113
Palearctic region 32-47
wildwood 28
Wilpattu National Park, Sri Lanka (Yala Park) 230, 230-1
Wisent 32, 32, 33, 35, 236
Wolverine 35, 236, 237
wolves 32, 60, 63-4, 68, 72, 77, 79, 106
wombats 190, 190, 233
wood, world consumption of 10
Wood Anemone 28
Wood Bison 77, 79, 237
Wood Buffalo National Park, Canada 79, 237
wood nightjar see potoos
Wood Stork 65-6
Woodland Caribou 237
woodlands 85
  acacia and eucalypt 180
  Africa 122-3
  ancient 28
  managed 26
  second-growth 54
  temperate, deciduous 89
Woodlark Island Cuscus 186
woodpeckers 62-3, 68, 103, 233, 234
Woolly Monkey 99, 99
Woolly Spider Monkey 98, 239
Worm-eating Warbler 85
worms, nemertine 45
Wrangel Island Reserve, USSR 231

Yacare Caiman 111
Yeheb Nut 123
Yellow Baboon 228
Yellow-footed Rock Wallaby 189
Yellow-tailed Woolly Monkey 96
Yellowstone National Park, USA 225, 237
yews 56
Yosemite National Park, USA 59, 225, 225, 237

zebra 132, 132-3, 138, 226, 228, 229

Quarto Publishing plc would like to thank the following for providing photographs and for permission to reproduce copyright material:

Cindy Buxton, Survival Anglia Ltd 131(r); Phillip Cribb 153; Stephen Davis 177, 178; Ian Edwards 121(1), 121(r), 122; Paul Glendell 214(t); David George 170(br); Nick Hanna 173(b); Paul Kay 214(b), 215; Sabina Knees 57(b), 92(t), 92(b), 127, 183; Royal Botanic Garden, Edinburgh 120; Philip Steele/ICCE 180; Ruth Taylor 150, 151.

All other photographs supplied by Bruce Coleman Ltd

Quarto would also like to thank Graeme George and Verna Simpson for technical and editing advice respectively on Australasian Wildlife.